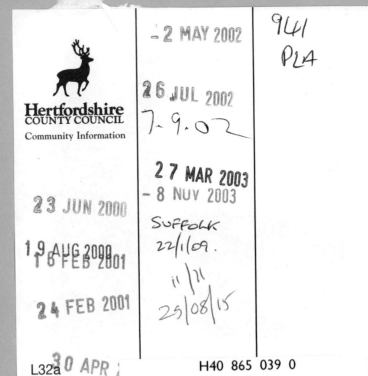

THE ORDNANCE SURVEY GUIDE TO
SMUGGLERS' BRITAIN

THE ORDNANCE SURVEY GUIDE TO

SMUGGLERS' BRITAIN

RICHARD PLATT

CASSELL

For Mary

Cassell Publishers Ltd
Villiers House, 41/47 Strand, London WC2N 5JE

Copyright © 1991 Richard Platt

Maps produced by the Ordnance Survey.
Copyright © Crown Copyright 1991

First published 1991

Distributed in the United States by
Sterling Publishing Co. Inc.
387 Park Avenue South, New York, NY 10016-8810

Distributed in Australia by
Capricorn Link (Australia) Pty Ltd
PO Box 665, Lane Cove, NSW 2066

All photographs by the author
Engraving on page 10: Mary Evans Picture Library
Photograph on page 60 courtesy of Parham Park, West Sussex

British Library Cataloguing in Publication Data
Platt, Richard
Smugglers' Britain.
1. Great Britain. Coastal regions – Visitors' guides
I. Title
914.1040858

ISBN 0304 340650
ISBN 0319 002608 (Ordnance Survey)

Typeset by Tradespools Ltd, Frome, Somerset

Printed in England by Clays Ltd, St Ives plc

Half-title illustration: Pepper Cove, Cornwall (photograph by Richard Platt)

CONTENTS

KEY TO LOCATION MAPS

RELIEF

Feet	Metres
3000	914
2000	610
1400	427
1000	305
600	183
200	61
0	0

·274 Heights in feet above mean sea level

Contours at 200ft intervals

To convert feet to metres multiply by 0·3048

TOURIST INFORMATION

✝ Abbey, Cathedral, Priory
ɱ Ancient monument
🐟 Aquarium
⛺ Camp site
🚐 Caravan site
🏰 Castle
Cave
Country park
Craft centre
Garden
⛳ Golf course or links
Historic house
Information centre

Motor racing
Museum
Nature or forest trail
Nature reserve
☆ Other tourist feature
✕ Picnic site
Preserved railway
Racecourse
Skiing
Viewpoint
Wildlife park
▲ Youth hostel
Zoo

ROADS Not necessarily rights of way

M 1 — Motorway with service area, service area (limited access) and junction with junction number

M 62 — Motorway junction with limited interchange

M 42 — Motorway under construction with proposed opening date where known

A 1 (T) — Trunk road with service area

A 15 Dual carriageway — Main road

A 15 — Roundabout or multiple level junction

B 676 — Secondary road

Road under construction

Toll — Toll   Road tunnel

A 855   B 885 — Narrow road with passing places

Other tarred road   Other minor road

Gradient 1 in 7 and steeper

18   23 — Distances in miles between markers

The representation on this map of a road is no evidence of the existence of a right of way

GENERAL FEATURES

Buildings

Wood

⟂ Lighthouse (in use)   ⟂ Lighthouse (disused)

✗ Windmill   ⟂ Radio or TV mast

Youth hostel

⊕ Civil aerodrome { with Customs facilities
·   { without Customs facilities

Ⓗ Heliport

☎ Public telephone

Motoring organisation telephone

ANTIQUITIES

❋ Native fortress   Castle · Other antiquities

✕ Site of battle (with date)   ------ Roman road (course of)

CANOVIUM · Roman antiquity

ɱ Ancient Monuments and Historic Buildings in the care of the Secretaries of State for the Environment, for Scotland and for Wales and that are open to the public.

WATER FEATURES

(boat)   (hovercraft)   Ferry routes for vehicles (subject to change)

Short ferry routes for vehicles

Canal

Lake

Marsh

Bridge   Ferry

Cliff
Slopes
Flat rock
Transport for vehicles
Light-vessel
Low water mark
Foreshore
High water mark
Dunes

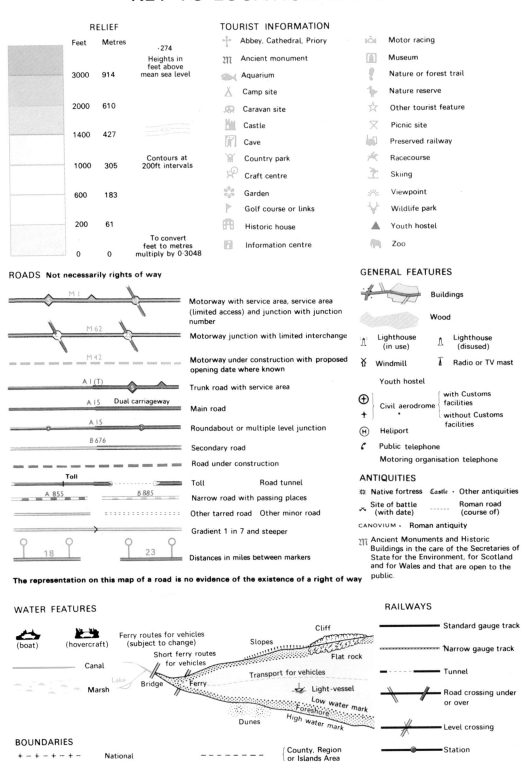

RAILWAYS

—— Standard gauge track
===== Narrow gauge track
-·-·- Tunnel
✕✕ Road crossing under or over
✕ Level crossing
——●—— Station

BOUNDARIES

+ - + - + - + - National

- - - - - - - - { County, Region or Islands Area

⑪ Site mentioned in the text

| 10 | 5 | 0 | Kilometres | 5 | 10 | 15 |

| 5 | 0 | Miles | 5 | 10 |

4 centimetres to 10 kilometres (one grid square)

1 kilometre = 0·6214 mile   1 mile = 1·61 kilometres

INTRODUCTION

The explosion of import smuggling that took place in the eighteenth and early nineteenth centuries has been absorbed into the public consciousness leaving only the vaguest of traces. The smugglers gave us phrases such as 'on the spot' and 'the coast is clear', yet they remain, at least in most people's minds, shadowy, romantic figures. I became interested in this period of Britain's history while researching a popular magazine article on the subject, and though I found the story fascinating, I was surprised and disappointed to discover that there were no books in print on smuggling. *The Ordnance Survey Guide to Smugglers' Britain* is an attempt to remedy this situation.

In researching the book, I read many volumes that purported to be histories of smuggling. In reality, most of them were histories of the prevention of smuggling, or of the customs and excise services. This is perfectly understandable—historians prefer to work from primary sources whenever possible, and by the very nature of the game, smugglers left few accurate and detailed records of their activities. Their adversaries in the service of the Crown were, by contrast, prolific correspondents, and in the public record office at Kew there are hundreds of thousands of letters and other documents that deal with the minutiae of life in the country's custom houses. I am not a historian, and early on I came to the conclusion that the story of smuggling is far more interesting than the story of its prevention. I have therefore tried whenever possible to view smuggling from the point of view of those who broke the law, not those who enforced it.

To find this perspective, I left the carefully paved and well-signposted road of official revenue records, and branched off onto the muddy and rutted paths of traditional yarns, folk tales, and recollections-of-the-oldest-inhabitant. The result will, I hope, please those who are fascinated by tales of smuggling and smugglers, and who wish to follow in the footsteps of the men and women who profited from Britain's punitive taxation laws. By the same token, this book will probably infuriate the historian. I have shamelessly included a great deal of hearsay and many unverified assertions, and for the sake of clarity, I have used a few revenue terms—such as preventive—in a rather loose way.

This is not to say that I have accepted as fact every yarn I heard and read. On the contrary, I have more often tended towards scepticism. For example, if every yarn about a smugglers' tunnel was true, the coast of southern England would resemble Swiss cheese, and most cliffs would collapse into the sea. If a story seemed plausible, I've said so.

In the course of researching the book, I visited and photographed most of the places on the mainland and the Isle of Wight that are covered as main gazetteer entries. The exceptions are remote areas, and those where I found little evidence of smuggling. Specifically, I stayed south and east of a line drawn between Stranraer and Inverness, and I omitted most of the west coast between Liverpool and Carlisle.

I received an enormous amount of help in writing this book, but I am indebted to a few people in particular.

Helen Denholm, Helen Douglas-Cooper, Rosemary Amos and Lesley Levene at Cassell deserve special thanks for turning my unruly and undisciplined manuscript into a book and Christine Wood for designing it.

The staff of the British Library at Bloomsbury helped me track down hundreds of obscure references, and branch librarians all over the country responded to my letters with photocopies of their local archives. The staff of the Customs and Excise Library at King's Beam House helped me in the early stages of my research.

Ilford Ltd generously provided me with film with which to shoot the colour pictures.

Robin Wood provided some early encouragement, and the list that follows is as complete as I can make it in the space available.

Many thanks to Blue Circle Heritage Trust; Flat Holm Project; Foulkes-Halbard of Filching; Margate Caves; Parham Park; Post Office Postcode Services; The Three Daws Inn, Gravesend; the many people who allowed a complete stranger to photograph their homes, and who shared their knowledge of the smuggling trade; and the friends who provided meals and beds during my travels, and endured my countless smuggling yarns!

UNDERSTANDING MAP REFERENCES

Many of the places in the book are marked on the location maps. Thus 1 at the start of an entry means that you will find the approximate location marked with number 1 on the location map. To locate places with more precision, you'll need an Ordnance Survey Landranger or Pathfinder series map, and you'll also need to understand map references.

These are usually provided in the text in the form, say, 29-NJ547342. The first number is the Ordnance Survey sheet number from the Landranger series. The letters and numbers that follow are a grid reference that allows you to pinpoint the spot to within 100 metres.

The grid in question is a series of imaginary squares that divide up the country. Forty-eight of these carve up Britain into 100-kilometre-square regions, and each is given a two-letter code. The NJ part of the map reference above, for example, locates the spot close to the north-east coast of Scotland. The remaining part provides the location with greater precision. The first three digits of the number give the distance that the spot lies from the left-hand edge of the 100-kilometre square. The first two numbers, 54, give you the location to within 1 kilometre, using the numbers marked along the bottom and top edges of the map. The fourth and fifth numbers, 34, give the distance from the foot of the 100-kilometre square, using the scales marked up the sides. These two pairs of numbers identify the place to within a 1-kilometre square. The other two numbers, 7 and 2, narrow the search down to 100 metres. However, to use these last two digits you'll need to imagine a grid of lines placed over the 1-kilometre square on the map, as shown within the enlarged circle in the diagram All measurements within the text are given in miles. To convert miles to kilometres, multiply the number of miles by 1.6, thus 5 miles = 8 kilometres.

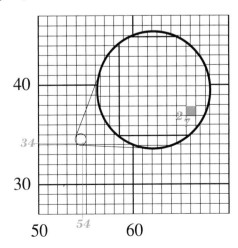

A SMUGGLING RUN

Ask anyone to describe an eighteenth- or nineteenth-century smuggler, and the chances are that you'll get a reply that goes something like this: he was a jolly figure—probably a Cornishman called Tom—dressed in long boots and a striped jersey. He rolled a couple of kegs of brandy up a moonlit beach, hid them in a cave, then returned the next night with ponies to collect them, and hawked the brandy round the village. Everybody knew him as Tom the Smuggler, and his neighbours took it in turns to distract the revenue man at the front door while Tom rolled his barrels out of the back.

How accurate is this traditional picture of the smuggler? In some ways it is hopelessly romanticized. In other respects it is a generalized impression that doesn't conform to the historical fact about smuggling at any one place or time. Worst of all, it is especially misleading because it omits important (and unsavoury) details about the smuggling trade. Nevertheless, this thumbnail sketch contains a few grains of truth. It can be argued that the substance (though not the letter) of this popular smuggling image captures the flavour of the extraordinary climate which supported a vast expansion of illegal imports in the eighteenth and early nineteenth centuries.

But before considering the true story, let us look briefly at the errors. For a start, our real smuggler was just as likely to have been called Jacque or even Hans as Tom; the story would probably have taken place in Kent on a stormy, pitch-black night, rather than on the Cornish coast floodlit by a full moon. There was a good chance that the contraband was tea, not cognac, and the cave was probably romantic embroidery, too. As for the revenue man, he was more likely to meet with a bump on the head than a discreet diversion. However, as for Tom's (or Jacque's) relationship with his customers, and their attitude towards the revenue man, there is every reason to believe that, for many years and in many places, the picture is an accurate one. Now let's look beyond the myths, at what really happened . . .

In the eighteenth century illegal trade across England's coast mushroomed. A trade that previously existed as simple small-scale evasion of duty turned into an industry of astonishing proportions, syphoning money abroad, and channelling huge volumes of contraband into the southern counties of England.

Even by modern standards, the quantities of imported goods were extraordinary. It was not unheard of for a smuggling trip to bring in 3,000 gallons of spirits; to picture this in your mind's eye, imagine some 1,500 cases of brandy stacked in your garage. Illegally imported gin was sometimes so plentiful that the inhabitants of some Kentish villages were said to use it for cleaning their windows. And according to some contemporary estimates, four-fifths of all tea drunk in England had not had duty paid on it.

Statistics like this are even more extraordinary when seen in the light of the time. The first steam-powered ships did not appear until the early years of the nineteenth century, so sailing ships brought the goods from the continent, and kegs and bales were manhandled—often up sheer cliffs—to a waiting file of men. These carriers then transported the goods either in carts or caravans of ponies, or lashed the tubs to their own backs for a journey inland.

Whole communities connived in the trade, and profited from it. The Isles of Scilly, for example, were totally reliant on smuggling for their survival, and the islanders were brought to the point of starvation when preventive measures were stepped up in the area. A large cargo drained capital from the area where it landed: in Shetland, and around Falmouth, there were times when every available penny had been spent on contraband (see pages 107 and 211). And there were numerous instances of whole communities uniting and taking up arms to reclaim cargoes that had been seized by the revenue.

This extraordinary situation was not the result of some plan, or a plot hatched in a smugglers' tunnel. Rather, it was a natural and inevitable result of punitive taxation imposed by a succession of governments, each more desperate for revenue than the last to pay for costly wars in Europe.

Eighteenth-century taxation fell into two categories, each administered and collected by a separate government department. *Customs* duties had a historical precedent in that the English Crown had for centuries claimed a proportion of all cargoes entering the country or a financial levy in lieu of the fine wine or bolts of fabric. In 1688, though, the customs duties were streamlined and restructured into a form that would—in theory at least—generate more revenue for the Exchequer.

The other type of duty had its origins in the Civil War: a tax on land took the place of two older taxes—wardship and the parliamentary subsidy—and a new tax, *excise*, was levied specially to pay for the war. Excise was a tax on domestic consumption, and during the years of the Civil War it covered many different items. Its scope was reduced ten years later to cover just chocolate, coffee, tea, beer, cider and spirits. However, after 1688 it was progressively widened again to include other essentials such as salt, leather and soap.

The separation of these two taxes mattered not a jot to the common man, who knew only that he had to pay more for what he bought. And as the eighteenth century progressed, the slice taken by the Exchequer increased sometimes steadily and progressively, sometimes by leaps and bounds, as the conflicts with France ebbed and flowed. By the middle of the century, the tax on tea was nearly 70 per cent of its initial cost, and the double burden of customs and excise duties was widely resented by a rural population often close to starvation.

Collection of the customs duties was haphazard and bureaucratic and was largely based on a system, established in the thirteenth century, of *custom-houses* at ports around the coast. In the ensuing centuries a creaking and corrupt hierarchy grew up around the custom-houses. The collectors and comptrollers of customs and their multitude of functionaries were primarily concerned with taxation on the export of the wool that made England wealthy. However, the dawn of the eighteenth century heralded heavy taxation on imports and the system was ill-fitted to combat the spirited efforts of large numbers of Englishmen determined to defraud the King.

We will return to look in more detail at the historical background of smuggling. To understand how smugglers operated, it is enough to know that they were opportunists taking advantage of a demand for heavily-taxed luxury goods and the state's almost total inability to collect those taxes.

WHO WERE THE SMUGGLERS?

If you've ever spent time delving into the local history of a coastal area, you'll sooner or later have come across notes to the effect that 'everybody in these parts is a smuggler' or 'every house is a smuggler's', and while many such reports were wildly exaggerated, it is probably true that, at certain times and in certain areas, everybody really was involved in smuggling in one way or another, or at least stood to benefit by the continuation of smuggling. The menial farm labourer helped carry goods inland; the parson bought cheap tea and wine; the local squire lent his horses for transport; the wealthy merchant obtained cut-price supplies of silks and lace; and members of the gentry conducted foreign business through intermediaries involved in smuggling.

This universal involvement in the 'free-trade', as it was euphemistically and generally known, creates the real problem in identifying the smuggler, because the term covers all manner of sins, embracing not only the mariner whose boat actually transported the goods across the water, but also the wealthy landowner who supplied the capital for the operation, and the thug who protected the cargo as it came inland. 'Smuggler', in fact, is about as specific as crook, villain, or blackguard, and the profession could potentially be minutely split up into numerous specialists, as we shall see as the tale continues.

If we confine the question to the men who actually made the trips abroad, identification becomes much simpler. Most sea smugglers were seafaring men who had a sense of adventure or an eye for a quick profit. They were fishermen, or crewed colliers, coasters and river vessels. When times were tough, they'd look for a novel way to use their knowledge of navigation and sailing.

From what little verifiable information we have about the lives of smugglers, it seems that they slipped in and out of the trade. Jack Rattenbury, for example (see page 96), started life learning fishing, but got bored and joined a privateer. This semi-piratical pursuit perhaps pushed him towards smuggling, but he plied an honest trade

from time to time too, running a pub, and working as a pilot. This last employment is particularly telling, since it highlights the extraordinarily detailed knowledge of the sea that smugglers possessed, especially of localized coastal conditions.

The stereotyped sea smuggler, of course, is easy to picture. He wears enormous seaman's boots, perhaps a smock or a striped jersey, baggy trousers, a heavy overcoat, a sou'wester, and maybe a handkerchief round his neck. In fact, this was the traditional garb of the sailor of the eighteenth and nineteenth centuries, so while the outfit looks distinctive today, it was hardly exceptional 200 years ago.

Surprisingly, perhaps, there was a good chance that the smuggler was a foreigner. After all, smuggling was only an illegal form of the import/export business, and wasn't restricted to English citizens. In times of peace, the market-places of coastal towns rang with many different foreign accents, and a French or Dutch smuggler taking orders for his next trip could easily merge with the crew of a legitimate vessel out getting drunk on the local strong ale. In times of war (and these were frequent) a little more caution was in order, but it usually wasn't difficult to arrange for a school of small English boats to meet a larger vessel from the (nominally) enemy power, a few miles off-shore.

The sea-going men were just one side of the story, though. Face away from the sea, and the land party comes into view: a group of shadowy figures who skulk around the coast waiting to land the cargo and protect it on the journey inland. These people were usually labourers who would supplement their paltry agricultural wages with a little fetching and carrying, to make ends meet. Only 20 per cent of the eighteenth-century population lived in towns and cities, and a quarter of the rural population was made up of landless labourers, many of whom lived in a condition that we would today describe as grinding poverty. According to one estimate,[1] a fifth of the population occasionally received parish relief—the equivalent of today's social security benefit.

Working hours were long, typically twelve or thirteen hours a day Saturdays included, and though wages may have been sufficient to buy food, they often didn't cover the cost of cooking it. Vast tracts of woodland had been cut to build ships and to provide fuel for the glass and steel industries. As a result, firewood was scarce, and as transport —except by water—was very costly, so coal was not yet an economical substitute for wood. The poor commonly ate food, such as cheese, that did not require cooking.

Calais was a major source of the contraband smuggled into the south of England. One distiller from the town built and fitted out ten smuggling ships a year, each capable of carrying 400 casks of brandy. Crews were on commission only—some were even paid in brandy.

For these people, the job of tub-carrier or bat-man (the thugs who made sure that the King's men didn't interfere) must have seemed like an easy way to cook the chicken. For those who could get it, a week's work on the fields paid 7s or 8s (35-40p), but a successful 'run' of a smuggled cargo could bring between 5s and 7s 6d (25p-37.5p) for a night's exertion. For those turned out of work—for example, by the contraction of iron-smelting in the Kentish weald—smuggling may have been the only source of income besides the parish.

The term 'smuggler', though, extended even to people who distributed the contraband inland, and these included not only landless labourers, but also a broader section of the working classes including skilled trades-people. A roll-call of unfortunate Dorset land smugglers whose cases came up in Lyme Regis court makes revealing reading:

Anthony, John	*quarryman*
Bagwell, Maria	*dressmaker*
Charles, Emmanuel	*tin-plate worker*
Dowall, George	*ferryman*
Etchcock, Richard	*labourer*
Ford, James	*cooper*
Gummer, Ann	*needlewoman*
Hatton, Robert	*butcher*
Jerrard, John	*flax dresser*
Kearley, George	*innkeeper*
Lumb, Martha	*chairwoman*
March, David	*pig jobber*
Oxford, William	*miller*
Powell, William	*shoemaker*
Rutledge, Levia	*twine spinner*
Sceard, James	*fell-monger*
Trim, William	*bricklayer*
Vivian, Martha	*labourer*
Way, Mercy	*twine spinner*
Zeally, Thomas	*labourer*

Significantly, 'squire' and 'parson' do not appear among the occupations listed, so it's safe to assume that the customers for the smuggled goods did not run the same risk as those supplying them!

FINANCING THE 'ADVENTURE'

People paid for their illegally imported goods on delivery, so clearly a would-be smuggler had to find finance to buy the goods abroad. There were so many ways of financing a smuggling trip that it's difficult to make any accurate generalizations about how the capital was raised. Every possible form of transaction short of credit cards was pressed into use at one time or another, but the earliest method of funding was probably simple barter. The Kentish and east-coast smugglers would ship

Flushing as it appeared in 1790. The Dutch port was the centre for tea smuggling, and whole industries developed to supply the smugglers' requirements. Oilskin bags, for example, were mass produced to protect cargoes from the weather.

out bales of wool to a destination in Normandy; these same ships would return packed to the gunwales with tubs of wine or bales of silks and lace. No money changed hands—it was a simple and direct arrangement.

The smugglers might themselves have bought the wool in England, but this would obviously have involved a considerable capital investment beyond the means of a rough-and-ready fisherman/smuggler. More likely, amateurs and dabblers in the free-trade acted as haulage contractors, taking cargoes of wool on trust, returning with other contraband, and either paying off the farmer when the incoming cargo had been sold, or just paying in kind, and keeping a share of the contraband as a fee for the trip.

As the trade developed, a number of new patterns started to emerge, partly because export smuggling declined in favour of a growing volume of imports. In the West Country, finance remained predominantly small-scale, with smugglers operating a sort of club scheme in the neighbourhood: everybody bought a share in the trip, each according to their means, and probably paying the organizer in currency. This system had much to recommend it. If the trip went badly wrong, no one person was ruined; and since the whole community had a stake, the risks of the game being spoilt by an informer were slight.

In the south-east of England the arrangements were somewhat different. Kent and Sussex smugglers had access to London, that den of iniquity, and the wealthy home counties. Here trips were more likely to be financed by individuals or by smaller numbers of merchants. A London draper, for example, might stock his shop from smuggled silks and

This genre scene shows how smugglers carried barrels of spirits on slings over their shoulders. However, the artist took liberties with the size of the casks, which would actually have held a little over 4 gallons—about twice as much as the average watering-can.

gloves, and a publican with substantial cellars would be able to dispose of a cargo of wines and spirits across the bar.

These are examples, though, of natural business arrangements in which the financier was also the retailer. There is additionally a suspicion that in the later years of the eighteenth century smuggling was bankrolled by highly-placed figures who never actually saw the contraband any more than one of today's speculators on the futures market ever expects to physically take delivery of a ton of pig-bellies.

Direct evidence of big-business finance for import smuggling is hard to find; like the apparently legitimate businessmen who 'launder' the profits of modern crime, the people involved took care to keep their hands clean. However, Napoleon implicates city folk in his memoirs when he describes how he arranged for gold to be smuggled out of England to support the franc:

> I got bills upon Vera Cruz . . . the bills were discounted by merchants in London, to whom ten percent, and sometimes a premium was paid as their reward. Bills were then given by them upon different bankers in Europe for the greatest part of the amount, and the remainder in gold, which last was brought over to France by the smugglers.

Another approach was for the suppliers of the contraband on the Continent to finance the venture by organizing speculative smuggling trips. French brandy distillers, for example, and Dutch gin manufacturers bought their own ships, and transported goods to within a few miles of the English coast, where they traded with small boats that flocked out from the fishing communities dotted along the shore.

But the most common source of venture finance for smuggling was probably a small consortium of home-counties land smugglers, well placed on the route from the coast to London. These individuals had sufficient capital between them to front the money for the purchase of contraband abroad, and would receive payment when the goods had been sold on the informal wholesale market that thrived on the outskirts of London. The Hawkhurst and Hadleigh gangs (see pages 47 and 163) are examples of this method of capitalization.

For every consortium bringing in vast shipments, there were thousands of petty smugglers who shipped goods across the Channel on small fishing vessels. At times when profits in the business were high, and preventive measures unsuccessful, finance was not a problem. A menial deck-hand on a smuggling ship might be paid in contraband and could amass a tidy sum from a few trips; enough, perhaps, to buy his own vessel and start trading on his own account.

BUYING THE CONTRABAND

With finance found, a representative appointed by the entrepreneur of the smuggling trip often travelled with the outgoing ship to the Continent to purchase the contraband. However, this was not always considered necessary, and the purchase might have been entrusted to the ship's master. A common arrangement was to have agents abroad, who could strike a bargain with the suppliers, and have a cargo stacked ready for loading on the quayside when the tide brought the vessel into port. Another option was for a representative to cross the Channel alone by some legitimate vessel such as a postal packet, and then on arrival to charter a French or Dutch boat and crew.

Finding transport wasn't difficult. At the height of the smuggling era, in the middle and late eighteenth century, some Continental ports reaped vast profits from the smuggling trade, and an enormous industry grew up in supplying the goods demanded by the British market and shipping them over. The most important suppliers were based in Flushing (now Vlissingen in the Netherlands), and Calais, Boulogne, Dieppe, Dunkirk, Nante, Lorient and Le Havre in France.

It is no coincidence that some of these are now familiar destinations for cross-Channel travellers; then, as now, the ports were conveniently situated for a short crossing, and had fine harbours. To a certain extent, each served a different part of England, with Calais and Boulogne supplying Kent and Sussex, and Cherbourg stocking the West Country. The Channel Islands enjoyed unrestricted trade, and were used as a staging post until 1767 when the British government imposed restrictions. At this the French responded by developing Roscoff into a major depot for the supply of Devon and Cornwall, and:

> Roscoff, till then an unknown and unfrequented port, the resort only of a few fishermen, rapidly grew into importance, so that from small hovels it soon possessed commodious houses and large stores, occupied by English, Scots, Irish and Guernsey merchants. These on the one hand gave every incentive to the British smugglers to resort there, and on the other hand, the French government afforded encouragement to the merchants.[2]

This cooperation is hardly surprising, because smugglers and their agents were big spenders. For example, one day in 1766 an enterprising smuggler bought at a Nantes warehouse 229,282 livres (nearly 110 tons) of tea.[3] Furthermore, it cannot be said that the French and Dutch supplied goods in all innocence, because the smugglers' needs were quite different from those of legitimate traders. An honest importer required goods in the largest possible containers, so as to make economies of scale at the dockside: the hogshead was a standard packaging size, and could hold up to 140 gallons, though 54 was more usual. Large packages like these were impossible for smugglers to conceal or to land without winches, so contraband was packed in much smaller quantities. Tobacco came in bales of a convenient size for a one-man lift, and wrapped in oilskin to make a virtually watertight bundle. This approach was highly effective, and bales of tobacco tossed overboard by smuggling ships in an attempt to destroy the evidence stayed afloat in the sea for hours. People in coastal towns were quick to seize this jetsam when it was washed up, since the bundles contained a substantial core of smokable product to which the sea-water had not penetrated.

Tea was protected in a similar way, and spirits were packaged in small barrels or 'tubs' called half-ankers, which contained a little over 4 gallons. Ankers, holding $8\frac{1}{3}$ gallons, were less commonly used. The coopers made both sizes of barrel with flattened sides for easier carrying, and usually supplied them slung together in pairs on ropes. This arrangement meant that 'tub-men' on the English side of the Channel could easily carry a pair of half-ankers across their shoulders, one at the front and one at the back. When pony transport was available, the rope slings on ankers fitted neatly across the beast's back.

The land-party on the cliff-top watched for a flash from the smuggling vessel, and answered with a similar signal, or fired a furze beacon if the coast was clear. The print is a romanticized Victorian view of the free-trade, but it probably also gives a fair indication of how eighteenth-century sea smugglers dressed.

To save tubs, and space in the ships, spirits were supplied just as they came out of the still: over-proof and virtually colourless. Dilution prior to sale was, at least theoretically, a simple matter, but who would buy crystal-clear brandy? To solve this problem, the French distillers offered burnt sugar, to be added to the kegs along with the water.

Over-proof spirits as they came out of the keg were just about drinkable, but lethal in any quantity. There are numerous stories of people opening washed-up or seized barrels and dying of the effects of the drink (see, for example, page 162).

These bundles and barrels were perfectly adequate as long as the smuggling-vessel was not subject to close scrutiny by the revenue men, but as preventive efforts were stepped up, such security could not be guaranteed. The suppliers of contraband responded with extraordinary ingenuity by packing their goods in disguised form. For example, tobacco was made up into ropes, and some warehouses supplied as stock items a whole range of such ropes, from thin cord right through to hawsers as thick as your arm. Innocently coiled on the deck, or tossed casually into a locker, these illicit packages aroused little suspicion. Similarly, spirits were stored in barrels with false bottoms—the tub was then topped up with drinking water, or perhaps with wine, on which lower duty was payable.

When the English customs men got wise to the trick, and resorted to dipping the barrels to find the true depth, the cunning French coopers constructed the hidden compartments at either end of the barrel, tapering away from the official's stick.

A smuggler on a shopping trip was as keen as a modern day-tripper to save money, but eighteenth-century bargains make our duty-free allowances look stingy. The profit margin varied with the prevailing rates of duty, but typically tea cost 7d (3p) a pound on the Continent, and could be sold in England for 5s (25p). Tobacco cost the same, and fetched 2s 6d (12½p) at home. A tub of gin or brandy cost £1, and found English customers at £4 even before 'letting down' to a drinkable strength. Diluted, the profit would have been even greater.

How was all this paid for? In the early years of the eighteenth century smugglers paid in cash only, but as the trade assumed greater proportions and the transactions became almost routine, the merchants began to settle their accounts by cheque or bank draft. This in itself points to a sophistication not popularly associated with rough rude smugglers, and confirms that a well-oiled organization backed up the men who got their hands dirty.

THE CROSSING

With contraband safely stowed, the smugglers awaited the tide for the return trip. In the harbour, the ship would rub shoulders with all manner of other smuggling vessels, from tiny deckless boats with a small sail, right up to large, well-armed cutters.

These smuggling craft had one thing in common: they were all fore-and-aft rigged. That's to say, they had sails like today's yachts. This form of rigging originated in Holland in the sixteenth century, and gradually superseded the square rig for coastal traffic all over Europe in the next three centuries. The difference between the two forms of rigging is not just of academic interest to naval historians: without the development of the fore-and-aft rig, it's fair to say that smuggling could never have developed on the scale that it did.

A vessel with square sails has to have the wind coming from behind to make any progress as it cannot move across the wind or into it. By contrast, a fore-and-aft rigged vessel travels most quickly across the wind, and can move into the wind by tacking. This is a process of sailing across and slightly up-wind, then turning and heading diagonally in the opposite direction, but again slightly up-wind. The ship thus progresses in a zigzag manner.

Clearly, a square-rigged vessel that enters a creek with the breeze behind it cannot get out until the wind changes; trapped in the falling tide, such a vessel would be easily seized. A fore-and-aft rigged vessel,

on the other hand, can sail nimbly up the same creek, discharge the cargo, and then scoot away on the same tide.

In the early eighteenth century when prevention was mainly land-based, small smuggling vessels were popular because they were highly manoeuvrable, and because losing one of several small ships was less damaging than losing a solitary large one. The vessels were commonly less than 50 tons, and were simple luggers or gaff-rigged luggers. A lugger had the mast positioned close to the bows, and a sail hung from a diagonal spar. The gaff rig adds a second, triangular sail in front of the mast.

Later in the eighteenth century smugglers began to use larger vessels which could travel faster and carry heavier cargoes. They chose wherries and cutters, which were gaff-rigged but with the addition of an extra sail on a taller mast above the main lug-sail, and another one at the bows, attached to a spar, the bowsprit, that extended straight forward from the bows. A long bowsprit gave a cutter great speed, and at one time only revenue vessels were permitted to use this spar to gain an extra bit of speed.

As prevention developed, ships were custom-made for the trade. To get maximum possible speed, they were carvel-built: each board of the hull was lapped up against the adjacent one, giving very smooth lines that slipped easily through the water. By contrast, the revenue men more often had slower, clinker-built vessels. These were constructed with each board of the ship's hull overlapping the one below. This form of construction increased the ship's resistance to the flow of water, and slowed it down.

The purpose-built smuggling vessels were made from fir, which was extremely cheap compared to traditional English oak and lighter, giving the vessels that much more of a competitive edge in eluding the King's men. To weight the dice still further in their favour, the smugglers armed their ships to the teeth with carriage guns and smaller swivel guns.

Crossing the Channel in these large sea-going vessels was not exactly routine, but was at least relatively safe. The same could not be said of sailing for England in one of the smaller ships in use in the early part of the century. The smugglers performed amazing feats of seamanship in bringing deckless ships as small as 9 tons across from France in atrocious weather, and in every season of the year. If anything, smugglers favoured bad weather, since it reduced the risk of detection, and in winter vessels sometimes arrived with the rigging festooned with and partly disabled by ice.[4]

There were other dangers besides the weather and the sea. As the century progressed, and the preventive service developed, more and more customs and excise cutters appeared on the scene. Small unarmed smuggling ships could do little when approached by a speeding revenue sloop, which by 1760 averaged around 50 tons, and had a modest complement of carriage guns.[5] For the larger smugglers, though, such a challenge from the customs authorities could be, and was, dismissed with a wave of the arm.

Military superiority partly accounted for this casual attitude. Smuggling ships of 80 tons were commonplace late in the century, and they easily outsailed and outgunned their opponents. However, there were other reasons why the smugglers often made light of the customs and excise ships. The King's crews were frequently second-rate in every respect: the commanders were timid and often poor seamen, and the other crew-members may have been the dregs of the navy, or serving the King against their will. By contrast, the smugglers were highly motivated, highly skilled at handling their vessels, and spoiling for a fight. It's therefore not surprising that on many occasions the hound turned tail and was chased by the hare.

In all fairness to the revenue sloops, there were some fearless crews who terrorized the smugglers they pursued and caught; and when pay was good and the ships well equipped, the government had no difficulty in securing a better class of sailor. However, until the end of the Napoleonic wars, the smugglers ruled the waves more often than the revenue vessels.

LANDFALL

A skilled master of a free-trade ship was expected not only to bring the cargo to English shores, but to do it to a timetable that would make even the Swiss look unpunctual. The success of a smuggling trip hinged on bringing together the contraband and a large group of men to carry it, at a spot where there would be no significant opposition. This was possible only if the time of arrival of the ship was known with some precision.

If the estimated time of arrival was fixed, the landing point certainly wasn't. Careful observation could establish the routine movements of land-based preventive men, but there was always a chance that an eager young officer would appear on the scene at an inconvenient moment. To prepare for this eventuality, smugglers invariably arranged several possible landing points spaced at intervals along the shore. When the ship appeared off the coast, accomplices on land could make a last-minute check on the opposition, then finalize the landing point.

As long as the preventive forces were stationed on land, this system worked well. A smuggling vessel could travel very much faster along the coast than a mounted officer could on shore, and by taking advantage of any coastal feature, smugglers made sure that it was a very un-even match (see page 131, Aberthaw entry). A typical trick was to bring the ship in to the mouth of an estuary, establish which side was most heavily protected, then land on the other side. Since the lowest bridging point was usually a long way upstream, the contraband was nowhere to be seen by the time the hapless custom-house officer arrived on the spot.

Responsibility for bringing the ship in to the right section of coast lay with the spotsman. He had an intimate knowledge of every creek and beach on his patch of the coast, and could instinctively make out features inland on even the darkest night. The spotsman would guide the vessel into a position from where all the pre-arranged landing points—or a signal from some high-point—could be seen.

As the vessel approached the shore, communication with the land party became vital. Smuggling ships were frequently painted black, with dark sails to hinder identification at night, and without a moon they were all but invisible. To indicate that they were off-shore, the spotsman showed a light. On a clear night, spark from a tinder-box would be enough to alert the men on the beach, but another popular signalling method was a 'flash'—a flint-lock pistol without a barrel. When the pan was charged with powder and the trigger pulled, it produced a distinctive blue light that was unmistakable on shore.

An answering flash from the land party indicated that the coast was clear (a phrase that is still used in a wider context), and indicated which beach or cove had been chosen for the landing. This signal was at first given openly by waving a lantern, but as stiff penalties were imposed for signalling to ships at sea, a degree of cunning was brought to bear on the problem. Houses were built with small windows high in the roof, as at Herne, where a lamp could be placed and seen only from the sea. Similarly, a lantern in a cave was invisible from the land. Technology came to the rescue, too, in the form of the spout lantern. As the name suggests, this had a long spout in front of the flame, sometimes with a bull's-eye of glass to focus the beam. An even more distinctive lantern used a primitive rotating shutter to produce a regularly flashing light.

If there was a risk of discovery, the land party might fire a furze beacon to warn the vessel off. This too was forbidden by law, and smugglers resorted to desperate measures to circumvent the regulations. At least one cliff-top house nearly burned down when the occupant stuffed the grate with enough tinder to send flames from the chimney as a signal that the preventives were about.

Daylight landings were not unknown, especially in remote areas, and by day fire from beacons was invisible. However, the smoke wasn't: wet gorse or bracken thrown on the flames formed conspicuous plumes. In some parts of the country a bed-sheet stretched over a peat stack or across a thatched roof confirmed plans for the landing. Other methods were more devious (a farmer at Looe either rode or led his horse along the shore to indicate the state of alertness of the revenue men, see page 104).

Once the crew of the vessel knew they were 'on the spot' (another phrase that's passed into the vernacular) they put on all sail, and headed for the coast. When they reached the shore, responsibility passed to the

Large ocean-going vessels such as the three-masted ship shown here in the background required proper port facilities for a landfall, which would make a search by the customs authorities inevitable. So when the ship's sails appeared on the horizon, a flotilla of small boats would put out from the shore to unload contraband goods at sea.

waiting *lander*. He had the job of mustering the muscle to get the goods out of the hold and inland as far as a place of safety. The lander organized ponies, horses and carts for transport, or in particularly difficult areas, tub-carriers to hump the barrels and bales quickly away from the sea.

The size of the vessel and the characteristics of the chosen spot dictated the nature of the landing. Small ships could be just run against the beach and the contraband thrown overboard onto the shingle. In other places the tubmen might have to wade through the surf to reach the ship. Larger vessels moored a little way off-shore, and an army of tub-boats shuttled to and fro to pick up the cargo.

In very isolated spots, all this urgency would have seemed out of place. At some locations on the east coast the sea ebbs for miles, and smugglers simply moored in the shallow water and waited until the flat-bottomed ship settled into the sand. Then kelp carts came out from the villages nearby and were loaded up with tubs, which were concealed under a superficial layer of seaweed.

In most places on the south coast, though, time was of the essence, and no sooner was the contraband on the beach than it was whisked away into the hinterland. The real beasts of burden were the tub-men, who carried 2 kegs each weighing about 45lb, one on the chest, and one on the back. This was no simple task, and the combined pressure of the two tubs apparently made breathing difficult and caused permanent injury to some of the tub-men. Nevertheless, these athletic figures were capable of moving their 90lb burden at a pace described as a very brisk walk for 10 miles or more.

If the landing took place at the foot of a cliff, the tub-men might additionally have to negotiate several hundred feet of swaying rope ladder before making off into the dark—a challenge that most of us would decline even in daylight without a load.

Clearly, effective self-defence was not a practical proposition for a man burdened with two barrels of gin, so 'bat-men' defended the tub-carriers. These hired thugs equipped themselves with a variety of weapons, such as stout oak clubs, flails or hand guns, and when called upon didn't hesitate to use them. When opposition was expected, two rows of bat-men stood back-to-back a couple of yards apart to form a corridor stretching inland away from the beach, so that the tub-men could run unhindered for safety.

Violent clashes with the revenue forces were inevitable and numerous, and there was loss of life on both sides. The customs men were greatly outnumbered most of the time, and when a patrol of two or three chanced upon a smuggling run in full flow, there was little they could do except signal for assistance and then watch and wait. Often even this was not tolerated, and revenue men were constantly threatened with physical violence and death. Some of the pluckiest preventives refused to be intimidated, and took on gangs of smugglers against quite overwhelming odds. Frequently these brave (some would say foolhardy) young men paid a high price.

Harsh laws against smuggling made the revenue man's task more dangerous; until the late seventeenth century the penalty for smuggling—as for many petty crimes—was death, so a smuggler caught in the act tended to deal out violence on a wholesale basis. Whether he killed his opponent or not hardly mattered, since if convicted of either smuggling or murder the result in court would be the same.

Force of numbers was the best defence against capture, and in any case a large cargo required an army of helpers to unload it. When smuggling reached its zenith in the middle of the eighteenth century, some gangs were indeed capable of mustering hundreds of labourers in a couple of hours (see page 40). This involved considerable organization, and the most successful gangs of land smugglers all had at their heads individuals with a flair for what could be loosely called management. George Ransley of Aldington, who came to dominate Kentish smuggling in the 1820s, was one such figure; and 80 years earlier, Arthur Gray organized another Kentish gang, based in Hawkhurst, with similar though more ruthless skill.

These men and others like them precisely synchronized shipping movements and large bodies of labour, but they also had access to professional skills. At a time when illiteracy was almost universal among the poor, the pen-pushers who kept accounts and wrote letters for the smugglers would be drawn from the ranks of the lower clerks, and often from the clergy—a surprising number of vicars feature in smuggling yarns. Some gangs even maintained surgeons, as at Brooklands in Kent, and solicitors for defence in court.

Personnel management wasn't the only task, though; transport inland was a good deal easier using ponies, horses and wagons. A few smuggling gangs maintained large numbers of horses specifically for transport, using a legitimate trade as a cover. For example, the north Kent Seasalter Company loaded contraband onto horses that were legally used by day for shifting timber in the nearby Forest of Blean, probably to supply oak bark to the many tanneries in the area. Other gangs simply dispersed horses and ponies across the misty marshes; grazing in twos and threes, the beasts attracted little attention, but mustered together, they formed a caravan sometimes 200 strong.

There are countless stories about the smugglers' horses, their intelligence, training and ingenuity. The tale that occurs most frequently is of a caravan of ponies being ambushed, the nags with their burden of tubs being released and whipped away into the darkness. When the exhausted owner arrives home at dawn, he finds his four-legged friends standing dutifully by the door. Interesting and amusing variations on this tale crop up in Scotland (see page 190) and on the Isle of Purbeck.

Smugglers, we are told, shaved their nags and soaped or oiled them to make capture more difficult; they muffled the hooves and the wagon wheels with rags for silent progress through the dark. Many a smuggler trained his horse to stop on the command 'Gee-up', and to bolt when told 'Whoah'. Under instruction from a suspicious revenue man, the smugglers could then pull in the reins and innocently call 'Whoa' to provoke a headlong and apparently spontaneous dash into the night.

Extra transport could also be 'borrowed' from farmers and landowners. A farmer close to the coast knew that a meaningful wink from one of his fisherman friends indicated that the stable doors should be left unlocked or the key hidden under a milk-churn. In the morning, the horses would be back in the stall, muddy and exhausted, but there would be a keg of the best brandy in the corn bin.

This arrangement sounds like a cosy bargain, but horses and other facilities were not always willingly loaned. A winded horse was worthless for ploughing, and an exhausted farm-hand of little more value. Farmers who rebelled against the smugglers using their horses and labourers for transport, and their barns for storage, were kept in line by systematic intimidation resembling today's protection rackets. Sheep would fall unaccountably ill; a hayrick would catch fire; or, returning late from the market, the farmer might ride at speed into a strong black cord stretched between two trees. Before long, the free-traders extracted the grudging cooperation they needed to operate.

TEMPORARY HIDING-PLACES

To a land smuggler, the eventuality to be avoided at all costs was to be caught in possession of the incriminating tubs, so hides and dumps near the coast were of great value. This of course is the origin of the many legendary smugglers' caves, and certainly, where coastal topography created caverns, some of these were used for short-term storage. However, few caves around the coast of Britain make really suitable warehouses: many are very shallow; others are so easily accessible that they offered inadequate security; and most fill with water at high tides, precluding their use for the storage of dry goods. Even spirits would not be completely secure in a tide-washed cave; a heavy surf could dash stored tubs against the rock walls, smashing them into a pile of staves and rings in minutes.

Some caves, such as those at Samson's Bay in Devon, were certainly used for storage, but smugglers often preferred to excavate their own hides in the shifting sands that fringe so many beaches. Once the entrance to the cache had been hidden by the wind-blown dunes, only the smugglers, who had taken bearings on the spot, could find it once more. The preventive forces used long probes to search for hidden contraband in soft sand, but, as the description on page 203 outlines, there were ways to avoid detection by this method. The account also details the other extraordinary precautions which the smugglers took to protect their valuable cargoes.

The excavation of these temporary stores was perhaps the seed from which the ubiquitous story about the smugglers' tunnel grew. Virtually every village within 5 miles of the southern coast of England has a smugglers' tunnel, the location of which the locals will divulge over several stiff drinks about an hour after 'closing time'. Almost always, though, the entrances to the tunnels have been lost or bricked up.

Some tunnel stories turn out to be very plausible. For example, a tunnel at Hayle in Cornwall really does seem to have been built specifically for smuggling. In other instances the tunnel either doubles as a storm drain or some other functional channel, or else is an extension of a natural fissure in the rock, as at Methleigh Manor near Porthleven, and at Porthcothan respectively.

Unfortunately, true tunnel stories are in a minority, and on close inspection, most of the rest are the products of vivid imaginations. The hypothetical tunnels cut through unsuitable rock, or burrow along beneath the water table. If they were genuine, some such tunnels would be prodigious feats of engineering—one of Isaac Gulliver's shafts was rumoured to run from Kinson, now a Bournemouth suburb, to the coast some 4 miles away!

There are two possible explanations of the lack of evidence in support of smuggling tunnel yarns. One is that the word was very loosely used to include sunken roads, or field paths running between high hedgerows that almost met overhead. Such 'tunnels' would certainly conceal smugglers as effectively as a tunnel through rock. And indeed, in some places where a tunnel is supposed to exist, there remains a footpath on the surface. For example, at Hawkhurst a footpath links Island Pond and Hawkhurst Place, two locations that are reputedly connected by a tunnel. The other explanation is that, when witnesses to the movement of contraband were quizzed by revenue men, they preferred not to admit that they had turned a blind eye. 'I saw nothing that night . . . perhaps the smugglers rolled their barrels down a tunnel, out of sight.'

Most tunnel tales fail one crucial test: what did the smugglers do with the spoil? Rock doubles in volume when excavated, and even a short tunnel would yield vast quantities of rubble. Where the tunnel ends at a quarry, a cliff, or on a beach, the story is plausible, because spoil would be inconspicuous. Elsewhere, though, digging a tunnel would more often attract attention than aid concealment.

Besides, why dig a tunnel when the ideal hiding place was so close at hand? The sea surrenders its secrets reluctantly, and smugglers were quick to recognize that the highway that brought them over from France and Holland could also conceal their cargoes. If the revenue man appeared on the scene, tubs of spirits were tipped into the sea for later recovery. A weight anchored the barrel in shallow water, and an inflated bladder and a bundle of feathers tied to the tub-rope marked the spot.

There was a risk of course: if tubs could not be recovered, the seawater seeped through the cheaply-made barrels, rendering the spirit undrinkable. In the West Country, spoiled French brandy earned the nickname 'stinky-booze'.

What started as a convenient way of concealing incriminating evidence developed with time into a systematic smuggling technique. Barrels were lashed together to form a raft, weighted so that it floated just below the surface of the water; pushing the tubs into the sea was known as 'sowing a crop'. The tubs could either be collected later, or floated together to some convenient landing point. At natural harbours which filled with the tide, such as Christchurch, the flowing current would tow the raft of roped-together tubs to the landing point under the very noses of the preventives.

TRANSPORT AND SALE

Methods of moving smuggled goods from the coast to the customers inland varied with the vigilance of the revenue men. If there was little opposition, a chain of armed horsemen—sometimes 150 men and twice as many horses—prevailed by sheer force of numbers. However, in the early nineteenth century when the tide turned against the free-traders, more caution was called for. Distribution took place in the dead of night, and consignments might be split up to spread the risk. In the south of England, smugglers followed roads and tracks to villages on the outskirts of London, where they arranged rendezvous with city merchants in what amounts to a thriving wholesale market. In south London, Stockwell was the base, and elsewhere the heaths and woodlands which are now part of the greater London sprawl provided effective cover: Hounslow Heath and Epping Forest were depots to the west and east. In the home counties, similar markets took place on land that still retains much of its eighteenth-century character, such as Tiptree Heath near Colchester, and Daws Heath near Hadleigh in Essex. These areas were notorious as the haunts of vagabonds and villains, and smugglers were able to melt easily into the general criminal milieu.

The contraband was now nearing the end of its journey, and the final stage prior to retail was to convert the smuggled goods into a form that could not be distinguished from the legitimate article. With tobacco this meant processing into a smokable form, and to achieve this aim the bales would have been mixed in with leaf from a legitimate source. Tea simply had to be broken down into smaller packings, but was often adulterated with rose leaves to bulk it up and increase profits still further. Spirits were usually smuggled over-proof, so they had to be diluted to bring them to a strength that was both profitable, and would not sear the throats of drinkers. One writer who was peripherally involved in the free-trade described how as a boy he learned his 'first lesson in hydrostatics' by doing just this:

> I can well recollect large quantities [of over-proof spirits] being put into an earthenware pan, and diluted with water till reduced to the proper strength which was shown by floating glass beads properly numbered; it was my part to watch them and see when the properly numbered one came to the surface.[6]

This process of 'letting down' to drinking strength could be fraught with difficulties. The smugglers themselves generally spurned the extra profit to be made in dilution, on the grounds that they would have to collect extra tubs to hold the increased volume, so the spirit arrived at the capital in concentrated form. The water added to reduce the strength came from London's over-stretched wells, and frequently all manner of unpleasant substances flowed into the brandy along with the water. Some drinkers were permanently sick as a result.

In London, final retail and distribution of the smuggled goods was sometimes via apparently reputable dealers who, through offering smuggled goods, were able to undercut the competition. At other times, the goods would be hawked round the public bars, or sold through the many gin houses.

In rural areas final distribution of spirits was sometimes carried out by concealing a pig's bladder full of the stuff under a woman's clothing—pregnancy explained away a particularly large swelling. In the event of capture, a quick stab with a knife was all that was needed to dispose of the contraband, albeit with a soaking into the bargain. The 'clome pitcher' was another way of moving small quantities of liquor around. A false bottom contained the spirits, and water or milk poured in on top hid the secret below.

HOW SMUGGLING DEVELOPED

In setting the scene, this introductory description of a smuggling run draws together elements that might have been separated in time or geography, and gives no sense of how smuggling methods evolved in the course of the eighteenth and nineteenth centuries. Furthermore, the rest of the book is organized geographically, and again the chronological context is not stressed. So it's worth now turning briefly to look at how changing patterns of taxation and prevention shaped smuggling practice.

Obviously, smuggling as a business proposition requires something to smuggle—contraband that on crossing a border is taxed, or levied, subject to a duty, or even banned and impounded. Broadly speaking, then, smuggling is the evasion of a levy imposed, or the movement of prohibited goods. English society prior to the twelfth century was substantially self-supporting, and cross-border trade so insignificant that it did not attract the attention of the administrators of the day. Since trade was unregulated, the smuggler as a character didn't really exist.

The growth of trade with Europe brought an end to this import/ export idyll, and provided the smuggler with his first opportunity. There had always been a small-scale cross-Channel trade, largely in luxuries such as wine that could not be produced satisfactorily in England. However, with a growing rural population, and improved methods of agriculture, England began to develop an agricultural surplus that could fill the returning French and Dutch boats. The biggest export was wool.

The English climate and topography are particularly well suited to the sheep, and traditionally the animal has fed and clothed most of the nation. Flax certainly grew in Ireland, and in parts of England and Wales, but common people were clothed in wool and leather. Wool production gathered momentum throughout the 1200s, and by the century's end exports amounted to 30,000 sacks a year. Some large English estates specialized in wool production. Abbey flocks at Crowland in Lincolnshire numbered in excess of 4,000 sheep.

English wool was highly valued abroad; it was tough, and the fibres were long, making them easier to spin. English fleeces made for good fabric, and the surpluses found ready buyers among the merchants of Flanders and Italy. Fleeces were transported to the 'staple'—the only place where they could be legitimately traded with foreigners—and there they were taxed and sold. The staple was often moved from place to place, but in 1347 Calais became a British possession and remained the staple for over 160 years. When the port fell to the French, the staple moved to Middelburg, and then to Bruges. Though much wool was exported, there was a small but expanding domestic fabric industry. Water-powered mills were speeding production, and by 1300 there were important wool-manufacturing centres in the south-west and south, and in Yorkshire and Cumbria.

Locally-produced wool cloth was of a poor standard, and those who were wealthy enough imported foreign wool fabric for making up into fine garments. The best cloth came from the Low Countries, so in the mid-fourteenth century Edward III encouraged immigration by skilled weavers from these areas, and thus provided a much-needed stimulus for the domestic wool-processing industry. The weavers were given considerable protection—both physically, from their xenophobic English neighbours, and more important, in business, from foreign competition.[7]

The plague of 1349 further stimulated wool production. The black death reduced the population of England from about 4 million to 2.5 million in little more than a year, and landowners looked for a form of agriculture less labour-intensive than the manorial system that had prevailed earlier. They found it in sheep-farming. The land that had been open to all was ditched and hedged, and herds of sheep put to graze where serfs had once sweated. Wool production rose dramatically, and with it, the potential tax revenue to the crown.

This lucrative source of income had been spotted long before the wool trade expanded in fourteenth-century England. Wool was the first product on which export duties were levied as far back as 1275. In that year Edward I taxed wool exports to raise revenue for a hard-pressed crown. The charge amounted to half a mark, or 6s 8d on a 26-stone sack. The same charge was levied on each 300 wool-fells (wool still on

sheep skins) and 13s 4d on 'each last of 200 hides'.

At the same time as imposing the duty, the King also recruited the first customs staff to collect the dues. This small full-time staff was simply involved in collecting the revenue; they didn't have the time or the resources to make sure everyone paid up. Within a few years of the imposition of the duty, it was quite clear that there was a considerable amount of evasion going on. This had serious consequences for the king, who needed the income from the duty to finance a succession of wars in Europe.

This connection between duties and wars occurred with monotonous frequency down the centuries. When Britain embarked on the Hundred Years War with France in 1337, Edward III taxed imports and exports to pay for the costly campaign. The King imposed a tax on wine—called 'tunnage'—at 3s 4d per barrel to fund the navy's defence of the trade fleet, since the war with France was partly to protect England's exports of wool to Flanders. Other duties imposed at the same time covered the export of wool cloth. Many goods were taxed by value, at 5 per cent.

Tunnage was not the only tax imposed on wine imports. If a ship brought in more than 20 tuns, the King claimed his 'prise' of 2 tuns, one taken from before the mast, one from behind. Prisage was paid only by English ships; foreign vessels instead paid tax, or 'butlerage', of 2s a barrel.

The pattern of spiralling taxation imposed by successive monarchs continued. The Hundred Years War was followed by similar territorial conflicts between England and her continental neighbours. To pay for the wars, each administration imposed ever more complex regulations and prohibitions; or they simply increased the level of existing duties.

This happened, for example, in the middle of the sixteenth century, when debasement of the coinage reduced the revenue generated by import and export duties. Tunnage was increased dramatically in 1558, from 3s 4d to 53s 4d, and Queen Mary's reign saw the introduction of a new book of rates, which set out the duties payable on each item. This greatly increased the duty by 1s in the pound, on many of the liable goods.

But why choose the import or export of goods as the taxable activity? Why not tax the sheep themselves on the hoof at the place they were grazing, for example? The answer is simple: coastal trade is conspicuous, so the coastline was the natural place for the authorities to try and tax the trade, or to stop it altogether. Being an island, Britain's borders are graphically defined and (relatively) unshifting. The movement of goods across England's borders was therefore an obvious business; the sails of a ship signalled its approach on the horizon even before the vessel itself was visible.

Other factors also made the movement of shipping easy to see. The ebbing and flowing of the tide regulated sailing times. In these days of deep-water harbours we tend to forget that for millennia shipping had to wait for the tide before sailing, and at low water boats simply grounded in the mud at the foot of the quay. Wind was a factor, too. The square-rigged sailing ship that dominated until the advent of fore-and-aft rigging was restricted by the wind. To leave a port, such ships needed a breeze blowing them out to sea.

All these factors meant that trade across England's coastline was easy to spot. Taxation of such obvious activity therefore must have seemed a natural way to earn revenue for the crown. Unfortunately, imposing a tax and collecting it are two different matters. When Edward I created the customs service, he did little to ensure that the customs dues were actually paid; he simply provided the apparatus of collection, in the form of a custom-house with a small staff at various points around the coast. This laissez-faire approach to the gathering of revenue prevailed for some considerable time, but by the early fifteenth century, the rudiments of enforcement were beginning to appear.

At this stage, legal import of goods meant using an official port—there were thirteen of these, each serving one section of the coastline. Goods could be landed elsewhere, but only with the explicit permission of the authorities at the main port. Naturally it was impossible for a handful of officials to control a whole stretch of coast from a single point. The East Anglian coast, for example, was controlled from Yarmouth, but the customs authorities there were expected to keep watch on nearly 90 miles of coastline, up as far as Blakeney and right down to Woodbridge.

At each of these key ports there were two principal officials responsible for the collection of the customs dues. The *collector of customs* was the official who had to actually do the work, but he was overseen by a *controller of customs*. Between them, the two men were supposed to collect the dues payable, and sign and seal the relevant receipts and other export documents. This two-part arrangement was designed to ensure the honesty of the officials, and a further precaution was that the port seal was made in two halves. Each official had half the seal and all documents had to carry both halves to be legal. Each of the two officials was separately accountable for the transactions of the port.

These customs officials were very badly paid, but they benefited from seizures of smuggled goods, and made a charge on every receipt sealed. Nevertheless, the temptation for the two men to cooperate with smugglers must have been irresistible, and the sealing of blank receipts soon became a problem. Signed and sealed, the piece of parchment was filled in by the merchant with whatever he chose. Blank receipts were so commonplace by 1433 that the practice was discussed in Parliament. However, even the stiff penalty—three years in gaol plus seizure of all belongings—proved little deterrent. In an attempt to enforce honesty on controllers and collectors, a third official was appointed. The *surveyor of customs* at each port was supposed to monitor his colleagues as they worked.

Backing up these three officials was a minor army of lesser bureaucrats. The *tide-waiter's* task was to board incoming vessels arriving on the high tide and check that they tied up at the appointed place on the quay. The tide-waiter joined London-bound boats, for example, at Greenwich, and made sure that the cargo was not unloaded on an isolated jetty out of sight of the waiting triumvirate of controller, collector and surveyor (all eyeing each other suspiciously, no doubt). To ensure the honesty of the tide-waiter there was another official, the *tide-surveyor*.

When these functionaries had safely guided the boat to dock in the right place, other officials took over. The *coast-waiter* supervised the unloading of cargoes from home ports; the *land-waiter* watched over loading and unloading of ships from foreign ports; the *land-surveyor* similarly kept an eye on both the land- and coast-waiters. At the bottom of the ladder the *searcher* was responsible for checking that the boat's cargo tallied with what was on the receipt; the *weigher* unpacked the cargo and weighed it; and the *tidesman* stayed with the vessel until the unloading was complete.

This hierarchy of officials had to administer a welter of complex laws

In 1724 Defoe counted 2,000 ships in the Pool of London, and at times it was impossible to see across the river for the forest of masts. Little wonder, then, that evasion of customs duty was simple, and that bribery of the officials who collected it practically undetectable.

that were added to the statute book over the centuries to protect the wool industry. The restoration of the monarchy in 1660 added still more laws and additionally jacked up the penalties for illegal export of wool. In 1660 all export of wool was forbidden, and soon afterwards further legislation ensured that those who smuggled out wool risked the gallows for their sins. Some of the measures taken seem extraordinary: a 1666 statute even obliged everyone to be buried in a shroud made of pure wool cloth!

These restrictions outraged wool producers, who, faced with low prices in England, naturally turned to the export trade to stave off starvation. This was hardly a new situation. As early as 1390 there was a stockpile of unsold fleeces amounting to three years' output. However, as the seventeenth century came to a close, export of wool from England's southern counties was getting seriously out of control, with fleeces disappearing to Flanders by the thousand almost as soon as they had been separated from the sheep's back. According to one estimate, 120,000 packs of wool annually were exported illegally.

The centre of the trade was Kent, where the wool exporters were known as 'owlers'. As restrictive laws strangled the owlers' trade, they became progressively more bold, and pooled their resources on the grounds that there was safety in numbers. Soon an owling venture involved hundreds of armed men.

Something clearly had to be done to stop the rot. In 1671 Charles II had set up the Board of Customs, and by 1685 there were ten smacks patrolling the coast between Yarmouth and Bristol. On land, a force of mounted customs officers—called riding officers—was established in 1690. However, the riding officers could hardly be described as an effective opposition, since there were just eight of them to patrol the whole of the Kent coastline. Their burden of work was made even greater by further restrictive legislation on the wool trade. The 1698 Wool Act obliged all producers with farms within 10 miles of the coast to register their annual production with the local custom-house immediately after shearing. The Act also controlled the movement of wool close to the coast.

The riding officers not only had to contend with the owlers, but with the growing tide of smuggled imports. The most recent war—again with the French—had necessitated a further hoisting of import duties, and the smugglers now found they could make a profit on both legs of their cross-Channel journey. Ships that went out loaded with wool came back groaning with foreign luxuries.

The inadequacy of the eight brave men of Kent was recognized in 1698, when the scope of the force (now called the landguard) was expanded and numbers increased to 50 and later to 300. However, the riding officers were hampered by the fact that they were land-based. Smugglers at sea had the benefit of much greater mobility, and could simply land goods at the point where the preventive effort was weakest. The sea-based preventive effort had been abandoned in 1690 with the appointment of the eight riding officers, and for the next eight years the custom-houses relied on the navy to oppose the smugglers at sea. At the turn of the century, though, the waterguard was established, with 21 vessels stationed all the way around the coast.

These twin forces were to be the principal opponents of the smugglers for the next century or so, and their effectiveness varied according to the calibre of the officers, their pay and conditions, and other factors. When pay was good, and the service was able to hire committed and diligent officers who could call on the military for assistance, the preventive effort could be remarkably effective. Regrettably, this seemed to be the case for only a fraction of the time. The job of riding officer in particular was not well paid, and out of their £42 annual salary, the officers also had to buy and maintain a horse. The temptation to turn a blind eye to a smuggling venture in return for payment of a small fee was irresistible for some.

The difficulty was exacerbated by the fact that the riding officers lived in the hearts of the communities they were supposed to be policing. If they were diligent in their efforts to prevent smuggling, they were ostracized and persecuted (see page 44); the alternative was collaboration with the smugglers, an easy life, and a regular supplement to the meagre pay. The easy option must have seemed attractive indeed.

SMUGGLING EXPANDS

In the absence of really effective opposition, it was inevitable that wholesale evasion of duty would expand. The process was accelerated in the early years of the eighteenth century by widespread support for the Jacobite cause. Smuggling was seen not just as a business transaction, but also as an act of rebellion and support for the Old Pretender. Some of the smuggling gangs openly supported the Jacobites and drank

The old London custom-house burned down in 1814, and was replaced by a new building on Thames Street. This illustration shows how the building appeared in 1828.

their health; the Oak and Ivy inn where the Hawkhurst Gang met takes its name from the Jacobite emblem. Jacobite sympathies manifested themselves in more tangible ways, too. Jacobites travelled secretly between France and England on smuggling boats, and some smugglers are known to have acted as spies and double agents for the cause.

The government responded to the widespread evasion with a rash of legislation, clamping down on smuggling in every imaginable way. The 1718 Hovering Act made it illegal for vessels smaller than 50 tons to wait within 6 miles of the shore, and brandy imported in smaller ships (under 15 tons) was also liable to seizure. Vessels involved in these offences were impounded and destroyed, usually by being sawed up, and their ropes unravelled. The divided vessels were useless at sea, but often found uses on land. Peggotty's house, of Dickens fame, was the remains of a smuggling boat.

Other legislation passed soon afterwards outlawed Kent and Essex boats with four or more oars, in an attempt to prevent contraband from being rowed across the Channel. Transportation to the colonies was simultaneously introduced as a penalty for smuggling, and the scope of the Act was cast to include virtually anyone carrying firearms, or wearing a mask to hinder identification.

However, it was legislation of 1736 that perhaps set the scene for the appalling violence that characterized mid-century smuggling in the south-east. A Parliamentary Committee of Enquiry investigated the free-trade, and painted a damning picture that demanded immediate action from the government. The result was the introduction of the death penalty for injuring preventive officers in the course of their duty, and heavy fines for bribery. Even an unarmed smuggler resisting arrest

faced transportation. The legislation was called the Act of Indemnity, and it was indeed the indemnity clauses that perhaps most provoked smuggling violence in the subsequent decades. A smuggler who revealed the names of his collaborators was granted a free pardon, making virtually anyone involved in the free-trade who turned King's evidence a mortal threat to his companions.

These new laws had little effect on the level of smuggling, and three years later the outbreak of the War of Jenkins' Ear against Spain pushed the already over-stretched government resources almost to breaking point. The situation worsened when the conflict became a mere sideshow to the War of the Austrian Succession, and when Jacobite sympathies exploded into full-scale rebellion. By the 1740s smuggling by large forces of armed men had reached a climax.

The threat to public order posed by the smugglers was now as much an issue as the loss of revenue, and in 1745 the tax on tea was radically reduced in an attempt to cut the profits of the smuggling gangs, and to eliminate them by economic means rather than by force. However, this move was only a partial success, since the smugglers merely turned to new forms of contraband, notably spirits, and tea duties were in any case raised again soon afterwards.

The government passed still more draconian legislation in 1746, and once more failed to back it up with greater resources for the preventive forces. Like the Act of Indemnity ten years earlier, these laws aimed to undermine the smugglers' power base in the countryside by providing an inducement to inform; and again, the smugglers responded with a further escalation of violence and intimidation of witnesses and jurors.

The core of the 1746 act was the publication of the names of known

Convicted smugglers and other prisoners awaiting transportation were housed if they were lucky in the filthy and cholera-infested cells of London's Millbank Prison. The unlucky ones rotted on prison hulks.

smugglers in the London Gazette. A smuggler thus 'Gazetted' had 40 days to turn himself in, and at the end of that period he was effectively outlawed, with a bounty of £500 on his head. The death penalty was extended to cover not just smuggling, but assembling in preparation for a run, and even the harbouring of smugglers. The bodies of smugglers who killed officers were to be hung on gibbets around the coast.

The new laws sparked bestial violence (see page 59) by gangs who aimed to obtain silence from witnesses either by intimidation or, if necessary, by murder; but if anything, the terrorism that followed was counter-productive. There was widespread revulsion at the activities of the gangs, particularly after the trial of Hawkhurst gang members revealed every gory detail of tortures and executions. By the mid-century the largest smuggling gangs had lost much of the local support they once enjoyed and indeed needed, and had been broken up.

Smuggling continued, however, and further conflicts abroad over the next three decades both provided a periodic distraction from the problems posed by the smugglers, and exacerbated the loss of revenue caused by the free-trade. For example, the cost to the Exchequer of the Seven Years War which started in 1756 was considerable, because 200,000 troops were being paid. Land Tax had been a shilling in the pound in the 1740s, but had quadrupled by the end of the war. The government was forced to borrow £60 million to finance the conflict, but they also looked to import duties to pay for it: duties on tea that had been cut in 1745 from 4s 9d a lb to 1s, were in 1759 raised again. This of course created a renewed demand for contraband tea, which the smugglers were only too happy to satisfy.

The outbreak of the American War of Independence in 1776 had a similar effect, as troops that had been assigned to guarding the coast in peacetime were again whisked away to fight abroad. By 1782, shortage of manpower induced the government to take a softer line on smugglers in an attempt to woo them into the service of the crown. The Act of Oblivion allowed a smuggler to wipe the slate clean by volunteering for the armed forces. Smugglers' skills as seamen were especially prized, and even their most vigorous opponents in the revenue services occasionally felt honour-bound to express admiration for the men's ability.

The effectiveness of this new law was, however, reduced by a clause that allowed substitution. A smuggler who could find two others willing to take his place would be released from a previously-imposed penalty up to £500, and four men were sufficient to repay any smuggling crime except the killing of a revenue officer. Substitution particularly affected

rich smugglers such as Isaac Gulliver (see page 82), who could afford to buy the services of others, and people even placed advertisements offering themselves as substitutes on payment of a fee.

By the 1780s, the free-trade had once more reached alarming levels, with smugglers trading unhindered on the continent. The revenue cutters put up a spirited defence at sea, but the wages of crews had fallen behind those paid on merchant ships, and the quality of seamen attracted to the service was lower as a consequence. Once goods had been landed in England, the run inland took place virtually unhindered, and smuggling gangs had once more sprung up to defy the authorities.

In response to this crisis, the government set up yet another committee of enquiry in the early 1780s, which came up with the blindingly obvious conclusion that the prevalence of smuggling could be attributed to high duties. William Pitt took note of the committee's report, and in 1784 slashed the duty on tea from 129 per cent to 12.5 per cent, and thus, at a stroke, rendered tea an unprofitable cargo. As in the past, though, this simply caused a shift into other forms of contraband, and the trade went on largely unabated.

The turn of the century was marked by still more conflict with Britain's European neighbours. The French revolutionary war began in 1792, and continued until 1802, and there was then a one-year lull before the beginning of the Napoleonic wars which continued until 1815. The wars once more drew preventive forces away from Britain's coasts, and again proved a financial drain. And as in other conflicts, smugglers played a role that was at best ambiguous, and often downright treacherous.

Smuggling ships traded freely with French ports through the wars, and often took reports of English conditions over to the enemy, returning with letters to spies in Britain. A flourishing export trade in smuggled gold grew up, as Napoleon struggled to pay his mercenaries while the economy collapsed around him. Vast galleys, rowed by dozens of men, propelled the gold across the Channel at speeds that would look respectable to a modern day-tripper (see page 27). In all fairness, though, some of the smugglers probably also acted as double agents, and some certainly remained loyal to the Crown, bringing back to England intelligence about French shipping.

Smuggled cargoes of this period frequently included French fugitives. During the revolutionary war, aristocrats fleeing the tumbrils sought refuge in England, often choosing a passage on a smuggling ship

Opposite: *Flintlock and percussion-cap pistols were notoriously unreliable, and even when they did work, the weapons were inaccurate and fired only once per loading. Hand-to-hand fighting between revenue men and smugglers as depicted in this illustration was therefore common, and one man can be seen with his pistol raised as a club.*

Left: *Officers limping past a prevention post must have been a common sight. Clashes with smuggling gangs were an occupational hazard, and the valiant preventives were often outnumbered.*

as the route least open to discovery. In the Napoleonic wars, the traffic flowed in the opposite direction, with escaped French prisoners fleeing from the north Kent coast, leaving behind the prospect of lingering death on a rotting prison hulk.

In the short term, the Napoleonic war made smuggling considerably more difficult, because preparations for the expected invasion also protected the coast from the attentions of the free-traders. This was most marked in the south-east, where in 1806, the construction of Martello towers provided purpose-made look-outs for the forces of law and order. In Kent, the Royal Military Canal effectively cut off Romney Marsh from its hinterland, so that Kentish smugglers no longer had easy access to the beaches they had traditionally favoured.

A reorganization of the preventive services also made life difficult for the free-traders. In 1809 the Preventive Waterguard was established. This brought the cutters and small rowing boats of the customs service under more central control, and provided greater coordination. Pay was raised to a higher level than that for comparable posts in the navy.

These changes improved morale in the service and a gradual decline in free-trade activity began. However, when the battle of Waterloo in 1815 brought the Napoleonic wars to an end, the decline in smuggling halted as enormous numbers of military personnel returned to a civilian life that must have seemed dull by comparison with the excitement of battle. Many of these men were skilled seamen, and Britain's fishing and merchant fleets couldn't hope to absorb such an influx of labour. Smuggling seemed like an attractive option.

This new breed of free-trader nevertheless faced highly organized opposition, and smuggling methods began gradually to change in response to the stepping up of preventive efforts. Concealment took the place of force. On the simplest level, smugglers would hide the illegal imports under a legitimate cargo such as coal, timber or stone. But human ingenuity knows no bounds, and as the customs men got wise to the smugglers' tricks, so the hiding places became more difficult to find. Masts and spars were hollowed out and stuffed with contraband; some vessels even had double hulls, with space for contraband between the two skins. The old days of smuggling runs succeeding by sheer force were well and truly over.

Two years after Waterloo, the preventive effort was stepped up yet again, with the introduction of the 'Coast Blockade' between North and South Foreland on the east Kent coast. The blockade was a force of land patrols commanded by Captain 'Flogging' Joe McCulloch, and though it was an effective deterrent, the blockade men had little enthusiasm for their task. They were frequently involved in skirmishes with smugglers, and were considered fair game for bribery in cash or contraband. The blockade men were stationed in the Martello towers, and in watch houses a few miles apart, and the blockade was soon extended to Seaford, and then round to Chichester.

Almost simultaneously, the Coast Guard was established on sections of the coast where the blockade men did not patrol, and by the end of the 1820s the effectiveness of the two forces was beginning to bite. In 1831 the coastguard service replaced the blockade all the way round the coast, and thus laid the foundations of the preventive force that we know today.

The coastguards and blockade men drove the smugglers underground (or more accurately underwater, since the sinking of tubs became the standard method of concealment), but it was economics that finally signalled the end of the great smuggling era. In the 1840s Britain adopted a free-trade policy that slashed import duties to realistic levels. Within ten years large-scale smuggling was just a memory.

Fears of a Napoleonic invasion prompted the construction of a chain of solid blockhouses, or Martello towers, round the south of England in 1806. After Waterloo, the towers were turned into watch-houses and guard posts for the prevention of smuggling.

THE SOUTH-EAST

LONDON TO CHICHESTER

A glance at an atlas is all that's needed to see the advantages that the south-east of England offered to the enterprising smuggler. To the east, within sight on a clear day, lies northern France, the source of much of the contraband; and to the north and west lie rich farm land, and the wealthy capital—ready markets for the fine laces, wines and brandy that the smuggler obligingly shipped across the Channel.

Smuggling, however, began not as the import activity that we know today, but as an export business. And in a sense, the south-east might be regarded as the cradle of big-business smuggling for the whole of the British Isles.

You only need to drive across misty Romney Marsh to see why this was so. Contented sheep still chomp the salty grass of the marshes, just as they have done for centuries, and it was the wool from their backs that was carried out of the country by the ton to the waiting weavers on the Continent. Even in the thirteenth century massive taxation on wool exports made the rewards from illegal wool export well worth the risk of capture.

The wool smugglers of Kent generally, and Romney Marsh in particular, were called 'owlers'. There has long been debate about how they acquired this name, and people have advanced various romantic theories, mostly centred around owls. The smugglers hunted at night, so they took the name of the nocturnal bird; or they signalled to each other by hooting like owls. The most prosaic explanation, and probably the most likely, is that 'owler' is just a corruption of 'wooler', which was a common name for anyone processing wool.[1]

The wool smugglers of south-east England, and their successors, the import smugglers, developed a reputation for savagery that is often used as a yardstick by other counties claiming a 'gentle' nature for their own smugglers. Certainly the horrific killings of Galley and Chater (see page 59) and the thuggish activities of the Hawkhurst Gang lend weight to this opinion, but it's possible to cite evidence of matching barbarity from other counties; for example, the way in which Jeremiah Gardener lost his nose near Snape in 1727 (page 166).

One possible explanation for the fearsome reputation of the Kent and Sussex smugglers is that their activities were more widely advertised than those of smugglers from other counties. The book that chronicles the torture and savage murders of Galley and Chater was first published in 1749, shortly after the trial, and reprinted four times in that year alone.[2] It has appeared in full and abridged forms many times since. Furthermore, it contained graphic engravings of the men's last moments which would have impressed even the illiterate. Perhaps if some Cornish smugglers had received an equally bad press, that part of Britain would not now pretend that smuggling there was a harmless fraud that hurt only the King's purse?

However, assuming that the smugglers of the south-east really were more violent than their fellows, are there any genuine reasons why this should be the case? Perhaps the long history of smuggling in the area goes some way towards explaining its savage nature. In the heyday of smuggling—the late eighteenth and early nineteenth centuries—the trade was carried out by large and highly organized gangs that landed

their goods mostly by brute strength. Men with cudgels and firearms lined the beach in such numbers that preventive forces could only stand and watch. This form of smuggling was not unique to Kent and Sussex—certainly the Essex gangs landed goods in this way—but it was more prevalent in the south-east than elsewhere. In other parts of Britain smugglers seem more often to have favoured the clandestine landing of a smaller cargo, and to have enjoyed the benefits of greater secrecy. By their very nature, open landings demanded greater force.

The size of the cargoes may also have been a factor: Kentish smuggling was on a scale that demanded large amounts of venture capital. Such sums were often raised not locally but at some distant point, usually London. Outside investors would want to protect their cash, and would not have been averse to hiring hoodlums to do it. By contrast, the financing of smuggling in other parts of Britain was more often on a cooperative basis, with each villager buying a share in the run. This ensured not only total support in the locality (hence less need for violence), but also that the loss of a cargo was a burden shared by all, and easier to bear as a result.

Besides having an aggressive streak, Kentish smugglers possessed one or two other quirks and wrinkles not shared by their counterparts in other areas of the British Isles. The most extraordinary is probably the practice of rowing cargoes across the Channel. This was most popular during the Napoleonic wars for shipping gold to pay Napoleon's armies, and the boats were monsters, up to 40 feet long and 7 feet wide.

The port of Deal specialized in building these boats. A dozen oars each side pulled them over to France in less than five hours during calm weather; and even with a head-wind, the Kentish oarsmen were no slouches. On one occasion a rowing-boat leaving Dover had difficulty getting out of the harbour because of the wind, and had to hitch a tow from a steamer. Once they had left the cliffs behind, though, the oarsmen overtook the steamship, and beat it to the French coast.

Pursuit of these galleys in a sailing vessel was futile, as a preventive officer succinctly summed up when he described such a chase as 'sending a cow to catch a hare'. Little wonder that the construction of 'Guinea boats', as they were called, was eventually forbidden in England.

Prohibition didn't deter the Guinea smugglers of Deal, Dover and Folkestone. Laughing at the authorities, they simply built their boats across the Channel, under the self-interested protection of the French government. The boats were so cheap that they could almost be considered expendable at the end of a trip: a 24-oared galley cost £40 or so to build, a small sum compared to the £30,000 worth of gold that the smugglers might be carrying on a single trip. There's a modern-day parallel here, in that drug smugglers think nothing of abandoning a light aircraft once they have ferried in their deadly cargo.

Kent became such a centre for smuggling activity that it is hardly surprising to find the earliest preventive efforts concentrated in the south-east. In 1690 an unstoppable force of eight men was stationed in the towns of Lydd, Romney, Hythe and Folkestone in an attempt to prevent wool exports from these areas. These 'Riding Officers' patrolled

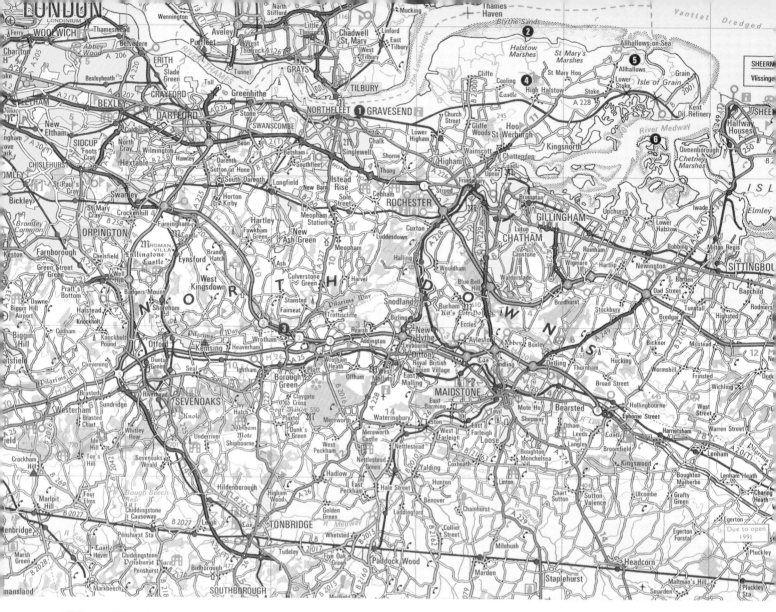

the area on horseback to detect and deter, but the smugglers would perhaps have outnumbered them a hundred to one.

In 1816 the Kent coast blockade scheme started between North and South Foreland. In 1824 this was extended north round to Sheerness, and south to Beachy Head, and in 1824 round as far as Chichester. Preventive measures existed in other parts of the country, but were never as strong as in Kent.

THE THAMES ESTUARY AND NORTH KENT

The Thames estuary today has a hard-edged, definite outline imposed by the high sea wall, but a couple of centuries ago the coast was not nearly so well defined. Ships heading for London threaded their way through treacherous channels and numerous mud-banks to find a safe harbour, and many made unscheduled stops in the sticky mud.

Sometimes these halts were the legitimate result of bad navigation. Frequently, though, the overnight wait for the tide was simply an excuse to unload half the cargo into a necklace of small boats that appeared as if by magic from the reedy margins of the river as soon as the ship grounded. Throwing parcels of tea from the deck of a large ship to a passing rowing-boat was a simple matter; in the unlikely event that the preventive forces were watching from the shore, the ship's master could always excuse himself by claiming that the off-loading was

necessary in order to float the ship off the mud. Once ashore, pursuit was virtually impossible, since the low-lying land was studded with brackish pools and broad drainage dykes, and the safe routes to dry land were known only to the locals.

GRAVESEND ■1

177/178-TQ6474, 7m NW of Rochester.

All vessels that managed to negotiate the twisting channel tied up at Gravesend on their way to the capital. This was the theory, at least. At the bustling Gravesend quayside, a customs officer boarded incoming vessels in order to escort the cargo safely to an official wharf in London. This practice revealed abuses of the system long before the heyday of smuggling: as early as 1410 a monk boarding a ship moored here was 41caught carrying a gold ring and a substantial sum of money. The same year a Flanders woman, Petite Gerderoic, was searched under similar circumstances at Haarlem, Gravesend, and caught carrying 21 gold rings, a block of gold, jewellery and rare books with coral-encrusted bindings.

THE SHIP AND LOBSTER

Approaching from the W, follow the A226 right through Gravesend, then take the second exit at a mini-roundabout, down Ordnance Road. Follow the road round through an industrial estate until you see signposts to the

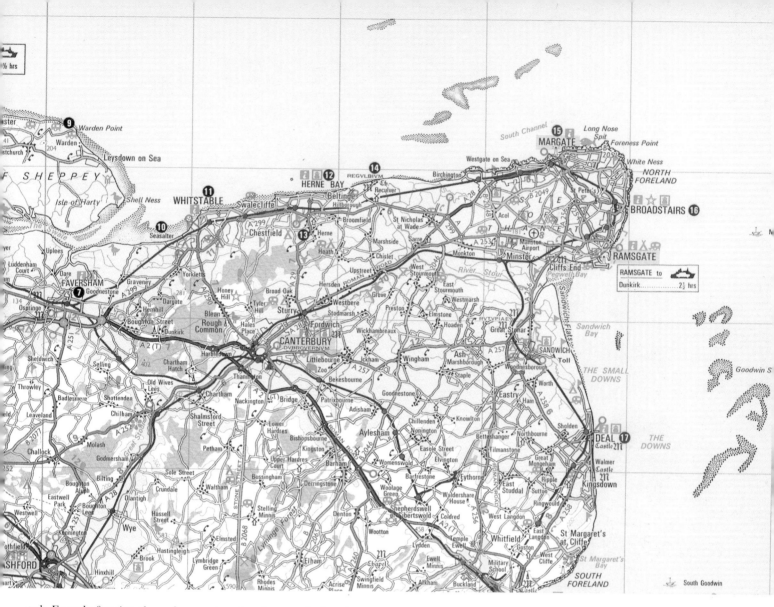

pub. *From the first sign, the road weaves in and out between the factories to the pub by the waterside.*

There are many stories associating the Gravesend area with the free-trade, and though some are demonstrably untrue (see below), the smuggling pedigree of the Ship and Lobster is impeccable. The pub is now hidden among container depots and modern jetties, yet this setting is nothing new. Even in the eighteenth century, it was situated in an industrial area, sandwiched between a windmill and a sulphur mill. The sulphur mill was very probably a blind for smuggling operations; contraband was reputedly unloaded from ships at Folkestone and carried overland to Denton, to be hidden in tunnels under the mill.

Some credence was added to this story when the Strood canal was being built: workers fell into one of the tunnels as they were digging. More confirmation comes from Dickens, who used the Ship and Lobster as the model for the inn he described in *Great Expectations*:

> At length we descried a light and a roof, and presently afterwards ran alongside a little causeway made of stones that had been picked up hard by. Leaving the rest in the boat, I stepped ashore, and found the light to be in the window of a public house. It was a dirty place enough, and I dare say not unknown to smuggling adventures; but there was a good fire in the kitchen, and there were also eggs and bacon to eat, and various liquors to drink . . .
>
> I lay down with the greater part of my clothes on, and slept well for a few hours. When I awoke, the wind had risen, and the sign

of the house (The Ship) was creaking and banging about, with noises that startled me.

The Ship and Lobster is not the only Gravesend pub with smuggling connections. Before alterations the Three Daws on the waterfront boasted seven staircases to ensure that the local smugglers always had a handy escape route. The pub retains much of its charm.

GRAVESEND TUNNELS

A recurring theme in smuggling stories is that of secret tunnels, and in the Gravesend area one such story suggests that several local landmarks are linked by tunnels. Though much of the tale is demonstrably untrue, it is nevertheless interesting, because it throws light on how smuggling tales in general become distorted and exaggerated with time. It has been recorded by a local historian:

> There are good reasons for believing that an extensive system of underground roads existed at one time or another for more or less illicit purposes. Some sections of these have been supported by proof of a reasonably reliable kind during excavations.

He goes on to say that there were tracks cut in the chalk.

> from Cobham Hall in the South-East to Wombwell Hall; to Swanscombe Wood, where Clapperknapper's Hole is regarded as the exit in the extreme southwest: to Parrock Manor, or

Parrock, or both; to the river bank at the old sulphur mill, near the Ship and Lobster; and to an unknown destination from an unknown source at Pelham Road—Old Road—Perry Street.[3]

Certainly the reference to the Ship and Lobster pub bears up under close scrutiny, but the other references are more dubious. Clapper-knapper's Hole, which has now been destroyed by quarry working for the cement industry, was a small indentation in the ground in Swanscombe woods. However, at that point at least 50 feet of sand lay over the chalk. Digging a vertical shaft in such soft ground would have been virtually impossible—a local geologist[4] commented, 'You'd need to cut down all of Swanscombe woods to make pit-props'. Many of the other tunnels are supposed to have run for several miles through hard chalk and crossed a watercourse. Digging such tunnels would have required a phenomenal amount of labour, and a string of windmills to drain them.

EGYPT BAY AND SHADE HOUSE, COOLING ▪2

178-TQ777782, 7m E of Gravesend. Park near Marshgate Farm in Cooling, and leave the road via gate to the left of the Cooling Cricket Club sign. Walk through the fields following well-defined raised paths. The square brick outline and white shutters of Shade House soon come into view on the right. Walk for about 3/4 mile until the house is directly on your right, then go through two gates on the right, and follow a metalled road to approach the house. Egypt Bay is 1/2m N.

Egypt Bay on the Hoo Peninsula was a typical Thames estuary landing spot, though its soft and changing outline has now been made regular and permanent by the concrete sea defences. Inland from the bay, though, there is still a reminder of the smuggling activity that was once rife here. Shade House was built specifically to aid the landing of contraband on the southern shores of the Thames. Significantly, all the windows of this peculiar box-like building face inland, to provide a good view of anyone approaching within a mile or so.

The cottage is even now extremely isolated, but would have been more so in the eighteenth century. The marshes were malarial, and most people lived on higher ground farther inland. Local stories tell of vaulted brick tunnels leading from Shade House towards the river, but there is no visible evidence today to back up these tales. However, we do know that the North Kent Gang (see page 35) used Shade House in their smuggling activities, driving the many marsh sheep along the trails they had followed inland so that there would be no tell-tale footprints.

WROTHAM AND VIGO ▪3

Wrotham lies 8m N of Tonbridge in a quiet backwater close to the junction of the M20, the A20 and the A227. At the pair of roundabouts where these roads meet, follow the local signs to Wrotham. The Bull is on the right, at 188-TQ613592, and the stone referred to below is set into the wall to the left of the pub. The Vigo Inn is on the right of the A227 from Wrotham to Meopham at 188-TQ632611, near Trottiscliffe (pronounced Trosley locally).

Not all contraband was water-borne. Some consignments followed inland routes, often via traditional trackways such as the Pilgrims' Way that traces the foot of the North Downs from Canterbury to Winchester. Wrotham, not far from Gravesend, was a major staging-post for the caravans of horses travelling up from the coast, and the Bull Inn there functioned as the headquarters of a gang led by one Lieutenant Colonel Shadwell. Shadwell met an untimely end—he was shot by army deserters, and a memorial to him can still be seen in the village. A mile or so away on the Gravesend road, the little hamlet of Vigo had an equally convenient resting-point for the London-bound convoys. The pub of the same name in the village once boasted a concealed hiding place for contraband that was revealed by building work on the substantial hearth. Though the pub is still redolent with the atmosphere of the eighteenth century, the hidey-hole has now been all but forgotten locally.

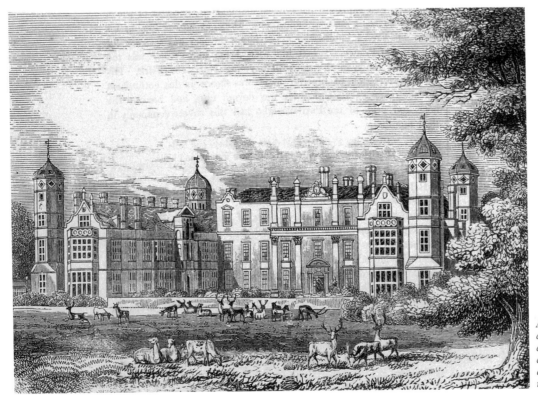

According to local legend, smugglers dug a network of tunnels in the Gravesend area to conceal the movement of their cargoes inland. One tunnel allegedly emerged here at Cobham Hall, some three miles south-east of Gravesend quay.

The Bull Inn at Wrotham was a centre of smuggling activity in the eighteenth and nineteenth centuries.

HIGH HALSTOW ∎4

Northward Hill is at 178-TQ7876 5m NE of Strood. The wood is now a National Nature Reserve administered by the RSPB. Park at the end of Longfield Avenue in High Halstow and walk through the fenced alley to Forge Common. Cross the stile and bear left across the common to the wood.

One smuggling trip in this area is particularly well documented, and especially interesting because of the insight it provides into the organization of smuggling in the early eighteenth century.

The story is told in a deposition made in 1728 by a couple of Medway men.[5] They travelled across the Channel in February 1728, and bought tea in Ostend. It was a very small-scale operation, since in all the men brought back just 400lb, plus a few yards of calico and some silk handkerchiefs. There were seven men on the ship, *The Sloweley*, and the trip was organized rather like one of today's cross-Channel shopping excursions: everyone bought tea, and paid for their passage in tea as well.

Once the goods had been landed, they were carried to Northward Hill, and concealed in the woodland that you can still see on the hill. By

the time the tea and fabric had been hidden it was three in the morning, and two of the group departed, leaving some of their fellows on guard—perhaps the plan was to rendezvous the following day to divide up the profits. After a long night in the cold, the three men who were left behind went into the village to get food, and when they returned to the hiding-place two more of their fellows joined them. By this time, though, the silk and calico had disappeared, and since the tea was in six bags, it proved impossible to give each man his exact share.

The delay in distribution provided the preventive forces with an opportunity—there is a suggestion that one of the group was an informer—and at five o'clock four customs men arrived. We will never know what sort of a deal took place in the gathering dusk on Northward Hill, but whatever happened it was not entirely to the benefit of the customs authorities. They took three-quarters of the tea, but the smuggling conspirators kept the remainder and were never prosecuted. The most likely explanation is that the customs men were 'squared', and simply sold the tea they had seized in order to line their own pockets.

The mastermind of this and many other similar trips was one Edward Roots of Chatham. Though this small trip was organized on a cooperative basis, most of the others followed more conventional business lines, with a London financier, and a 'fence' in Blackheath who had organized an efficient distribution system through the pubs of Deptford.

It is no coincidence that High Halstow is within sight of Shade House. In fact, the whole of the Hoo Peninsula played an active part in the free-trade, aided by the area's reputation as a malarial and mist-shrouded swamp. Smuggled goods were commonly landed on Chalk Marshes, and at Cliffe, and often stored near to Chalk Church, and at Higham.

ALLHALLOWS AND GRAIN ∎5

Avery Farm, Allhallows, is at 178-TQ841785. Go into Grain village, TQ8776, on the main road (A228/B2001) and you can't miss the Hogarth Inn, which is on the left of the High Street.

Not all smuggling stories from the Hoo Peninsula are as specific in detail as the tale of Edward Roots and his team. The local headquarters for the smuggling fraternity was said to be the Lobster Inn, some three-quarters of a mile north-east of Allhallows church. The pub is now a private house at Avery Farm.[6]

A local legend tells of a tunnel passing underneath the Hogarth Inn in Grain village; and according to another tale, contraband was hidden on the island of Gantlebor near Yantlet Creek, which divides the Isle of Grain from the rest of the peninsula. The creek itself made a discreet anchoring point even for quite large vessels engaged in the smuggling trade.[7]

THE MEDWAY AND MAIDSTONE ∎6

Penenden Heath is 1m N of Maidstone, at 178-TQ7657. On mid-nineteenth-century maps the area that is now Heathfield Road was marked as 'Gallows Hill', and the Chiltern Hundreds public house, on a roundabout signposted to Boxley on the A249, stands close to the site of the old gallows. Pistols reputed to have been used by members of the Hawkhurst Gang are on display at Maidstone museum, and the collection also includes a blunderbuss with similar origins. Burntwick Island is at the mouth of the Medway at 178-TQ8572.

Between the Isle of Grain and the Kent mainland lies the Medway, and at its mouth are dozens of tiny creeks and low-lying islets. One of these, Burntwick Island, was the headquarters to the North Kent Gang in the early nineteenth century (see page 35), and the gang skirmished with the preventive forces in Stansgate Creek nearby.

Though there was a garrison posted at Sheerness, some ships would use the cover of darkness to slip past the military into the river, perhaps to ferry goods up-river to Maidstone or further. Some contraband, though, would be landed on the banks of the Medway estuary—Cockham Woods, Upnor is mentioned[8] as one such landing-point.

Maidstone's connection with smuggling is principally through prevention and punishment of the perpetrators. Many smugglers danced 'the hempen jig' on a gallows at Penenden Heath on the northern outskirts of the town, and the gaol in Maidstone housed more. A few of the condemned prisoners escaped execution—in November 1747, 'Twelve armed and disguised men broke open Maidstone (on the Medway) gaol, and rescued the notorious prisoners, carried them some distance where twenty horses were in readiness to aid them in the escape'.[9]

FAVERSHAM ▪7

178-TR0161, 12m N of Ashford.

Faversham was notorious for its smugglers, and many of the fine buildings that can be seen there today were constructed from the proceeds of the free-trade. Daniel Defoe remarked on the town's reputation when he wrote his *Tour through the Whole Island of Great Britain* in 1824-6:

> . . . I know nothing else this town is remarkable for, except the most notorious smuggling trade, carried on partly by the assistance of the Dutch, in their oyster boats . . . the people hereabouts are arrived to such proficiency, that they are grown monstrous rich by that wicked trade.

Defoe singles out the Dutch for special condemnation (xenophobia is always a reliable ally when you want to pass the buck), but much of the contraband that was sold and distributed through Faversham would have been landed by red-blooded Englishmen on the open beaches to the East. Some also came in from the Swale, the channel dividing the Isle of Sheppey from the mainland. Ships sneaked past the Sheerness garrison into the mouth of the Medway, and then headed into the Swale before pushing onwards to Faversham. This circuitous route to the town is easily explained: coming into the Swale by the back door allowed smuggling cutters to avoid the vigilant preventives at Whitstable.

THE ISLE OF SHEPPEY

178-TQ9770, 5m NE of Sittingbourne.

The inhabitants of the Isle of Sheppey used historical precedent as an excuse for their smuggling activities. The town of Queensborough was granted a charter by Edward I, allowing them to import and export goods free of duty. This convenient loophole was stopped in 1575, but the spirit of free enterprise far outlived the letter of the privilege.

MINSTER ▪8

178-TQ950735. Drive into Minster, and follow signs to the hospital along Union Road. Just before the hospital, the road makes a sharp left turn: instead go straight on down Love Lane. The tombstone is in the far corner of a small park a little way down on the left.

The Minster smugglers took care to keep their activities well hidden. A pathetic gravestone here illustrates that they were quite prepared to use force when necessary:

> O EARTH COVER NOT MY BLOOD
> SACRED TO THE MEMORY OF A MAN UNKNOWN, who was found MURDERED, on the Morning of the 22nd April 1814, near SCRAPS-GATE in this PARISH, by his Head being nearly Severed from his Body. A SUBSCRIPTION was immediately entered into, and ONE HUNDRED GUINEAS REWARD offered on the conviction of the PERPETRATORS of the HORRIBLE ACT, but they remain at present undiscovered.

According to local legend, the unfortunate man was mistaken by smugglers for an informer, and dealt summary justice on the spot. That the reward should have failed to bring the villains to justice is hardly surprising; it's said that the smugglers themselves carried out the collection to conceal their guilt. They also paid for the memorial stone, which used to stand in the churchyard.

Kent smugglers who had the misfortune to be captured frequently ended up in Maidstone gaol, awaiting trial at the assizes. A guilty verdict provided Maidstone residents with grisly entertainment: in April 1824, a crowd of 40,000 watched the execution of four smugglers on Penenden Heath, just a mile or two from the prison.

WARDEN ■9

178-TR016725. Turn N off the B2231 at the crossroads at Eastchurch, then take a right turn after about ¹/₂ mile. Warden Manor is a white house on the right, close to the coastguard station.

At the far eastern end of Sheppey, Warden Manor was once the home of Sir John Sawbridge, a respectable magistrate who dabbled in smuggling in the late eighteenth century. He cleverly incorporated into his house a novel signalling mechanism that innocently alerted him to the arrival of his kegs of spirits. A pigeon-loft in the house could be observed from the smoking-room, and the smuggling vessel released a homing pigeon as the contraband was dumped overboard at the mouth of a nearby creek. The tide swept the barrels in, and the cooing messenger warned the magistrate to collect the goods before anyone else found them. Legend has it that tunnels joined the manor house to the local church, and to the pub, the Smack Aground (now a private house).

SEASALTER ■10

179-TR0965, 2m W of Whitstable.

As it is today, Seasalter in the eighteenth and nineteenth centuries was little more than an isolated hamlet. This isolation was turned to advantage by a smuggling fraternity, who based their operations in the area.

Wallace Harvey has investigated the business of 'the Seasalter Company' as he calls it, with great thoroughness, and by tracing property transactions and marriage certificates, has built up an intriguing picture of flourishing commerce.[10]

During the eighteenth century the coast at Seasalter was an ideal spot for landing goods. The beach consisted of mud and shingle, so there was little risk of damaging beached vessels, and open marshland backed onto the shore. The nearby Forest of Blean provided plenty of cover for the landed goods.

The *modus operandi* of the Seasalter company was to land goods close to the Blue Anchor pub, then ship them inland to Lenham, where heavy carts could load up with the brandy and tobacco for onward shipment to the major markets in London. Blue House Farm was the base at the Lenham end, and Seasalter Cross Farm and Pink Farm (which benefited from cunningly concealed compartments, windowless rooms, and secret shafts) were both used as coastal storage depots. The headquarters of the Seasalter Company was Seasalter Parsonage Farm, now a private house in the village.

The route the smugglers took from the coast was via Pink Farm, Yorkletts, Dargate, Hernehill, to Whitehill along Brogdale Road, and then on to Lenham. At Seasalter Cross, cargoes of tobacco were stored in greatly enlarged haystacks (though this ruse would have worked only when the wind was blowing in the right direction, for the aroma of tobacco would have alerted a customs man standing 50 yards away).

It seems that the Seasalter Company were either in league with the preventive forces, or at least had developed a policy of peaceful coexistence. One tale serves to illustrate how this worked: one of the company would stand close to the coastguards' cottages at Seasalter, and bellow 'The coast is clear' at the top of his voice. In what was clearly a well-rehearsed pantomime, this would lure the 'suspicious' coastguard into pursuing the 'smuggler', who would of course head away from the true landing-point. In order to make pursuit more difficult, the decoy carried a long plank, which he used to bridge the numerous dykes. The panting coastguard had to take the long way round, and the cat-and-mouse game kept suspicious eyes off the truly dubious activities on the coast.

In the course of time the Seasalter Company had cause to take more care in its illegal activities, and eventually developed an elaborate signalling system. A chain of houses had rods running up either a chimney or a tree outside, with a broom attached to the top. By pushing the rod up the chimney someone could raise the broom and the signal was copied down the line. The signalling points were Moat House in Blean, Frog Hall, Honey Hill Farm in Blean, a house at Pean Hill built by the company, Clapham Hill Farm, Martin Down Mill, and on to Borstal and eventually to Whitstable. At night a lantern in a window replaced the broom in the chimney.

The Seasalter Company flourished for over a century from 1740, and must have made many fortunes for its partners. Certainly one man, William Baldock, benefited to an unprecedented degree: when he died in 1812, he left over a million pounds—a staggering sum of money even by today's standards.

WHITSTABLE ■11

179-TR1166 6m NW of Canterbury.

Whitstable played a full and active part in the free-trade. This is unsurprising, but what makes Whitstable more unusual was the trade in smuggled prisoners of war that was carried on in the area. During the Napoleonic wars the enormous numbers of POWs put a considerable strain on the country's resources, and led to a vast prison building programme (including Dartmoor). Many French prisoners lived in appalling conditions in prison hulks—filthy, overcrowded and disease-ridden vessels anchored off-shore. Through an elaborate network of contacts and safe havens, prisoners who succeeded in escaping from the hulks would be brought to London, then smuggled on a hoy or an oyster-boat to a timber platform at the low-tide mark near Whitstable.

This platform was a mooring for the oyster-boats and fishing vessels that were prevented from reaching the true shoreline at low-tide by the 2-mile wide ribbon of mud that fringes the beaches there. Mingling with fishing folk and wildfowlers, the French escapees were able to make their way back to the shore, rest up and hide for a few days, then make a clandestine departure one dark night from Swalecliffe Rock—a shingle spit close to the Herne Bay road. Relatives of the wealthier prisoners would no doubt have paid handsomely for their safe return, and the arrangement no doubt suited the smugglers, who would otherwise have had to pay for their returning cargo of contraband in currency, rather than bodies. The trade continued between 1793 and 1814.[11]

This period was an exception, though, and smuggling in Whitstable generally followed the national pattern, with smugglers moving the familiar cargoes of brandy, tobacco, lace and gin using bribery and violence. Bribery worked when there was little opposition: officialdom at Whitstable at the end of the seventeenth century was represented by a single corrupt boatman who took so much money in bribes that he was able to build a fine house on the proceeds.[12]

Violence worked when there was greater resistance. In February 1780 the Supervisor of Excise set out from Whitstable for Canterbury, with 183 tubs of gin that had been captured earlier. The caravan was guarded by a party of 8 troopers and an officer, but 50 smugglers attacked at Borstal Hill, the steep road that crawls up out of Whitstable. In the battle, two soldiers were killed, and Joseph Nicholson, the Supervisor, fled with the survivors. A fat reward induced an informant to supply the name of an 18-year-old (John Knight) who had played a minor role—this man was executed at Penenden Heath, Maidstone, and later hung in chains at Borstal Hill.

NORTH-EAST KENT

In the early years of the eighteenth century, smuggling on this part of the Kent coast was very much a small-time affair, played to rules that both the smugglers and preventives understood and adhered to. Later in the century, though, larger cargoes began to be brought in, and the increased scope for profit brought with it a totally different breed of smuggler. The new entrepreneurs were not local men supplementing a meagre income from fishing and farming, but professional smugglers, such as members of the notorious Hawkhurst Gang, based inland. The large out-of-town gangs were by mid-century gathering in groups of 150 and more, and carrying off their goods in long caravans of packhorses.

These groups used the north Kent beaches of Birchington, Reculver and Herne Bay, and protected their business enterprises with brute force when necessary. This had some sorry side-effects, including the loss for a Whitstable vicar of a very useful supplement to his stipend. The Rev. Patten had become accustomed to charging a tithe from the local smugglers, but discovered in 1746 that the 'rugged colts', as he called the new breed of smuggler, would not pay up. In a fit of pique, he informed the local customs authorities of the activities of these less generous souls.

The destruction of the Hawkhurst Gang (see page 63) provided some respite from the worst of the smugglers' violence, but armed clashes between the preventives and their north Kent adversaries continued spasmodically. The establishment of the blockade in the early nineteenth century caused a renewal of aggression. The most celebrated battle took place at Herne Bay, and culminated in the death of a young midshipman who dared to challenge the North Kent gang as they tried to bring their goods ashore.

HERNE BAY ■12 AND HERNE ■13

Herne Bay 179-TR1768 is 7m N of Canterbury. The Ship Inn on the seafront is an attractive white-painted building. Herne village, where Sydenham Snow was buried, is about 2m inland. Turn off the A299 along the A291 at a roundabout, signposted Herne and Sturry. The windmill can be reached along Mill View Road, a turning to the left. The mill (telephone 0227 368511 or 0227 364660) is open to the public between April and September on Sundays and Bank Holidays; in July and August it is also open between 2 p.m. and 6 p.m. on Thursdays. In the village visit the churchyard, where the grave of Sydenham Snow can be found at the very foot of the tower on the west side. Facing the church, directly across the road from the Red Lion pub is a row of smugglers' cottages in a terrace that directly adjoins another pub, now called the Smuggler's Inn. Look up at the chimneys of the cottages, and you'll see a small triangular spy-hole that looks out down the road leading to the coast.

The North Kent Gang were unloading a boat on the beach at Herne Bay in the small hours of Easter Monday morning, 1821, when they were disturbed by a patrol of blockade men. The leader, Sydenham Snow, challenged the smugglers, who outnumbered the preventive men by some twenty to one. The smugglers fired on Snow, but he was unable to return their shots, because his gun misfired; so he drew a knife and charged on the gang. Pistol balls in the thigh and shoulder soon brought Snow down, and the smugglers then reloaded their weapons and kept the other three members of the patrol at bay until the run was complete.

Snow wasn't dead, though, and his colleagues carried him to The Ship nearby, where a naval surgeon made a vain attempt to help him. Snow died the next day, but on his death-bed he was able to provide information that led to the arrest of five gang members. Ironically, his killers got off scott-free because prosecution witnesses broke down under cross-examination.

The valiant Sydenham Snow was buried in Herne churchyard, where his grave can still be seen. Much of the rest of the village has smuggling associations, too: about 200 yards further up the hill (but still overlooked by the church) there is a row of old houses leading off the main road to the left. The street includes one house called the Box Iron, on account of its pointed shape. Excavations early this century uncovered a network of cellars which were admirably suited to the needs of a smuggler. Windmills in the Herne area—there is still one on the hill above the village—were used by smugglers for signalling purposes.

Left: *Gallant preventive Sydenham Snow lay bleeding to death here in the Ship Inn on the Herne Bay shore.*

Below: *An inconspicuous window built into the roof of this cottage in Herne provided a perfect spot for smugglers to hang a signalling lantern or to keep watch.*

THE NORTH KENT GANG

The smuggling gang that shot Sydenham Snow (see under Herne Bay above) had its roots in the smaller companies operating in the North Kent area in the eighteenth century. By the early years of the nineteenth century, though, these independent operators were faced with a concerted official attempt to strangle their business—and perhaps they drew together to counter the threat. The group were initially based on Burntwick Island, a patch of land that stands little more than a few feet above the mud of the Medway estuary.

As an organized force, rather than as individuals, the gang seems to have attracted little attention until 1820. In the spring of that year they clashed with two blockade men at Stansgate Creek, which flows sluggishly between the gang's island base and Chetney Marshes on the mainland. The gang, who were unloading a cargo in the creek, escaped by attacking one of the blockade men, wounding him seriously.

This escapade possibly emboldened the gang, for just a year later they landed a cargo directly opposite Herne Bay blockade station. With extraordinary cheek, the 50-strong force of smugglers tied up the two duty blockade men while they unloaded their goods from a French boat. The Easter clash in which midshipman Snow lost his life followed shortly afterwards.

The trial for Snow's murder seemed set to break the back of the gang and this was exactly what the authorities wanted. Five of the gang had been accused of the killing, including the leader, James West, and three more had turned King's evidence to save their necks. Having as witnesses not only three of the gang but also Snow's comrades on the patrol, the Crown were confident of a prosecution. However, the defence vigorously questioned one of the gang, George Griffiths, and he proved a poor witness. The North Kent five were acquitted despite overwhelming evidence of their guilt.

This coup made James West a local champion, and just a week or two after the trial, it was business as usual. In mid-June a run at Reculver was interrupted by blockade men, and in the battle both sides sustained casualties. The contraband got through, and none of the gang was captured, but their luck didn't hold; soon afterwards, two were taken prisoner during a run at Whitstable. The prisoners were taken to Faversham gaol, but their stay was to be be brief. They were sprung just eleven days after their arrest, when their colleagues arrived with pickaxes and clubs, and broke open the gaol to release the captives.

Other clashes led to the arrest of small numbers of the gang, but the round-up started in earnest in the spring of the following year at Margate (see page 36). The three gang leaders were eventually executed on Penenden Heath (see pages 31–2), but the other fifteen were transported.

RECULVER ■14

179-TR2269, 3m E of Herne Bay.

This was one of the North Kent Gang's favourite landing-places and the spot was immortalized in verse by the Rev. Richard Barham in his well-known *Ingoldsby Legends*. Barham was inspired to write *The Smuggler's Leap* by an entry in a history of Thanet, which he quotes at the start of the poem:

> Near this hamlet (Acol) is a long-disused chalk pit . . . known by the name of 'The Smuggler's Leap'. The tradition of the parish runs that a riding officer from Sandwich, called Anthony Gill, lost his life here . . . while in pursuit of a smuggler. A fog coming on, both parties went over the precipice . . . . The spot has, of course, been haunted ever since.

Barham embroiders his story to feature Lucifer and a demon horse that spouts flame when shot, but the tale begins at Reculver:

> The fire-flash shines from Reculver cliff,
> And the answering light burns blue in the skiff,
> And there they stand, That smuggling band,
> Some in the water and some on the sand,
> Ready those contraband goods to land:
> The night is dark, they are silent and still,
> At the head of the party is Smuggler Bill.

Though written as a satire of the epic style, Barham's lines often read like doggerel today:

> Manston Cave was Bill's abode,
> A mile to the north of the Ramsgate road,
> (Of late they say It's been taken away,
> That is, levell'd and fill'd up with chalk and clay, By a gentleman there of the name of Day)
> Thither he urges his good dapple-grey.

The cliff-top spires of Reculver church acted as a prominent sea-marker on the north Kent coast, and the beach was therefore a popular landing-spot. Bribery and intimidation secured the silence of local people: one Reculver man told revenue officers that, 'ye gang will bourn down his house and barn if he should discover (identify) any of them . . .'

The poem must have played a major part in the romanticization of smuggling that arguably began in the late Victorian era. And though the chase ends in death, the poem succeeds in making exciseman Gill's job sound almost exciting.

The reality was very different. Life for exciseman Gill and his colleagues meant many hours of excruciating boredom shivering in the cold, interspersed with brief and probably terrifying encounters in which they were out-gunned and outnumbered by the smugglers. Little wonder that so many excisemen preferred to take two barrels as a bribe, hand one over as confiscated booty, and sit snug in the watch-house drinking the other.

East of Reculver, shingle and mud beaches give way to chalk cliffs that the smugglers reached by gaps, stairs and cart tracks. Though modern development has led to many of these sheltered beach access roads being covered in concrete, it is still possible to imagine chains of pack-horses hauling sweet-smelling tobacco bales up to the main road. Much of the contraband landed here would have found its way to Canterbury, either as a final destination, or *en route* for London. Some smuggled goods made the journey along the coast road, via Herne and Faversham.

THE ISLE OF THANET

The importance of Thanet as a mid-eighteenth century smuggling area was emphasized by the supervisor of customs in Canterbury, who reported daily visits to the town by smugglers, and described how they openly carried arms, defied authority and bullied locals into supplying them with fodder and fresh horses.

Gaps and caves all along the Thanet coast were used for access and storage, and this was one place where tales of smugglers' tunnels stand up to close scrutiny; not only did preventive officers discover a 300-yard long tunnel that started at a Ramsgate house in 1822, but they actually caught the 'mole' red-handed. Significantly, the tunnel ended at the beach, thus neatly solving the problem of disposing of the spoil; it could be tipped in the sea. Contemporary estimates put the cost of the digging at £200.

MARGATE ■15

179-TR3570, 15m NE of Canterbury. Before visiting the smugglers' caves at 1 Northdown Road, phone 0843 220139 to check opening times.

A bloody confrontation at Marsh Bay near here proved the downfall of the North Kent Gang. A blockade man recognized one of the gang, and called out his name. At this, all resistance evaporated as the smugglers fled. This was just the beginning of the story, though. The matter was put in the hands of a Margate solicitor, John Boys. Amazingly, pursuit by the legal process succeeded where the gun and pistol had failed. Through Boys' tenacious efforts eighteen members of the gang were brought to book, and a Maidstone jury convicted all eighteen for armed assembly.

The conviction and break-up of the gang is especially remarkable because of the intimidation that went on in the lead-up to the trial. The unfortunate solicitor:

> Was the object of general hatred in the town of Margate; he was placarded on the walls as an informer and a hunter after blood-money, his house was frequently assailed, his windows broken, his person assaulted in the dark, the fruit trees in his garden destroyed.[13]

Boys was probably not the only one intimidated, either. Jury nobbling was commonplace, and the Maidstone jury were putting themselves at considerable risk by bringing in their guilty verdict.

Smugglers used caves in Margate to store their goods, and the earth-works remained a closely-guarded secret until they were revealed by sheer fluke: a gardener working at Trinity Square disappeared in a fatal fall when his spade penetrated the roof of the long-forgotten cavern. The owner of the site presumably mourned the loss of his employee for only a token period, for the cave was soon opened as a tourist attraction. You can still visit the caves today.

BROADSTAIRS ■16

179-TR3967, 2m N of Ramsgate. To reach Botany Bay take the B2052 from Margate to Kingsgate. The road makes a sharp turn to the right. The

Kingsgate, close to Broadstairs, was one of many cart gaps cut through the cliffs to bring goods (both legal and otherwise) off the beaches. Joss Snelling's gang landed goods at Kingsgate, probably very much as shown here—contraband could easily be passed directly from the beached boat down to horse-drawn farm carts.

Broadstairs smuggler Joss Snelling is commemorated in the name of his favourite landing site, Joss Bay. A beach nearby was the scene of a running battle between smugglers and excisemen.

Captain Digby Inn is on the bend. Joss Bay lies just below the Inn.

Continue towards Broadstairs, past the lighthouse, and turn right into Lanthorne Road. Stone House on the corner of the road was used by the Callis Court Gang for storage, and a tunnel linking the house to the coast was revealed when it collapsed under the weight of a bulldozer in the 1950s. Farm Cottage, where Snelling himself lived, is further along on the right. At the far end of the road, a right turn takes you along Callis Court Road. The Fig Tree is on the corner of the road of the same name, and is now a private house with a copper cupola. Continue along Callis Court Road, and either follow the road round to the left to enter Reading Street, or continue straight ahead into Elmwood Avenue. In the garden of a thatched cottage halfway down is a row of caves that once hid contraband.

In Broadstairs itself, the Bleak House Museum (phone 0843 62224) contains smuggling replicas and tableaux.

Thanet smugglers mostly emerged into the limelight briefly and reluctantly, and often transportation or an engagement with the hangman precluded further appearances. However, one character from the area lived to a ripe old age, and in his dotage was presented to a young Queen Victoria as 'the famous Broadstairs smuggler'. He even gave his name to a local cove—Joss Bay—though some believe that he took his own name from that of his preferred landing-site.

Joss Snelling was born in 1741, and lived to the extraordinary age of 96. He had brushes with the law from time to time in the course of his career, and was fined £100 for smuggling at the age of 89, but he seems to have been wily enough to avoid the setbacks that hampered his fellow free-traders. It's tempting to speculate on the reasons for Snelling's good fortune. One explanation might be that he avoided the armed confrontations that left other smugglers mortally wounded or behind bars. However, an incident in 1769 rules out such an hypothesis.

That spring Snelling's company, the Callis Court Gang, were unloading a cargo at Botany Bay when they were surprised by a preventive patrol. Five members of the gang fled from the beach, either up Kemp's stairs or by scrambling up the chalk. Unfortunately, their troubles had only just begun, for they were challenged on the cliff-top by a riding officer. To effect an escape, they shot him, and the dying man was taken to the nearby Captain Digby Inn. To locate the killers, the authorities mounted a search of the area, concentrating on nearby Reading Street. In Rosemary Cottage there they found two dead smugglers and one mortally wounded.

In all, the Battle of Botany Bay, as it came to be known, claimed the lives of fifteen of Joss's gang. Nine died of their wounds, and six were later hanged at Gallows Field, Sandwich.

EAST KENT

As any modern traveller knows, the shortest Channel crossing is from the east Kent coast to northern France, and this obvious fact had not escaped the early smugglers either. The gently curving coastline between Romney Marsh and the Isle of Thanet was well supplied with shingle or sand beaches on which it was simple to draw up a boat. This whole area was steeped in the free-trade from the very beginning: east Kent was notorious for wool exports long before import smuggling began.

DEAL ■17

179-TR3752, 8m NE of Dover.

The town of Deal had become a notorious haunt of smugglers as early as 1745, and well deserved to be dubbed 'a sad, smuggling town' by an eighteenth-century writer.[14] That smuggling was going on there was obvious not from activity in the town, but from lack of it:

> There are said to be in the town of Deal, not less than two hundred young men and sea-faring people, who are known to have no visible way of getting a living, but by the infamous trade of smuggling ... This smuggling has converted those employed in it, first from honest industrious fishermen, to lazy, drunken and profligate smugglers.

Deal men were well known for their skill both as boat-builders and as seamen—some Deal smugglers served as pilots for Nelson—so it is hardly surprising that they turned their hand to rapid cross-Channel trips for a hefty profit. It was at Deal that the 'Guinea boats' were

constructed to ship gold across the Channel (see page 27).

By 1781, the notoriety of the town was such that the authorities felt obliged to act against the Deal smugglers. A hundred mounted soldiers and nine hundred infantrymen moved in on the town, expecting to find £100,000 worth of contraband concealed there. The troops didn't bother with the formalities:[15]

> Some flint and many stones came at the windows and many shots were fired by the soldiers but most miraculously nobody was killed and only one man considerably wounded who, having thrown a mattock-iron [a pick, with an adze blade at one end] from a garden at the officers, a Middlesex militiaman fired at him as he was scrambling over a wall.[16]

The troops left with perhaps a tenth of what they'd expected, probably because an informer had forewarned the Deal men, who had spirited the goods back to their source on the Continent for the duration of the raid. This slap in the face for the authorities evidently made them all the more determined, and three years later, William Pitt sent in troops again. The townspeople were once more forewarned (by carrier pigeon this time), and turned out in considerable numbers to resist the raid. However, the military prevailed by sheer force of numbers, and after resting overnight, they marched down to the beach where the smugglers had pulled their boats well above the high-water mark to secure them from the storms. After a cursory 'anti-invasion drill' a pre-arranged signal initiated the coordinated destruction and burning of the boats, in front of the very eyes of their outraged but helpless owners.

Despite this setback, smuggling soon resumed in the town. In 1801 smugglers had no trouble in enlisting the help of Deal residents when the revenue men forced a smuggling lugger onto the town beach. The mob attacked the luckless preventives, and brought ashore the cargo of tobacco, playing-cards and bolts of fine cloth. And sixteen years later, blockade men who were attempting to arrest some local smugglers were set upon by a mob of local people, and had to shelter in a shop. To add insult to (near) injury, the mayor of Deal ordered the arrest of the Midshipmen, accusing them of assault on the free-traders! Smuggling even continued in the town in a small way into the last quarter of the nineteenth century, long after the free-trade had been effectively snuffed out elsewhere.

When Pitt sent troops to Deal in 1785, the residents immediately (and correctly) suspected that there was a plan to stamp out smuggling in the area. All inn signs were taken down, and the commanding officer had considerable difficulty in finding billets for his men. Nevertheless, the troops were eventually accommodated, and the following day they burned all the boats drawn up on the town beach. The incensed Deal people were held back at bayonet-point during the operation.

DOVER ▪18

179-TR3141, 15m SE of Canterbury.

The white cliffs soaring high above Dover form a landmark that is visible on all but the darkest of nights. However, smugglers returning to Britain would have taken pains to avoid the town itself, since Dover was a local centre for the preventive forces, and soldiers from the castle were always on hand to strengthen the arm of the customs officers or blockade men.

Perhaps because of the deterrent effect of so many representatives of the forces of law and order, accounts of smuggling in Dover itself are few and far between. However, the Aldington Gang (see page 40) are known to have used the beach here, and what started as a routine landing of contraband for the gang in 1826 ended in disaster. Two blockade men were on patrol among the bathing-machines which then lined the beach when they spotted the attempted landing. One of the pair, Richard Morgan, fired a shot to summon help, and the smugglers returned fire, killing Morgan and injuring his colleague.

With the killers still at large, the dead blockade man was buried in St Martin's churchyard, but the incident sparked off a concerted attempt to round up the gang and bring them to justice. A £500 reward was offered for the arrest of George Ransley and the rest of the gang he led. One smuggler turned King's evidence, and the whole group were eventually rounded up and tried for a variety of offences: Richard Wire was charged with pulling the trigger. Though convicted, they narrowly escaped the gallows and were transported to Tasmania the following year.

Morgan's killers didn't hesitate to use violence when their livelihood was threatened, and armed clashes were becoming increasingly common at the time of his death. However, this doesn't seem to have isolated the smugglers from the local community, since the reward failed to elicit any information about the crime. The impression of solidarity is reinforced by another incident just six years before when the population had turned out in force to free a group of smugglers imprisoned in the town gaol. A revenue officer called Billy 'Hellfire' Lilburn had caught eleven Folkestone and Sandgate smugglers on a run, and had them locked up in Dover gaol. Word soon got around, and the prisoners' fellows raised a huge mob which quickly broke down the door of the gaol. When it was discovered that the captured smugglers had been moved to the most secure cells, the mob started literally to pull the prison apart, pelting the troops that had by now been called in with a hail of stones and tiles. The mayor of Dover arrived, but when he attempted to read the riot act, he was set upon, and gave up. By this time, Hellfire Lilburn himself had appeared, and tried unsuccessfully to persuade the commanding officer (reputedly 'Flogging Joe' McCullock, the founder and mentor of the Blockade) to fire on the crowd.

Eventually the smugglers were released, and made good their escape in hired horse-drawn carriages—the fore-runners of today's taxis! They stopped at the Red Cow to have the conspicuous and unwieldy chains removed from their hands; meanwhile, the mob continued to rampage through the town, smashing windows.

The gaol was damaged beyond repair and a new one had to be constructed. The whole event was commemorated in a folk-song.

FOLKESTONE ▪19

178/189-TR2236, 14m E of Ashford.

Local customs authorities here were quite clear about the allegiances of the Folkestone people. One commented, 'As most of the Inhabitants of Folkestone, Sandgate and Hythe are in the confidence of the smugglers, no information can be expected of them'.

In the seventeenth century the headquarters of the smugglers in the area was The Warren, just east of the town. Four secret passages led from a house here into a nearby wood, and the premises were considered such a problem that in 1698 the government bought the lease to the house.[17] The smugglers commonly brought goods ashore at East Wear Bay, then moved them up to The Warren, and on to the Valiant Sailor Inn nearby for onward distribution and local sale.[18]

The area was still fequented by free-traders in the nineteenth century. One story tells of the interrupted sleep of a couple from The Warren who were roused when a gang of smugglers burst into their home

The good harbour at Dover long ago made it a favourite arrival point for passenger traffic from the Continent. Like the modern trippers going through the green channel with their extra bottles of spirits, early travellers couldn't resist packing a few illicit luxuries. Consular couriers were among the worst offenders, using the diplomatic bag for cover, and items seized by Dover customs in the 1830s included musical snuffboxes, human teeth, vultures' feathers and dubious foreign books.

Engraved from a drawing by Turner, this illustration shows smugglers burying tubs on the cliffs above Folkestone.

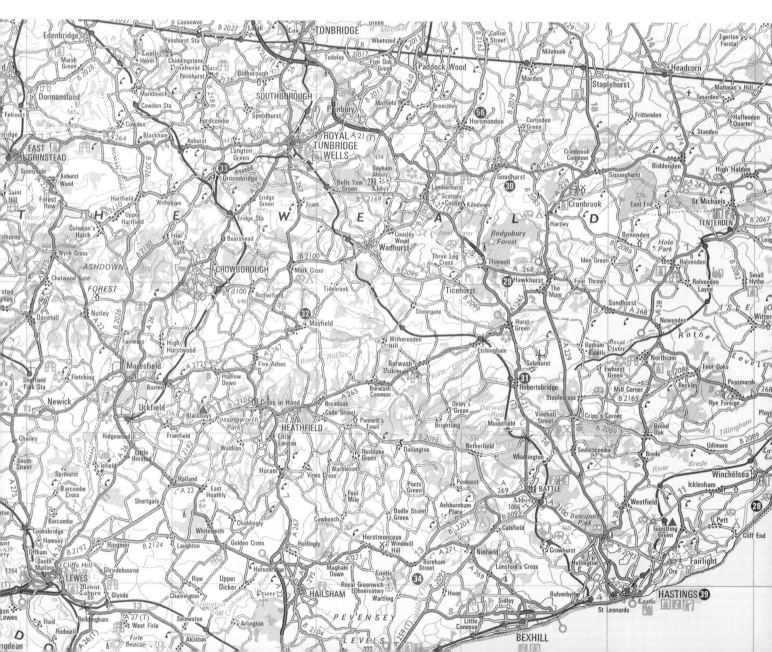

searching for a place to hide part of a cargo of gold. They chose the four-poster bed, concealed the goods, and took their leave, urging these law-abiding (and yawning) citizens to say nothing about the visit. Soon afterwards the customs authorities arrived, and searched the house, fruitlessly. Finally the smugglers returned to collect their goods, and offered the couple a payment for the inconvenience. This was haughtily declined.

An incident that took place at West Pier in 1820 gives some indication of the popular support that local smugglers enjoyed. A blockade man caught a smuggler red-handed, and marched him and the incriminating evidence—a tub of spirits—to a nearby watchhouse. However, before the blockade man, one John Kelty, had the opportunity to take his prisoner to more secure accommodation in Dover, a mob armed with clubs, rocks and pistols closed in, freeing the smuggler and injuring the blockade man.

THE ALDINGTON GANG ▪20

Aldington 179/189-TR0636 is 6m W of Hythe. Leave the A20 at Smeeth 179/189-TR0737, and turn down the B2069 (signposted to Aldington). On reaching Aldington turn right at a T-junction. The Walnut Tree 179/189-TR063366 is a short way down on the left. To reach the Bourne

Tap, take a left turn at the pub (B2069) then take the first on the right. At the T-junction turn left, then follow the road as it veers round to the right, then to the left. At the next T-junction turn right (signpost Mersham), down a hill then up the other side—the Bourne Tap 179/189-TR046365 is near the brow of the hill on the left.

The story of smuggling in east Kent in the 1820s is largely dominated by the activities of a gang based in Aldington, who worked the stretch of coast between Deal and Rye. They were nicknamed 'the Blues'—supposedly because they wore blue smocks to work—though the customs authorities simply named them after the parish in which some members lived.

However, it would be wrong to suggest that every member of the Blues was from Aldington. The gang could with ease turn out hundreds of workers to unload a cargo, and to supply this amount of labour would probably have meant enlisting the help of half the parish. Rather, the nucleus of the group came from Aldington and they picked up help from a much broader area of the county.

Early reports of the gang's activities find them plying from Boulogne to Sandgate, with a cargo of tobacco, spirits and salt. On arrival, the waiting land party of 250 or so formed the customary corridor of armed men running about 40 yards inland from the galley; protected by this cordon, the contraband was moved quickly and relatively safely away.

This operation was noted in detail by the preventive forces who sustained several casualties, so it's fair to assume that the group had been operating on a smaller scale, or undetected, for some time prior to the 1820 report.

This run took place in late autumn, and the company didn't come to the attention of the authorities again until the following February. When they did, it was in a dramatic and especially violent way. A blockade patrol spotted the gang at Camber Sands, and within a short time a running battle had started as the smugglers retreated across Walland Marsh towards Brookland, firing repeatedly at the blockade men. The confrontation was bloody and bitter, leaving four smugglers and one blockade man dead, and many injured.

Two of the Blues were caught in the 'Battle of Brookland', as it came to be known. According to some accounts the smugglers' leader, Cephas Quested, was found after the battle lying dead drunk on his back in the marsh. When his case came to court, one piece of evidence against him was particularly damning, and probably sealed his fate on the gallows: in the thick of the battle, he mistook a blockade man for a smuggler, and handed him a pistol, suggesting that the man should 'blow an officer's brains out'. The other man arrested claimed to have been an innocent bystander, and attributed the gunpowder stains on his skin to a rook-shooting trip. The gullible (or terrified) jury believed this alibi and acquitted him.

The trial was a setback for the gang, and further reports of their activities don't appear for another five years. By this time, George Ransley had assumed the mantle of leadership. The Ransley family hail from Ruckinge, and were originally farmers, though George Ransley apparently gave up the plough for smuggling when he accidentally stumbled on a hidden cargo of spirits. The proceeds from the sale paid for his house at Aldington, the Bourne Tap, and capitalized his ventures into smuggling. Other legends that surround the family and the activities of the gang contained the usual mixture of truth, exaggeration and simple fiction, but what doesn't seem to have been exaggerated is the violent nature of the gang's activities, and the viciousness of some of the batmen that protected the cargo. George Ransley's second-in-command

was his father-in-law, who was reputedly always armed with a threshing flail—a vicious instrument when used to crush skulls instead of corn husks. Circumstantial evidence suggests that the Blues forced cooperation from the more unwilling of the local farmers.

Ransley organized his business methodically and professionally. He retained a surgeon, Dr Ralph Papworth Hougham, to attend to wounded smugglers; his solicitors in Ashford, Langham and Platt (sic), defended him in court just as they would the most respectable banker; and because Ransley took care of the families of those unfortunate enough to die on active duty, he seemed able to command considerable commitment from those he led.

At Aldington, the gang used the Walnut Tree as their headquarters, but George Ransley also made a considerable profit by selling smuggled liquor from the Bourne Tap. The house was notorious not only for drunkenness, but also for the scenes of unbridled sexual licence that took place on the premises. Local legend has it that George Ransley did not himself take part, but sat sober outside the house during these orgies.

Ransley's long and distinguished career in the service of free-trade finally ended at his home one stormy night in 1826. The gang had been running wild locally, terrorizing the neighbourhood, and generally making themselves unpopular. The killing of Richard Morgan on Dover beach (see page 39) had lost them considerable support, and the preventive authorities finally grasped the nettle and took on the gang. A party of blockade men aided by a couple of Bow Street runners encircled the house, cutting the throats of the guard-dogs. George Ransley was in bed when the doors were smashed down, and was taken to Newgate prison to await trial, the local gaols being considered too insecure for such a big fish in the smuggling world. Seven more of Ransley's gang were taken in a simultaneous swoop, and another eleven were arrested soon afterwards. At their trial a form of plea-bargaining seems to have secured the lives of the gang; though all were sentenced to death, the punishment was reduced to transportation. George Ransley thrived in Australia, and some tales suggest that he sneaked back as an old man to die in England.

The Ransley family who played a leading role in Kent smuggling in the 1820s hailed from Ruckinge, where the family grave-board can still be seen. Though George Ransley was transported to Australia for his crimes, local legend asserts that he returned to England to be buried in the family plot.

RUCKINGE ■21

189-TR025335, 2m E of Ham Street.

The Ransley family graveboard can be seen in the graveyard behind the church of St Mary Magdalene here.[19] Walk round the back of the church—the board is on the SW side. William and James Ransley, who were hanged in August 1800 for highway robbery, are buried here, and some believe that George Ransley joined them.

ROMNEY MARSH

It would be fair to say that Romney Marsh was the birthplace of smuggling in southern England. The fertile land reclaimed from the sea made fine grazing for hundreds of thousands of sheep, and the export of the wool from their backs was for centuries both highly taxed and badly policed—almost an open invitation to smuggle.

In 1275 the government introduced a tax of £3 a bag on wool leaving England and illegal wool exports from the Marsh probably started the very day that this tax was imposed. The tax was doubled in 1298, and successive administrations tinkered with the laws and duties according to their need for funds. Wool smuggling from Romney Marsh—and elsewhere in Britain—fluctuated in response to the laws, and to market forces; high demand at home meant there was less incentive to smuggle. In the fifteenth century, though, the reverse happened, and as wool prices fell, the producers found it harder to make a living from the home market. The expansion of smuggling was inevitable.

It was in the seventeenth century that the problem assumed epidemic proportions, and attention was focused firmly on Romney Marsh as the centre for the trade. In 1660 wool exports were forbidden, and two years later the death penalty was introduced for smuggling wool. The legislators of the day probably saw this as a major deterrent, but if anything, it simply made the owlers of Romney Marsh more desperate still. If you're to hang for smuggling wool, why hesitate to shoot your pursuer?

Public opinion on the Marsh generally sided with the owlers, but in other circles there was outrage at the scale of illegal wool exports. The most vocal and aggressive opponent of the thriving free-trade in wool was William Carter, who set himself up as a one-man preventive force and propaganda machine. In 1671 he published a tract, *England's Interest in Trade Asserted*, in which he alleged that the owlers exported wool not just from the marsh, but from a catchment area some 20 miles in diameter. Carter also documented the armed guards that the smugglers used to protect their cargoes.

In all fairness, William Carter cannot be described as an independent witness. He was a clothier, and was therefore concerned that foreign competition should not affect his own trade. Nevertheless, Carter went to extraordinary lengths to stamp out owling, often risking life and limb in the process. In 1669 he obtained a warrant from the King, and armed with it, arrested the master of a smuggling ship berthed at Dover. Carter planned to take his prisoner to Folkestone for trial, but the mariner's wife rode ahead and mustered a large stone-throwing mob to greet Carter when he arrived. The would-be smuggler catcher fled, releasing his prisoner.

Carter was nothing if not persistent. He was still enthusiastically pursuing the cause nearly twenty years later. With some assistance from his friends, he arrested ten owlers on the marsh, and took them to Romney for trial. However, the trade enjoyed such popular support that the Mayor of Romney hesitated to proceed, and he had the ten men released on bail. The outraged owlers naturally set out to extract revenge, and William Carter was chased to Lydd. There the smugglers attacked by night, and the Mayor of Lydd suggested that these freelance preventive officers should make haste to Rye to save their skins. Carter and his group were followed by 50 armed men as they headed for Guldeford ferry, planning to get a boat from there to Rye. However, they never reached the ferry. At Camber Point they were so terrified of capture that

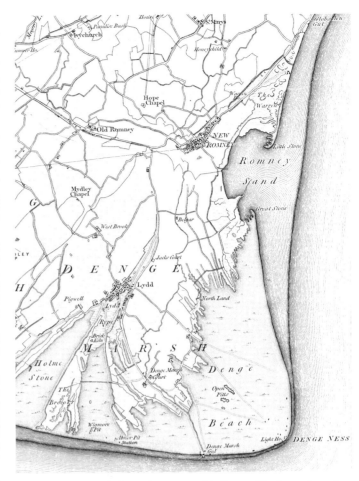

An early 19th-century Ordnance Survey map of the Romney Marsh area shows the marshland and coastline much as the smugglers would have known it.

they abandoned their horses, and climbed into the nearest available boat to make good their escape. A contemporary account says, 'had they not got into the boats, Mr Carter would have received some hurt, for many of the exporters were desperate fellows, not caring what mischief they did.'

LYDD ■22

189-TR0421, 4m NW of Dungeness. The George Inn is on the main street.

Lydd was notorious for its smuggling sympathies, and though today the town is landlocked, in 1688 when the unfortunate Mr Carter tried to take refuge there, the sea still washed against the town boundaries and the locals launched smuggling boats from the beach. Besides Mr Carter's close shave, other incidents from the period serve to reinforce the town's reputation.

Around the turn of the century two smugglers were captured as they disembarked from a French sloop at Dungeness. Taking no chances, the customs authorities took them to the George Inn at Lydd, and locked them in a room guarded by six men, their twenty 'firelocks' charged and ready. Even these precautions didn't deter the locals, though: nine of them burst in and rushed the room, firing their weapons as they charged up the stairs. Outside, 100 reinforcements stood by in case help was needed. Against such odds the guards stood little chance, and the two smugglers escaped.

The town became especially prominent in the late 1820s and early

The silting of the River Rother made Rye's harbour useless for ocean-going ships long before the heyday of smuggling. However, once the smaller vessels favoured by Marsh smugglers had evaded patrols at Camber sands and at the mouth of the river, they had little difficulty in mingling with the other coastal traffic that clustered round the quays at the foot of this historic cinque port.

1830s when increased preventive efforts around Dymchurch forced the owlers to move their operations from there to a cooler spot. On decamping to Lydd they lost no time in making their intentions known to the local riding officers: 'they have drove Mr Darby and his wife and family from their habitation, threatening to murder him if they can catch him'.

The smugglers at this stage still felt sufficiently confident to flaunt their trade. In 1829 when they openly paraded a convoy of contraband through the middle of Lydd, the streets were lined with cheering crowds. Ironically, though, this was to be the last open landing in the area.

RYE ■23

189-TQ9220, 9m NE of Hastings. Rye gets very busy during summer weekends and bank holidays, so if possible visit at other times. The Old Bell Inn and the George are both on the High Street, from which Mermaid Passage takes the visitor through to Mermaid Street and the famous inn. Look for the concealed door in the bar, which provided a handy bolt-hole from one of the bedrooms above. Farther down Mermaid Street on the left is Trader's Passage. The building on the corner (now a private house called the Old Trader) was once the London Trader Inn, a popular watering-hole for local free-traders. The Flushing Inn is in Market Street.

Rye in the eighteenth century was connected to the rest of Romney Marsh only by the ferry at East Guldeford. The Mermaid Inn was even then such an established hostelry that it would be surprising if it did not have smuggling associations. In fact it was a well-known haunt of free-traders, and recurs frequently in smuggling episodes involving Rye.

The notorious Hawkhurst Gang enjoyed a drink at the Mermaid, and drew outraged comment when they sat imbibing at the windows of the pub with their pistols cocked on the tables; but such was the gang's notoriety that the locals felt powerless to act. The gang ensured that they maintained their fearsome reputation by a variety of rowdy

activities; carousing in the Red Lion, they fired their pistols at the ceiling specifically to intimidate the other drinkers.

Another of the Mermaid's eminent guests was Gabriel Tomkins. Tomkins was a reformed smuggler from Mayfield, and in 1735 when he stayed in Rye he was wearing the hat of bailiff of the Sheriff of Sussex. He was in the town on business, so to speak: he had arrested Thomas Moore, a local smuggler. However, like his fellows at Romney, Moore was bailed by the magistrate, and he returned to the Mermaid to find Tomkins. With the aid of the landlord, he smashed his way into Tomkins' room, dragged him through the streets and on board a boat,

On this old street plan of Rye, the London Trader, where the town's smugglers slaked their thirst, still appears as an inn.

probably with a view to landing him in France and leaving him to fend for himself. However, the local revenue men intervened, searching vessels berthed at Rye, and Tomkins thus narrowly avoided involuntary emigration.

Other officials were not so lucky. The luckless John Darby, who had been threatened and bullied in Lydd, found himself enjoying a weekend break in France in 1742. He and one other officer had tried to impound some tubs of brandy but—as usual—they were heavily outnumbered. The smugglers kidnapped the two men, and hustled them on board a French boat from which they had just unloaded tea. This story has a surprising ending: with unusual courtesy, the smugglers made sure that when the two men had secured a passage home from the Continent, their horses were waiting for them at the Old George Inn in Rye.

Other Rye pubs are just as intimately tied up with the free-trade, though few are as picturesque as the Mermaid. The Olde Bell Inn once had a revolving cupboard for rapid exits to the street, a connecting door to the adjoining building, and a tunnel leading to the cellars of the Mermaid Inn nearby. When Rye was still bordered by the sea the Flushing Inn backed onto the water, and smuggled goods were conveniently brought straight into the pub after landing by the back door.

OTHER MARSH LANDMARKS

Rye and Lydd may have been the smuggling capitals of the Marsh, but numerous other spots are equally steeped in the traditions of the free-trade. Finding favoured landing-sites on this part of the coast is easy, since almost all of the low coastline was used.

The picturesque Mermaid Inn at Rye was the setting of several smuggling incidents. The Hawkhurst Gang once sat drinking in the bar with pistols cocked on the tables in front of them.

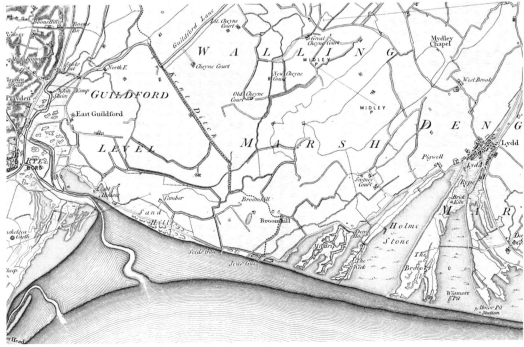

An 1816 map of Rye and the surrounding marshland and coast.

DUNGENESS ■24

189-TR0917, 8m SE of Lydd.

The isolation of Dungeness proved an irresistible lure to smuggling gangs: the absence of prying eyes and wagging tongues meant that they could carry on their work undisturbed. In a single week of 1813, free-traders were known to have landed 12,000 gallons of brandy here. Nor was this the first cargo of spirits to cross the coastline illegally at Dungeness; 180 years earlier the local smugglers lured aground a Spanish vessel, *Alfresia*. They murdered the crew and looted the cargo of spirits.

CAMBER AND ADJOINING BEACHES ■25

189-TQ9518, 6m E of Rye.

Camber beach had one unique feature that made it a particular favourite: the dunes. In the high sand-hills, it was possible to conceal large numbers of tub-carriers and bat-men while waiting for an incoming boat. The convenient dunes perhaps explain why the last smuggler to die 'in the course of duty' fell at Camber. Thomas Monk, a fiddler (*sic*) from Winchelsea was shot here by the coastguard in 1833. Closer to Rye, Jew's Gut (now Jury's Gut) was also widely used, and Fairlight beach to the west of the town was popular too. However, erosion has greatly altered the landscape in that part of the Marsh, making some of the smuggling beaches inaccessible.

MARSH CHURCHES

None of the Marsh churches is hard to find, since the land around is so low. Ivychurch ■26 is 3m NW of New Romney 189-TR0227. Inside the church look at the hudd, an eighteenth-century graveyard shelter, used to protect the vicar's wig from the rain.

Snargate ■27 is 2m E of Appledore at 189-TQ9928. Hope All Saints church is just off an unclassified road at Ivychurch 1m NW of New Romney at 189-TR049258.

Most of the Marsh churches have stories to tell. Almost all of them were used at one time or another for storing contraband, though there are specific yarns associated with a few of them. At Ivychurch there was a vault under the nave that was used for storage, and cargoes of tobacco stored at Snargate church smelt so strongly that in the Marsh mists the vicar was able to locate the church with his nose. The vicar was R.H. Barham who wrote the smuggling poem that appears in the Ingoldsby Legends. Snargate church is particularly interesting to visit today, since there is a wall-painting of a ship—an owler's coded symbol marking a place of safety.

At Dymchurch the ruined church of Hope All Saints was a smugglers' meeting point. The churchyard at Dymchurch itself was the final resting place of smuggler Charles Keely, who was killed in a skirmish with blockade men in the last days of 1825. Richard Morgan, who fired the fatal shot, was a midshipman from *HMS Ramillies*, and had been leading a patrol when one of its members, a 'landsman', was attacked by

Hope All Saints church was a meeting and signalling point for 18th-century smugglers.

a gang of smugglers that he had surprised. As the gang closed in, the landsman tried to shoot at his assailants, but neither his pistol nor his musket would work. Richard Morgan's first pistol wouldn't fire, either, and had his second gun failed to function it would not have been smuggler's blood spilled on the Marsh that night. When they saw one of their team shot dead, the remainder of the gang fled into the darkness, leaving behind the body and their booty. Morgan was himself shot by the Aldington Gang the following July.

THE ROYAL MILITARY CANAL ■28

At Pett Level the canal lies 5m NE of Hastings at 189-TQ9016.

The Royal Military Canal is a prominent feature on the Marsh, and its construction in the first five years of the nineteenth century must have caused some consternation among the Marsh smugglers. The canal was intended to prevent a French invasion, but it was equally effective at stopping the movement of contraband from the Marsh coast to the markets inland. Some parts of the canal were shallow enough to ford, but these points weren't always easy to locate. Several smugglers drowned at Pett Level when they were chased into the water by the preventive services; evidently they searched unsuccessfully for a safe crossing-point. Toot Rock nearby was a rendezvous for the smuggling fraternity, so perhaps a free-trader's business discussion had been rudely interrupted.

THE HAWKHURST GANG ■29

188-TQ7630, 12m NW of Rye. The Oak and Ivy Inn is about ½ mile east of Hawkhurst village on the A268 to Rye. Seacox Heath is on the Flimwell Road two miles west of Hawkhurst at 188-TQ730308.

Much of the contraband entering the country across the sand and shingle coasts of Romney Marsh was shipped on packhorses to London, soon passing through the sleepy hamlet of Hawkhurst 10 miles or so inland. In the 1730s this collection of scattered farms and houses was the headquarters of the most notorious gang in the history of English smuggling.

As outlined earlier in the chapter, the Hawkhurst Gang probably don't hold any special records: other gangs were longer-lived; a few could probably muster as many tub-carriers and bat-men on the beach; and it's likely that individuals in other smuggling gangs were equally violent. However, the Hawkhurst Gang had the questionable benefit of especially good (or bad) public relations. The account of the trial of two of the gang members for the torture and murder of two men in 1748 makes grisly reading, and almost certainly played a major part in turning the tide of public opinion against the smugglers.

The Hawkhurst Gang formed as a separate entity in the mid-1730s. An isolated reference to the gang appeared in 1735, and within five years the company had been consolidated into the powerful fighting force that was to dominate Kentish smuggling for the next decade.

In 1740 the gang ambushed a group of customs officers at Robertsbridge, and recovered a cargo of contraband tea that had been seized in a barn at Etchingham (see below). The gang soon escalated their operations, and perhaps because of the sheer scale of the landings, they cooperated with other local smugglers. However, these joint ventures were somewhat unequal partnerships, and it was always clear who was in command. When the Hawkhurst and Wingham gangs joined forces in 1746 to unload 11½ tons of tea, an uneasy alliance evidently turned to open warfare. The Wingham men tried to leave the landing-site at Sandwich Bay prematurely, and were set upon by their collaborators. After a sword-fight in which seven of the Wingham men were injured, the Hawkhurst Gang left the scene taking with them 40 horses belonging to the other gang.

In Hawkhurst village, the gang operated from the Oak and Ivy Inn, but various prominent members owned property in the area that was

extensively used—or even purpose-built—for smuggling activity. Highgate House (now Highgate Hall, on the north side of the main road just east of the traffic lights in the centre of the village) used to be a hiding-place for contraband; Hawkhurst Place at TQ767304 was said to have had a tunnel linking it to Island Pond. The pond is probably the overgrown pool at Guns Green (TQ773308); and Tudor Hall (now the Tudor Court Hotel at TQ769304) was supposedly linked by another tunnel to the Home Farm on the Tonges Estate, also at Guns Green. Tubs Lake, which is 2 miles north of the village on the Goudhurst Road, and Smugley, on the outskirts of Goudhurst, at TQ726366 were staging posts for contraband coming up from the coast. However, the most imposing monument to the profits to be made from smuggling was probably the mansion built by the gang's financier Arthur Gray at Seacox Heath (the smugglers were known locally as 'Seacocks'). The mansion, nicknamed 'Gray's Folly', incorporated various hiding-holes for smuggled goods, and even a bonded store. Unfortunately the grand mansion has been demolished, but Seacox Heath still remains.

By the late 1740s, the Hawkhurst Gang had developed an unprecedented degree of power, and boasted that it could assemble 500 men in the space of a couple of hours. In the absence of any effective policing, this disreputable group soon became a canker on the face of the Garden of England, taking without payment whatever they wished from the local farmers and merchants, and answering tolerance and patience with aggression and insult. Their activities did not go entirely unresisted, though. The most spectacular instance of rebellion by the much-abused people of Kent came in 1747, with a showdown at Goudhurst (see below).

The gang suffered a humiliating defeat at the hands of the citizens of Goudhurst, but the battle proved to be only a temporary setback, and the Hawkhurst men continued to operate in the area—albeit with a lower profile. The final break-up came only in 1749, as the result of the murder of a minor customs official and an innocent shoemaker (see page 59).

GOUDHURST ■30

4m NW of Cranbrook at 188-TQ7237. The Star and Eagle still sits cheek-by-jowl with the church at the top of the village. Spyways is a short distance down the hill on the same side of the road. A stout oak door up a few steps reminds the visitor that the house once served as the village gaol. The battle took place at the top of the village, along the road leading in from Hawkhurst.

The Star and Eagle Inn was a meeting place for the Hawkhurst Gang in the 1740s, when they terrorised the citizens of the village of Goudhurst. A pitched battle in the churchyard beyond finally ejected the smugglers from the village in 1747.

By 1747 the Hawkhurst Gang had extended their sphere of influence to include this pleasant village, where the gang used 'Spyways' on the main street, and the Star and Eagle near the church. The unfortunate citizens of Goudhurst were, it seems, able to do little but comply when the Hawkhurst Gang demanded horses, help or just money. Eventually, though, the villagers rebelled, and organized a vigilante group to defend themselves from their unpopular neighbours. In April they formed the Goudhurst Band of Militia, an armed self-defence group led by a recently-discharged soldier. Despite attempts to conceal these plans, news of the Goudhurst group reached Hawkhurst, and the leader of the gang vowed to sack the village of Goudhurst and murder all the inhabitants. With extraordinary arrogance, the gang leader Thomas Kingsmill even named the day—20 April.

When the Hawkhurst men appeared, stripped to the waist and armed to the teeth, Goudhurst was ready. G.P.R. James gives a dramatized account of the battle in his novel *The Smuggler*. He describes how the villagers united, and prepared to defend themselves with ancient (and inaccurate) fowling pieces. On the day of the battle the women and children were sent to the next village, and the men gathered on the porch of the church, and cast bullets in the churchyard. The battle was short-lived: it's clear that the smugglers expected little resistance from the village, and turned tail when they suffered a few casualties.

ROBERTSBRIDGE ■31

199-TQ7323 5m N of Battle.

This village was the scene of a bloody battle involving members of the Hawkhurst Gang. One of the gang (nicknamed 'Trip') discovered that 15 cwt of tea which had been seized earlier was on its way back to Hast-

ings under guard, and rode around the neighbourhood drumming up support for a rescue attempt. About 30 smugglers assembled, fortifying themselves with a drink and an oath before ambushing the wagon-load of tea on the steep hill at Robertsbridge. In the battle for the tea a customs officer was shot dead and the party of dragoons taken captive, one of them being seriously injured.

The choice of Robertsbridge as a point of ambush was a shrewd one, since the hill there was notorious, and the town well-known for its smuggling inhabitants, as Horace Walpole wryly observed:

> We got up, or down, I forget which, a famous precipice called Silverhill, and about ten at night arrived at a wretched village called Robertsbridge . . . But alas! there was only one bed to be had; all the rest were inhabited by smugglers, whom the people of the house called mountebanks . . . We did not take at all to this society, but, armed with links[20] and Lanthorns, set out again on this impracticable journey. At two O'clock in the morning we got hither to a still worse inn, and that crammed with excise officers, one of whom had just shot a smuggler.

HAUNTS OF THE EAST SUSSEX GANGS

The smuggling beaches of east Sussex were largely controlled by highly-organized gangs. Of course the Hawkhurst Gang used many of the Sussex beaches, but there was no shortage of home-grown talent, either. The smuggling companies were frequently based in coastal hamlets, but were as likely to conduct their business operations from an inland centre on the route to the main market in London. The core of

gang members would thus not have been seamen, and farmed out the Channel crossing to others—often local fishermen—or to French ships. As landsmen, the gang's talents lay in raising capital and arranging distribution.

MAYFIELD ■32

199-TQ5826, 8m S of Tunbridge Wells. Take the A267 into Mayfield from Tunbridge Wells; on entering the village the road veers sharp right into the High Street, but instead turn left down Fletching Street to find the locations described at the end of the first paragraph.

The village of Mayfield was the base for a powerful company that flourished for a few years in the early part of the eighteenth century. The group was led by Gabriel Tomkins (who later turned from poacher to gamekeeper—see page 44). They landed contraband along the length of the Sussex coastline, and into Kent. Favourite haunts included Lydd, Fairlight, Hastings, Eastbourne, Seaford and Goring-by-Sea.

Tomkins was suspected of the murder of a riding officer in 1717, and his fellow gang members were scarcely less desperate. When two of their number were captured at Dungeness and imprisoned at Lydd, the Mayfield smugglers charged up the stairs firing their pistols and released the pair. Tomkins himself was wounded in this affray.

Such extreme measures weren't always needed. Faced with opposition on the beaches where they landed goods, the Mayfield gang preferred simply to restrain the customs men rather than beat them senseless. Gabriel Tomkins' half-brother was at one point wanted for tying up a customs officer on Seaford beach during a run, and on another occasion the gang did the same to a preventive on Goring beach, throwing him into a ditch for good measure.

The Mayfield Gang landed their goods on the coast below Fairlight Down, and in shipping the contraband inland, they would have welcomed the concealment provided by the wooded valley shown here. Hastings can be seen on the left of the picture.

49

The gang were slippery customers, and narrowly evaded conviction several times. Sensibly, they would resist arrest when possible, but even if detained the group had a handful of aces up their sleeves. Frequently they won the sympathy of the local magistrate, who dismissed the case and sometimes even ordered the imprisonment or flogging of the arresting officer. And behind bars the Mayfield men found ways of securing their freedom—they often bribed the gaolers, or were rescued from the prison cells by their colleagues.

Gabriel Tomkins was first brought to justice in 1721, when he was captured at Nutley after a chase from Burwash. Though he bribed his gaoler and escaped, he was caught again and stood trial in London. On conviction he was sentenced to transportation, but provided the authorities with so much useful information that they freed him—only to re-arrest him three years later, and again in 1729. This time he gave evidence to an inquiry into corruption in the customs service, and clearly made a great impression on his captors. Far from being punished for his claims to have smuggled 11 tons of tea and coffee in a year, Tomkins was rewarded with the post of riding officer, and within six years had risen to a high rank in the customs service.

However, old habits die hard, and Tomkins slipped quietly out of his job in 1741 to resume activities on the wrong side of the law. In 1746 he robbed the Chester Mail, and the following year helped the Hawkhurst Gang in a robbery at Selbourne. It was the mail robbery that proved to be his undoing—Tomkins' long and chequered career ended on the gallows in 1750.

There are still a few reminders of smuggling days in Mayfield, though none that can definitely be connected with the gang. A little way down Fletching Street on the left, there is a curious tall house built like a layer cake—masonry at the bottom, then half-timber and brick, then clapper-board, and tiles on up to the roof. This building was cleverly equipped with two cellars in order to fool the excisemen. Stop at the Carpenter's Arms and walk down the side road facing the pub. Smugglers' Lane, an overgrown footpath leading downhill on the left just before a white clapper-board house, was a regular trade route for taking goods inland.

GROOMBRIDGE ■33

188-TQ5337, 4m W of Tunbridge Wells.

The Groombridge Gang rose to prominence in the 1730s, landing contraband at Lydd, Fairlight, Bulverhythe and Pevensey. Like other gangs, this team revelled in nicknames: Flushing Jack, Bulverhythe Tom, Towzer, Old Joll, Toll, The Miller, Yorkshire George, and Nasty Face all humped kegs and bales off the beaches or stood guard. These names weren't just familiarities—they served the valuable role of hiding the true identities of the people involved.

Official records first feature the Groombridge men in 1733. Thirty of them were ferrying tea inland from Romney Marsh via Iden in a convoy of 50 horses when three preventive men, two dragoons and a foot soldier made the mistake of challenging the convoy at Stonecrouch. For their interest the customs men were disarmed, and their guns made useless; they were then marched at gun-point for four hours to Groombridge, and on to Lamberhurst, where their weapons were returned to them after they had promised not to renew the pursuit.

By 1737 the gang were said to be terrorizing the area, and the military were sent to Groombridge to restore order. In the same year an informer who signed himself simply 'Goring' provided a detailed insight into the gang's activities, referring directly to an armed class at Bulverhythe:[21]

This is the seventh time Morten's people have workt this winter, and have not lost anything but one half-hundred [weight] of tea they gave to a Dragoon and one officer they met with the first [run] of this winter.

... When once the Smuglers are drove from home they will soon all be taken. Note, that some say it was [Thomas] Gurr that fired first. You must well secure Cat or else your Honours will lose the man; the best way will be to send for him up to London [for trial] for he knows the whole Company, and hath been Moreton's servant two years. There were several young Chaps with the smuglers who, when taken, will soon discover [identify] the

Smugglers certainly used the ruins of the castle of Herstmonceux and may have been responsible for the various ghosts that terrified local people nosy enough to investigate the nocturnal goings-on: a phantom drummer patrolled the south gallery, and a grey lady also appeared from time to time.

whole Company. The number was twenty-six men. Mack's horses, Moreton's and Hoak's were killed, and they lost not half their goods. They have sent for more goods, and twenty-nine horses set out from Groombridge this day . . . all the men well-armed with long guns.

. . . I will send your Honours the Places where [you] will intercept the Smuglers as they go to Market with their goods, but it must be done by soldiers, for they go stronger now than ever.

. . . The first [run] of this winter, the Groombridge Smuglers were forced to carry their goods almost all up to Rushmore Hill and Cester [Keston] Mark . . . but tea sells quick in London now, and Chaps from London come down to Groombridge almost everyday, as they used to last Winter. When once [the smugglers] come to be drove from home, they will be put to great inconveniences, when they are from their friends and will lose more Goods than they do now . . . Do but take up some of the servants, and they will rout the masters, for the servants are all poor . . .

Young [John] Bowra's house cost £500 building, and he will pay for looking up. Moreton and Bowra sold, last winter, some-ways, about 3,000lb weight a week.

In 1740 the Groombridge gang were implicated in the attack at Robertsbridge on the customs men carrying seized tea to Hastings, and they continued to operate up to the end of the decade, when an informer provided information that led to the round up and subsequent trial of the majority of the gang's leading lights.

HOOE AND AREA ■34

199-TQ6809, 4m E of Hailsham. Boreham Street (199-TQ6611) is on the A271 Bexhill Road—the Smuggler's Wheel restaurant is in the middle of the village on the main road. Herstmonceux church (TQ6410) is close to the castle and observatory, at the end of a turning off the main A271.

The informer who painted such a detailed picture of the Groombridge company's efforts also pointed the finger at a smuggling company from Hooe, nearer the coast, and though we know little about this group, it's clear that the two gangs cooperated in landing goods on the Sussex coast. In Hooe village the Red Lion Inn was the gang's headquarters. The lime trees that still stand outside signify—like the ship fresco in Snargate church—that this was a safe haven for smugglers.

Numerous places close to Hooe are known to have been used for concealing contraband, so perhaps the gang were among those who used the ghostly reputation of Herstmonceux churchyard to deter visitors while they stored goods in the table-tombs there. In a house at Boreham Street, closer still to Hooe village, you can still see a shaft and winch that smugglers used to lower goods down into a cellar. The house is now a restaurant that takes its name from the winch wheel, and in the restaurant garden are the remains of a tunnel leading away from the cellar.

CROWLINK AND BIRLING GAP ■35

Leave the A259 close to the church at Friston 199-TV552983. There is a NT car park, and walks to the sea. Birling Gap, where the Jevington smugglers landed their goods, has suffered from coastal erosion, and the beach is now approached down a flight of steps. The gap is at a bend in the minor road leading from Eastdean to Beachy Head (199-TV554960). There is a large car-park and a café.

Two centuries of erosion have changed the shape of the Sussex coast, creating cliffs where once were Britain's most famous cart gaps. Crowlink, as it was called, provided easy access to the sea, and the east Sussex gangs from Alfriston, Jevington and farther inland took full advantage of the spot and of nearby Birling Gap to haul contraband from their

beached ships. Crowlink gave its name to the illicit brandy that entered England here: 'Genuine Crowlink' was a guarantee of a good drink. During a period when illegally imported goods could be legally sold over the bar, some landlords even chalked this slogan on the brandy barrels.

ALFRISTON ■36

199-TQ5203, 5 miles NE of Seaford. The pub is in the centre of the village. Parking is restricted; avoid the village at popular tourist times.

Market Cross House (now Ye Olde Smugglers Inn) in the centre of Alfriston was the headquarters of one of the lesser east Sussex gangs. Though the house was standing well before the eighteenth century, it lent itself admirably to the gang's purposes, since it had at one time 21 rooms, 6 staircases and 48 doors. The maze of passageways and doors made escape easier in the event of an unwelcome caller, and tunnels reputedly led away from the house to nearby buildings and off to Wilmington.

The leader of the gang, Stanton Collins, seems to have used the house to great advantage, since the gang was singularly successful at eluding the customs authorities:

For years they defied the law, and although many outrages committed at the time were attributed to them, they plied their trade with so much caution that no real evidece could be brought against them. No doubt this was in a measure owing to the connivance of the inhabitants (of Alfriston).

The table tombs in Herstmonceux churchyard were widely used to store contraband in the eighteenth century.

One of the 'outrages' referred to was the death of a patrolling customs man at Cuckmere Haven. Fearing that his attentions would interfere with their landing, the gang moved the lumps of white chalk that the officer used as way-markers for his moonlight sorties along the cliff-edge. Instead of leading him safely along the coast path, the stones lured the poor man over the parapet. Hearing his cries as he tumbled over the precipice, the gang emerged from hiding, only to find the man desperately hanging by his fingertips. Deaf to pleas for mercy, one of the gang cynically trod on their adversary's finger-tips, sending him tumbling to the rocks below.[22]

The break-up of the gang came only when their leader was transported for seven years for stealing sheep.[23]

JEVINGTON ■37

199-TQ5601, about 5 miles NW of Eastbourne. Thorpe cottage is almost opposite the pub in the centre of Jevington; it is now renamed King's Farthing. The Rectory is a little way south of the Eight Bells. Filching Manor (199-TQ569030) is a beautiful and ancient building about 1¹/₂ miles N of the village.

The Jevington smugglers used Crowlink, and also landed goods at Birling Gap. They were led by James Petit or Jevington Jig who, like Gabriel Tomkins of Mayfield, tried his hand at many occupations. His regular trade was as innkeeper at Jevington, but smuggling came a close second, and he also turned to horse stealing and various other petty crimes. Again like Tomkins, Jevington Jig turned his coat at various stages in his career. He acted as an informer (for which treachery he nearly paid with his life when chased by a mob at Lewes), and cooperated with customs officers in 1792 in the seizure of a haul of tobacco.

Jevington Jig probably regarded collaboration as a last resort; he was certainly nothing if not resourceful in avoiding this undesirable option. On one occasion he disguised himself in women's clothing and rushed in theatrical hysterics from his inn when it was encircled by the authorities. Only his heavy boots, which showed beneath the petticoats, gave the game away.

The Jevington gang left their mark on the buildings in the village; there was once a tunnel linking the Eight Bells to Thorpe Cottage, and to the nearby church; tombs in the churchyard were reputedly once used to store contraband. Filching Manor has a subterranean passage leading away from its cellars, and a concealed cupboard in what is now the drawing-room. Jevington Rectory also had large cellars that formed a convenient storage spot.

THE SUSSEX COASTLINE

Inland gangs were not the only Sussex smugglers, but after two centuries they are perhaps the simplest to identify. Consequently, it is only too easy to focus on land-based companies, and overlook the vast volume of small-scale smuggling that went on all along the east Sussex coastline.

As in other parts of Britain, wholesale customs evasion was probably almost universal here until preventive efforts were stepped up. While it was safe to land goods openly, Hastings, Bexhill and Eastbourne beaches were all widely used, and there were dozens more suitable sites stretching away to the west: Pevensey Bay was a popular spot, as was Norman's Bay (then called Pevensey Sluice).

The modern visitor to many parts of this stretch of coast—and especially the towns—might have difficulty in picturing a smuggling run amid the piers and ice-cream stalls. However, it is important to remember that the area was virtually untouched in the eighteenth century as the resorts and spas for which the south coast became famous did not really develop until sea-bathing (or Thallasotherapy) became fashionable in the early nineteenth century. Throughout the eighteenth century much of the Sussex coast was relatively isolated, with just small hamlets looking out towards northern France. On the quiet sand or shingle beaches, landing un-customed goods would have been almost a leisurely affair.

With increasing preventive efforts, though, the local free-traders had to become more wily and resourceful, making landings less public. Usually this simply meant bringing the goods in at a time when the neighbourhood riding officer was known to be occupied elsewhere on the coast, but as the net tightened, the Sussex smugglers went to extraordinary lengths to avoid detection and capture. Derricking, for example, was a technique used to bring goods up a cliff from

Opposite above: Despite the watchful gaze of the preventive forces in their chain of Martello towers overlooking the beach at Pevensey Bay, this spot continued to be used for landing contraband as late as 1833.

Left: Ruined even in smuggling days, the crumbling turrets of Pevensey Castle made a convenient hiding-place for contraband brought ashore at nearby Pevensey Bay.

When derricking was impractical, tubs of spirits were slung across the shoulders of the smugglers, and carried up the cliffs on swaying rope ladders—a hazardous business that claimed the lives of many men.

CUCKMERE HAVEN ■38

The most attractive approach to Cuckmere Haven is from the overlooking South Hill, and there is a car-park there, close to Seaford golf course. However, the route to the spot passes through a maze-like residential estate, and it is easier to park at the Seven Sisters Country Park car-park (199-TV520995) and walk along the valley of the Cuckmere River.

This beautiful bay is probably one of the best-preserved smugglers' beaches on the east Sussex coast. Cuckmere Haven figures prominently in the records of the customs authorities right from the earliest days, when wool exports were more important than import smuggling. Goods were landed there throughout the eighteenth century, as this extract from a letter, dated 18 September, 1783, illustrates:

> On Tuesday evening, between two and three hundred smugglers on horseback came to Cookmere [*sic*] and received various kinds of goods from the boats, 'till at last the whole number were laden, when, in defiance of the King's officers, they went their way in great triumph. About a week before this, upwards of three hundred attended at the same place; and though the sea ran mountains high, the daring men in the cutters made good the landing.[24]

an inaccessible beach below. The contraband was landed on the beach, and stacked in baskets or on some sort of pallet—often a farm-gate. Using a horse-driven winch or windlass on the cliff top, the smugglers then hauled the contraband up the face and unloaded at the top. The derrick itself was purpose-built, and could be trundled quickly into position, or wheeled off equally rapidly at the sign of danger. There are records of this happening at numerous spots, but notably Rottingdean, Newhaven, and Birling Gap.

The undetected distribution of contraband could be a more difficult task than landing it in the first place. Sussex smugglers from Alfriston and Jevington used the Cuckmere River to bring goods inland from Cuckmere Haven.

Even in the nineteenth century, when preventive efforts were at their height, the smugglers still favoured the flat beach at Cuckmere. By that stage, though, a little friendly persuasion was necessary if the goods were to come in safely, as this description of a bribery attempt (told by a local customs man) illustrates:

> I was posted as sentinel on duty at the point near the mouth of Cuckmere Haven when two men came up to me. One of them, who has since called himself John Clare, laid money on the beach, desiring me to pick it up. I told him I did not want it. The two men then sat down for some time underneath the cliff when John Clare put on a lump of chalk £20 and pointing to it said there should be twenty pounds for me and a cart in readiness to carry me to what part of the country I pleased admitting them to work tubs, asking me at the same time which was the most convenient place for that purpose.[25]

It is easy to pick out Crowlink cart gap on this old map, though today coastal erosion has consumed all traces of Crowlink and Birling Gaps.

HASTINGS AND ST LEONARDS ▪39

199-TQ8109, 24m SE of Tunbridge Wells. See map on page 40.

Some of those smugglers crippled by cliff falls and derrick accidents were 'electrified' by John Banks, a Hastings schoolteacher (and evidently a man of many other parts) who had the foresight in 1871 to set down many of the smuggling stories associated with the town.[26] He had plenty to choose from; one native of the town[27] commented:

> No business carried on in Hastings was more popular and extensive as that of smuggling. Defrauding the revenue, so far from being considered a crime, was looked upon as a laudable pursuit, and the most successful 'runners' were heroes. Nearly the whole of the inhabitants, old and young and of every station in life, were, to some extent, engaged in it.

From his own experiences, John Banks paints a vivid picture of smuggling in an era when prevention was at its height, but he also reminisces about the earlier era when most of the smuggling activity at Hastings and St Leonards took place on the beach. In these colourful tales the smugglers rely for their safety and that of their cargoes on their traditional allies of darkness, brute force, and the incompetence or corruptibility of the revenue services. The custom-house officers could usually be expected to make themselves scarce at the prearranged time of landing, but things didn't always go according to the timetable. Banks describes one embarrassed encounter and the final resolution with characteristic humour.

The boat landing the goods near the centre of St Leonards was owned by one Jemmy Roper, and he made the mistake of beaching the boat before his reception committee had arrived. Worse, a custom-house officer appeared. The two men exchanged curses, and the officer told Jemmy he was a fool for arriving early, and that he would now be obliged to seize the cargo. Jemmy replied 'If you be a man, act like one'. In the meantime, the owner of the cargo had arrived, and negotiations began. The custom-house officer agreed that in exchange for seizing 10 tubs of spirits, he would allow the crew to ship the rest inland. The boat was quickly unloaded, and when the 'gentlemen' had melted away into the darkness, the officer fired his pistol into the air to summon help in carrying the seized goods back to the custom-house.

This transaction must surely have been typical of many thousands of such 'accommodations' reached between the opposing forces of smugglers and preventives, but not all encounters were so amicable, and there was violence on both sides.

During the early 1760s one particularly notorious gang of Hastings smugglers and privateers, 'Ruxley's crew', would board ships in the Channel on the pretence of doing legitimate business (then a common practice). Once on board they would lock up the crew, kill anyone who resisted, then remove the cargo and scupper the boat with all hands. Such behaviour was perhaps not all that outrageous at a time when a licence to attack foreign vessels could be bought from the government (this indeed was the essence of privateering). However, the gang overstepped the mark when they killed the master of a Dutch ship by break-

The Hastings Arms has a dusty memento of smuggling ingenuity: copper pipes carried draught brandy from this concealed barrel to the bar on the floor below.

ing his back with an axe, then later drunkenly bragging about 'How the Dutchman wriggled when they cut him down the backbone'.[28] The act caused public outrage, and the Hastings population persistently demanded to know what was going to be done. When the mayor could not come up with a satisfactory reply, he was attacked violently. In response the government stationed a man-of-war offshore, and sent in 200 dragoons. The gang was arrested and tried in London (the authorities feared that a local jury would not dare convict) and four of the crew were hanged as pirates at Execution Dock.

The most celebrated example of violence at Hastings, though, was perpetrated by the preventive forces. Joseph Swaine, a fisherman, was shot in 1821 by an exciseman who was intending to search his fishing boat. There was a struggle, during which the excise officer's gun went off (accidentally, he claimed). The incident was the flash-point for seething discontent among the fishermen, in a dispute that was focused on the searching of their boats. The increasing vigilance of the government's anti-smuggling campaign had forced the free-traders to rope together tubs into rafts, which were anchored off-shore and (allegedly) recovered by the local fishermen. Fishing boats were so numerous that a thorough and methodical search of each one was impossible, so the customs men resorted to poking a metal spike through the piles of net to feel for barrels concealed beneath. According to the fishing folk, the prodding damaged the nets, and Swaine was shot while trying to prevent such damage to his tackle.

Swaine became a local martyr, with the Hastings mob baying for blood. The excise man, George England, was convicted of murder, despite desperate and heart-rending pleas from the dock as the sentence was read:

> ... you be taken from hence ... *Consider I was in execution of my duty* ... to the place whence you came ... *Gentlemen of the Jury, pray consider your verdict again* ... and from thence to the place of execution, on Friday next, where you are to be hanged by the neck until you are dead, and may the Lord have mercy upon your soul ... *Oh Gentlemen of the Jury, pray consider your verdict again!*

The sentence was never carried out, for England was reprieved soon afterwards, much to the fury of the residents of Hastings. After the shooting there had been considerable civil disturbance locally, and dragoons were sent in to restore order. The reprieve caused a renewal of rioting, and if England had returned to his former posting, the mob would almost certainly have taken the law into their own hands and carried out what they saw as a just sentence. Instead, England was discharged from his job and spirited out of harm's way.

For the visitor to modern Hastings, there are still plenty of reminders of the smuggling era. The Old Town retains many of the buildings that would have been part of Joseph Swaine's landscape, and the fishermen's net houses remain in their original condition. Up above the beach, two local pubs have smuggling associations. The Hastings Arms in George Street has a brandy barrel concealed under a window ledge on the first floor (not in a public area, unfortunately) which was once linked by pipes to a tap above the bar so that 'genuine Crowlink' could be dispensed from the wood without attracting undue attention. And the cellars of the Stag Inn on All Saints Street were once linked by a tunnel to a cave on the hills towering above.

JOHN COLLIER

Hastings House, at the top of the Old Town facing the church, was the home of one of the most resolute opponents of smuggling. John Collier was mayor of Hastings, and surveyor-general of the Kent riding officers for fifteen years from 1735. Over this period he was a prolific correspondent, and the 2000-odd letters he wrote form perhaps the most important surviving account of eighteenth-century smuggling and its prevention.

SUSSEX WEST OF THE OUSE

Between the River Ouse and Selsey Bill, nineteenth- and twentieth-century building work has largely transfigured the coastline into widespread areas of housing, and little remains to remind us of the lucrative smuggling runs that took place here. The once isolated beaches are now hemmed in with tarmac and concrete, and it takes a considerable imaginative leap to picture Kipling's five and twenty ponies trotting through the dark. However, some of the quainter spots demand less suspension of disbelief than others.

Cow Gap below and just to the east of Beachy Head was a landing-point favoured by eighteenth-century smugglers. A cart gap there provided a simple route inland for the tub-men, and a light on the famous headland could be seen miles out to sea, making signalling simple. The coast here was treacherous to those who did not know the tides and currents, and wrecks such as this one were common. Before the first lighthouse was constructed in 1831, a lantern hanging in an enlarged cave served to warn mariners of the dangers.

ROTTINGDEAN ■40

198-TQ3703, 4m E of Brighton. The picturesque village attracts large crowds on summer weekends.

Stretching out north from the coast road, Old Rottingdean still retains some of its original character, and when Kipling stayed there the tales of the older inhabitants must have provided ample inspiration for his *A Smuggler's Song*. The windmill was used both for the purposes of storage and signalling, and the Black Horse Inn on the High Street was an informal HQ for the smugglers. Townspeople of all social classes were deeply involved in the free-trade, from the local vicar to the butcher who lived at Whipping-Post House close to the pond, almost opposite the Olde Place Hotel.

BRIGHTON ■41

198-TQ3005. The Ship Hotel is on the sea front, close to the Pavilion (Ship Street).

At Brighton, the lanes remain much as they were in the eighteenth century, when goods were landed on the beach and carried straight up for sale and distribution from shops and inns among the winding alleys and narrow courtyards. The Old Ship Hotel nearby has changed little since the day of George IV's coronation in 1821, when it was the scene of an admirable bit of smuggling opportunism. While the town celebrated elsewhere, the free-traders took advantage of the empty streets and moved tubs of spirits out of the pub stables completely unobserved.[29] Today it's one of the town's better hotels,

Like their colleagues elsewhere, members of coastguard patrols in the Brighton area were instructed to disguise themselves in a manner that would make them indistinguishable from their adversaries—they wore white smocks and hat covers. However, their superior officers also saw fit to warn them of dangers peculiar to the town, such as women who came to their posts to distract them from duties!

with an air more of smugness than smugglers.

It's less easy to picture the open runs that took place on the beach at Brighton, and more difficult still to imagine some of the other activity that went on where deck-chairs now stand. In 1794 several officers heard a commotion on Brighton beach, and went to investigate. They found a gang of smugglers landing 400–500 tubs of gin, and with the help of troops stationed nearby, the officers dispersed the free-traders, and seized the cargo. However, *en route* for the Shoreham custom house, two of the soldiers tucked into the barrels. They drunk themselves insensible, and were found comatose on the beach the following morning. One, who was due to be married that day, was quite literally dead drunk—he never recovered from his over-indulgence.[30]

HOVE ■42

198-TQ2805, W suburb of Brighton. The church is on Church Road, near the junction with Vallance Road. The Ship Inn is on Hove Street close to the sea front.

The coast at Hove, Shoreham-by-Sea, Worthing and Goring-by-Sea was used for beaching smuggling ships, but even the beaches themselves scarcely resemble their eighteenth-century counterparts: the sea defences and groynes have turned them from flat expanses of sand and shingle to shelving staircases. It's difficult to believe that coaches would travel along the flat beaches at low tide in preference to the appalling roads of the day.

At Hove, St Andrew's Church and the early eighteenth-century Ship Inn are the only remaining smuggling landmarks; both were used for storing contraband. The church was reputedly stuffed with tobacco and brandy every other week, since the parish shared a vicar with Preston church, and services alternated between the two. Inevitably, perhaps, the story is told of how a confused vicar got his preaching timetable wrong, and arrived at Hove to find a congregation of bales and barrels.[31]

SHOREHAM-BY-SEA ■43

198-TQ2305, 5m W of Brighton.

Shoreham-by-Sea had long-standing connections with the trade, and a writer noted in 1785 that Shoreham boats no longer went to the Yarmouth fishery, because they had taken up the more profitable pursuit of smuggling.[32]

It should therefore hardly come as a surprise to find that there is a crop of local smuggling ancedotes associated with the area—some of them more likely than others. The most fascinating one concerns a circus and wild-beast show that visited Shoreham in August 1855. Complimentary tickets were handed out to important folk in the area, and also to the valiant preventives stationed in the town. As the proceedings reached a climax, the streets were emptied of people, so few noticed a suspicious-looking ship on the town quay. Before the tide had even begun to ebb, the cargo of tobacco had been unloaded into barges and was on its way up the Adur River to Upper Beeding. Though the plan was discovered, little of the cargo was ever found, and as a result of their negligence, virtually all of the Shoreham coast guards were replaced.[33]

WORTHING AND STEYNING ■44

Worthing is at 198-TQ1503, 10m W of Brighton. To reach Steyning take the A283N from Shoreham; in Steyning turn right down Tanyard Lane (signposted health centre and library) to St Andrew's church at 198-TQ178114. William Cowerson's grave is just to the left of the path, a short way from the lower gate.

A local preventive force and a cutter were stationed at Worthing, and an early chronicler of Worthing history[34] recorded that in February 1832 he was:

> ... aroused by an uproar in the High Street and the sound of firearms. A big cargo of spirits had been landed and was being taken up the High Street towards Broadwater while a number of men armed with stout staves had come down from the country to protect the smugglers and their cargo. The Preventive Force got wind of the affair, and attacked the procession as it made its way up High Street, and there was a running fight all the way up the road. At the top of High Street was a footpath leading to Broadwater, closed by a gate which happened to be padlocked, so that only one man could get over at a time. The staff men, as they were called, closed round the smugglers and laid about vigorously with their staves in order to hold off the Preventive men. The latter drew their pistols and fired into the crowd, hitting and killing a young man named William Cowerson.

Cowerson, a stonemason, was buried in the churchyard at Steyning, his home town. His grave can still be seen there, though the inscription on the tombstone is now only partly legible. A local churchwarden[35] recalls that it ran:

> Death with his dart did pierce my heart
> When I was in my prime,
> Weep not for me my dearest friends
> For 'twas God's appointed time.

GORING-BY-SEA AND FERRING ■45

198-TQ1203, 3m W of Worthing centre.

At Goring-by-Sea, Smuggler's Walk is not named on the romantic whim of a modern planner, but actually stands at the centre of an area that was once used for storing smuggled goods. But Ferring, a little way to the west, has some still more tangible links with eighteenth- and nineteenth-century smugglers. In Ferring Street, Smuggler's Cottage and Annex were both used for storage, as was the building that is now The Tudor Close Restaurant in Ferringham Lane. Goods were brought up from the beach along the Rife—a small river that passes close to the building (though it now flows in a culvert). Landfalls, also in Ferring Street, served a similar purpose.

Ferring's major claim to smuggling fame, though, lies buried on Highdown Hill overlooking the village. John Oliver was an eccentric local miller who ran a profitable sideline in smuggling. He died in 1793, but had made preparations for his departure from this life some 30 years earlier. He had a tomb built close to his mill on the hill, and his coffin was stored under his bed.

When Miller Oliver died, he had made sure that everything was ready: the lavish funeral was a cheerful affair attended by 2,000 brightly dressed people. Local gossip has it that the miller was buried face down in his coffin, because he believed that when the Last Judgment came the world would be turned topsy-turvy—and he would be the only one facing right-side-up.

CHICHESTER AND AREA

The far west of Sussex has a particularly black reputation in the history of smuggling, on account of a number of particularly brutal murders that took place here. (See Barbarous Usage, page 59.) However, these notorious incidents were in some respects the doing of strangers to the area, and by contrast the local people kept a characteristically low profile in their smuggling activities.

They were aided in this by the nature of the coastline, which changes progressively west of Bognor, from straight flat beaches to a fretwork of sandy inlets and natural harbours. The proximity of the Isle of Wight was an added bonus, as outlined in the following chapter.

PAGHAM HARBOUR

For Pagham ∎46 (197-SZ8897) leave the B2166 at Lagness along a minor road. To get to Sidlesham ∎47 and Church Norton ∎48 from Pagham is perhaps quicker on foot (there's a path round the harbour) than by car; follow the road almost to Chichester, then take the B2145 Selsey road.

Pagham Harbour, the most easterly of the inlets in the Chichester area, is today choked with mud and weeds, but in the eighteenth century it was still a working port, with channels to the quayside both at Sidlesham and Pagham. The tide flowing into the harbour created sufficient current for rafts of tubs to float through the inlet unaided and usually unnoticed—a technique used to great advantage farther west. When vessels brought contraband into the harbour, it would have been a simple matter for accomplices on shore to pinpoint the preventive forces, so that goods could be landed on the distant side; crossing the 3/4-mile wide harbour in a boat was far quicker than negotiating the 5-mile circumference on horseback. Smugglers made good use of this topographical advantage in 1830, luring revenue officers to Sidlesham with a decoy light, then landing 700 tubs from a galley at Pagham.

The silted harbour is now a beautiful nature reserve, and the creeks unnavigable, but there is still a row of attractive old buildings close enough to the Pagham quayside to make a convenient temporary hiding place for contraband. At Church Norton, on the west of the harbour, you can see the remains of a church that was once linked by a tunnel to the old rectory.

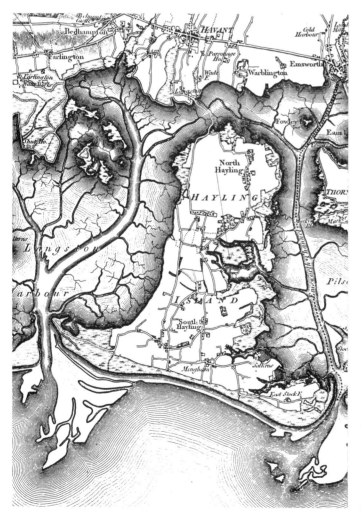

SELSEY BILL ∎49

197-SZ86, 3m S of Chichester.

Two centuries ago Selsey Bill was very much more isolated than it is today, and the sand spit extended farther out into the Solent. Selsey was linked to the mainland by only a causeway, so the approach of the local riding officer would have been conspicuous in the extreme. The rectors of Selsey reputedly claimed a tithe on all kegs landed there, and stories also tell of a passageway leading from the Old Rectory to the Mound. The course of the tunnel was marked by a depression on the surface of the ground as late as 1911.[36] In the 1720s one Selsey man ran a regular ferry service to France, travelling back and forth every five weeks, and other prominent Selsey figures made considerable fortunes just from part-time work in the free-trade. Landings weren't confined to Selsey itself: in a single run in 1743 2,000 lb of tea were brought inland at West Wittering some 6 miles away.

HAYLING ISLAND ∎50 AND THORNEY ISLAND ∎51

Much of Thorney Island is now an army camp, and entry by car is at the discretion of the military as it is a 'restricted' area. Ask for permission at the gatehouse, or walk around the island on the public footpath. Contraband most often came ashore near the church 197-SU770025.

To the west of Selsey Bill, the harbours of Langstone and Chichester, together with Emsworth Channel, form a huge natural basin with a wild and convoluted border. The single riding officer assigned to the area in the mid-eighteenth century would have found it difficult to patrol just one of these harbours efficiently, let alone all three. Hayling and Thorney islands were widely used for landing goods rafted into the harbours on the fast-running tides, or rowed across the narrow strip of water that separated the coast from the Isle of Wight.

Hayling Island was approached along a causeway before Victorian times, and until the contraband could be inconspicuously moved along this link to the mainland, the kegs and bundles of tobacco were stored in vast depots dug in the sandy soil of the low island. A writer commented in 1826 that:

> When this nefarious and demoralizing system was at its height ... Many subterraneous caverns were known to exist along the south beach, for the reception of contraband goods.[37]

By 1826 most of the caverns had disappeared, with the exception of one, 'not far from the new buildings'. On an old map, these can be seen one-third of the way along the south shore travelling west to east.

Left: The sandy beaches of Hayling Island, shown on this map dated 1810, offered a safe and sheltered landing point for smugglers. Even the local gentry were not above taking advantage of the sea's bounty from time to time. Lord Norfolk of Arundel Castle claimed salvage rights to 143 barrels of wine that were washed onto the beaches in 1753 to the consternation of the local customs officials, who demanded that he pay duty on them.

Opposite: The mill at Langstone Harbour served local smugglers well as it was one of the few buildings which could be locked without suspicion. Its sails were also used for signalling.

LANGSTONE AND EMSWORTH ■52

Langstone is at the end of the causeway to Hayling Island 197-SU719049. The mill and the Red Lion are at the waterside, set back from the road. Parking restricted at summer weekends. From Langstone, Emsworth is just a 2m walk to the east along the mainland, and has many smuggling associations detailed on the town information board; the pharmacy, for example, was once linked by a tunnel to cellars of a house on the waterside.

The villages of Langstone and Emsworth were both notorious haunts of smugglers. At Langstone, the mill on the coast path to Emsworth was used both for signalling (it was worked by both tide and wind, so the sails could be easily positioned to form a pre-arranged code) and for storage. The bar of the Red Lion on the waterfront saw many a smugglers' conference, and there are stories of a tunnel linking the pub to the mill.[38] Such a passage would have been so close to sea level that keeping it dry would have presented formidable problems—though perhaps the mill was used for pumping out when the tide filled the tunnel.

BARBAROUS USAGE
(Tales of torture and sadism)

Sussex was the setting for two of the most horrific tales in all the history of smuggling—events that were to lead to a public outcry, and ultimately to the destruction of the big eighteenth-century gangs.

This ugly chapter in the smuggling story centres on the activities of the Hawkhurst Gang—or around certain members of it, since only a handful of smugglers were involved in the murders that so shocked public sensibilities. The stories are recounted here in detail because the events described played a key role in changing the public image of smugglers, and because the brutality of the murders gives the lie to the 'harmless smuggler' myth that has grown up in the last two centuries.

The first incident was centred on the village of Slindon. This was the home of Richard Hawkins, a farm labourer, whose body was found weighted with rocks in the pond at Parham Park, some 12 miles away in the spring of 1748.

Hawkins made the simple mistake of getting on the wrong side of a group of smugglers. John 'Smoker' Mills, and Jeremiah 'Butler' Curtiss suspected Hawkins of stealing two bags of tea, and went looking for him on the farm in Walberton where he worked. Hawkins denied all knowledge of the tea, but evidently the two men didn't believe him. Hawkins was hoisted into the saddle behind Mills, and taken off to the Dog and Patridge Inn at Slindon. There it appears there was a smugglers' court, with Hawkins on trial, and Mills, Curtiss and two other smugglers as judge and jury.

When Hawkins denied that he had anything to do with the missing tea, Curtiss shouted, 'Damn you, you do know, and if you do not confess I shall whip you till you do, for damn you, I have whipped many a rogue, and washed my hands in his blood.' At this point the landlord of the inn appeared, and remarked, 'Dick, you had better confess, it will be better for you'.

When Hawkins continued to protest his innocence, he was whipped and beaten, then forced to strip to the waist; and despite his begging for mercy, the smugglers continued to whip, punch and kick him so hard that they had to pause for breath. In the course of the torture, though, Hawkins let slip, 'My father and my brother'.

At this, the beating stopped, and two of the torturers rode off in search of further victims. The respite came too late for Hawkins, for he died soon after the men had left.

At this the two smugglers who had stayed at the inn locked the room and rushed after their colleagues, meeting them as they returned to the pub with the dead man's father-in-law and brother. Realizing the danger they were in, the four smugglers released their prisoners, swearing them to secrecy; then they returned to the Dog and Partridge, picked up the corpse, and rode to Parham ■53 (2m W of Storrington at 197-TQ0614). They weighted the body with rocks, and dumped it in the lake.

The murder hunt started when the body was found, and one of the four—Mills—was cleverly captured by a fellow Hawkhurst gang member who negotiated a pardon in exchange for this service to the Crown. One of the accused smugglers who had not actually taken part in the whipping gave evidence against Mills at the trial, and thus saved his own skin. Curtiss escaped to France before he could be brought to trial.

This violent story was by no means an isolated incident. Indeed, had Hawkins lived, it's unlikely that any of the torturers would have been brought to justice. And for 'Smoker' Mills, it seems, torture and violence were a way of life, for Mills was part of a group that committed

Smugglers John Mills and Richard Rowland whipping Richard Hawkins to death at the Dog and Partridge Inn, Slindon Common. Jeremiah Curtis and Thomas Winter watch in the background.

The lake at Parham Park in West Sussex where the body of Richard Hawkins was found, murdered by the Hawkhurst Gang.

two even more grisly murders less than a fortnight later.

However, this second story actually started four months earlier, with a smuggling trip in September 1747. The voyage was organized by two groups acting in concert: the Hawkhurst Gang that we have already met; and a group from Dorset. The gangs sent a representative to Guernsey on a Rye boat, to buy about 2 tons of tea and 30 casks of spirits. These were duly loaded, and the vessel set off for the planned rendezvous in Christchurch Bay near Lymington.

However, things went badly wrong. The smuggling vessel was seized at sea by a revenue ship, and although the crew escaped, the contraband was taken to a government warehouse in Poole. The principal sponsors of the trip were naturally dismayed by this turn of events, and at a meeting in Charlton Forest they resolved to take back the tea in a raid on the custom-house. This they did on the night of 6 October.

The 30 smugglers had met at Rowland's Castle the previous night, then ridden from there to Poole, resting *en route*. When they arrived at the town, an advance party went forward to assess the risk of capture, and returned with the bad news that there was a naval guard in the harbour, with guns trained on the doors of the custom-house. This caused some discussion and argument—the faint-hearted Dorset men wanted to abandon the enterprise, but the Hawkhurst contingent said they would go it alone if their co-conspirators backed out. This threat, and the fact that the falling tide had put the custom-house out of sight of the

The Hawkhurst Gang break open the Poole custom-house to recover their confiscated tea.

battleship, persuaded the party to go on. They left their horses with two of the gang, and broke open the strong-room with crowbars and axes.

This part of the raid went entirely according to plan. The smugglers took virtually all the tea, leaving behind the brandy, perhaps because they had insufficient transport. The heavily laden convoy then set out for Brook in the New Forest, where they planned to weigh the tea and share it out: each man was to get a little over a hundredweight.

At no point had the smugglers been opposed, and it seems likely that they were elated by their success. As they passed through Fording-bridge, a fine crowd turned out to watch the caravan passing, and it was there that one of the gang made a fatal error. Hawkhurst man John 'Dimer' Diamond spotted a familiar face in the crowd: shoe-maker Daniel Chater. The two men had worked together to get the harvest in and Diamond shook the other man's hand and threw him a small bag of tea.

The convoy then rode on to divide up the spoils, and Chater, perhaps basking in reflected glory, chatted innocently to his neighbours, saying he knew Diamond. This was to be his undoing, for when the authorities started investigating the theft, they soon began to view Chater as a key witness.

Diamond, meanwhile, had been arrested on suspicion of his involvement, and was in Chichester gaol. To prove the case against him, the collector of customs at Chichester had to get the cobbler to positively identify the smuggler.

So it was that on Valentine's Day, 1748, William Galley, an ageing minor customs official, set out with the shoe-maker on what was to be a fateful journey. They left Southampton heading for the home of a JP near Chichester, carrying a letter with instructions that Chater should go to Chichester gaol to identify Diamond.

They soon lost their way, but were guided by a couple of local men as far as the White Hart Inn at Rowland's Castle. This was an unfortunate place for the two men to break their journey, for it was owned and run by a family who were in league with the smugglers. The landlady became suspicious of the intentions of the travellers, and sent for William Jackson and William Carter, who lived close by. Before these two smugglers arrived, though, Galley and Chater wanted to press on; an excuse about lost stable keys delayed them just long enough for the other smugglers to arrive.

At this point the danger that the men were in started to become apparent. The reinforcements arrived, innocent witnesses were sent away from the pub, and the smugglers began to drink heavily. Jackson took Chater aside, and asked him what was happening: Chater replied regretfully that he was obliged to give evidence against his friend Diamond. At this point, rightly suspecting that his witness was being intimidated, Galley emerged, only to be hit in the face by Jackson. The three men came indoors together, with Galley protesting, 'I'm a King's officer, I'll not put up with such usage'. 'You a King's officer,' Jackson

spat back at the bloodied customs man, 'I'll make a King's officer of you; and for a quatern of gin I'll serve you so again'. Jackson raised his fist, but a bystander sprang forward and grabbed his arm, crying, 'Don't be such a fool, do you know what you are doing?'.

This calmed things down a bit, and the smugglers apologized. They persuaded the two men to drink with them, and soon Galley and Chater were drowsy with the drink, and went to sleep in an adjoining room. As they slept, the smugglers crept in and took the letter.

The contents plainly spelt out the intentions of the men, and the smugglers held a council of war. A great deal of drinking went on, and there were various proposals as to what they should do with the prisoners. The most humane was to send them to France, but for the wives of two of the smugglers, no punishment was severe enough. They egged their husbands on, crying out, 'Hang the dogs, for they came here to hang us'.

When this conference ended Jackson put on his spurs, and woke the sleeping men by getting on the bed, spurring their foreheads and whipping them, providing a foretaste of the torture that was to follow. Soon the men were taken outside, and put together on a horse, with their legs tied under the horse's belly. One man led the horse—the road was too

Galley (in front) and Chater set out on their last painful ride through Sussex. Jackson and Carter, who led the torture of the two men, are fourth and third from the right respectively. Steel, who turned King's evidence, holds the horse's head.

rough for all to ride—and the rest of the gang followed.

They hadn't got more than a hundred yards when Jackson shouted, 'Whip them, cut them, slash them, damn them!' and for the next mile five of the smugglers attacked Galley and Chater so badly with whips that the two men slid sideways, so they hung beneath the horse; at each step one or other was kicked in the head by the horse's hooves.

Galley and Chater had their feet tied together, so that when they became too weak to sit upright, they slid down under the horse's belly. At each step the horse kicked them in the head.

'William Galley, brought lying cross a horse to a sand pit where a deep hole is dug to bury him in.'

'The unfortunate William Galley being put by the smugglers into the ground and as is generally believed before he was quite DEAD.'

By now the captives were so weak that they couldn't sit in a saddle unaided, so they were separated, and each sat behind one of the smugglers. The other four took off their prisoners' jackets and rained blows on the pillion riders. The torment only stopped when the smuggler on the horse carrying Galley complained that many of the whiplashes were striking him, as well as their intended victim.

The company moved on as far as Harris's Well in Lady Holt Park, where they planned to kill both men and throw them down. Here Galley pleaded for a quick death, but this only provoked Jackson further, and he swore, 'No, God damn your blood, if that's the case, we must have something more to say to you.'

The party set off again, first with the helpless Galley on his belly across a saddle, then sitting in it, leaning forward on the horse's neck:

> . . . in this posture Jackson held him on for half a mile, most of the way the poor man cried out 'Barbarous usage! barbarous usage! for God's sake shoot me through the head'; Jackson all the time squeezing his private parts.

Galley eventually fell from the horse, apparently lifeless, but probably only temporarily unconscious. His captors slung him across a horse, and the grisly caravan trudged on. They reached the Red Lion at Rake in the early hours of Monday morning, after stopping briefly at the house of another reputed smuggler who '. . . imagining they were upon some villainous expedition . . .' refused to help them.

At the inn, Chater was still capable of standing, and he was taken out and chained up in a skilling—a place where turf was stored. The smugglers hid Galley's body temporarily in the brew-house attached to the pub, and later that night carried the 'corpse' about ¾ mile to Harting Coombe. There they enlarged a fox-earth, bundled the old man into the hole, and tipped the soil back on top.

When the corpse was found some time later, it was apparent that Galley had recovered consciousness after being interred, for he was standing almost upright, and had raised his hand to cover his eyes and keep out the dirt.

For the smugglers, there was still the problem of Chater. He remained chained in the turf house for three days, too ill to eat. After a secret meeting on Wednesday night, it was resolved that Chater should be murdered and his body dumped in Harris's Well as originally planned. The gang went out to the turf house, and one of the group, Tapner, ordered the shoe-maker '. . . down on your knees and go to prayers, for with this knife I will be your butcher.' As Chater knelt, Tapner slashed the man's face twice, completely cutting through his nose, and virtually blinding him.

Chater, chained in the turf house, prays for mercy as Tapner carves his face with a knife.

Eventually they set off for the well, with Tapner continuing to whip Chater, and threatening him with all manner of tortures if he spilt his own blood on the horse's saddle! The party eventually reached the well, and after an unsuccessful attempt to hang Chater with a rope that proved too short, they dumped his body into the well, and threw in rocks and timbers until there was silence.

Though they had disposed of the bodies, there were still two dumb witnesses—the men's horses. One had strayed, but the other was knocked on the head, flayed, and the hide cut into small pieces.

The two victims were soon missed, but the murderers had concealed the bodies carefully, and despite a strenuous investigation, months passed with no progress. Eventually, though, an anonymous letter led to the discovery of Galley's body, and a second letter named William Steel as one of the murderers. (Some accounts[39] say that Galley's body was found by a man walking his dogs on the common.) On his arrest, Steel turned King's evidence, and named all the others involved. Another smuggler who had played a minor role in the affair surrendered himself, and also turned King's evidence. Soon virtually the whole gang had been rounded up.

At the Chichester Assizes all the seven men were sentenced to the gallows, but Jackson cheated the hangman by dying in gaol before sentence could be carried out. (Though he was ill, it is said that the shock of being measured up for gibbet chains hastened his end). The other six were taken up the Midhurst Road and executed on the Broyle, and the bodies of the five principal murderers were hung in chains—one on the Portsmouth Road near Rake, two on Selsey Bill, one on Rook's Hill near Chichester, and one at Horsmonden.

The passage of two centuries has changed the setting of this grisly story very little, and it's still possible to trace the last painful steps of the two unfortunate victims. Harting Coombe where Galley was buried is criss-crossed by footpaths, and foxes still make their earths in the sandy banks there. Lady Holt Park ■54 is now a Forestry Commission estate. Leave Petersfield on the A3 Havant road, and take the first left after the B2146, down a minor road about a mile outside Petersfield town centre. Follow the road through Buriton, and under the railway.

After about 3 miles the road joins a larger road and swings left over a railway bridge. At the junction immediately after the bridge continue straight on down a rough track. Ladyholt estate is on the left. Stop at the gate on the left signed Barnett Copse and follow the track through woodland. Keep left at the first junction, then down a hill past another junction. About 1¼ miles from the road at 197-SU753172 you will find the well set a few yards to the left of the path, some 50 yards beyond a track on the left marked 'No riding'. At the time of the murder, the well was dry, and Chater's makeshift grave is now just a shallow dent in the ground.

At Chichester ■55, the site of the execution on the Broyle was marked by an inscribed stone which can still be seen. Leave Chichester on the A286 Midhurst Road. The stone is some 200 yards past the Wellington pub, on the other side of the road, backing onto the barracks, 188-SU859065.

At Horsmonden ■56 the gibbet where the body of one of Chater's killers was displayed used to stand on the right of Gibbet Lane just as you turn the corner. Horsmonden is 4m SE of Paddock Wood, straddling the B2162: when approaching from the N, Gibbet Lane is a turning on the right about ¼m before the village green, 188-TQ7040. See map on page 40.

The bungling smugglers try to hang Chater in a well, but find their rope is too short.

Eventually the smugglers throw the shoemaker down the well and stone him to death.

SOUTHERN ENGLAND

CHICHESTER TO LYME

The south of England was not as close to the sources of smuggled goods as were Kent and Essex, but the coast here had other compensations: the Channel Islands made a very favourable staging post; there were many fine beaches and inlets for landing goods; the winds were favourable; and—at least initially—the coast was less well guarded than that of Kent or Sussex. In addition, in comparison to the treacherous Cornish and Devon coasts, the beaches of Hampshire and Dorset are quite benign.

Contraband came in to the south principally from France, though often via Jersey and Guernsey, or the smaller Channel Islands. Some more exotic imports also arrived on ocean-going vessels heading for Southampton; the crews of East Indiamen in particular openly traded with the small boats that clustered around the vast hulls in the Solent.

Oriental luxuries were the exception, though, and in the early years of the eighteenth century the staples of the Hampshire and Dorset smugglers were wine and brandy, along with miscellaneous items wide in variety but small in quantity, such as playing-cards and handkerchiefs. During the 1730s there was a shift away from kegs, and the principal contraband became oilskin bags of tea. During the Napoleonic wars a few of the south-coast towns, notably Christchurch, exported gold, but the so-called 'Guinea run' was never carried on to anything like the same extent as in Kent and Sussex.

The techniques for landing smuggled goods in the south closely paralleled those in other parts of Britain. Until about 1700, the bribing of customs officials was regarded almost as a simple business transaction, and was a great deal easier than landing goods at some inconvenient spot in the middle of the night. But as corruption and nepotism began to be ferreted out by diligent government officials, this approach became closed to the merchants of the south.

It was replaced initially by open landings at a discreet distance from the official ports, because the government of the day was preoccupied with the wars in Europe, and did not have the will to deal with minor domestic problems. However, when peace broke out in 1713, the preventive effort began in earnest, and the smugglers united to protect their cargoes. Defiance was the order of the day, and the smugglers prevailed by sheer force of numbers, often landing goods in full view of the customs authorities. The smugglers wore masks and other disguises to prevent identification by the officials, who in small towns might well have been their next-door-neighbours.

Brute-force landings like this waxed and waned; they flourished when the stakes were high enough, when the risks of capture were slight, and the punishments meted out not too severe. But when the net tightened, or declining taxation cut profits, subterfuge began. The free-traders' objective was wherever possible to sneak the goods in unobserved. Tubs were sunk from the large smuggling luggers some distance off-shore, then collected inconspicuously by small fishing boats. Where the tides were favourable, barrels could be roped together

and rafted in from the open sea to the inland harbours with which the south coast was so well supplied. This method was used to great effect at Portsmouth, Langstone and Chichester harbours, and to the west at Christchurch and Poole. Dorset and Hampshire smugglers caught in the act of sneaking their goods in would destroy the evidence or simply flee if they ran the risk of the gallows or transportation.

Some of the contraband landed in southern England was consumed locally. Many a farming fortune was made by tilling the rich soil a little way inland, and just as the squire demanded the best brandy, so too his daughters expected the best French lace. However, there is evidence that the smuggled imports would have often found their way to London. A trail of stories of smugglers' hidden depots points to a cross-country highway that channelled goods from the coast to the markets in the capital.

Amazingly, some contraband made its way to London from as far afield as west Dorset. In 1719 a merchant at Lulworth was importing cocoa beans at a time when there was a taste for drinking chocolate only among the smarter London set. Some contraband travelled long distances inland for different reasons. Cargoes of brandy landed in Dorset in the early nineteenth century were of such poor quality that they were virtually unfit to drink, and the kegs were carted a safe distance from the coast to undergo a further distilling process, before being sold in the town taverns.

London was not the only inland market: sophisticates in Bristol (formerly England's second port) and in the country houses of Gloucestershire and Worcestershire were also supplied with contraband landed on the south coast, and moved inland through Dorchester and Sherborne. Though land transport was vastly more expensive than water, the inland route would have proved much less risky as preventive measures were stepped up.

Parts of the Dorset and west Hampshire coasts were flanked by untamed heath and woodland that made concealment easy and pursuit difficult. Some regions of the New Forest were effectively no-go areas, and once a cargo entered the Forest, it was usually safe from the clutches of the revenue men. Even Bourne Heath, where Bournemouth now stands, at one time had a fearful reputation, and the dense woodland of Cranborne Chase was felled because it provided a haven for smugglers and other undesirables.

Although the larger and more powerful smuggling gangs from the south-east spread their tentacles out as far west as Poole, native Hampshire and Dorset smugglers seem to have preferred persuasion to compulsion in their dealings with the local population (though not the revenue men). One figure in particular, Isaac Gulliver, had such a non-violent reputation that he was nicknamed 'the Gentle Smuggler', though in fairness, such gentleness was relative. His gang was reputedly forbidden from carrying firearms, but they probably weren't averse to swinging a weighty club when met by any of the King's men.

THE ISLE OF WIGHT

In Hampshire, the smuggler's job was made especially easy by the proximity of the Isle of Wight. The island had a well-developed trade in wool exports, and until the late eighteenth century, its coasts were only lightly guarded against the attentions of free-traders. Any ship's master with sufficient navigational ability would have been able to slip into one of the island's bays or creeks with little risk of losing a cargo to the land-based forces.

A chase at sea was perhaps more of a risk, but in the early eighteenth century, the smugglers relied on their superior seamanship to evade the preventive forces. The south-east side of the island is fringed with treacherous rock platforms, notably Rocken End, and the risk of a wreck was not something that the master of a revenue cutter contemplated with pleasure. Any smuggler who knew a way through the rocks, and was prepared to ride out the ferocious south-westerly winds that batter this part of the coast was unlikely to be followed too far.[1]

There seem to have been no large gangs on the island, and the free-trade apparently enjoyed the support of many of the inhabitants. To a certain extent this may reflect the fact that many local people despised rule from the mainland—until the end of the thirteenth century Wight had been an independent principality, and even at this early date, export smuggling of wool was already taking place on the island and the mainland.[2] Little wonder that the islanders were disrespectful of the customs authorities!

Smuggling yarns are widespread on Wight. Rookley, situated at the epicentre of the island, claims the crown as smuggling capital. Chale on the south coast was the home of a notorious smuggling family called the Wheelers, who lived in Box Cottage, and Chale churchyard had a reputation for other-wordly happenings that were probably deliberate scare tactics to keep nosey locals away from stored tubs. Bembridge was famous for its small boats that crossed to Cherbourg and Harfleur, and the Bembridge windmill, which still stands above the village, served as a useful marker for incoming vessels.

This nineteenth-century engraving of Arched Rock on the Isle of Wight depicts an unopposed smuggling run with a fair degree of authenticity. The small tubs—light enough to be carried over the shoulder—are the incriminating evidence. Legal imports were packed in very much larger containers.

At Ventnor the museum of smuggling history merits a visit. There are tableaux and replicas, together with original exhibits. The museum is in the grounds of the botanical gardens on the outskirts of the town. Bembridge windmill is $^1/_2$ m S of Bembridge at 196-SZ639874.

THE CHINES

Coastal erosion has truncated many of the chines at the seaward end, and modern development has dissipated the essential character of others. However, the wooded slopes of Shanklin Chine at 196-SZ585812 retain much of their original atmosphere, despite the tarmac path and entrance fee.

The high cliffs close to Blackgang Chine gave the land party a fine view of approaching smuggling craft. Treacherous off-shore rock ridges meant that the masters of revenue vessels were reluctant to pursue local men when they went in to make a landfall at the foot of the chine.

When the chance of detection was slight, most free-traders preferred to land goods on the south-west coast of the island. Here there are a few more accessible landing points than the south-east, and they were all pushed into use: notable landing points were Blackgang Chine, Walpan, Ladder, Branes, Grange, Chilton, Brook, Shippard's and Compton Chines, Freshwater Bay and Scratchell's Bay. The chines in particular were valuable points of entry, because most featured a safe beach on the coast, and a secure path inland, hidden from view by dense brushwood and small trees.

BROOK ■1

Brook Chine 196-SZ385835, S of the A3055 5m E of Freshwater is less spoiled than most.

A favoured way to get contraband up the cliffs was to haul the tubs up on ropes, and a local story[3] tells how a group of smugglers were caught red-handed doing exactly this. The local riding officer spent much of his time patrolling the coast on a white horse, and the yarn tells of a Brook man who enjoyed similar excursions on his *black* mount. Anxious to avoid being confused with the hated customs officer (thus risking a bump on the head from his smuggling pals), the Brook man had developed an elaborate code. On reaching a hill, he would gallop up and walk down. So one time when the smugglers were hauling tubs up the cliff face they saw no danger at the approach of a man on a black horse who galloped uphill and walked down. Only when the riding officer was close enough to be recognized did the lookout realize his mistake—and by then it was too late. The riding officer was not on his usual mount, and only coincidence made him gallop up the hill and walk down. Most of the gang were at the top of the cliff, and got clean away; but the man loading tubs at the bottom spent a year in prison for this unfortunate error.

COWES AND THE NORTH COAST ■2

Cowes is at 196-SZ5096 at the northernmost tip of the island.

The south of the island had the advantage of being ill-policed, but the landing-places there were really suitable only for small craft. Bigger ships had to travel round to the north side to unload. Here smuggling sometimes took a different form. East Indiamen would anchor in the Yarmouth Roads and openly do business with small boats that rowed out. By the 1780s, the smugglers had become quite brazen, and were ready to unload cargoes within sight of the preventive forces; they even

When the Wight smugglers were most active the only remaining inhabitant of Shanklin Chine was the keeper of the Chine Inn. Contraband was carried inland and dispersed, or, if there was danger, buried in the sand between the ledges.

formed convoys of small vessels guarded by well-armed cutters and luggers (200–300 tons). Frequently 200 to 300 men met the boats to unload the goods.

Such open flouting of the law could not be tolerated forever, and the preventive effort was stepped up. Cowes was the centre for the operation, and in September 1777 William Arnold took up the post of collector of customs there. He was extremely diligent and devoted to the cause of stamping out smuggling, but his pleas for more help in the war against the smugglers fell on deaf ears in London. Undaunted by this, Arnold resolved to rent, fit out and crew a vessel at his own expense. He chose the *Swan*, but this was soon wrecked in a ferocious storm. It was replaced by more ships—this time supplied by the Admiralty—which had an impressive effect on smuggling in the area. A succession of battles at sea proved successful for the preventives, and before long the large and well-armed smuggling craft had moved to less well-protected areas, or to ports where the customs officials were easier to bribe.

Smaller craft were more difficult to deal with, particularly on the rocky south coast, and when Arnold reinforced the land-guard in these areas subterfuge became the rule. The smugglers hid their goods under legitimate cargoes, and landed them in the north-coast ports.

In common with other parts of the south coast of England, tubs were also sunk off-shore, though this was practical only in the Solent, since surf on the south of the island would soon set tubs adrift. Recovering sunken barrels was unlikely to arouse suspicion: crabbing and lobster fishing were major industries on the Isle of Wight, and 'creeping' for tubs could easily be passed off as the baiting of pots, or checking the catch.[4]

NITON ■3

196-SZ5076, at the southernmost point of the island.

Of Niton:

> The whole population here are smugglers. Everyone has an ostensible occupation, but nobody gets his money by it, or cares to work in it. Here are fishermen who never fish, but always have pockets full of money, and farmers whose farming consists in ploughing the deep by night, and whose daily time is spent standing like herons on lookout posts.

Dobell, a nineteenth-century writer, also commented that the men of the village had a variety of pseudonyms, a characteristic shared by smugglers elsewhere in the country.

MOTTISTONE ■4

196-SZ4083, 4m SE of Freshwater.

At Mottistone a large tomb, excavated for the bodies of seven sailors washed ashore from a wreck, was used for storing contraband (a theme that recurs in every part of Britain). The tower of the church was probably also used as a landmark and lookout point, and the local gang used caves in the cliffs above the beach for storage; cottages looking out to sea reputedly have small windows to carry lanterns for signalling. The manor at Mottistone was pressed into service, too: tubs were stored in the large loft, 'and although the revenue men often looked in at the clap door, they did not dare venture up the rotten ladder'.[5]

BINSTEAD ■5

The Church of the Holy Cross, Binstead, is at 196-SZ575928 down Pitts Lane, which is a turning on the right of the A3054 just before the Post Office on the way out of Ryde. The grave is on the right, about 10 yards from the path leading to the church door.

Today most of the smuggling landmarks on the island are topographical

A revenue man who took too close an interest in the smuggling activities at Brook Chine was reputedly murdered near the old Post Office and his body left to rot under a heap of mangolds.

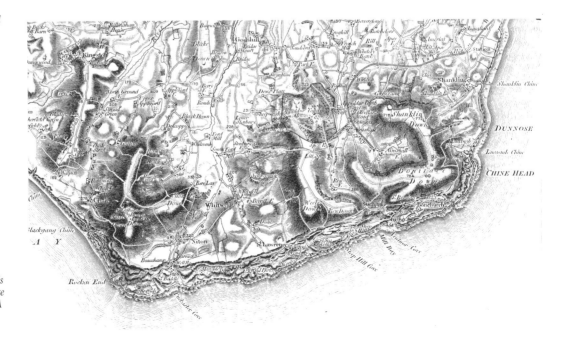

In 1801, less than a decade before this map was drawn, the smuggling village of Niton numbered just 52 families. A visitor commented that they were 'offensively rude to strangers'.

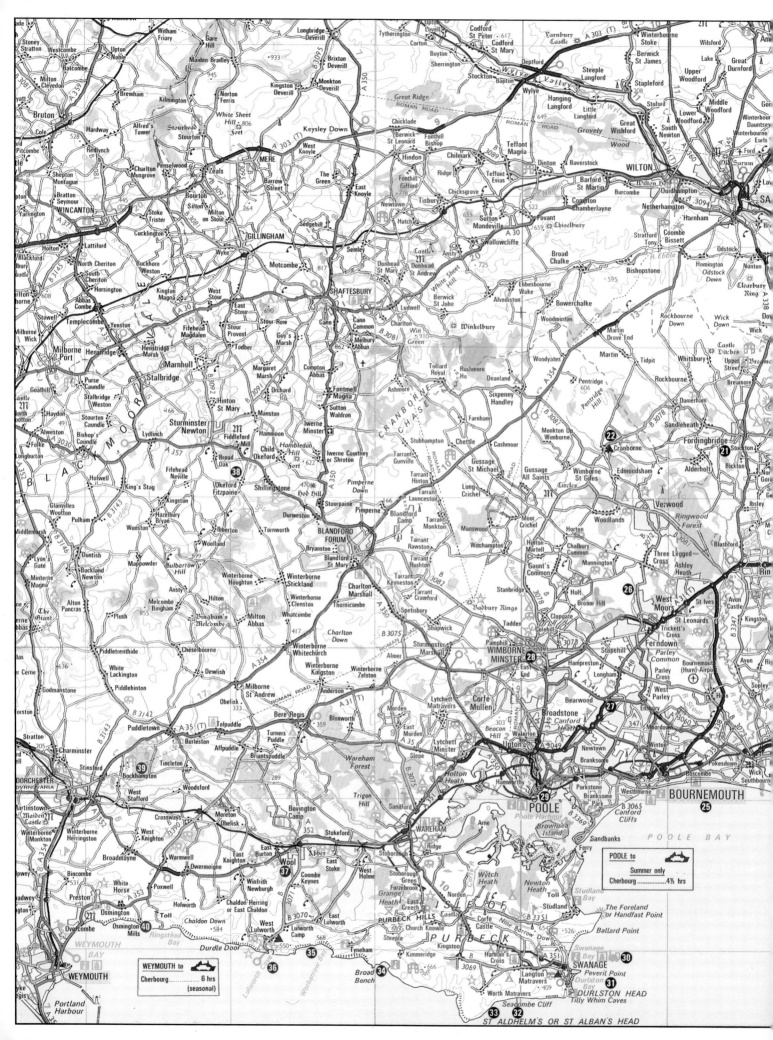

features of buildings, but at Binstead is the grave of suspected smuggler, Thomas Sivell. He was a Solent ferryman who was shot by the preventive forces in 1785. According to some stories he was innocent of smuggling, but others relate that he was shot while being chased in his smuggling vessel, and that he tossed nearly 70 barrels of spirits overboard to evade capture, along with a considerable quantity of tea! His epitaph tells the smuggler's side of the story:

> All you that pass pray look and see
> How soon my life was took from me
> By those officers as you hear
> They spilt my blood that was so dear
> But God is good, is just and true
> And will reward to each their due.

EAST OF SOUTHAMPTON WATER

Contraband crossing the Solent from the Isle of Wight was landed in Hampshire both east and west of Southampton Water. On the east side, the miles of coast between Langstone and Chichester harbours provided ample opportunity for an inconspicuous landing. Portsmouth harbour was a different matter. The long-standing naval presence there would seem at first glance to discourage smuggling, but this is really a considerable simplification. The truth was that smuggling simply took on different forms here. Naturally, the military presence prevented smugglers from organizing the classic run, with the cargo collected by hundreds of men and horses on shore. Instead, contraband at Portsmouth probably came in through semi-legitimate means: as the

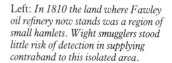

Left: *In 1810 the land where Fawley oil refinery now stands was a region of small hamlets. Wight smugglers stood little risk of detection in supplying contraband to this isolated area.*

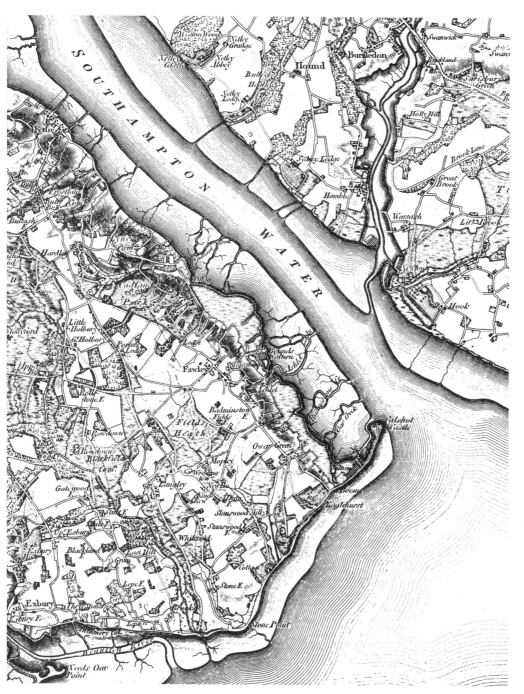

Opposite: *A garrison was stationed at Netley until 1627, but the Tudor castle was subsequently used by smugglers. It provided a strategic view up the Water towards Southampton, and down towards the Solent.*

personal property of the crews on the naval vessels themselves, and on East Indiamen. The East Indiamen were generally escorted to Spithead by naval vessels, and lay at anchor there with a handful of customs officers on board to prevent the cargo from falling into the wrong hands. However, the system was not perfect, and there were plenty of opportunities for abuse.

Corruption in the customs and excise at Portsmouth was probably as widespread as elsewhere, and even honest officials had numerous other duties besides the suppression of smuggling. In this context, it's hardly surprising to find stories of smuggling passed down by word of mouth all over east Hampshire. Many yarns concern not the runs themselves, but transport and storage inland. The passage of time has erased most evidence to support these stories, and though the place names remain, the casual visitor is unlikely to find the depots, tunnels and hidey-holes that the tub- and tea-carriers used for storage.

One route ran along the Meon River, and at Soberton ■6 in the church of St Peter and St Paul there was once a vault used to conceal contraband, with its entrance close to the chancel door. Another route used to bring contraband north from the coast passed through Cheriton, where a farm called East Down was reputedly used by smugglers to keep an eye on the activities of the customs authorities.

Cheriton ■7 is at 185-SU5828 on the B3046 E of Winchester. Leave Bramdean on the Cheriton Road. Take the first fork on the right. The farm is on the left.

At Medstead ■8 185-SU6537 were depots for storing silk, lace and brandy—in a cave, according to rumour, and in the church tower. The church can still be seen, but today the cave remains only a memory.

And at Preston Candover 185-SU6041 two wells were used for the concealment of contraband. Near the mouth of one was a cave big enough to accommodate a coach and horses. Again, the wells are no longer shown on maps, and there is no trace of the storage depots on the spot.

In Southampton itself, the history of smuggling goes back a long way, but is primarily concerned with wool export. There are records of the bribery and corruption of local officials, and even one story of how a Genoese merchant whose bribe had been spurned kidnapped the incorruptible official, and dumped him on the Isle of Wight.

NETLEY AND HAMBLE ■9

Netley Abbey is 3m SE of Southampton centre at 196-SU453089.
Hamble is 2m further SE at 196-SU4806.

Just to the south of Southampton on the east side of Southampton Water, Netley Abbey and Castle were rumoured to have been used by smugglers. One local story tells how a Netley smuggler who was planning a run lured the local customs officers away from the landing-point by sending a second vessel up Southampton Water to unload its cargo. The unfortunate customs officers pounced near Netley, only to discover that the 'barrels' were straw replicas.

Hamble, just a little way to the east, was the home of a smuggling gang led by a man named Sturgess, who bought in 1783 a huge 20-gun cutter called *The Favourite*. His choice of base was understandable —contraband could be shipped cheaply and safely up the branching Hamble River. Recognizing the value of the route, the preventive forces stationed dragoons here as early as 1723.

SOUTHAMPTON TO BEAULIEU

Immediately to the west of Southampton Water the mainland forms a kind of peninsula, hemmed in on the west side by the Beaulieu River. This remote spit of land was ideal smuggling country: at its closest point, the Isle of Wight is less than 2 miles away, making the crossing quick and simple. And over such short distances, a signal flashed from a lantern instantly warned of danger, so that a landing could be diverted to a safer spot.

This area of land was all but impossible to police; even within living memory the roads were little more than muddy tracks, and visits to the coastal hamlets were easier on water than by land.

FAWLEY ■10

Fawley is next to an oil refinery off the A326. Ashlett Creek is part of the yacht-club marina (196-SU4603). Badminston Common is at 196-SU4501.

Strategically situated on the west of Southampton Water, Fawley was once a den of smugglers; Ashlett Creek there was a favourite landing-point. Smugglers recruited labour from the villages nearby, and this earned Sprat's Down the nickname 'Lazy Town', on account of the

habits of the smuggling population, who spent all day asleep. Caves in Sprat's Down Wood were used by smugglers for storage, and a cottage in the wood was also used to conceal contraband under the stone floor.[6] There were reputedly other storage depots on Badminston Common.

EAGLEHURST ■11

Park at Calshot 196-SU480014 and walk SW along the shore. The tower is visible through the gate, as is a heavy wooden door guarding a 60-foot tunnel reaching out from the foot of the tower towards the shore.

Smugglers bringing goods across from the Isle of Wight found their landing points on the mainland with the aid of sea markers, and at Eaglehurst, near Calshot, a folly called Lutterell's Tower was certainly used in this way. Though the reasons for building the tower are uncertain, it may have been employed as a lookout point by the land party waiting on shore. The tower was probably built in the second quarter of the eighteenth century, at the behest of Temple Simon Lutterell, who died in 1803 in a French prison. Local tradition asserts that this shadowy figure was himself a smuggler, bringing in the finest brandy from France, and supplying even the Royal Family.

BEAULIEU AND THE RIVER ■12

Beaulieu is at 196-SU3802, 8m due S of Southampton; Buckler's Hard is 2m SE of Beaulieu.

The western boundary of this smugglers' haven is marked by the Beaulieu River, which was itself a useful highway for shipping contraband goods far inland without the expense of tub-carriers or carts. Contraband was landed in many places along the thickly wooded banks, and according to one account:

> All the farms along the river were more or less concerned in the traffic . . . At Ginn's Farm . . . a gentleman rode up and said to the servant girl 'Do you ever see anything of the smugglers about here? If you can give me any information, I will give you a sovereign'. The girl was not likely to betray her friends, and replied 'Smugglers Sir! Why we be always all in bed by nine o'clock'. A few minutes later the handmaiden found her master entertaining the stranger, who was deeply interested in the contraband trade, and who had only been trying to test the girl's fidelity. He at once gave her the sovereign, not for giving information, but for withholding it.[7]

Buckler's Hard on the river was a major landfall for the contraband trade: the cottage that is now a chapel was a centre of operations. In Beaulieu itself Palace House made a convenient warehouse, since it was frequently unoccupied. To discourage unnecessary interest, and ensure that the premises remained vacant, smugglers laid on a variety of stage ghost effects—clanking chains, hair-raising screams in the night, and mysterious apparitions.

The shore to the west of the Beaulieu River is lined with treacherous mud-flats, which acted as allies for wily free-traders: an unwary revenue man could easily be sucked to his death when pursuing a smuggler through the unfamiliar creeks and rivulets. The local smugglers avoided the same fate by strapping planks or barrel-staves to their feet.

At East Boldre, some 2 miles west of Buckler's Hard a persistent story relates how, when a tub of brandy fell from a horse and smashed on a rock, the whole party took off their shoes, and drank their fill using these as improvised cups![8]

Badminston Common was used by smugglers as a convenient temporary storage site for contraband pending distribution and sale inland.

This splendid folly at Eaglehurst looks out across the Solent towards Cowes and was used as a sea-marker by smugglers crossing to the mainland.

BEAULIEU RIVER TO LYMINGTON

Leaving Buckler's Hard going S towards Lymington, Sowley Pond ■13 is some 3m away at 196-SZ3796. Pitt's Deep ■14 is at the end of a turning off to the left of the same road some ¹/₂m further on, at 196-SZ372958. Pylewell House and Home Farm ■15 are 2m due E of Lymington at SZ 3595.

Safe landings on this coast are few and far between, but there was one at Pitt's Deep, a winding creek that cuts through the mud-flats. Here a jetty, Pitts Deep Hard, provided a berth for even quite large ships. The deepest part of the trench cut by the brook flowing into the sea at this point was used for sinking tubs when danger loomed, and won the nickname Brandy Hole. Pylewell Home Farm nearby was also used as a storage place by smugglers, and Tanner's Lane in the same area was a popular route inland, '. . . owing to being near the forest'.[9]

Sowley Pond once overlooked an inn, the Forge Hammer, which boasted numerous hiding-places. However, when contraband overflowed into the regular cellars, ingenuity was needed to prevent discovery. A raid by the coastguard caused vigorous activity in the bowels of the pub, and the landlady was despatched to divert the coastguards while the tubs were removed from their hiding-place in the chimney to the safety of a nearby copse of trees:

The landlady advanced upon them. Singling out one of the officers who owed her a score for . . . liquid refreshment, she abused him roundly for not paying his debts.

When the contraband was safe, the landlady admitted the coastguards, who found nothing and were once more abused for interfering with the business of honest citizens.[10]

LYMINGTON ■16

196-SZ3295 15m E of Bournemouth. The Angel Inn is on St Thomas' Street (the principal road up the hill in the town), and the Nag's Head at number 34, almost opposite The Angel, is now shops.

The inhabitants of this town were so busy smuggling when Daniel Defoe visited that he noted:

I do not find they have any foreign commerce, except it be what we call smuggling, and roguing, which I may say, is the reigning commerce of all this part of the English coast.[11]

If the number of smuggling yarns circulating about a town is any reflection of the importance of the place in the free-trade, then Lymington would have been the centre for the whole of Hampshire. In fact, there's probably no such correlation, and some of the yarns told of Lymington recur in very similar forms all over the country. One local tale bears a remarkable resemblance to stories related in the vicinity of Helston in Cornwall, and at Lowestoft.

A ship moored at Lymington, and weeping passengers and downcast crew came ashore with the sad news that the captain had expired during the voyage. A doctor was called, and he duly certified the captain as deceased, and called the undertakers. Soon a sombre procession (including the local customs men) headed up the main street. To drown their sorrows, the mourners called at the Angel Inn, where the King's men were especially well treated. The cortège continued, in a slightly less dignified manner, but as soon as there was a clear road, the hearse sped off at a pace that was far from funereal, and the coffin and its contents of contraband were spirited away to a safer spot, no doubt to the benefit of undertakers, doctor and all of the mourners.

There is good reason to believe that this ruse would have been successful even if the customs men had not had their brains fuddled by drink. The vicar was in league with the smugglers, and allowed the tower of St Thomas' church to be used for storage.[12].

The Angel Inn features strongly not only in this tale, but in other local legends. According to one, a tunnel from the shore led up the hill

Smugglers used the reedy Lymington River to move goods away from the coast to markets inland.

to the Angel, and from there to the Nag's Head. This legend possibly has its origins in the existence of storm drains: the course of the tunnel would have been a logical one for a rainwater or flood drain, so perhaps the smugglers simply made enterprising use of existing facilities.

Close to Lymington, a cave called Ambrose Hole was used as a storage depot by a gang of thugs who dabbled in smuggling, but who were best known for brutality and murder. When troops were called in to put down the gang:

> Booty to an enormous extent was found. The captain turned King's evidence, and confessed that he had murdered upwards of 30 people, whose bodies were found in a well down which they had been thrown.[13]

BOLDRE AND ST AUSTINS ■17

Boldre Church is 2m N of Lymington at 196-SZ323993. St Austins is to the W of the A337 some 2m N of Lymington, at 196-SZ312980.

The route taken by contraband moving inland from Lymington was probably via the Lymington River. This was formerly navigable for a much greater length of its course, and along its banks there is a tradition of smuggled goods being stored in all manner of places. At Boldre, the church was used for storage, as was one of the table tombs in the churchyard.

At St Austins there are stories of a tunnel leading down from the ruined monastery chapel to the waterside. Unlike many tales of smuggling tunnels, there is some evidence for the St Austins story: in dry summer weather, the meadow grass changes colour in a strip that marks the route of the tunnel. (Sceptics suggest that the line shows where the monks spread gravel to form a path.)

TOM JOHNSTONE

Lymington's most famous smuggler must be Tom Johnstone. He was born here in 1772 and was brought up as a fisherman by his smuggling father. By twelve he had already developed formidable skills of seamanship, and knew the south coast of England well enough to act as a pilot virtually anywhere. By fifteen he was a smuggler himself.

Descriptions of him are probably tinged with romanticism: he was said to be over 6 feet tall, with handsome, clear-cut features, dark curly hair and vivid blue eyes. 'Women, children, dogs and horses adored him'.[14] Whatever the facts of his personal appearance, he undoubtedly had a great deal of charisma, backed with some low cunning. His life story is a long saga of dramatic escapes and successes, interspersed with spells in prison, injuries and personal disasters. He turned his coat several times, working both for the French and English governments when they were at each other's throats, playing alternately the role of smuggler and revenue man. He had an easy manner that gained him the loyalty of the roughest seamen, and also enabled him to mix on equal terms with the wealthy and titled in England, France and Holland.

When he was 21 Johnstone joined the crew of a Gosport privateer to fight the French, and this led to one of his early spells in prison: he was taken prisoner by the French, and briefly languished in a French gaol. He soon negotiated his release, agreeing to carry messages on board a smuggling cutter to a spy in England. However, his jubilation at being released was short-lived, for the cutter was intercepted by a naval vessel during the crossing. Though Johnstone managed to avoid arrest by handing over the package of letters, he was grabbed by the press-gang as soon as the ship docked at Southampton.

In true *Boy's Own* style, our hero fought free of the press-gang and escaped—but was effectively an outlaw. Having nothing to lose, he

Built in 1544 from the stones of Beaulieu Abbey, Hurst Castle had a mixed history. For most of the eighteenth century the castle harboured smugglers, and only in 1803, when preparations began to make the country safe from Napoleonic invasion, did the Crown finally eliminate all smuggling activity.

returned to smuggling, initially with some success. He ran a succession of cargoes, including the export of a French double agent released from prison in England, but in 1798 was captured by a riding officer at Winchelsea along with another smuggler. Imprisoned in the New Gaol, the two of them conspired to bribe the turnkey and Tom escaped to Flushing where he lay low for a while.

Returning to England despite the price on his head, he volunteered a year later as a navy pilot in the campaign to drive the French out of Holland. His skill as a navigator to the expedition won him a cheque for £1,000—a staggering sum in those days—a free pardon, and a personal letter of gratitude from the commanding officer.

With these advantages, Tom was able to set up a fashionable household in London, and he began to lead a profligate lifestyle, running up debts of £11,000. In 1802 his creditors caught up with him, and Johnstone was thrown into the Fleet prison. No prison could hold him for long, though. This report soon appeared in a newspaper:

> Johnstone, the notorious smuggler, this morning effected his escape, notwithstanding he was confined in a strongroom with a double door. At the top of each door was a pannel[15] instead of glass. By forcing out these and creeping through them, Johnstone was able to reach the gallery, and from thence the high wall that surrounds the prison. There he found a rope ladder which his friends outside had provided for him. In the evening he arrived in a chaise and four on the coast near Brighton where a lugger was in waiting for him, in which he embarked for Calais, on his way to Flushing. He had a severe wound in the thigh, which he received in the following manner. He had got on top of the last wall that separated him from the street 70 feet from the ground. A lamp was set in the wall, some distance beneath the place where he was. He let himself down, so as to fall astride the bracket supporting the lamp. In so doing, a piece of iron caught his thigh above the knee, and ripped it up almost to the top. At this moment he heard the watchman crying the hour; and had so much fortitude as to remain where he was, bleeding abundantly, till the watchman had gone his round, without perceiving him. Immediately after, he let himself down and crawled to where the post chaise was waiting in expectation of his escape.[16]

Johnstone recovered from his wounds in France, and was persuaded to take up the Guinea run (see page 27), smuggling gold from England to pay Napoleon's armies. Significantly, Johnstone does not seem to have regarded this activity as unpatriotic, despite the fact that England and France were then at war. However, the Hampshire smuggler evidently had some scruples, because he soon afterwards turned down the Emperor Napoleon himself when asked to lead the French invasion fleet to the shores of England. Johnstone's genius as a navigator had evidently reached the ears of the Emperor, who clearly believed he was in a position to make him 'an offer he couldn't refuse'. The plan was for Johnstone to have a free pardon in an England under French rule (plus a substantial fee, of course).

Declining the offer led to another spell in a French gaol, and this time it was nine months before he escaped. He managed to hitch a ride to New Orleans on an American ship, but by 1806 had secured yet another pardon from the English, and was working for the Admiralty once more, with the American inventor Robert Fulton. The project was the development of limpet mines, and an attempt in 1806 to blow up the French fleet in Brest using these devices was a failure in spite of Johnstone's leadership. However, three years later a successful attack on Flushing harbour earned the smuggler a pension of £100 a year.

The final phase of Johnstone's career was to earn him the lifelong hatred of his fellow smugglers: he became the commander of the revenue cutter *HMS Fox*, pursuing his former comrades with all the vigilance of a poacher turned gamekeeper. He eventually retired with a navy pension at the age of 44, but his retirement was not entirely without incident. He dabbled with submarines (another Fulton invention) and almost drowned during a demonstration of the first practical model, the

Nautilus. He was also approached by the French to rescue Napoleon from St Helena, again using the submarine. Johnstone died—remarkably peacefully after such an active life—at the age of 67.

HURST CASTLE ■18

196-SZ3189, 3m SW of Lymington. The castle is reached on foot from Milford-on-Sea (2m), or by ferry from Keyhaven.

Standing far out in the Solent at the end of Hurst Beach, Hurst Castle was at one time a centre for the contraband trade, despite the fact that it was a stronghold of the Crown, complete with a garrison. It seems, though, that the smugglers had reached an accommodation with the officers stationed there, because William Arnold, collector of customs at Cowes, considered it necessary in 1783 to request:

> a King's cutter also in Hurst Road . . . to keep off the large cutters from landing their goods for three or four days at a time . . . to ruin the Trade, because the expense of keeping a large number of men and horses collected together waiting the arrival of goods must materially diminish the profits arising from their sale.[17]

Specifically, Arnold suspected a Christchurch smuggler by the name of John Streeter. According to information supplied to Arnold, Streeter was using the castle as a rendezvous—a clearing-house visited by smaller vessels from Christchurch itself. This is highly probable, for Streeter reappears in various guises at Mudeford and Christchurch (see page 79).

MILFORD-ON-SEA TO CHRISTCHURCH ■19

Chewton Bunny is at 195-SZ218932.

'Bunnies' or ravines between these two towns were used to bring contraband up from the sea: Milford Bunny, Becton Bunny and Chewton Bunny were all used. Milford Bunny runs past Milford Church, which was used for storage and for observation by the smugglers, but Chewton Bunny had several special attractions. It featured a heavily wooded path leading from the coast; and at its foot was an area of quicksand—all but the most knowledgeable locals therefore kept away from the area at night. Naish Farm is said to be linked to Chewton Bunny by a tunnel.

Hurst Castle, on the peninsula facing Worsley's Tower, provided the smugglers who used it as a base with a 360° view over the Solent and inland.

THE NEW FOREST

Contraband run all along this stretch of coast quickly found its way up to the New Forest.[18] The wilds of the forest provided a haven for smugglers and in 1748 'We hear from the New Forest in Hampshire that Smugglers have got to such a height in that part of the country that scarce a week passes but great quantities of goods are run between Lymington and Christchurch'.[19]

During the same period '. . . every labourer was either a poacher or a smuggler, very often a combination of the two'.[20]

The forest glades were also used for boat-building, and some spots far from the sea are still known locally as 'the Boatyard'—presumably to the puzzlement of visitors.

BURLEY ■20

Burley lies 4m SE of Ringwood at 195-SU2103. The Warne family mentioned below is commemorated in Warnes Lane at Burley, and in the Warnes Bar at the local Queen's Head Inn—secret cellars were discovered at the pub during building work. The most remarkable sight, though, is the Smugglers' Road, which can be reached from the car-park of the same name at 195-SU188040. Here, sunken roads criss-cross the heath-land— reputedly constructed so that smugglers could move contraband unobserved. Crow-Hill Top and Knaves Ash are close by at 195-SU182038. Vereley Hill, where Lovey Warne wore her red cloak as a warning signal, is at 195-SU1904. Ridley Wood, at 195-SU2006 was a smuggler's market-place.

Places all over the New Forest are traditionally strongly connected with the free-trade, but none more so than the Burley area. This was the home of the Warne family, John, Peter, and the strangely-named Lovey, their sister. They lived at Crow-Hill Top, in a house called Knaves Ash, just outside Burley. The most picturesque yarns are associated with Lovey Warne. Legend has it that when the revenue men were abroad in the forest, she would parade across Vereley Hill wearing

Above: *A deep ditch conceals from view the smugglers' roads such as this one that criss-cross the New Forest. A caravan of heavily-laden ponies could safely canter along, unseen by revenue men just a hundred yards away.*

Left: *Formerly more densely wooded than today, the New Forest concealed and protected both the smugglers and their contraband. The Forest also provided transport: New Forest ponies could carry 6 tubs of brandy apiece, three times the burden that an unaided tub-man could manage.*

a red cloak, as a warning to smugglers on the coast to avoid the area. At night smugglers living at a cottage on the hill would hoist a lantern up a nearby oak-tree to give the warning signal.

Lovey Warne's role in smuggling didn't stop at signalling. According to legend, she would visit ships in Christchurch harbour, undress in the privacy of the captain's cabin, and wind herself with valuable silks before getting back into her clothes—somewhat fatter. Evidently the sudden gain in weight passed unnoticed, since Lovey would walk straight past the revenue men without arousing suspicion, and return home to be unwound and relieved of her burden. This clever ruse apparently had to stop when one of the revenue men invited Lovey for a glass at the Eight Bells in Christchurch. Emboldened by drink, he became amorous and started to explore Lovey's fine thighs with his hand. A swift jab in the eye deterred his amorous advances, but Lovey was retired to the smuggling equivalent of a desk job on Vereley Hill.

FORDINGBRIDGE ■21

195-SU1414, 6m N of Ringwood.

This town, which was once called Forde, was a notorious smuggling centre, and a local saying runs, 'keystone under the hearth, keystone under the horse's belly', since these were two favourite places for hiding contraband—under the stable floor, and under the hearth, with a fire burning innocently on top. When opposition at Fordingbridge got really intense, smugglers would sink tubs in the River Avon.[21] A favoured route for contraband from the town ran via Redbrook,

Stuckton and Frogham, and it is significant that when the Hawkhurst Gang rescued a cargo of contraband from Poole custom-house, their convoy came through Fordingbridge, where the population turned out to watch and cheer (see page 61).

CRANBORNE AND CRANBORNE CHASE ■22

195-SU0513, 8m NW of Ringwood. The exciseman's house is on the corner of the street opposite the present Post Office.

Like the New Forest, and bordering on it, Cranborne Chase had also become a notorious haunt of smugglers, cutpurses and other brigands, and the situation there became such a threat to law and order that it was cut down in 1830.[22] Of Cranborne itself, a tale is told of how one of the local men, known as Dan, was cutting turf when his brother-in-law rode up to tell him that the exciseman had searched Dan's house and found 11 tubs hidden in the cellar. Dan then returned to Cranborne, and took up his habitual (and inconspicuous) seat in the bar of the Flower De Luce. Eventually the exciseman appeared, bragging that he had seized the tubs, and stored them at his house. At this, Dan slipped unnoticed from the bar, and tore off to rally support. A gang of smugglers returned at midnight, and Dan went into the town and chalked a mark on the exciseman's door (presumably so that he would not have to attend in person).

A map of the New Forest dated 1890.

Being made sure of their prize the ruffians soon followed, and one of them beat in the door with the sledge hammer, whilst another stood in the street with a loaded horse pistol, threatening to blow out the Exciseman's brains, or of any other person who offered to resist them. Having secured the 'goods' they soon loaded their carts and horses, and with one outrider in front, armed, and another in the rear they galloped away with them; nor had the incident any unpleasant sequel so far as I ever heard, and it only afforded a subject of gossip in the Public-houses of Cranborne.[23]

A search of the parish registers suggests that the Dan mentioned in this quote was probably Daniel Sims, who died in 1826 from injuries caused by a fall from his horse.

THE WILTSHIRE MOONRAKERS ■23

173-SU0364, Bishops Cannings is 3m NE of Devizes. See map on page 77.

For obvious reasons, smuggling stories are most abundant on the coast, but in a few instances the yarns penetrate very much further inland. The story of the Wiltshire moonrakers is a case in point. According to legend, smugglers who lived in the village feigned stupidity to conceal their activities, and put it about that they spread manure around the church tower to make it grow taller. They also told strangers that every inhabitant of the village had once walked to Devizes to watch an eclipse of the moon. But the most celebrated story tells how several villagers were caught one night in the act of raking the village pond to haul out tubs that had been sunk in the brackish water. The excisemen who demanded to know what was going on were told by the smugglers, who pointed at the moon's reflection in the water, that they were raking the pond to recover the 'big yellow cheese' that was floating in it.

CHRISTCHURCH AND MUDEFORD ■24

The battle of Mudeford took place on what is now a car-park at Mudeford Quay (195-SZ1892). Nearby is Haven Point and Haven House, where the body of George Coombes, who was convicted of murder after the battle, hung in chains on a gibbet. The Haven House is alongside the Run at the harbour entrance. Mother Siller's Channel lies between Grimsbury Marsh and Pound Hill, and is crossed by a bridge at 195-SZ168918. Also see Smugglers' Ditch at 195-SZ165919 on the west side of the harbour. The Eight Bells is now a gift shop, but you can still drink in the Ship in Distress at Stanpit.

When the vicar of Christchurch told his Parish Clerk in 1776 what a grievous sin it was to smuggle, the clerk replied, 'then Lord have mercy on the town of Christchurch, for who is there here who has not had a tub?'[24]

This assessment seems to be born out by the wealth of evidence linking Christchurch to the free-trade. Numerous writings refer to the smugglers; there is a flourishing anecdotal tradition on the subject locally, and the official records tell a similar story. In the town itself there are still many buildings that once harboured smugglers or contraband—and usually both.

Christchurch had a number of natural advantages for smugglers. The only land approaches to the town were across two bridges, and one of these was frequently out of use. The other could easily be blocked —perhaps by a herd of sheep—when there was a sign of danger, giving the smugglers time for a leisurely escape.

Another plus was the conjunction of the rivers Stour and Avon, which flow into Christchurch harbour. These were major arteries for contraband, at a time when transport by water was very much faster and cheaper than overland movement of goods.

Finally, there was the harbour itself. At the seaward end the sole entrance to the harbour is a narrow channel, the Run, which was negotiable only with extreme care. It was doubly difficult to sail into the harbour because of sandbanks that could shift overnight. To the smugglers, most of whom were superb seamen (and who could in any case afford to lose a vessel or two), the harbour entrance was an open gate. But to the less skilled sailors on the revenue cutters, the Run acted as a barrier that they feared to pass.

On land, the Run was carefully guarded as a matter of priority, but plenty of contraband sneaked through the gap into the harbour using a variety of ruses. Brute force was one of these, but subterfuge was possibly more important. At high tide the currents flow through the Run at alarming speed, and a raft of sunken tubs could be swept into the harbour right under the noses of the unsuspecting preventive men. The weighted tubs were released just off-shore, and often guided into the run by a strong swimmer. Abe Coates (or Coakes) was possibly the last of the Mudeford smugglers to make an honest living as a human tug-boat: he would ferry the tubs into Mother Sillers' Channel, or even to Bergman's Mill on Christchurch quay, a distance of 6 miles.[25]

Mother Siller's Channel is today barely a creek cutting through the Stanpit marshes, though two centuries of silting have probably greatly reduced its width. The channel led to a pub called The Ship in Distress, and it was the landlady of the pub, Hannah Seller, who gave her name to the creek. Hannah had been married to the landlord of the Haven House at Mudeford, and on his death she took over the inn, later moving to The Ship. It appears that Mrs Seller was deeply involved in the free-trade: she allowed both pubs to be used for storage, and would turn out her customers to assist smuggling vessels in trouble.

When Hannah Seller was landlady of the Haven House, her pub played a central role in a drama that rocked Christchurch in 1784, and that became known as the Battle of Mudeford. The story starts—as so many smuggling tales do—with a run. Two smuggling luggers had shipped across from the Channel Islands a huge cargo of tea and brandy, and on 15 July a crowd of some 300 people were busy unloading the luggers at Mudeford beach, just east of the Run. The goods were being loaded into about 50 carts, drawn by 300 horses, but things did not go according to plan. A navy sloop, *HMS Orestes*, rounded Hengistbury Head with two escorting revenue cruisers.

When the 'philistines' appeared on the scene, there was pandemonium. John Streeter, a Christchurch man who had crewed on one of the two luggers, rode to the Haven House and herded the customers out of the pub and down to the beach. The luggers had by this time been beached on the shingle, and the patrons of the Haven House helped to strip the luggers of all their lines and rigging. Meanwhile, the cart-loads of contraband were moving away from the shore.

At sea, activity was just as frenetic. Seeing what was happening ashore, the captain of the *Orestes* resolved he would seize the cargo if possible, or failing that destroy the luggers. The sloop of war and the escorts lowered six rowing-boats filled with intrepid sailors armed to the teeth, and the boats closed in rapidly on the beach. As they neared the shore, Mr William Allen, the master of the *Orestes* shouted to the smugglers remaining on the decks of the ships to surrender. The reply was a deafening fusillade, and Allen fell back in the boat, mortally wounded. Still some 200 yards from the shore, the naval and revenue men returned fire. A running battle ensued, but it was hardly a fair fight: the smugglers were firing from trenches that they had dug along the beach, whereas the preventive forces had to take aim from rocking open boats with no cover.

When the boats landed, the smugglers retreated to the Haven House, and continued firing from there. The fighting continued for some three hours (some accounts say for fifteen hours) during which the guns of the *Orestes* were trained on the Haven House. Somewhat inaccurately, it would seem: stray cannon-balls actually struck the Christchurch Priory two miles away.[26] Eventually the revenue and navy men captured the two luggers and a number of small boats that the smugglers had scuttled in shallow water.

The price of the seizure was high. While the preventive forces were pinned down on the beach they suffered many casualties in addition to the death of one of their number. By contrast, the smugglers had secured their cargo, estimated (probably generously) at 120,000 gallons of spirits and 25 tons of tea, and had for the most part melted away into the surrounding countryside. It is not known whether any of them were injured.

Three men were eventually arrested on a murder charge, but two were released for a technicality. Eventually the might of the British legal system descended on the shoulders of one George Coombes, who was hanged at Execution Dock and his body hung in chains at Haven House Point until sympathizers cut it down and gave him a decent burial.[27]

John Streeter escaped punishment, and continued to operate as a smuggler, using as a cover a tobacco processing plant adjacent to the Ship in Distress. The authorities hounded him, and in 1787 William Arnold, the collector of customs at Cowes, commented that Streeter was:

> Supposed to be now in the Island of Guernsey or Alderney, but occasionally [returns] to the neighbourhood of Christchurch, where Streeter narrowly escaped from being retaken by disguising himself in woman's clothes.[28]

The Mudeford battle focused public attention on the Christchurch smugglers, but the incident was exceptional only because of the violent resistance the smugglers put up. There is little evidence to suggest that the cargo was anything out of the ordinary. One writer described how on another occasion he saw . . .

> a procession of twenty or thirty wagons, loaded with kegs of spirits, an armed man sitting at the front and tail of each, and surrounded by a troop of two or three hundred horsemen, every one carrying on his enormous saddle from two to four tubs of spirits, winding . . . along the skirts of Hengistbury Head, on their way towards the wild country to the north-west of Christchurch.[29]

Hengistbury Head was a favourite landing-point, and compared to Mudeford beach the Double Dykes there provided much more cover for the land party awaiting the arrival of a smuggling lugger.[30]

Those residents of Christchurch who were not directly involved in the free-trade provided help and support when called on; local people with special skills learned that if they helped out and kept their lips buttoned, they'd be rewarded in due course. A local surgeon, Dr Quartley, cited this example from his own experience: soon after setting up in the town he was woken by a loud rapping on the door in the middle of the night. On opening it, he was greeted by a pair of horsemen, who told him that his skills were needed urgently and that he should saddle a horse and follow them.

The surgeon wasn't really given any choice, so he did as he was told and followed the horsemen (who were soon joined by others) out of the town and to Bransgore. There he was shown into a small cottage, where a smuggler lay, severely wounded. The doctor quickly removed a musket ball from the man's shoulder and told companions of the injured man that he should not be moved, but should get some rest. At this news, one of the uninjured smugglers turned to their groaning colleague and asked, 'Well, Tom! Willst thee stay here and be hanged, or shall we tip thee into a cart?' The lad preferred to die of his wound than at the end of the rope, and was duly carted off into the forest (where he later recovered) as the learned doctor was escorted back to Christchurch. Dr Quartley's reward was a keg of brandy left anonymously on the doorstep, chalked with the legend, 'Left there for the doctor's fee.'[31]

Dr Quartley's doorstep can still be seen on Castle Street at the end of one of Christchurch's bridges, and many other Christchurch landmarks have connections with the free-trade: both the Old George Inn and the Eight Bells in Church Street were haunts of smugglers, and had tunnels leading to the priory. Associated with the Eight Bells is another version of the popular story about tubs of spirits hidden under the voluminous petticoats of the lady of the house. According to Christchurch legends, Kate Preston sat on a brandy tub bathing the baby while revenue officers fruitlessly searched the inn.[32]

Cottages in Whitehall and Silver Street were also used as refuges, and for the storage of contraband. Strangely, the Priory itself seems to have been overlooked by the smugglers—unlike their contemporaries elsewhere in England.

Mother Siller's (or Seller's) Channel in Christchurch harbour took its name from the landlady of the nearby Ship in Distress Inn. Though the channel is now silted up, it was once a watery back door through which the landlady imported all her foreign spirits—duty free, of course.

BOURNEMOUTH ■25

Hurn Court is at 195-SZ122958, 1m S of Bournemouth airport.

The coast west of Christchurch is now dominated by the town of Bournemouth, but this is a relatively recent development and just a century and a half ago the area around the mouth of the Bourne River was wild and desolate. The open country inland was known as Bourne Heath. Smuggling was rife: the first Earl of Malmesbury remarked that:

> All classes contributed to its support, the farmers lent their teams and labourers, and the gentry openly connived at the practise and dealt with the smugglers. The cargoes, chiefly of brandy, were usually concealed in furze bushes that extended from Ringwood to Poole, and in the New Forest for thirty miles.

The creation of the town of Bournemouth is generally credited to Lewis Tregonwell who, in 1810, built a holiday home (now part of the Royal Exeter Hotel) in the Bourne Valley. However, there is speculation that the highly respectable Tregonwell was himself a smuggler.[33] This theory is a little far-fetched, but was fuelled by the discovery in 1930 of a hidden chamber on the site of Portman Lodge, a thatched house that Tregonwell had enlarged for the use of his servant. *The Times* reported:

> The underground chamber . . . is about 10 ft long, 7 ft wide and 6 ft high and the only entrance to it is a trap door. It is a kind of arched chamber and was found about three feet below the level of the ground.

The concealed chamber would have made an admirable hiding-place for Tregonwell's flunkeys to conceal smuggled goods, and the holiday home provided the ideal excuse for their master to visit the coast and supervise operations.

There is also evidence that other worthies of the area were involved with the trade, or at least turned a blind eye. One amusing story tells how a commissioner of customs, Edward Hooper, was entertaining Lord Shaftesbury, the Chairman of the Customs and Excise, at Hooper's home, Heron Court (now Hurn Court). The house lay directly alongside one of the major routes used by smugglers to bring contraband spirits inland, but Hooper was clearly reluctant to lose the goodwill of his neighbours by interfering with the trade. So the host sat with his back to the window during dinner, and did not turn round when six or seven wagons noisily rolled past, loaded with tubs. Shaftesbury sprang from his seat to look at the spectacle, staggered by his host's

complacency. When the meal was interrupted again, by a party of dragoons in hot pursuit of the smugglers, the old squire could truthfully assert that he had seen nothing. His guest followed his example.[34]

Prior to the development of Bournemouth, one of the few buildings in the area was a house close to Coy Pond. The site of this lies between the War Memorial and the Square, and the name is a contraction of decoy: the pond had a wildfowl trap on it, and decoys led the birds inside. The house, called Bourne House, had an evil reputation, and was almost certainly owned or rented by smugglers, though some assert that it was simply a shelter associated with the trap.[35] From here they organized trips abroad, kept an eye on the landings—and plotted revenge on their enemies. In 1762 the Bournemouth smugglers suspected one Joseph Manuel of Iford, near Christchurch, of informing against them, and they decided to teach him a lesson. The lad was kidnapped and taken to Bourne House, then severely beaten and transported on a lugger to the Channel Islands. He managed to escape with his life, and returned to England. A £50 reward brought information about the crime, and four years later one of the smugglers responsible was captured in Swanage.[36]

The technique used by smugglers landing goods in the Bournemouth area was simple—and one that worked with equal success in other parts of Britain. A lugger would hover off-shore, and a signal from the coast would indicate whether or not it was safe to land. In the event that the preventive forces were patrolling, the lugger could move far more quickly by sea than the customs or excise men could ride. A riding officer's journal explains how this was done:

October 4th 1803
. . . set out with Mr Bacon to the West Coast on discoveries . . . In the Heath at Bourn we saw a fire lighted up, and immediately went to the spot, by the time we got there the fire was out, the smugglers flashing and striking up light with flint and steel all night in different parts of the heath and on the cliffs.

October 5th
Early in the morning Mr Williams, mate of the Batt cutter, called to inform me that smugglers were working to the east, so I set out with Mr Bacon and party and examined the cross roads through the forest leading from Highcliffe and Barton.

October 6th
Mr Williams . . . informed me that there had been a run of goods, about three or four hundred casks . . . Traced the smugglers into the country and at Hinton searched several suspected places. No success.

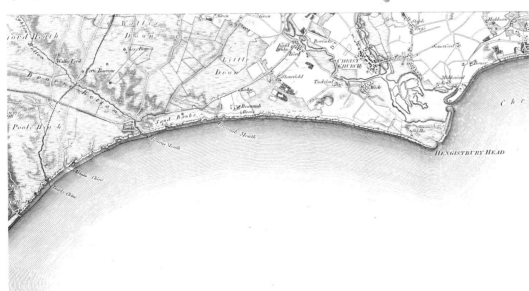

This early 19th-century map of the coast where Bournemouth now stands vividly illustrates how isolated the area was until recently. The chines marked on the map are now the only reminders of the Bourne Heath of the smuggling era.

E. Russell Oakley, in his book *The Smugglers of Christchurch*, explains that the lugger had probably been hovering off Hengistbury Head while the unhappy riding officer was patrolling near East Cliff. On seeing the flashes, fires and sparks, the ship would have landed the cargo between Highcliffe and Barton. To make an interception, the customs officers would have had to ride across the heath, following winding country lanes and crossing narrow bridges to Christchurch, via Iford, then to Somerford and on to the coast. The lighting of fires on the heath was probably a diversion to attract the officers to Boskum (Boscombe).

ISAAC GULLIVER

Many places associated with Gulliver's story can still be seen: one of his farms is on the B3072 just N of West Moors ■26 at 195-SU0703. At Kinson ■27 the tower of the church of St Andrew (195-SZ064964) was used for storing contraband, and grooves cut by smugglers' ropes could at one time be seen. Ledges on the tower have also been damaged by the hauling of kegs.[37] The table tomb at the foot of the tower was supposedly purpose-made for the storage of contraband. On the N side of the church is the grave of Robert Trotman, the head of a gang of smugglers shot by the customs men in 1765.

Woodlands, the Dower House, Ensbury vicarage and Kinson House are also said to have had smuggling connections. At Wimborne Minster ■28 (195-SU0100) Gulliver's House can still be seen at 45 Westborough, at the junction with School Lane, and his tombstone can be seen in the Minster Church.

Bournemouth's most famous smuggler was Isaac Gulliver, who achieved almost legendary status. He's the archetypical smuggler, a real lovable villain. And in one respect at least, Gulliver is different from other partners in the free-trade: he claimed never to have killed a man in the course of a long career.

Unlike some smuggling heroes, such as Sam Hookey, who was created in the 1950s to advertise a holiday camp, it is clear that Gulliver really did exist, and carried out some extraordinary exploits. While on the one hand there is ample documentary evidence surrounding his life, on the other it's certain that many of the tales about Gulliver have been embroidered to a greater or lesser extent. So in the account that follows, I have tried to differentiate between the facts and the legends.

Though Gulliver spent much of his life in Dorset and Hampshire, he wasn't born in either of these counties. His family were from Wiltshire, and Isaac was born in Semington, near Melksham, on 5 September 1745.

We know little about his youth, though one Isaac Gulliver does occur in the custom-house records for 1757: in March, four customs officers found a cargo of spirits and tea at the foot of Canford Cliffs Chine in Bournemouth (it was then called Bitman's Chine). The contraband was guarded by a handful of smugglers, and three of the revenue men seized the goods while their colleague went for a cart to transport the cargo. Before he returned, the smugglers were reinforced, rescued the cargo and beat off the customs officers. An informant later alleged that 'Isaac Gulliver, very often at . . . the New Inn within the Parish Downton' was one of those responsible.

Our Isaac Gulliver was then only twelve, so it seems likely that the man accused (he was never convicted) was the boy's father.

As he grew older, young Gulliver developed attributes that were to stand him in good stead in his smuggling enterprises; he was described as strong in physique and with great determination of character. In adulthood, he was credited with a genius for speculation, and certainly he grew to be a very wealthy man.

Of his early smuggling enterprises we know little, but it seems likely that he was already established by the time he married Elizabeth Beale in 1768. The union doesn't seem to have been entirely domestic, for his wife's father, William, was later suspected, along with Isaac, of 'running great quantities of goods on [the] shore between Poole and Christchurch.'

This stretch of coast, in fact, was Gulliver's favourite landing-place: he used Branksome Chine, Canford Cliffs, and Bourne Heath.

While he developed his smuggling skills, Gulliver had to have an alibi. His ostensible profession was as an inn-keeper, and the year he married he took over the tenancy of the Blacksmith's Arms, the pub run by his father-in-law at Thorney Down, in the parish of Handley, on the Salisbury to Blandford road. The location of the pub may itself be significant, for Tidpit, some 6 miles away, has a reputation as a clearing-house and distribution centre for contraband.

Gulliver changed the name of the pub to the (possibly ironic) King's Arms, and remained the tenant for ten years. Over this period, he seems to have prospered to an extent that could hardly be explained by the turnover of the small pub, and the farming of the little land around it. In 1777, he had enough money to lend £300 as a mortgage to a farmer near Shaftesbury.

And though there is no direct evidence to connect Gulliver with particular incidents in the area, smugglers were certainly active around Thorney Down. The excisemen seized ¾ ton of tea and 9 casks of spirits there in 1778, and stored the haul in the house of the supervisor of excise at Thorney Down. Their glee at the seizure must have been short-lived, for:

> About seven o'clock the same evening a large body of smugglers came with pistols etc, on horseback, forced their way into the house, and carried the whole off in great triumph, shouting along the street, and firing their pistols into the air. While they were loading, they gave two casks of liquor to the mob to amuse them.

In the churchyard at Kinson, Robert Trotman's epitaph serves as a reminder that tea was sometimes as important a contraband item as brandy, lace and tobacco. He was felled by a revenue man's pistol ball.

From Thorney Down, Gulliver moved to Longham, close to Kinson, and bought the White Hart Inn. Bournemouth now occupies the shoreline to the south of Kinson, but when Gulliver lived there in the late 1770s, the area was desolate. He landed goods all along the coast, but favoured Branksome Chine in particular, moving goods inland along a track that passed through Pug's Hole in Talbot Woods.

Exactly when Gulliver began to organize his 'gang' on methodical lines is not entirely clear, but according to one nineteenth-century description Gulliver:

> kept forty or fifty men constantly employed who wore a kind of livery, powdered hair, and smock frocks, from which they attained the name 'White Wigs'. These men kept together, and would not allow a few officers to take what they were carrying.[38]

Gulliver may have used Kinson church for the storage of contraband —certainly the tower was used by other smugglers for that purpose.

When Gulliver sold the White Hart to move into Kinson itself, he significantly also auctioned off 'Twenty Good Hack Horses'—hardly a necessity for a publican. With the proceeds, he set up a regular alcohol emporium—a wine merchant's, a malt-house and wine-cellars. From this base he traded quite legally for three years.

In 1782 the government offered a pardon to smugglers who would join the navy, or who could find substitutes to perform military service on their behalf. For a man of Gulliver's means, buying a substitute was no problem (the going rate was £15), and he thus wiped the slate clean as far as his smuggling record was concerned.

At this point Gulliver expanded his business interests, setting up another wine and spirits business in Teignmouth, and, it appears, simultaneously expanding his smuggling operations. He bought Eggardon Hill near Dorchester as a sea-marker for his ships, and planted trees on the summit to make the spot more prominent.

However, he maintained his links with Kinson, and continued to land goods on the coast south of Bourne Heath. Apparently he moved from the spirits business into wine, which was considered a far less reprehensible form of contraband. The Poole customs house reported in 1788 that:

> but a few years ago the said Gulliver was considered one of the greatest and notorious smugglers in the West of England and particularly in the spirits and tea trades but in the year 1782 . . . [he] dropped the branch of smuggling and after that year confined himself chiefly to the wine trade . . . having vaults . . . situated in remote places and we are well informed that he constantly offers old wines considerable (sic) under the fair dealer's price from which circumstances there is no doubt that he illicitly imported that article.

The report went on to add that Gulliver had retired from smuggling, but there is a possibility that the author was in collusion with the subject of his letter because the Poole official who dealt with this sort of correspondence was sacked soon after for passing information to smugglers.

The reference to vaults in the report has fuelled speculation that Gulliver built a network of tunnels. One was supposed to run from Kinson to Poole, though this stretches credulity to the limits.

In 'retirement', Gulliver seems to have constantly bought and sold property, frequently moving round the Kinson district. He had a farm at West Moors that can still be seen, he had land at Handley, and at one time lived in Long Crichel, close to Thorney Down. Towards the end of his life he moved to Wimborne.

According to an 1867 magazine report, Isaac Gulliver ran his last cargo of contraband at the turn of the century:

> His crowning achievement took place on the beach where the pier is now situated, when three large luggers, manned by determined crews and deeply laden with silks, tobacco and other valuables successively ran their respective cargoes; and it is in the

recollection of an old inhabitant of the place, that the cortege conveying the smuggled goods inland extended two miles in length, at the head of which rode the old chief mounted on a spirited charger . . . Thus ended Old Gulliver's smuggling career; he 'coiled up his ropes' and anchored on shore in the enjoyment of a large fortune.

Though the legends that have sprung up around Gulliver have doubtless been exaggerated, they are too persistent to ignore. One tells how, when his house at Kinson was searched, he dusted his face with chalk and lay in a coffin feigning death. Another story tells that the pardon he received was in gratitude for saving the King's (George III) life, by revealing an assassination plot; yet another that Gulliver was pardoned for passing on to Nelson intelligence regarding the French fleet.

Gulliver lived until 1822, and was interred in Wimborne Minster.[39]

POOLE AREA ■29

Poole lies 5m W of Bournemouth at 195-SZ0090. The custom-house on the quayside is a replica of the custom-house broken open by the Hawkhurst Gang and their confederates in 1747.

The town of Poole had an evil reputation in the eighteenth century. Children from the surrounding area would chant:

> If Poole was a fish-pool, and the men of Poole fish
> There'd be a pool for the devil, and fish for his dish.

There were preventive stations on Brownsea Island and at Poole to keep a wary eye open for smuggling vessels sailing into the vast natural harbour.

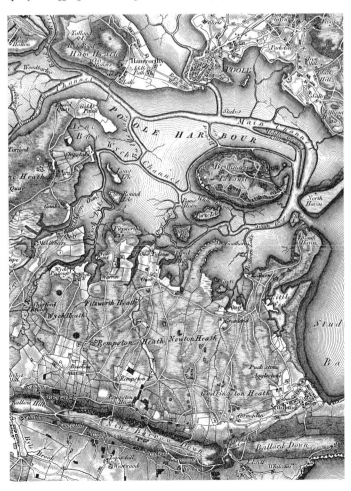

If the incident that took place in Poole in 1747 was anything to go by, the smugglers of the town amply deserved this reputation. In that year a substantial gang broke open the custom-house on the town quay, and recovered a considerable cargo of tea that had been impounded there. They later went on to torture and murder an informer and an innocent customs man in the most horrible manner (see page 59). However, to be fair to the home-grown smugglers, these grisly acts were perpetrated by men from Kent—the Hawkhurst Gang.

Poole's enormous harbour would seem to present the local smugglers with a considerable advantage, but it's hard to tell to what extent they made use of the many miles of creeks, saltings and inlets. Certainly in the seventeenth century, the most cost-effective way of smuggling goods into the town was by bribing the corrupt officials on the quay.

A less brazen way to go about the process was to unload the contraband into 'dragger' boats—boats with a shallow draught designed for use on the oyster-beds. The draggers then took the contraband to stores on Brownsea Island, and from there to Poole and the hinterland. This approach was made impractical by the stationing of a crew of preventives on Brownsea.

Poole smugglers made good use of the town drains, dragging contraband from the quay directly into the cellars of the town pubs. When there was a good flow of water through the pipes after a rain-storm, the task was made considerably easier, because the smugglers could stand high up in the town and let the water wash a rope down the channel to their colleagues at the quay. Contraband was then tied on, and the rope hauled up against the flow of water.[40] It's said that when the customs men got wise to this trick, they waited at the harbour end for the rope, tied on a tub chalked with the legend 'The end is nigh', then gave a tug to signal that the load was ready. The tub was hauled into a cellar of one of the town pubs, and the smugglers read the appropriate message at the very instant their adversaries burst in upstairs.

In the late seventeenth century an investigation into the operation of the Poole custom-house revealed many abuses, but it also pinpointed the key operators in the area. The most prominent smuggler was John Carter. His usual technique was to arrange for his ships to hover a little way off-shore, where they could be unloaded by the dragger boats. Once on land, Carter had countless stores and hiding-places, and as a legitimate merchant he also ran a variety of covers for his illegal operations: a windmill, a malt-house and a brewery, a shop, various stables, cellars, barley lofts, woodyards—all were used for hiding contraband. When Carter's men travelled through Poole, they disguised themselves in masks and women's tall hats. The substantial clubs they carried encouraged rapid memory loss in witnesses.

When the preventive forces began to be more effective, guarding the harbour entrance was a simple enough task, and the preferred method of import was to land the cargoes on Purbeck, then carry them to the shores of the harbour for a sheltered crossing to the town itself in small boats. This subtle approach wasn't always necessary, however. When the odds were stacked in the smugglers' favour, they got their cargoes to Poole quite openly. In the 1780s cargoes were being landed daily in broad daylight . . . 'for such is their numbers and insolence that the officers of the revenue dare not attempt to approach them'.

Though Poole had a deep channel leading to the quayside, smugglers preferred to land contraband from a small boat with a shallow draught. These vessels could be rowed right up to the extensive shoreline at high tide, to land goods at distant inlets.

PURBECK TO WEYMOUTH

To the west of Poole harbour lies the Isle of Purbeck, famous for its marble workings. The Purbeck marble quarries were a gift for the local free-trading population. Much of the marble was extracted by sea, so there was constant activity all along the coast, and an extra ship or two berthing alongside the stone ships passed almost unnoticed. The workings themselves formed a maze of passages and trenches, and a pursued smuggler could dart down a tunnel and soon be hidden behind a pile of rubble, or a slab waiting to be dressed. (The outlawed heroes of Faulkner's novel *Moonfleet* used this ruse to avoid capture.) The quarrymen were doubtless amply rewarded for assisting the smugglers and cooperation was the rule on the island.

Locally, contraband was landed from large fishing boats, and from luggers of 20–40 tons. The main imports in the early eighteenth century were tobacco and spirits, though tea became more popular in the later part of the century. When the revenue men were abroad, tubs were sunk in Swanage, Studland and Kimmeridge Bays. Studland Bay was particularly popular, because it had a safe, sandy bottom, and because Studland itself was very isolated. Goods landed there were concealed in seaweed or bracken, then taken inland, and shipped across the harbour in ones and twos, using the Poole dragger boats.

Though the Purbeck smugglers landed goods on the island, this was often only a temporary resting place. The larger markets for their goods lay to the east, in Poole and beyond. From Purbeck, the kegs and bundles made their way by sea to Parkstone, Hamworthy, Lytchett Bay, West Holton, Keysworth, and the Rivers Piddle and Trent. Transport inland then continued by cart. The simpler option of shipping goods directly overland was too risky, since the land routes off the island were carefully guarded.[41]

SWANAGE ■30

8m S of Poole at 195-SZ0278.

Purbeck harbours the usual complement of smuggling yarns, and though the following story of a Swanage smuggler is totally impossible to verify, it is worth repeating anyway. The story[42] concerns a smuggler quarryman who lived in Station Road, Swanage. This man had the misfortune to have for a neighbour 'a zealous Customs House Officer'; not an unusual situation in a small town. The smuggler worked his quarry with the aid of an old and faithful nag, and the horse had been trained to find its own way home, with a cargo of tubs across its broad back. On reaching the smuggler's house, the horse would wait patiently in the porch until the door was opened, and some kind soul unloaded the night's goods. One particular night, the horse was perhaps affected by the rich aroma wafting up from the tubs, and turned into the wrong porch. Hearing a clatter of hooves, the customs officer got up from his chair and discovered a windfall seizure waiting on the doorstep. The horse, relieved of his burden and doubtless horrified by the mistake he'd made, crept back to the correct house hanging his head.

DURLSTON BAY ■31

195-SZ0377, 1m SE of Swanage centre.

The sea bed at Durlston Bay was covered in soft silt, making tubs difficult to recover if they were sunk in the usual way, and the technique used there was to attach the tubs to a plank, which was weighted so that it floated some 6 feet off the bottom. This kept the tubs clear of the mud. To mark the position of the tubs, the Purbeck smugglers used a bottle-cork tied to a piece of cord—pulling on the cord would bring to the surface a stouter line attached to the string of tubs. Lobster-fishing provided the cover for recovering tubs, and the smugglers took care that their floats were indistinguishable from the markers used for lobster pots.

This habit had on occasion dire consequences—a local yarn tells how a well-bred lady was travelling to Poole in the market boat, and noticed the bobbing corks. She asked the captain what they were for, and on learning that they marked lobster pots, she exclaimed that, although she had eaten lobster, she'd be fascinated to see how they were caught. When the obliging captain hauled in the pot to satisfy the woman's curiosity, he was dismayed (but perhaps not surprised) to find a couple of kegs attached. As ill-fortune would have it, one of the other passengers was a custom-house officer from Swanage, who promptly chalked a broad arrow on each keg, and resolved the following morning to keep a weather eye on the lobster fishermen. He was not disappointed, and had the perverse pleasure of seeing the astonishment on one man's face as he hauled in tubs marked as seized by HM Government. On returning to the shore, a reception committee was waiting for the unfortunate fisherman.

When the coast was clear, the local men preferred to land goods directly, rather than risk a storm washing away their cargoes. Frequently they would moor at the very foot of the cliff, from Old Harry to Pondfield, and haul the tubs up the cliff. From Ballard Down a signal fire or flash could be seen out at sea miles away, so the risk of detection was slight. Goods brought up the cliff made their way across the down, then off to the west via Jenny Gould's Gate.

If cargoes could not be shipped inland from the Purbeck coast directly, they were easily concealed in the stone quarries. The quarry at Durlston Bay was particularly useful for this purpose on account of its size. From about 1700 the stone was worked from shafts or lanes that sloped steeply downwards, and at Durlston the lanes continued a long way inland. Many of the passages were interconnected, so that the knowledgeable smuggler could disappear down one shaft, and emerge some distance away. At times there were fourteen gangs of quarrymen working there, and with the crews of the stone boats milling around, it was impossible for the customs officers to keep an eye on what was happening, as they frequently complained:

Purbeck smugglers landed contraband at the foot of Old Harry Rocks, hauling it up over the cliffs on ropes. The local lobster fishermen also acted as useful allies, 'harvesting' tubs that the smugglers had sunk off-shore for safe-keeping.

One mile from Swanage Bay is Durlston. Here goods are very frequently landed and immediately concealed in the stone quarries where from their great number and extent it is wholly impossible to discover them.

Small quantities of contraband could be removed in the rush baskets which the quarrymen carried to work and back each day. Larger cargoes were frequently stored at the quarry until the coast was clear. A particularly effective hiding-place was inside a hollowed out block of stone: the small entrance was concealed by a pile of loose rocks. Customs men, ignorant of the intricacies of quarrying, were told that the rock was unsaleable, because there was no longer any demand for that kind of marble. Other hiding-places included a small cave near Durlston Head, concealed with a thin block that could be slid aside. This hiding-place was unfortunately sniffed out by a coastguard's dog. Other caves were pressed into service, too—one near Tilly Whim Caves had a narrow sea entrance just big enough for a small boat, but ample space inside for several burly smugglers.

DANCING LEDGE ■32

2m SW of Swanage at 195-SY995768. To reach Dancing Ledge, approaching from Swanage, turn left in Langton Matravers down Durnford Drove immediately after passing the C of E church. Follow the track through a gate and park at the farm (fee). The ledge is ³/₄m S.

This extraordinary rock platform is aptly named—it really is flat enough to dance on—and was a popular landing-point. Goods were taken up over the hill to Spyway Farm from temporary storage (on occasions it was guarded by a bull) and from there to the church at Langton Matravers, where tubs were stored in a void above the ceiling in the church roof. A local story tells that on one memorable Sunday the choir were singing from a psalm the words 'And Thy paths drop fatness', when the roof collapsed, bombarding the congregation with kegs.

Asked whether there was any truth in the smuggling connection with Spyway Farm, one local wryly observed 'I reckon as how it must be true, 'cos it's the only reason why a sane person would put a house on top of a hill where it catches all the wind'.

WINSPIT ■33

195-SY977761 3m W of Swanage. Drive to Worth Matravers, park, then walk the 1m S to the cove. Chapman's Pool is ¹/₂m NW.

This was another popular landing-site; a sheltered valley leads up from the sea there to Worth Matravers. Cargoes continued to be landed here and at Chapman's Pool until the smugglers overstepped the mark, binding and gagging the unfortunate coastguard who found them at work, then staking him to the ground before beating the man to within an inch of his life. After this incident, a permanent guard was stationed at the bay.

WEST PURBECK

Kimmeridge Bay ■34 is at 195-SY9079 8m W of Swanage, close to Kimmeridge via a toll road (map 195). Arish Mell ■35, 2m E of West Lulworth at 194-SY855803, is inaccessible, and a cliff-top path running above the cove is now part of an army firing range, and therefore closed to the public on weekdays and four or five weekends a year. The range office can give details: ring 0929 462721 extension 819. Approach from East Lulworth (map 194).

To the west of the marble workings of Purbeck, every point where there was direct access to the sea was pressed into service at one time or another. Tubs were sunk on the sandy bottom of Kimmeridge Bay, and landed at Brandy Bay to the east, though when it was clear what was going on, the revenue men began to use Clavel's Tower, overlooking Kimmeridge Bay, as an observation post. Worbarrow Bay was a popular landing-spot, with Arish Mell beach in the middle especially convenient. One run in 1719 was of spectacular proportions, with five luggers unloading together, and 'A perfect fair on the waterside, some buying of goods, and others loading of horses . . . there was an army of people, armed and in disguise, as many in number as . . . at Dorchester fair.'

Nearly sixty years later, a local newspaper reported that:

A Dunkirk schooner landed . . . upwards of twenty tons of tea, in sight of and in defiance of the Custom House officers as they were

The small beach of Arish Mell in the centre of Worbarrow Bay provided smugglers with a haven from mountainous seas such as those depicted in this nineteenth-century print. At the western end of the bay smugglers used a cave close to Mupe Rocks, and carefully cleared a path through the boulders to make access safer.

mounting twenty four-pounders, which they brought to bear on the beach. The smugglers on shore carried it off in three waggons and on horses, except twelve hundredweight, which the officers seized, and carried to a public house at West Lulworth ... but thirty or forty of the schooner's people, well armed, followed after, and broke into the house, beating and cutting the people they found there in a cruel manner, and carried off the tea.

LULWORTH COVE ■36

194-SY8279, 10m SE of Dorchester close to the village of West Lulworth. Mupe Bay is 1 mile to the E.

This picturesque spot makes a neat full stop at the western end of the isle of Purbeck. The cove has been described as the most beautiful in Britain, and makes an almost perfect circle, surrounded on all sides by cliffs. This extremely sheltered bay could therefore be used in virtually all weathers, and was of course the ideal spot to sink tubs. One, a hogshead of French red, bobbed up in 1717, and was promptly seized, though it proved to be 'poor thin stuff that will not keep'.

A couple of years later nearly a dozen smugglers were stopped near the cove as they tried to run wine and brandy in the early hours of a summer's morning. They fought like demons with flails, swords and clubs, and when it looked as if they would lose the cargo, the smugglers staved in some of the barrels, and made off with the remainder. The battle between smugglers and revenue men went on for some 12 hours, and attracted people from four parishes, who ran off with the abandoned barrels.

The coast around Lulworth was widely used by smugglers, and the cove itself provided their ships with a haven from even the fiercest storms.

In the early years of the eighteenth century the local venturer at Lulworth was one Charles Weeks, who lived at Winfrith, and who had developed a particularly shrewd way of defrauding the revenue. He would buy seized goods at legitimate auctions, and mix in the smuggled article for onward shipment, often to London. When an officer challenged Weeks to produce receipts showing that duty had been paid, Weeks could often do so. When he couldn't, he would threaten the officer with litigation; on the pittance paid by the government, no customs officer could afford a legal action, so the smuggler escaped.

Smugglers are said to have stored contraband in a cave at the most easterly point of Mupe Bay. In 1906 it could be reached

... by following the coast from Lulworth, and by descending the cliff the moment the bay is reached. The cave is at the foot of the precipice, at a spot where a little channel has been cleared between the boulders for a boat to land.[43]

The Lulworth men evidently took no chances of being identified by the local customs authorities: on a tombstone in Weymouth's Bury Street cemetery there is the following inscription:

Sacred to the memory of Lieut Thos Edward Knight, RN, of Folkestone, Kent, Aged 42, who in the execution of his duty as Chief Officer of the Coastguard was wantonly attacked by a body of smugglers near Lulworth on the night of 28th of June 1832, by whom after being unmercifully beaten he was thrown over the cliff near Durdle Door from the effects of which he died the following day.[44]

WOOL ■37

194-SY8486, 10m E of Dorchester.

The route that contraband followed inland from Lulworth went directly through the village of Wool, where in the 1820s the landlord of the Ship Inn, Tom Lucas, supervised onward shipment and storage. He was a formidable man, and his associates were notorious for their violence. Little wonder, then, that when the Bow Street Runners were called in to arrest Lucas, they took no chances. They arrived in large numbers, heavily armed, in the early hours of the morning. To gain entry to the inn, they chose the softly-softly approach. One of them knocked gently on the door, and when Lucas asked 'Who's there?', the officer replied in a child's high, squeaky voice, 'It's only me, Mr Lucas, Mrs Smith's little girl. I want a little drop of brandy for mother, for she is bad in her bowels'.

The subterfuge worked, and Lucas opened the door, only to be arrested by several burly sergeants and hustled to prison—he was later acquitted, by a jury perhaps fearful of the consequences of a guilty verdict.

ROGER RIDOUT

In charge of one of the overland haulage companies moving goods from the Dorset coast was Roger Ridout, who has since achieved legendary status in north Dorset. He lived at Okeford Fitzpaine ■38, a small village near Blandford Forum, and in an 1895 account of his activities, a local writer commented ...

[my] father stated that when a boy, in or about 1794, he had, when riding ... late at night seen the string of horses in the narrow road between Okeford Fitzpaine and Fiddleford with the kegs and other contraband goods on the horses. One or two men, armed, generally were in front and then ten or twelve horses connected by ropes or halters followed at a hard trot, and two or three men brought up the rear. This cavalcade did not stop for any person, and it was very difficult to get out of their way, as the roads, until the turnpikes were made in 1724, would only allow

for one carriage, except in certain places. The contraband goods were principally brought from Lulworth and the coast through Whiteparish and Okeford Fitzpaine, through the paths in the woods to Fiddleford, and thus distributed.[45]

The author of this piece was the grandson of a Sturminster Newton JP who was reportedly bribed by Ridout.

From baptism registers, it appears that Roger Ridout was born in Shroton (the parish of Iwerne Courtney) in 1736. He inherited a house in Fiddleford when he was ten and married when he was twenty. He earned a living as a miller, died in 1811, and was buried in Okeford Fitzpaine graveyard.

However, behind these bald facts lie numerous legends.[46] The Ridout of the oral tradition was a bold smuggler who brought contraband—notably brandy—from the coast, and stored it at the mill. Most of the tales tell the usual story of the exciseman outwitted, but their charm lies in the west-country flavour. For example, Ridout owned a horse known locally as Ridout's Ratted (or stumped) Tail, for reasons that probably need no explanation. Once, as he arrived in Sturminster Bridge Street a mob of rival smugglers gathered round the horse and rider, and tried to pull Roger to the ground. Ridout leaned forward and whispered to his nag, 'What'd 'ee do fer thy king?' On hearing this, the horse reared up and kicked in the door of a nearby house.

Other stories have Ridout being lowered from the back window of his house in a bed-sheet to escape the revenue men, and tricking them in other ways. Returning from Fiddleford brewery with a jar of balm, Ridout was met by a curious exciseman. Roger shook the bottle as the exciseman approached, and as the wily smuggler had expected, the officer asked about the contents of the bottle. Roger led him on: 'Would 'ee like t'smell 'un', and handed it over. When the officer pulled the cork he got a faceful of balm, and the smuggler pushed him into the ditch and went on his way.

Ridout is reputed to have been employed by Isaac Gulliver, and it is certain that he spent some time in Dorchester Gaol, languishing there until he could pay the fine. The local stories tell that he was fortified behind bars by his wife, who would walk a 40-mile round trip to the gaol with a concealed bladder of brandy, equipped with a tube that she passed through the bars so that her husband could have a drop of the right stuff.

HIGHER BOCKHAMPTON ■39

194-SY7292, 2m NE of Dorchester.

Thomas Hardy was born here, and described in his notebooks his grandfather's connections with the free-trade:

While superintending the church music (from 1801 onward to about 1805) my grandfather used to do a little smuggling, his house being a lonely one, none of the others in Higher, or Upper, Bockhampton being then built . . . He sometimes had as many as eighty tubs in a dark closet (afterwards destroyed in altering the staircase)—each containing four gallons. The spirits often smelt all over the house, being proof, and had to be lowered for drinking. The tubs, or little elongated barrels, were of thin staves with wooden hoops. (I remember one of them which had been turned into a bucket by knocking out one head and putting in a handle.) They were brought at night by men on horseback, 'slung' or in carts. A whiplash across the window-pane would wake my grandfather at two or three in the morning, and he would dress and go down. Not a soul was there, but a heap of tubs loomed up in front of the door. He would set to work and stow them in the dark closet aforesaid, and nothing more would happen till dusk the following evening, when groups of dark, long-bearded fellows would arrive, and carry off the tubs in twos and fours slung over their shoulders.[47]

OSMINGTON MILLS ■40

194-SY7381, 1m SE of Osmington, off the A353, 4m from Weymouth.

West of Lulworth lie high cliffs, but there is again access to the sea at Osmington Mills, backed by a sheltered valley hidden from casual gaze. An easy landing and a safe route inland made this a valuable landfall for import smugglers, and the thirteenth-century inn on the spot had a constant flow of visitors—both English and foreign—and smuggled liquor with which to supply them.

The landlord in the early nineteenth century was Emmanuel Carless or Charles,[48] who apparently imported brandy that was so disgusting that none of the locals would drink it. The spirit therefore had to be shipped inland disguised as luggage on the local mail coaches, then redistilled before it could be sold. Charles's accomplice—the sea-borne side of the partnership—was a Frenchman called Peter Latour, or French Peter. This intrepid mariner at one time had a price on his head, and a local anecdote tells how an innocent young preventive, John Tallman, visited the inn seeking information about French Peter. The landlord plied him with brandy and stories of French Peter's brave deeds and ferocious temper. With each glass the stories became bolder, and the young preventive's eyes wider. So when French Peter's ship, the *Hirondelle*, dropped anchor in the bay below the pub, Tallman was not quite so anxious to make his acquaintance. He turned to the landlord for help, and Emmanuel suggested he hide up the chimney in what is now the Old World Bar. No sooner had the lad hauled himself up the flue but French Peter came in the door. Peter's greeting, 'How do you fare, Manny?' wasn't met with the customary warmth. Emmanuel put his fingers to his lips, rolled his eyes, and pointed at the large fireplace, then asked Peter if he'd like his usual glass of gin. The Frenchman, who drank only cognac (presumably not the stuff he imported) was quick to sense that something was not quite right, and replied, 'I'm feeling a bit of a sea-chill today, Manny, perhaps I'll have a tot of brandy, and what about a warming fire in yonder grate?'

The two men set to work with damp twigs, heather and rotting leaves, and soon the choking smoke brought the unfortunate revenue man out of his hiding-place, much to the amusement of the watching locals. After another large tot of brandy, he was then dusted off and sent back to Weymouth.

WEYMOUTH TO LYME REGIS

Weymouth was the centre of preventive operations for the area, but from custom-house correspondence it would seem that the smugglers were not strongly opposed. At the end of the seventeenth century, the collector of customs at Weymouth was described in an official report in terms far from glowing. He had . . . 'a debauched life and conversation, seldom sober, and hardly ever goes to bed till three or four a clock in the morning and many times not all night'. The customs officers of Portland were of little help; of one was said, he 'never did any service, but rather the contrary'. Other staff seem to have included the handicapped and the lame: an official appointed in 1719 was 'an old man . . . [who] cannot see anything at a distance'.

The failings and corruption of the Weymouth officials had historic origins: even in the early sixteenth century the ironically named George Whelplay had difficulty making any progress against concerted local support for smuggling. He was originally a London haberdasher, but he contrived to make considerable sums of money by becoming a public informer. As such he was entitled to half of the fine levied on people caught as a result of his actions. Since smuggling amounted to a national pastime, this did not make him a popular man. He overstepped the mark in 1538, incurring the wrath not only of the crooked merchants, but also of the customs officials themselves.

He had uncovered a plan to export horses to France illegally, and had intercepted the cargo. However, he was also aware that three French

ships were at anchor in Weymouth harbour, ready to set sail with contraband on board. Whelplay had tried to enlist the help of local officials in rounding up the three French boats, but far from assisting, the controller, searcher and deputy customer joined a gang of merchants to set about the informer.

It appears he didn't learn his lessons easily—soon afterwards he tried again to intercept 200 horses bound for France. This time he was beaten with bills, swords and staves, again by customs officials among others.

WEYMOUTH AND PORTLAND ▪41

The Black Dog is in St Mary Street, Weymouth (next to Marks and Spencer).

The smuggler's grave is in All Saints Church, Wyke Regis, on the B3157, close to the junction with the A354 (194-SY665775). Enter the churchyard via the lych gate and immediately turn right, to walk parallel with the graveyard wall. The stone faces the ninth buttress on the wall (map 194).

With such a history of incompetence and dishonesty among the staff, and a determined band of local smugglers, it was inevitable that the Weymouth customs authorities would have problems, sometimes with tragic consequences. In June 1770 a large run of contraband was expected on the coast near Weymouth, and the tide-surveyor took a boat out to intercept the smugglers. According to stories related after the incident, the custom-house boat with its five crew was run down by a smuggling cutter (allegedly a Folkestone vessel). The witness to this event claimed that:

> he saw a cutter run down the King's boat . . . taking her upon the larboard quarter, and that he particularly saw Mr. John Bishop the tide-surveyor take hold of the Bowsprit shroud or Jibb jack in order to save himself, and on that, the people on board the cutter let go the shroud.

However, it has to be said that the witness was 'much in Liquor' when reporting the drowning. In another incident a custom-house officer was murdered at the sixteenth-century Black Dog Inn in the town while trying to arrest a smuggler who had taken refuge there.

The battle between the revenue men and smugglers was not entirely one-sided, as a tombstone on the outskirts of Weymouth testifies. In its shadow lies the body of a smuggler cut down by a shot from an excise schooner. His bitter wife had this epitaph carved on the stone.[49]

> Of life bereft, by fell design
> I mingle with my fellow clay
> On God's Protection I recline
> To save me on the Judgment Day
> There shall each blood-stained soul appear
> Repent, all, ere it be too late
> Or else a dreadful doom you'll hear,
> For God will soon avenge my fate.

CHESIL BEACH ▪42

W of Weymouth. Access to the beach from the Portland end via the car-park at 194-SY668754.

Weymouth smugglers had the unique advantage of Chesil Beach and the Fleet—the lagoon behind. This extraordinary bank of shingle stretches unbroken for nearly 17 miles, from Burton Bradstock to Portland. Smugglers landing on the beach in the pitch black of a moonless night were able to judge their position to within a mile or two by simply picking up a handful of shingle and gauging the average size of the stones. At the Portland end, the pebbles are the size of potatoes, and

An 1811 map of Portland Bill.

then progressively slim down to pea-shingle on the beach at Burton Bradstock.

Tubs landed here were humped over Chesil Beach, and sunk in the quiet waters of the Fleet for collection at a more convenient time. Landing, though, was not always straightforward, because in stormy weather a ferocious sea pounds Chesil Beach, often reducing vessels to matchwood, and on one memorable occasion lifting a 500-ton ship clean over the beach and into the Fleet. In 1762 a winter storm destroyed a Cornish ship, killing the crew and scattering the cargo to drift with the tide to Portland. There, custom-house officers were determined to seize the contraband spirits, and 150 local people were equally determined that they should not. After five hours of argument and battle, the fracas ended at 4 am with a score of Revenue: 26 tubs, Locals: 10. The 10 that got away were tossed back into the sea and collected the following day. This opposition from the Portlanders came as no surprise to the customs authorities, who were reluctant to visit the island 'for fear of being struck in the head by a volley of stones.'

If they were lucky, the customs officials suffered only insults. In 1822 a storm loosened a raft of tubs, which floated free, and a race between the revenue and the tubs' owners ensued, to see who could reach the contraband first. The revenue boat was in the lead, but the smugglers raised a sail and surged ahead. As they passed, the helmsman dropped his trousers, 'striking his posterior in derision' at the downcast revenue men in their slower vessel.

CHICKERELL AND MOONFLEET ■43

194-SY6480, 2m W of Weymouth on the B3157. The chapel is at East Fleet (194-SY635800).

The villages behind the Fleet developed a thriving commerce in spirits, tea, tobacco and lace. The community close to Chickerell is the best known today, since it provided the basis for J. Meade Falkner's novel *Moonfleet*. Though fictional, the story had its foundations in the trade that flourished here. In 1717, customs officials trying to prevent a landing on Chesil Beach reported that they were met by 30 men in disguise, who drove them away with clubs and other weapons. Some of the places mentioned in the book can be seen locally. The tiny chapel is especially atmospheric; it was in the chapel's flooded vault that the tubs of gin bumped together, making a noise that so frightened the congregation above.

ABBOTSBURY ■44

194-SY5785, 8m NW of Weymouth.

Abbotsbury boasts a dramatic chapel on the hill-top—a fine navigational marker—and the local smuggling HQ was the Ilchester Arms, once called the Ship Inn. In 1737 evidence of the Abbotsbury group's activities came to light at Bexington, on the Swyre road, where ¾ ton of tea was found under hedges, along with brandy, rum, silk, cotton and handkerchiefs.

BURTON BRADSTOCK ■45

Burton Bradstock is 12m NW of Weymouth at 193-SY4989. Eggardon Hill is at 194-SY5495, about 6 miles W of Dorchester. Turn N off the A35 towards Askerswell. The hill is signposted in the village.

Smugglers used the Dove Inn at Burton Bradstock as a rendezvous, and Isaac Gulliver himself probably drank in the pub, since in 1776[50] he bought Eggardon Hill, a prehistoric earthwork a little way inland, specifically to guide his ships to the coast. To make it more prominent, 'The small enclosure [on top] was prepared for a plantation to serve as a local mark for vessels engaged in the contraband trade.'[51] (The revenue men cut them down.)

The hill is impressive. It rises suddenly at the end of a long, flat plain, and a series of concentric trenches and embankments spiral around its circumference. From the top, it is possible on a clear day to look out over the sea some 5 miles away, and the hill gives a good view over all the surrounding countryside. In Shipton Gorge, Gulliver's Lane runs down from the hill.

Abbotsbury legend relates that even the vicar was implicated in the smuggling which took place along Chesil Beach, seen here stretching away to Portland.

Contraband barrels landed on Chesil Beach were easily concealed in the calm waters of the Fleet on the other side. The hero of the famous smuggling novel Moonfleet *describes the Fleet as 'a lagoon, being shut off from the open Channel by a monstrous great beach or dike of pebbles'.*

CHIDEOCK ■46

193-SY4292, 3m W of Bridport.

The villagers of Chideock were all allegedly involved in the free-trade, and one vicar of the town commented:

> The fishing interest seems to have slipped away with the dwellings at Seatown. Some say the fish have left the coast, but others . . . that in the old days the fishermen lived more by smuggling than by fishing.[52]

The Chideock smugglers landed goods between Charmouth and Seatown, and marked the hills above their favoured landfalls as Gulliver marked Eggardon Hill—with copses of trees. These grew at Stanton St Gabriel, Eype's Mouth, Seatown and Charmouth. The miller at Chideock hid his share of the contraband in a secret room under the floor of his living accommodation at the mill. When the revenue men found four tubs of spirits there in 1820, the cowardly miller tried to blame his servant Dido, saying the boy had told him several days earlier that the cellar was 'a really good place to hide tubs, master. The officers will never find them there'.

LYME REGIS ■47

193-SY3492, 20m SW of Yeovil.

The coast of Lyme Bay and the town itself were landing-places for Isaac Gulliver, but he was simply following in the footsteps of many who had gone before. Lyme has an especially long history of smuggling. Sixteenth-century merchants were suspected of smuggling bullion out of Britain, and in 1576 the suspicions became so strong that one Ralph Lane was despatched to the town to investigate, carrying a warrant to search ships that were alleged to be taking part. The result was a riot—the warrant was destroyed and Lane's deputy was thrown overboard.[53]

According to legend, the principal route taken by contraband was up the river Buddle where the buildings crowd in,[54] but the truth is more prosaic. Most contraband was probably just sneaked in under the noses of the preventives, who were frequently understaffed, and handicapped by ludicrous local bylaws about where their jurisdiction ended. Cargoes unloaded on the Cobb—the town pier—could not be inspected until they had been carried half a mile to the Cobb gate.

However, when caught red-handed, the Lyme smugglers were as resourceful as the next man. A tub-carrier who ran into a senior official of the custom-house reputedly exchanged warm greetings and put the tubs down at the officer's feet, telling him, 'The exciseman axed me to take these two tubs to you, and gied me two shillings for the job; but damn him! If I had know'd they'd be so heavy, and would ha' cut my shoulder so, I'd seed unto the devil afore I'd ha' touched o'em'. Whether or not the officer believed the story is unclear, but unable to carry the tubs himself, he eventually gave the man a further florin to carry them back to the custom-house, and strode off to await their arrival while the tub-carrier 'rested'. As soon as the officer rounded the corner, the man's exhaustion left him, and he effortlessly shouldered his burden and made off.

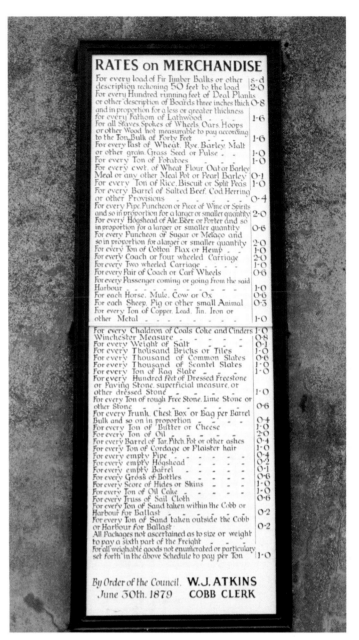

This table, on a wall of a building on the Cobb at Lyme Regis shows the rates of duty for imports.

SOUTH-WEST ENGLAND

LYME TO BRISTOL

The counties of the south-west, and Cornwall in particular, are so famous for smuggling that many people today believe this to be the only area of Britain where the activity took place. The traditional stereotype of the Cornishman—taciturn, suspicious of strangers and rather sly—owes much to the area's reputation in the free-trade. In reality, the men of Cornwall and Devon probably smuggled much less than their contemporaries in the south-east of England. The crossing to the Continent was very much farther; the market for smuggled goods was strictly local; and there were fewer suitable landing-places on the south-west coast.

However, smuggling in Cornwall and Devon was stimulated by a number of local factors, notably the lack of prevention, and extreme poverty. The alluvial tin-miners or streamers in the West Penwith area were especially active, because of the seasonal nature of their work, which caused them to be laid off in the summer when there was a shortage of water: '. . . A trip to Roscoff or Guernsey formed a pleasant change after a spell on tribute underground or working stamps.'[1] By contrast with this poverty-stricken existence, smuggling brought fantastic wealth into the area. One writer observes (with customary exaggeration) that:

> When smuggling was in full swing, money became so plentiful that neighbours lent guineas to each other by the handful, not stopping to count, or being so particular as to reckon by ones and twos.

In some parts of the south-west, smuggling was indeed the principal means of employment—the Isles of Scilly, for example, were brought almost to bankruptcy when the preventive net finally tightened.

As in other parts of the country, the early smugglers from Devon and Cornwall were not importing, but exporting. Here, though, the outgoing contraband was likely to be Cornish tin rather than bales of wool. Tin was one of the earliest strategic metals, and lined the holds of many vessels apparently loaded with other more innocent cargoes.

When increased duty made imports more important than the exported ore, Continental supplies for the south-west came mainly from Brittany and the Channel Islands. The trade from Guernsey was at least partly stopped when a preventive boat was stationed there in 1767, but this did not deter the French traders who were getting rich by shipping goods through the island. The French responded two years later by making Roscoff a free port; and within months the sleepy port was transformed into a hive of industry, supplying the tubs and bales needed for transport across to Devon and Cornwall. The historic link is still maintained, with a ferry from Plymouth plying the same route. The Channel Islands were soon back in business, though by 1775 it appears that the government's resolve had weakened, and reputedly many people from the island made fortunes in the latter part of the eighteenth century 'simply by manufacturing casks'.[2]

Financing arrangements in the south-west don't seem to have been quite so centralized as elsewhere in Britain. Instead of a 'Mr Big' bankrolling the whole operation, everyone took a share: 'the farmers, the merchants, and, it is rumoured, the local magistrates, used to find the money with which the business was carried on, investing small sums in each voyage'.[3] At Falmouth, where smuggling by postal packet-carriers was rife, local traders organized an extraordinary 'sale-or-return' agreement with ships travelling to Portugal.

Compared to their companions-in-trade from Kent and Sussex, smugglers from the south-west have a benign, rather jolly image. The accuracy of this is open to dispute, and it's possible to call up examples to support both sides of the argument. The pacifists maintain that West Country smugglers were not organized in gangs to anything like the same extent as free-traders in the east, and that this had some bearing on their reluctance to use force against their adversaries. Furthermore, some sources suggest that, whereas the boats used in the east of the country were generally large, purpose-built, and heavily armed, smugglers in the west tended to use fishing vessels and other small craft.

There is probably a germ of truth in this argument, and the pacifist point of view has been fostered over the years by several local legends. There is the example of 'the Gentle Smuggler', Isaac Gulliver, who earned his nickname for his reluctance to use force and his ban on the carrying of firearms by his followers.

However, the size of ships used, and their complement of arms, probably varied according to the degree of vigilance of the preventives and their strength. In the boom years of the free-trade, Cornish and Devon boats were probably every bit as big as those in the south-east and east of Britain. According to one authority[4] the vessels used here ranged from 50–250 tons, 'were often heavily armed', and had up to 1000 sq feet of canvas in the mainsail. As prevention developed, such a ship would have become too conspicuous to be of any practical use, and the smugglers began to favour smaller boats, masquerading as fishing vessels or coasters. Since these boats are more recent, they obviously figure more frequently in the oral history of the free-trade.

A further factor which must have influenced the lesser degree of violence used is the proximity of the sea. Only a small part of Cornwall is more than a day's walk from the coast and eighteenth-century claims that the majority of the population was involved in smuggling may have had some truth in them.

'The coasts here swarm with smugglers from the Land's End to the Lizard', one man wrote[5] in 1753, and with the active support of the local population these swarms would need to use violence only against the revenue forces—and the King's men didn't count anyway in the eyes of most otherwise law-abiding citizens.

When it came to dealing with the preventive forces, there is no evidence to suggest that smugglers from south-west Britain were any less violent than their fellows. If anything, accounts point in the opposite direction:

> A rough, reckless and drunken lot were these tinners, and if riots and bloodshed were more scarce in West Cornwall than in some parts, it must have been due to the judicious absence of the Custom House officials, and not to any qualities in the smugglers.[6]

The vicar of Morwenstow, who wrote much about local smuggling legends, described a conversation he had with one of his congregation concerning the hanging of a man who was wrongly convicted of murder. The local wished to know why it was that grass will not grow on the man's grave, and turf withers on the mound. When the vicar asked what crime the unfortunate man was alleged to have committed, he was told that the deceased '. . . only killed a custom-house officer'.

The account of the chase of the smuggling ship *Lottery* (see pages 105–6) also gives a vivid picture of brutality, and stories of other pitched battles reinforce this view. In 1735 a gang of armed smugglers attacked excisemen near Fowey when they tried to repossess some rum. The band had apparently acquired a local reputation for violence. A report on the clash observed that the revenue officers 'go in danger of their lives' if they try to seize the goods . . . the smugglers having entered into a combination to rescue any person who shall be arrested'.[7]

Even if they were caught, violent Cornish smugglers often got off scot-free. In 1768 smugglers brutally murdered an excise offficer, William Odgers, at Porthleven. A Gwennap man, Melchisideck Kinsman, was accused of the murder, together with other unknown people. His accomplices were initially thought to have fled the country to Guernsey or Morlaix, but were later reported to be hiding in the tin mines. The principal witness was offered a bribe of £500 to go abroad, and when this didn't work, he was threatened with physical violence, and could not work for fear of his life. He was later paid a state pension of seven shillings a week.

The tin mines of Cornwall provided willing, strong labourers to hump the smugglers' goods inland, as well as a ready market.

Three of the accomplices eventually surrendered, and agreed to track down Kinsman (presumably in return for leniency). They caught him, and all stood trial at the assizes, but to the astonishment of the judge, none was found guilty. The local collector of customs observed that three of the jury had disappeared after the trial, and suggested that they had been either bribed or 'nobbled'. Little wonder, then, that in the 1750s '. . . nobody can venture to come near (the smugglers) with safety while they are at their work.'[8]

The preventive forces sometimes offered violence to match that of their opponents. In 1799 two preventives accused fellow travellers between Bodmin and Truro of being smugglers. In the battle that ensued, the innocent travellers were killed, and the preventives absconded.

Though the south-western smugglers treated revenue men as harshly as their colleagues elsewhere in the country, it could be argued that informers received less brutal treatment. Compared to the torture and murder of Chater and Galley, the weapons used in the south-west seem positively benevolent. Social ostracism of the informer and his family were the rule, and in at least one instance (see page 100) the informer was simply burned in effigy.

WRECKING

The treacherous coasts of Devon and Cornwall are notorious for wrecks, and the local people did not hesitate to ransack a ship unfortunate enough to be smashed on the rocks. This is illustrated vividly by a story told of Portlemouth. The vicar of the parish church there was drawing to the end of a particularly dry sermon, and many of the congregation had dropped to sleep. The sound of a man opening the church door woke a few of them—a gale was blowing outside—and they welcomed the diversion as he walked up to the pulpit and whispered in the vicar's ear. The remainder of the congregation were immediately roused from their musings by the vicar bellowing, 'There's a ship ashore between Prawle and Pear Tree Point!' He started to tear off his vestments, continuing as he tugged at the encumbering garments '. . . but let us all start fair'. As one, the congregation rose and charged headlong to the beach with the vicar in the lead.

The legend goes on to relate that the parishioners ignored the cries for help from the drowning crew as they tried to salvage the cargo of the galleon. However, it is difficult to credit this account, just as it's hard to believe tales of ships being deliberately lured onto the rocks, and crewmen cynically drowned for fear they would testify about the plundering that took place. Most of the local inhabitants were seafarers themselves, and knew of the inevitable loss of life that followed a wreck. The villagers would also have to bury the bodies of drowned crew, and this was a highly distasteful task (see page 114). It would be fairer to say that the misfortune of the storm could sometimes be turned to advantage.

Wrecks were the scene of much dispute and argument, not least because dutiable goods washed up should theoretically have been declared at the local custom-house. The custom-house officers were therefore among the first on the scene, representing the interests of the Crown. Their chance of securing anything would often have been slight, because they were usually greatly outnumbered by the hundreds of villagers plundering the broken ribs of the beached ship. The searchers and gaugers nevertheless saw wrecking as a form of smuggling, and viewed it as their duty to levy the rightful customs charges (see pages 121–2).

There were other interests at odds with the wreckers. The crew of the ship itself—if they had survived—usually looked on helplessly while every item of value was dragged from the hold, or prised free of its mountings. But the biggest disputes were often between the wreckers and the owner of the stretch of coastline where the ship had foundered. These people had 'Royalty of Wrecks' on their land, and were generally entitled to half the value of the goods washed up. The other half went to the rescuer, but both sides were keen to take more than their share.

Often the rights to Royalty of Wrecks were disputed; such as at Porthleven in 1743. Edward Coode, son of the Lord of nearby

Methleigh heard of the wreck and went to the beach wearing only a greatcoat and gloves. He was met by a neighbour, Squire Penrose, with a gang of armed men who defied him to touch the cargo. The squire grabbed a musket and cried, 'Damm him, shoot him, or by God, I'll shoot him'. Ironically, all they were fighting over was a case of salted pork.

Though wrecking was counted as smuggling, a full study of wrecking could quite easily occupy a complete book, so I have generally not included wrecking stories in the text that follows.

THE SOUTH COAST

BEER ▪1

192-SY2289, 1m W of Seaton. Bovey House is now a delightful hotel on the road from Beer to Branscombe. Leave Beer on the B3174, and turn left 2m outside Beer.

This village at the extreme east of Devon was the headquarters of a gang of smugglers led by Jack Rattenbury, who was once dubbed 'The Rob Roy of the West'. Like the Carter family of Prussia Cove, Rattenbury probably owes his fame not so much to his actual exploits as to the diary and journal he wrote. This is essentially an autobiography,[9] and starts with his birth in Beer in 1778. As a child he intended to go into fishing, but found this rather a dull activity, and his real adventures began when he turned fifteen: he set out on a privateer, was taken prisoner by the French, and thrown into gaol in France: 'Instead of returning to our native country laden with riches and adorned with trophies, we were become . . . unwilling sojourners in a strange land'.

Rattenbury became a trusty inmate, though, and eventually managed to sneak away. Escapes of one sort or another soon became his forte. He described how a smuggling brig in which he was travelling was captured by a French privateer, and he was left at the helm to steer

for a French port while the crew got drunk below: 'I began to conceive a hope not only of escaping, but also of being revenged on the enemy. A fog too came on, which befriended the design I had in view.'

Rattenbury steered for the English coast, and when they came in sight of Portland Bill, he convinced the crew that this was Alderney; similarly, St Alban's became Cape La Hogue. When they got closer to the shore, Jack persuaded them to lower a boat and go and get a pilot—he eventually completed his escape by diving overboard and swimming into Swanage harbour. He hurried to the local customs authorities, who sent a cutter to recapture the brig from the French.

Rattenbury followed this with a series of daring escapes—from the navy, the press-gang, from privateers, from customs men. He hid up chimneys, in cellars, on board small boats, and in bushes.

Jack catalogued a series of adventures, some of them doubtless exaggerated, and most of them carefully drawn to show him in a heroic light. A typical story has him stripped to the waist, with a knife in one hand and a reaping-hook (hand-scythe) in the other, facing nine or ten soldiers who were determined to arrest him as a deserter. He took up position at the stable door to the cellar, closing the lower half:

> I declared I would kill the first man who came near me, and that I would not be taken from the spot alive. At this, the sergeant was evidently terrified, but he said to his men 'Soldiers, do your duty, advance and seize him;' to which they replied, 'Sergeant, you proposed it: take the lead' . . . no one, however, offered to advance.

The deadlock continued for four hours, and eventually a distraction gave Rattenbury the opportunity to dash through the crowd and make good his escape—by removing his shirt, he prevented the soldiers from taking a firm hold of him.

Reading through the short book, Jack's increasing wealth is abundantly clear. In the early days he hadn't two pennies to rub together, but by the age of 30, he had amassed sufficient money to trade in ships much as people today buy and sell second-hand cars. Even in the face of

The people of the south-west certainly profited from wrecked cargoes, but deliberate wrecking was probably rare. Villagers not only picked up the ships' cargoes, they would also have had to collect and bury the sailors' corpses.

Taken prisoner on a French privateer, the famous Devon smuggler Jack Rattenbury escaped his drunken captors by persuading them that St Alban's Head was actually Cape La Hogue. Then he steered the ship for Swanage harbour, and dived overboard when he was within striking distance of the shore.

Axmouth, Charmouth, Bridport harbour, Swanage Bay, Lyme, Christchurch, and Kingswear all feature. In 1820 one of his boats ran aground at Stapen Sands and was dashed to pieces, 'the greater part of her goods became the prey of the inhabitants'. One of his escapes was from a pub called The Indian Queen, a few miles from Bodmin. Though the pub has now been demolished, a village still bears its name. And at Beer itself, Rattenbury was reputed to have used a cave in the face of Beer Head.

Bovey House nearby may have been used by Rattenbury as a hiding-place for contraband. Certainly smugglers frequented this fine Tudor house, taking advantage of its reputation for hauntings, and of a passage that led down to Beer Cliffs. Even today, you can see a well with a hiding-place half-way down its shaft.

BRANSCOMBE ■2

192-SY1988, 5m E of Sidmouth.

This village was frequented by Rattenbury—local stories connect farmers from the neighbourhood with the famous smuggler, and the Three Horseshoes Inn was a local meeting-place. Branscombe men made a reputation for their skills in landing smuggled goods, just as other places specialized in different aspects of the trade: 'Sidbury financed, Branscombe landed, Sidmouth found wagons, and Salcombe carriers; but the six "escort-men" with blackened faces and swingle bats were always specialists from Yeovil.'[10]

Though this quote suggests that the violence was perpetrated only by Yeovil men, a table tomb in the Branscombe graveyard leads one to believe that local men also had a share in the murderous business.

adversity he had no trouble in setting up in business once again. He bought a leaky old tub, the *Lively*, and carried out several hazardous smuggling missions in her. Fearing drowning on further forays, Rattenbury beached the boat for repairs, and bought the *Neptune*. With the wreck of the *Neptune*, the *Lively* came back into use, but was in turn seized at Brixham, and Rattenbury forfeited a £160 bond. He commented that, on top of the loss of two boats the loss of the bond 'was a great shock to my circumstances', but continued in the next breath, 'Not long after this disaster, I bought part of a 12-oared boat, which was 53 feet keel and 60 feet aloft'. Clearly he was not short of cash.

Rattenbury's principal smuggling method in the early years seems to have been to buy tubs in the Channel Islands, and sink them off the English coast for later collection. As the nineteenth century proceeded, Rattenbury began to make trips direct to France—usually to Cherbourg. This in good weather took a day or less.

He didn't confine himself to smuggling conventional cargoes, but also considered other enterprises, some successful, some not so profitable. He was caught smuggling out French prisoners, but excused himself by saying he thought they came from Jersey. The magistrates ticked him off and sent him home.

Rattenbury's book also reveals much of the ups and downs of smuggling. He tried to give up the trade and run a pub, but this proved far from lucrative and in 1813 he shut up the pub, commenting, 'there was scarcely anything to be done in smuggling'. And in early 1814 'in consequence of the fluctuating nature of our public affairs, smuggling was also at a stand'. (At this time there was a temporary lull in the Napoleonic wars—Napoleon was in exile on Elba).

Rattenbury's shipping transactions cast an interesting perspective on the values of the day. Piloting proved very lucrative for him—sometimes paying £100 in a storm . . . he bought a boat for £200 . . . his bail was set at £200 . . . he payed a fine of £200. His fortunes seemed to vary wildly. At times he must have lived hand-to-mouth, because a two-month attack of gout is a considerable set-back.

All in all, though, Jack painted a swashbuckling picture of himself, and probably forms the model for many a fictional smuggler to this day.

Rattenbury mentioned many places by name in the text, but few that are specifically identifiable today: Beer, Brixham, Seaton Bay,

John Hurley, Custom House Officer ... was endeavouring to extinguish some Fire made between Beer and Seaton as a Signal to a Smuggling Boat then off at Sea. He Fell by some means or other from the Top of the Cliff to the bottom by which He was unfortunately killed.

The epitaph goes on to describe the officer as active, diligent and inoffensive. Evidently the local smugglers paid more attention to the former two attributes when they hastened his descent over the cliff.

The Branscombe smugglers hid contraband in a novel way that apparently has no parallel elsewhere in Britain. They dug a sloping tunnel leading to the centre of a field, then at its end hollowed out a circular pit, some 12 feet underground. The entrance to the chamber was concealed using earth and turf. These storage places have been repeatedly uncovered during farming, and in 1953 an estate map showed the location of no less than six of them, found between 1909 and 1939.[11]

Smuggling continued in the Branscombe area as late as the 1850s, and at that time the Brays of Woodhead Farm were deeply implicated. Samuel Bray was betrayed for his involvement, and served a prison sentence as a result, but young George Bray was taught his smuggling skills by an old farm-hand, and escaped capture on at least one occasion with aid from the old man. The two of them were returning from Budleigh Salterton one night in 1758 with a cart-load of tubs, when they heard the exciseman in hot pursuit, near the summit of Trow Hill, just outside Sidmouth. The 18-year-old took the reins and the old man hurled the tubs one by one into the ditch, then curled up under the tarpaulin and feigned sleep. When the preventive arrived, he cried triumphantly, 'At last I've caught you red-handed!' but was met by a blank stare from George, who replied, 'We be goin' t'Beer Quarry to vetch lime'. A search of the wagon needless to say revealed nothing, and when the coast was clear the two were able to retrace their steps and locate the barrels.

At Woodhead farm the tubs were concealed in a pit alongside the cowshed. This was covered by tree-trunks, and on this firm support was a hay-rick. To reach the pit, there was a tunnel leading under the cowshed.

OFFWELL AND WILMINGTON ■3

Offwell 192-SY195995 is 2m SE of Honiton. Batt's Close is at 192-ST193002, just off the A35. At Wilmington the School House is at 192-SY212999 on the A35, some 3m E of Honiton. The School House is next door to the old school—now the village hall.

This area provided many a tub-carrier for the smugglers of Branscombe and Beer.

A sunken lane at one time led towards the coast at Seaton, and joined up with the main London road close to Batt's Close, a cottage in the village. Though it has now been developed for much of its length, a section of the sunken road remains and is known locally as Featherbed Lane.[12] Sunken lanes are a fairly common feature in the south-west, particularly on routes leading down to coves from the cliff top. Embankments on either side conceal from view anyone passing down to the sea.[13]

A descendant of one of the Offwell smugglers described in 1953 how his grandfather had helped land cargoes. Tubs were off-loaded to a particularly inaccessible beach at the foot of a 400-ft cliff close to Branscombe and Salcombe Regis. The tub-men then appeared at the top of the cliff with a long rope, and tied a farm gate to one end. One of their number was then lowered to the beach, where he loaded the gate with tubs, and was hoisted up again. This system was not foolproof—on at least one run, the rope broke and the smuggler dashed out his brains on the rocks below. The recollections were in this case particularly vivid, and only third-hand (!), since the father and grandfather of the old man relating the story both lived into their nineties.

Batt's Close in Offwell at first glance appears pretty but unexceptional, built in a style typical of much of the vernacular architecture of Devon and Cornwall. Look more closely at the eastern gable end, though, and you will see a couple of glass bullseyes just below the eaves. These are bottle bottoms—a traditional sign that the house-owner was sympathetic to smugglers.

The house was in fact at one time the home of Jack Rattenbury (see page 96), and is also reputed to have been used at various times by other smugglers. At Wilmington there is a similar bottle in the eastern gable end of the old school-house.

Right: *Whole village communities were involved in smuggling and informers were often murdered. Here in Branscombe, punishment was more humane. Villagers formed an elaborate procession and then burned the informer's effigy on a bonfire.*

Opposite: *In Branscombe graveyard the inscription on a table tomb provides a poignant reminder that many customs officers died grisly deaths in the battle to prevent smuggling.*

SAMPFORD PEVERELL ■4

181-ST0314, 5m E of Tiverton.

Smugglers hid contraband in an elm in the churchyard here; in 1874 the tree was 'perfectly hollow', and the only entrance was from the top.[14]

Stories of hauntings were rife in the area in the early years of the nineteenth century, and one explanation is that the incidents may have been staged by the Beer smugglers, who were known to pass through the area, and who would have been anxious to draw attention away from their activities. The Old Haunted House, as it was called, was at the extreme north-west end of the village, and at the turn of the century was used as a bakery and grocer. The house was reputed to have double walls, which made it a fine place to store contraband. However, rolling barrels would have caused some considerable amount of noise, which—so the story goes—was concealed by the ghostly howls and thumps:

> The chambers of the house were filled, even in day-time, with thunderous noises, and upon any persons stamping several times on the floors of the upstairs room, they would find themselves imitated—only much louder—by this mysterious agency.

One owner of the house, in seeking to explain the noises, said that the sound was made by 'a cooper banging tubs with a broomstick'. For 'cooper' read 'smuggler' perhaps—a man equally likely to have a tub handy.

SALCOMBE REGIS ■5

192-SY1488, 2m NE of Sidmouth.

Branscombe and Beer smugglers used to land goods all along the coast between Lyme and Exmouth, and this village was widely used as a staging post. The church there made a handy storage place for contraband,[15] and an old sexton born in the parish in 1803 noted that:

> The main smuggler was Mutter of Harcombe, who kept a public [house] at Exmouth and when riding officers wanted to know if a run was on, they would go to his house for a pint, and if the old man could not show up it was look out for the next tide. He was more artful than Rattenbury. Two Branscombe farmers smuggled too. Dimond's brother kept Trow turnpike and informed against a wagon that went through with goods. A procession was made through the three parishes with his likeness and then burned. Williams and Bray paid for this.[16]

This account is particularly interesting for a number of reasons. First, it identifies the Branscombe farmers—the Brays—as those who partly paid for the procession and effigy, and confirms their involvement. The convicted smuggler was in fact Sam Bray, who went to prison on the evidence of the gate-keeper. Secondly, the effigy itself and the burning give credence to the widely held belief that West Country smugglers both enjoyed wider support than elsewhere in Britain, and were more humane. In other counties informers would almost certainly have been murdered.

The 'public' mentioned in the account was a cider shop which stood 'on the corner of Hamilton Road, just beyond Waterworks Cottage'[17] in Exmouth.

Another Salcombe man observed:

> I have carried scores of kegs up the cliff. We used to strike a match and hold it in our hands a moment to call the boats in. The loads were then shouldered into a pit with a lid at Paccombe Bottom, or by the turnpike in the hedge there, and waggoned on afterwards.[18] Once they were in Slade cellar but the [revenue officers] called and [the kegs] were only just in time started down the drain; it made the rats squeak. It was a pity for they were a nice lot of tubs . . . The goods used to come in a cutter called

Primrose . . . it was her J Rattenbury steered with his foot . . . She was taken often by the coastguards, but generally had her papers right. She used to bring potatoes from Guernsey, but one day they caught her in a gale without ballast; she had just started [discharging] her cargo and that determined them [identified the crew as smugglers]. They sawed her in half, for they said nothing else would stop her. I knew Rattenbury and have heard he cut the [responsible] officer up for crab bait, but [Jack] always laughed if it was thrown up at him and said it happened down Dawlish way by a Sussex man. The last cargo was Mutter's laid up under High Peak.[19] G Salter watched all day from under a furze bush but about 4pm a stranger (gentleman to look at) came under Cliff and strolled right up to the tubs. The man in charge got as mad as fire but he had to lump it for if he'd spoken they would have taken him.

SIDMOUTH ■6

Mutter's Moor lies just outside the town at 192-SY1087. Leave Sidmouth on a minor road heading W towards Otterton. After a steep climb over Peak Hill the road slopes down, and a track leading to Mutter's Moor leaves the road to the right on a sharp left-hand bend.

Mutter's Moor, on the fringes of Sidmouth, takes its name from the Abraham Mutter mentioned in both quotes above. Mutter was one of Jack Rattenbury's accomplices, and helped to distribute contraband. Mutter cut wood and turf at Peak Hill and carried the fuel into nearby towns for sale. This innocent activity acted as a convenient cover for the transport and sale of contraband, especially so since the biggest houses would consume large quantities of both fuel and brandy. Frequent visits by Mutter's carts and donkeys therefore aroused no suspicion. A newspaper story relates that:

> Rattenbury was at the peak of his career at about this time, and Mutter worked for him for years, so profitably, it appears, that when Rattenbury eventually retired, Sam Mutter, who was a lifelong sailor, stepped into his shoes and continued to provide the supplies for his enterprising brother, and later for John, who has also joined the business.[20]

Numerous stories surround the Mutter family. One tells how Sam was sent to prison in 1843 for smuggling, and his release was eagerly anticipated by friends and family. However, the star guest at the welcome-home party failed to arrive as scheduled. Fully three months passed before he reappeared once more—with a cargo of contraband. The Mutters' involvement apparently ended when the railway brought cheap coal to the area, killing off the convenient and effective cover.

EAST BUDLEIGH ■7

192-SY0684, 2m N of Budleigh Salterton.

Two of the vicars of this village were reputedly involved in smuggling, over the period 1741 to 1852, using the fifteenth-century rectory (since named Vicar's Mead) to plan landing of cargoes at the mouth of the Otter.[21] The room used for this purpose was the Parish Room, now a bedroom, and its thick walls conceal two secret passages, 18 inches wide, on the north and south sides. There are also rumours that a tunnel led away from the house to the church.

Opposite: *Today place names commemorate the era of smuggling on the sheltered estuary of the River Teign: you can still visit a Smuggler's Lane and a Smuggler's Tunnel, both within a couple of miles of Teignmouth town.*

DAWLISH AND TEIGNMOUTH ■8

The Mount Pleasant Inn is at 192-SX978782 in Dawlish Warren, 4m NE of Teignmouth. Smugglers Lane is on the left at Holcombe 192-SX955748 about halfway from Dawlish to Teignmouth on the A379. It winds down to the sea and the railway.

Smugglers sailing in to the Exe had the advantage enjoyed by anyone landing goods at an estuary: once the land-guard was located, the cargo could safely be run on the opposite shore, with the knowledge that the lowest bridging point was a long ride upstream. Bribing the ferry-man or getting him drunk was a useful precaution and on the west side of the Exe the ferry-men were frequently and lavishly entertained in the Mount Pleasant Inn at Dawlish Warren. Smugglers often used the pub, and stowed contraband in nearby caves that the landlord obligingly hollowed for them in the soft soil. The windows of the pub were also used for signalling with a lantern, presumably to indicate which side of the estuary was safe. Goods were brought to the pub from the beach at the Warren itself, which until the arrival of the railway was virtually a no-go area and a hide-out for villains, brigands and highwaymen of all sorts, quite apart from smugglers. Other landing spots nearby were at Teignmouth, where caves were used for storage,[22] and a narrow inlet at Holcombe, on the road to Teignmouth. A storage cave at Holcombe was destroyed when the railway was built, but the track leading down to the secluded inlet is still called Smuggler's Lane.

The free-trade era is also commemorated at Shaldon on the south side of the Teign estuary, facing Teignmouth. The sheltered estuary was a favoured landing spot,[23] and a smuggler's tunnel cuts through the cliff, leading to Shaldon beach.

ST MARYCHURCH ■9

202-SX9166, 1m N of Torquay town centre.

Next to the Post Office in Park Road there is a small house used by smugglers, where there was once a hiding-place under the hearth. Maidencombe Farm to the north, and Rocombe Farm, also had places for concealing tubs.[24]

Storing the contraband wasn't the end of the story for local smugglers: distribution was also open to detection. Some Devon smugglers made a habit of carrying illicit spirits in pig-skins. One man at least escaped conviction by puncturing the skins, thus destroying the evidence, when he saw a revenue man approaching. Women with a 'skin-full' of spirits about themselves had a particular advantage, for they could not be legally searched,[25] and a woman hawker from St Marychurch used this technique to great effect, hiding the skin under her shawl.

BRIXHAM ■10

202-SX9255, 5m S of Torquay. Berry Head is to the E of the town.

Smugglers here had a wily reputation: 'Resurrection' Jackman reputedly used his own funeral as a ruse for moving the goods inland. Revenue men appeared at the door of Jackman's house armed with cast-iron evidence against him, and were met by a house-full of wailing women. Jackman, they were told, was dead, and was to be buried in Totnes; the corpse was to be taken there the following night. However the custom-house officers were made suspicious by the vast size of the coffin, and decided to keep watch on the funeral cortege.

Brixham was home to several legendary smugglers, and was a regular port of call for Jack Rattenbury. The cutter in the centre of the picture is typical of the craft used by nineteenth-century smugglers.

Opposite below: Cawsand smugglers defrauded the revenue on a massive scale. One contemporary estimate puts the numbers of barrels imported illegally here in 1804 as 17,000.

The two officers assigned to the duty had difficulty making out the procession in the pitch black, but to their horror, they were soon met by Jackman himself—pale as death, and riding a spectral horse:

. . . The nag cocked his tale
like a harpooned whale
and snorted a crimson flame.

Screaming with fear, they fled. In reality, of course, the coffin contained brandy, which made its way safely on to Totnes—possibly to the Bay Horse Inn, which was a notorious watering-hole for smugglers.

Curiously, this legend crops up again, with small changes of detail, nearby. However, in the second version, the 'dead' man is Bob Elliot, who stored contraband in a cave at Berry Head.[26] The cave was said to be connected to the Laywell, a spring close to upper Brixham.

BURGH ISLAND ■11

202-SX6443, 5m S of Modbury. The island is accessible on foot at low tide. Tom Crocker's hole is accessible only by sea.

Burgh Island was the smuggling domain of Tom Crocker. He gave his name to a cave on the coast of the island, and spent most of the time when he wasn't at sea, in the Pilchard Inn.[27] However, little else seems to be known of the smuggler and his activities.

CAWSAND AND KINGSAND ■12

201-SX4350 on the W shore of Plymouth Sound. Approach the villages via the B3247, then on minor roads. Restricted street parking in the village centre during the summer season; use the car-parks or park outside and walk in.

The vast natural harbour of Plymouth had a naval presence throughout the eighteenth and nineteenth centuries which made smuggling activity more difficult, but apparently did not preclude it completely. The city itself formed the largest market for Devon and Cornwall contraband, so it's not surprising to find some notorious villages nearby. The twin villages of Cawsand and Kingsand owe their pre-eminence in the trade to their position: goods brought in there could be easily ferried across the harbour to Plymouth.

In the last years of the eighteenth century a visitor to Cawsand described it in vivid terms:

We descended a very steep hill, amidst the most fetid and disagreeable odour of stinking pilchards and train oil, into the town . . . In going down the hill . . . we met several females, whose appearance was so grotesque and extraordinary, that I could not imagine in what manner they had contrived to alter their natural

Dartmouth was a centre for the prevention of smuggling, but some port officials saw their positions as a licence to print money. Christopher Blackroller was collector of customs here, but his cellar was full of contraband goods which he had accepted as bribes.

shapes so completely; till, upon enquiry, we found that they were smugglers of spiritous liquors; which they were at that time conveying from cutters at Plymouth, by means of bladders fastened under their petticoats; and, indeed, they were so heavily laden, that it was with great apparent difficulty that they waddled along.

The main hazard to this trade, it appears, was not the customs authorities, but drunken sailors who delighted in puncturing the bladders.

Cawsand and Kingsand merge so seamlessly that it is difficult to imagine the bitter rivalry that once existed between the two communities. Both towns were hotbeds of smuggling—in 1804 the revenue services estimated that 17,000 kegs of spirits had been landed here in just one year.

Harry Carter (see page 112), a famous Cornwall smuggler, frequently used Cawsand for his illicit activities, and on one of these trips his boat was boarded by sailors from a man-of-war anchored nearby. In the hand-to-hand fighting that ensued, he sustained a cutlass wound that almost killed him.

Cawsand carried on legitimate business as a boat-building centre, but even this activity was not entirely innocent: the village was the source of many smuggling luggers. This design of boat drew very little water —very handy for trips up shallow estuaries with muffled oars.

Smuggling goods into the Plymouth Sound was a simple matter in the early part of the nineteenth century, despite the strong military presence. Before clearing customs in Plymouth, vessels unloaded their cargoes of illicit spirits at Cawsand, just a couple of miles from the spot where the unsuspecting dragoon idly chats in the picture here.

LOOE ■13

201-SX2553, 7m S of Liskeard.

The open beaches of Whitsand Bay made a fine landing when the coast was sufficiently clear for covert runs, but smugglers seeking a more discreet approach headed for Looe, and brought the goods ashore on Looe Island. There are various stories about the inhabitants of the island and their involvement in the trade. One story names them as Hamram and his daughter 'Tilda; another account makes them brother and sister —Fyn and Black Joan, who moved to the island from the Mewstone at the mouth of Plymouth Sound after their outlaw father died. They were said to have eaten every rat and rabbit on the island!

The pair stored contraband in a cave which was hidden even from the smugglers, who paid a fee for each tub concealed. The cave's custodians liaised with a farmer on the mainland. When he was able to divert the customs authorities, or when he knew they posed no threat to a landing, he would ride his white horse along the coast. This acted as a signal to the islanders, who would then use a lamp to tell the smugglers waiting off-shore that the coast was clear. If there was danger, the farmer would walk the horse home.

Some of these stories perhaps seem a little far-fetched, but locals repeating them back up the yarns by recounting how a picnic party on the island once rushed into a barn to shelter from a storm, and fell through the floor into a hidden cache of spirits.[28]

In West Looe Ye Olde Jolly Sailor was a smuggler's haunt, and here too the story is told of how the quick-thinking landlady once concealed an illicit keg beneath her petticoats during an unexpected raid. While the preventives searched, she calmly knitted.

TALLAND ■14

201-SX2251, 2m W of Looe on a minor road off the A387 to Polperro. Restricted parking near the beach (fee).

The village of Talland was at one time a thriving community, and the bay was a favourite landfall for smuggling boats from the Continent. All that now remains of the village is the church high on the steep hill above Talland Bay.

Near the door of the church in the south-west corner there is an interesting tombstone commemorating Robert Mark. Like others in the graveyard, this elegantly carved stone carries a rhyming epitaph:

Erected to the memory of Robert Mark, late of Polperro, who was unfortunately shot at sea, the 24th of January in the year of our Lord God 1802, in the 40th year of his age.

In prime of life, most suddenly,
Sad tidings to relate,
Here view my utter destiny,
And pity my sad state.
I by a shot which rapid flew,
Was instantly struck dead.

Lord pardon the offender who
My precious blood did shed.
Grant him to rest, and forgive me
All I have done amiss:
And that I may be rewarded
With everlasting Bliss.

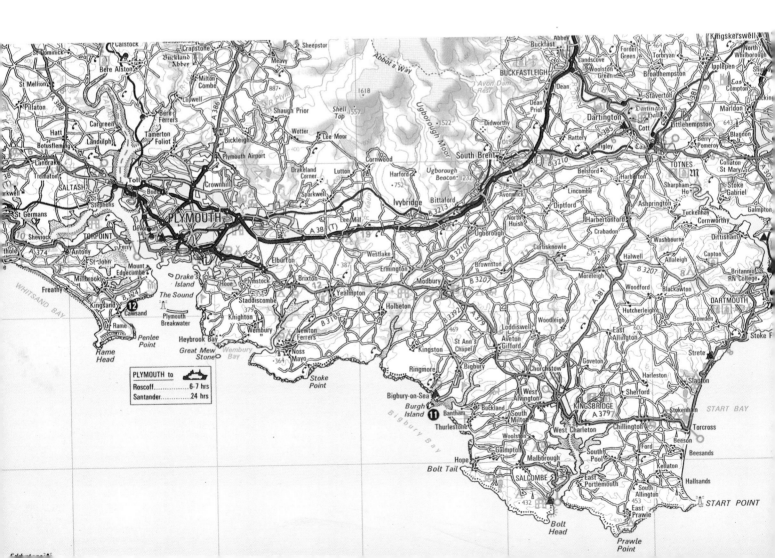

Here at Polperro, the observant visitor might catch a glimpse of the headless ghost of smuggler Battling Billy, as he drives his hearse-load of barrels down the narrow streets.

Local legends differ about Mark's identity. One story has it that while on a smuggling trip he died from wounds inflicted by a revenue man's pistol ball. This is borne out both by the details on the tombstone, and by the fact that a smuggler of the same name was sentenced in May 1799 for resisting arrest when the smuggling vessel *Lottery* (see below) was captured. However, another account makes him not a free-trader but a revenue man who was shot in a cellar on dry land; Jonah Puckey, the ringleader of a smuggling gang, reputedly fired the shot that killed him.

One of the vicars of Talland in the eighteenth century, the Rev. Richard Dodge, had a reputation for raising and laying ghosts at will. Parishioners were said to be afraid of meeting him at night for fear of his devilish accomplices. It seems likely, however, that he fostered these stories to keep people out of the way while the smuggling went on.

POLPERRO ■15

201-SX2051, 5 miles W of Looe on the A387. If possible, visit in the early morning to miss the crowds. Park on the cliff-tops on either side of the village, and approach the harbour using the South-west Coast Path. The Polperro smuggling museum houses a small collection of pictures and other items associated with the free-trade.

Polperro is a village of contrasts: Approach from the cliffs, and it is easy to imagine what this charming port was like when it was a favourite landfall for smugglers of lace, brandy and tea. The popular tourist approach, on the other hand, requires the visitor to run the gauntlet of chip and souvenir shops, and gives no hint of the treat awaiting at the foot of the hill. The harbour area survives almost intact, surrounded by white and pastel-painted houses looking out across the water.

A particularly colourful Polperro legend involves 'Battling Billy', who ran the Halfway House Inn. Faced with the perennial problem of transporting kegs of brandy inland without being detected by the preventive services, he hit on the idea of using a hearse. The ruse worked well for a while, but Billy ran into trouble when one cargo had to be unloaded by daylight. Just as the last keg was being pushed into the hearse, the revenue men arrived, and Billy whipped the horses into a ferocious gallop, shouting back 'If they shoot me dead, my body'll drive the load to Polperro'.

According to the story, this is precisely what happened: a bullet went clean through Billy's neck, so that his head hung limp and lifeless, but his whip-hand continued to urge the horses on. When they reached Polperro, the dead man drove straight down the main street, off the quayside and into the harbour. Battling Billy's ghost still haunts the narrow cobbled streets.

Rooted more in fact is the tragic story of the *Lottery*, a Polperro smuggling vessel much wanted by the customs authorities. The most well-known version of the story had its origins in a nineteenth-century history of the village,[29] and is sympathetic towards the Polperro smugglers' cause.

When the Cawsand customs men saw the ship becalmed half a mile from Penlee Point, they thought their luck was in, and in due course they put to sea in several rowing-boats. The crew of the *Lottery*, seeing that capture was imminent, set to work preparing for battle, and the preventive forces responded by opening fire when they were still some distance away. As the gap closed, a figure on the deck of the *Lottery* took aim and fired, and almost immediately one of the crew in the King's boat dropped at the oar, dying of his wounds. Seeing this, the boats headed back to port, and the incensed authorities put out orders to seize the crew of the *Lottery*.

The seamen became outlaws in their own village. Some lay concealed in cramped hiding-places in their homes; others fled. But eventually one of the *Lottery* crew, Toms, came forward and pointed the finger at Tom Potter as the man who pulled the trigger.

Potter was still free, and Toms became a marked man. As a key witness, he was taken on board a government cutter, and became—effectively—a prisoner himself. However, the Polperro men managed to lure him ashore by arranging a rendezvous with his wife, and Toms was seized at Lantick and spirited away to Guernsey, *en route* for America.

In Polperro, all eyes were on the patrolling dragoons, and the authorities initially had little success in tracing Potter. However, by raiding the town from the west, they managed to surprise the smuggler in his home, and he was taken to London for trial.

Meanwhile, Toms the informer had been tracked down in the Channel Islands, and was therefore able to give evidence at the trial. He never saw the shot fired, but claimed that Potter had come down from the deck and, swearing, said he had 'done for one of them'. On this evidence alone, Potter was executed.

In Polperro there was fury at the injustice of the conviction. According to one report, the slaughtered oarsman had been killed by a member of his own crew, and the musket ball had entered his body from the side facing away from the *Lottery*. Toms would surely have been murdered had he returned home, and since he would be a valuable witness in the trial of the other members of the crew (who remained at large) he was kept at Newgate. He was employed there in some menial capacity until his death.

There is, of course, another side to the story. Government records[30] and evidence at Potter's trial assert that the smugglers fired first, and the men in the custom-house boat opened fire only when one of their crew members had been shot. The crew-man who died was shot in the front of his head, and though some suggest that this is proof that he was shot from the *Lottery*, it is hardly conclusive. Certainly if he was looking at the smugglers' ship when he fell, the ball would have passed through his forehead. But pulling on oars, he would have faced away from the *Lottery*.

However, the most convincing evidence that the shot came from the *Lottery* is to be found in the records of the trial. The defence never argued that the boatman had been felled by a government bullet, which they would surely had done if there was thus any chance of avoiding the noose.

FOWEY ■16

200-SX1251, 6m E of St Austell. The town can be approached from either side of the Fowey Estuary. There is an all-year-round vehicle ferry service across the river, and a frequent passenger ferry nearby. Parking is difficult at busy times.

The story of an abortive landing in 1835 close to Fowey, and its court sequel, is especially interesting in that it illustrates how difficult it was for the customs authorities to secure convictions from a local jury, even when all the evidence pointed to guilt.

Two coastguards from Fowey went to Lantick Hill, and hid in bushes near Pencannon[31] Point. After a wait, at least 100 men arrived on the beach—20 of them bat-men. One of the coastguards went to get help, and meanwhile, the activity on the beach continued out of sight of his mate. When reinforcements arrived, the party of six plucky preventives

challenged the smugglers, and there was a fierce battle; one of the coastguards was knocked unconscious, but five smugglers were eventually arrested. A party from the revenue cutter *Fox* evetually met up with the six coastguards, and captured 484 gallons of brandy.

When the case came to court, the men were charged with 'assisting others in landing and carrying away prohibited goods, some being armed with offensive weapons'. The defence argued that the clubs were just walking sticks—this despite the fact that the group had been caught red-handed. The local vicar was called as a character witness from one of the accused, and local farmers vouched for the good name of the others. The judge pointed out when summing up that if the coastguard had been killed, instead of just being knocked out, the five prisoners would have been on a murder charge. Despite this, the jury acquitted, adding that they did not consider the clubs to be offensive weapons.[32]

Contraband from this abortive landing may have been headed for the Crown and Anchor Inn on the quayside at Fowey, since the smuggler Richard Kingcup was at one time the landlord there.[33]

MEVAGISSEY ■17

204-SX0144, 5 miles S of St Austell on the B3273. Parking very restricted.

Like Cawsand, Mevagissey was a town renowned for its ship builders. The large vessels built here in the eighteenth century when smuggling still took place relatively openly were capable of tremendous speeds, and could make the crossing from Roscoff in a day or less. Ship builders here also constructed vessels for the preventive forces, and the trade still continues at the port.

THE ROSELAND PENINSULAR ■18

204-SW8530, directly across the Carrick Roads from Falmouth. Topographical evidence would suggest that the boat mentioned below was carried from Towan Beach (204-SW872328) to the inlet at Froe, across what is now the minor road leading to St Anthony's Head.

Smuggling stories here centre on St Anthony's Head and the peninsula leading to it. At one point only a narrow strip of lowland separates the sea from the creek that flows into the Percuil River, and though the stories are told so as to make either the smuggler or the revenue service look foolish, a common feature is one side outwitting the other by carrying a light boat overland while the other side watches from the headland. One story tells of a St Mawes customs officer who realized that the Portscatho smugglers operating in Gerrans Bay kept watch on hills overlooking St Mawes harbour, so that they had time to disperse if a revenue boat approached around the headland. By carrying a small boat across the isthmus, he mounted a surprise attack.[34]

St Mawes was the base for Robert Long, a seventeenth-century smuggler who met an untimely end—he was executed, and his body was hung in chains on the road from the town to Ruan Lanihorne.[35]

THE FAL AND TRESILLIAN RIVERS

King Harry Vehicle Ferry ■19 now takes the B3289 from Truro to St Mawes across King Harry's Passage near Trelissick House at 204-SW8439. The ferry avoids a 30-mile detour through Truro, but the service is restricted outside the tourist season. Check locally for details, especially evenings and weekends.
Malpas ■20 (204-SW8442) is a small pleasant settlement about 2m S of Truro along a minor road. From the waterside, you can look out across to Sunset Creek (204-SW8442). The tombstone mentioned is in the churchyard at Mylor Churchtown ■21 (204-SW820352), at the intersection of two paths a little way from one of the waterside gates.

The tree-like branches of the creeks and tidal inlets of these rivers make communications difficult for the modern-day traveller, but the situation was completely the reverse for the waterborne smuggler, and there are many local reminders of the smuggling era. Close to Truro, Sunset Creek opposite Malpas was the site of Penpol Farm, which featured a sunken road and hiding-places in caves and woodland.[36] Tresillian creek to the east and Mylor Creek to the south were also popular landing-places. At Mylor there is a memorial dated 1814 to a fisherman who had the misfortune to be shot in error by revenue men. His epitaph reads:

> We have not a moment we can call our own.
> Official zeal in luckless hour laid wait
> And wilful sent the murderous ball of Fate!
> James to his home, which late in health he left,
> wounded returns—of life is soon bereft.

Just to the south of Mylor, at Penryn, local legend tells of a tunnel linking the shore of St Gluvias' Vicarage, and farther down the creek on the south side, there are two caves used for storage. A tunnel on the same site has now been blocked.[37]

Near to one of these creeks in 1801 a mounted smuggler carrying two ankers of spirits was surprised by a customs man. The incident occurred on the steep road leading down to King Harry's Passage. The two raced down the hill, the revenue man gaining all the time. The smuggler eventually plunged into the water to escape, but the exhausted horse was in danger of drowning, so the smuggler dismounted and cut free the barrels. Despite being relieved of its burden and aided by his rider swimming alongside supporting his head, the nag drowned. The smuggler escaped, but with the help of the ferryman the preventive rescued the barrels.[38]

FALMOUTH AREA ■22

Falmouth is at 204-SW8032. Helford lies some 4m SW at 204-SW7526.

The smugglers of this busy port operated on an extraordinary scale, and used a whole range of techniques from subterfuge through to bribery and outright thuggery. An incident in 1762 illustrates just one spectacular aspect of the local trade.

The crews of the East Indiamen returning to Britain habitually sold goods to visiting locals, but at Falmouth the practice was taken to extremes. Three ships from China anchored in the bay, and for a fortnight held a regular on-board bazaar, selling silk, muslin, dimities, china, tea, arrack, handkerchiefs and other goods. The town was filled with people of every rank who lived within a 20-mile radius, and the ships drained the area of cash; a writer estimated that through the private adventures of the East Indiamen's crews, £20,000 worth of business was concluded, and complained that 'a week after ye ships sailed I could not get a bill of exchange from any merchant in town'. He added, 'The captains and officers are allowed large priveleges (*sic*), and there are ways and means of dealing with Custom-house officers . . .'.

This ship entering Fowey harbour might well have been smuggling goods for the mayor. A search of his house in 1824 revealed a large cache of contraband. Investigating a cracking noise from upstairs, the customs men found that an accomplice had broken so many illicit bottles that the wine and brandy ran 3 inches deep on the floor.

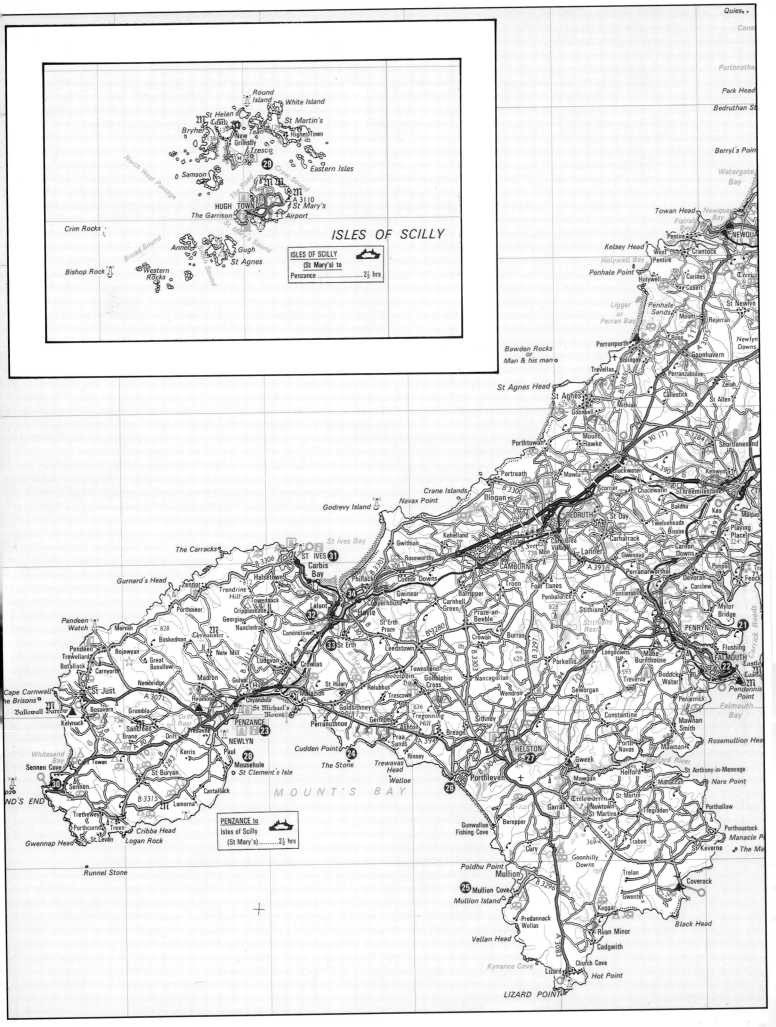

ISLES OF SCILLY

Quies

Const

Porthcotha

Park Head

Bedruthan St

Berry's Point

Watergate Bay

Towan Head Newquay Bay

Fistral Bay NEWQUAY

Kelsey Head West Pentire Crantock

Holywell Bay Pentire

Penhale Point Holywell Carines

Ligger or Perran Bay Cubert Trerice

Penhale Sands Mount Rejerrah St Newlyn

Rose Goonhavern Newlyn Downs

Perranporth Bolingey Zelah

Trevellas Perranzabuloe St Allen

Bawden Rocks or Man & his man Callestick

St Agnes Head St Agnes Mithian

Goonbell Shortlanesend

Porthtowan Mount Hawke Kenwyn

Portreath Mawla Blackwater Threemilestone

Crane Islands Scorrier Chacewater Baldhu

Navax Point Illogan Poole St Day Bissoe Playing Place

Godrevy Island REDRUTH Twelveheads Carnon Downs

St Ives Bay Kehelland Carn Brea Village Lanner Gwennap Penpol

The Carracks Gwithian Troon Carharrack Perranarworthal Feock

ST IVES Roseworthy CAMBORNE Penhalurick Mylor Bridge

Gurnard's Head Carbis Bay Connor Downs Barripper Stithians PENRYN

Zennor Phillack Gwinear Carnhell Green Burras Flushing

Trendrine Hill Hayle Praze-an-Beeble Stithians Resr FALMOUTH

Porthmeor Towednack Lelant St Erth Praze Crowan Mabe Burnthouse Castle

Pendeen Watch Cripplesease Leedstown Porkellis Longdowns Treverva Pendennis Point

Morvah Georgia Nancledra St Erth Townshend Ramey Buddock Water Falmouth Bay

Pendeen Boskednan Chysauster Canonstown Godolphin Nancegollan Penjerrick

Trewellard New Mill Ludgvan Crowlas Cross Wendron Constantine Rosemullion Hea

Botallack Madron Relubbus Sithney Porth Navas Mawnan Smith

Carnyorth Great Bosullow Gulval St Hilary Trescowe Mawnan

Cape Cornwall Newbridge Heamoor Marazion Goldsithney Germoe HELSTON Gweek Helford St Anthony-in-Meneage

The Brisons St Just Chyandour St Michael's Mount Perranuthnoe Ashton Breage Mawgan Manaccan Nare Point

Ballowall Barrow Bosaven PENZANCE Praa Sands Rinsey Trelowarren St Martin Porthallow

Kelynack Sancreed NEWLYN Cudden Point Tregonning Hill Garras (Newtown in St Martins) Tregidden Porthoustock

Brane Drift Paul The Stone Trewavas Head Porthleven Manacle P

Grumbla Tredavoe Welloe Berepper St Keverne The Ma

Sennen Cove Mousehole MOUNT'S BAY Gunwalloe Fishing Cove Cury Goonhilly Downs Coverack

Sennen St Clement's Isle Poldhu Point Traboe

LAND'S END St Buryan Castallack Mullion Trelan Gwenter

Trethewey Lamorna PENZANCE to Isles of Scilly (St Mary's) 2½ hrs Mullion Cove Kuggar

Porthcurno Treen Cribba Head Mullion Island Predannack Wollas Ruan Minor Black Head

Gwennap Head St Levan Logan Rock Vellan Head Cadgwith

Runnel Stone Kynance Cove Church Cove Hot Point

LIZARD POINT Lizard

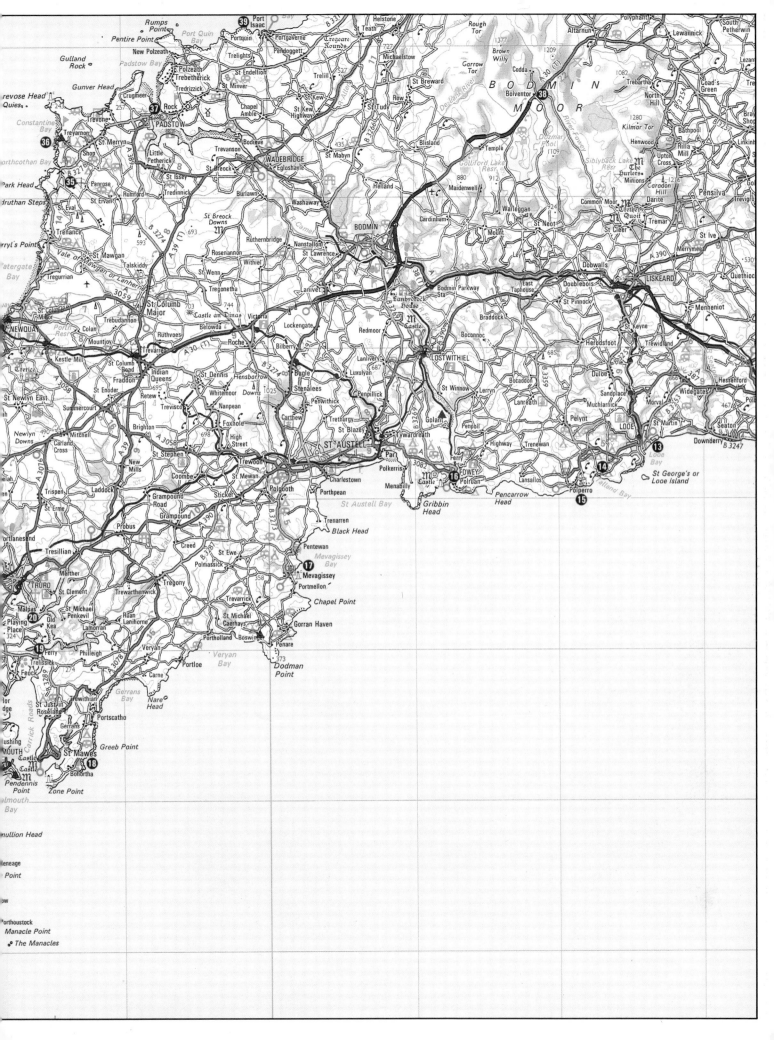

Clearly such ways and means were not universally effective, for when a similar incident happened three years later, an excise vessel came down from London and carried out several seizures. This in itself demonstrates how openly the trade was carried on, as a message had to be sent from Falmouth to London, and the excise vessel then had to return to make the seizure.[39]

The Falmouth postal packet ships were also heavily implicated in smuggling. The packet crews were not just entrepreneurs—they were so badly paid that they had little choice but to smuggle, just to live.

They ran what amounts to a mail order service. For example, the steward of the Manor-office ordered 24 hams from Portugal, and to reduce the risk of all being seized, he instructed that they should be sent in two consignments:

> . . . for as they are lyable to the Seizure of ye Custom house offic-ers, a greater number by one ship would be in danger . . . the best way to have them safe, I believe, will be to Send a trustey Servant for them, who will consult with the captain on ye safest means of escaping ye officers.[40]

War led to larger crews on the packet boats, and this in itself was good for trade in Falmouth. In 1739 one commentator could scarcely conceal his glee at the prospect of imminent war with Spain: 'There is something to be hoped, past experience teaching us that the Town will flourish in a French war'.

1743 brought an unexpected crack-down which strangled Falmouth trade. The same writer outlined the import/export service which the postal packet carriers had provided:

> . . . our shopkeepers . . . send over great quantities of woolen stockings, hatts, pewter and other goods to ye value of some thousand pounds by ye saylors for sale, upon getting a certain price upon ye goods to be paid for when sold (what the saylors make beyond the price set being their own), and if not to be returned. The Saylors on receiving ye money for ye goods at Lisbon lay it out in wines, Sugars, fruit and divers other things which they sell at an advantage when they come home, and so pay the shopkeepers either in money or in such Portugall comodityes as he deals in.

The writer then goes on to explain how the licensed wine-dealers and British traders in Portugal (who were, of course, being undercut) were spoiling it for everyone by complaining to the customs authorities, and as a result 'a pacquet on arriving would be rummaged and stripped of whatever goods were found in her'. This in itself was not usually a disaster, because under the former system, the customs men were gentlemen of honour, and the shopkeepers could get back the seized goods by:

> . . . gratifying ye officers who seized them, but this is now refused and severall bales of these goods bro't ashore from ye pacquets of late, are ordered to be condemned . . . The commissioners of the Customs are making sad work among our shopkeepers and pacquet people, and seem determined to break ye neck of the trade carryed on in these things, which I apprehend will be an ugly thing for the Falmouth people, this trade being ye best support of our shopkeepers.

The smugglers of Falmouth matched with cunning the vigilance of the collectors of customs. Newspaper reports from 24 May 1839 provide an interesting insight into the battle. A schooner loaded with coals docked in the harbour, and immediately attracted attention since the excisemen suspected the ship of being used for illicit activity, but had never been able to gather enough evidence. The coals were gradually unloaded, but the crew were so blasé about the operation that the customs authorities began to think they were barking up the wrong tree. However, when a customs officer set to work boring holes in the hull with a gimlet, the crew mysteriously melted away—obviously anticipating what was to happen next. Withdrawing the gimlet, the customs officer received a face-full of brandy from a tub stowed in a cavity between the false interior of the hull and the outside. There were 276 barrels of brandy and gin in the space, but the loss to the smugglers cannot have been too disastrous, since the ship had already been operating for three years without detection.[41]

The creeks south of Falmouth, notably at Gweek and Helford, also proved useful to smugglers seeking privacy for their activities, as did the beaches and small fishing ports at Porthallow, Porthoustock, Godrevy Cove, Coverack, Black Head and Kennack Sands. Smugglers from this area were apparently remarkably daring, and continued their

The deep water at Falmouth harbour provided a safe anchorage for even the largest ocean-going sailing ships, and much of the smuggling here was carried out by the crews of East Indiamen returning from the Orient.

St Michael's Mount was used by both smugglers and revenue men at different times in its history. In 1798 the customs authorities offered a reward of £50 for the capture of smugglers who broke open a cellar on the island and made off with four hogsheads of fine French wine.

activities even in the face of stiff opposition. In September 1840 a 30-strong gang of smugglers using several carts broke open the custom-house at Helford, and removed 126 half-ankers of brandy which had been confiscated a few days before at Coverack. They worked from 1 to 1.30, but generously left 3 barrels for the excisemen. The customs man on station heard the doors being forced, but was powerless to do anything as the nearest dwelling was ³/₄ mile away.

The tubs had been seized from the *Teignmouth*—they were lashed to the outside of the boat (although this technique was common in Kent, it was less convenient for the long crossing to Cornwall). When the vessel reached the beach at Gweek, the crew hailed two men on the beach for help. They proved to be customs officers, who drew their pistols and arrested crew, ship and cargo.[42]

MOUNT'S BAY

Beyond the Lizard from Falmouth is the golden curve of Mount's Bay, with St Michael's Mount set like a jewel on the western side. It is the most westerly point in the country protected from the Atlantic storms, and the natural shelter made the area especially suitable as a fishing base and, of course, for smuggling. The geographical situation lent itself to the free-trade in other ways, too. Mount's Bay was well-placed for trips to France, to the Channel Islands and the Scillies.

In the eighteenth and nineteenth centuries, the whole region was extremely isolated, and this helped the free-trade cause. Overland communication was very difficult, because the roads were little more than cart tracks. Prevention therefore centred on the sea, and Penzance, which looks out over the west side of the bay, was furnished with a revenue cutter at an early stage in the game.

PENZANCE ■23

203-SW4630.

The effectiveness of the Penzance force seems a little dubious, to say the least, and there are numerous accounts of how the laws on trade were flouted, often in front of the very eyes of preventive forces. In 1767 nine smugglers' vessels, including armed sloops, sailed from Penzance harbour in broad daylight; a man of war looked on, powerless to stop them. Five years later, a customs boat from Penzance was plundered and sunk by smugglers, and later the same year, another smugglers' ship captured the revenue cutter *Brilliant*, which was lying in Penzance harbour with seized goods on board.

The collector of customs at Penzance described how, in 1775, the smugglers worked in full view of the customs authorities:

Two Irish wherries full of men and guns (one about 130 tons, and the other less) came to anchor within the limits of this port, and within half a mile of the shore, and lay there three days, in open defiance discharging their contraband goods. We are totally destitute of any force to attack them by sea, and as the whole coast is principally inhabited by a lot of smugglers under the denomination of fishermen, it is next to an impossibility for the officers of the revenue to intercept any of these goods after they are landed . . . the officers, being on the look-out, saw a boat come off from one of [the wherries] and come ashore near where the officers had secreted themselves, and the crew began to land the goods. The officers interfered, and attempted to make a seizure of said boat and goods; but a blunderbuss was immediately presented to one of their breasts, and the smugglers, with great imprecations, threatened their lives.

On another occasion, a large wherry landed 1500–2000 ankers of spirits, 20 tons of tea and other goods on the beach here, and a local officer of the customs wrote the following plaintive letter to his superiors:

In the western part of this country, smuggling, since the soldiers have been drawn off, has been carried on almost without control. Irish wherries, carrying 14, 16 or more guns, and well manned, frequently land large quantities of goods in defiance of the officers of customs and excise, and their crew, armed with swords and pistols, escort the SS a considerable distance from the sea. In this way, goods are carried from one part of the country to another almost every night . . . The beach lies near a public road which, whilst the goods were discharging, was filled with armed men, in order to stop every traveller in whom they could not confide, till the goods were safely lodged in the country . . . A few days after, two officers got information that a very considerable quantity of goods was concealed in the house and premises of a well-known smuggler. They obtained from me a search warrant, but were forcibly hindered from executing it by four men, one armed with a pistol and a large whip, the others with sticks and bludgeons. They were told that if they persisted they would have their brains blown out. As the law now stands, I fear a criminal prosecution would have been useless for the reason, which it shocks me to mention, that a Cornish jury would certainly acquit the smugglers... These, my lord, are the facts. It would be mere pedantry to describe to your lordship the shocking effects, the moral and political consequences of smuggling carried to such a daring height, but I cannot help saying that perjury, drunkenness, idleness, poverty, and contempt of the law, and a universal corruption of manners are, in this neighbourhood, too plainly seen to accompany it.[43]

The principal reason for this unhindered activity was the weakness of the excisemen, the strength of the smugglers and the degree of local support. The trade involved the very cream of society, even up to the Lord Mayor's office: in 1770 the Mayor of Penzance was bound over with a large financial surety to cease smuggling.

Given the way the laws against smuggling were flouted in the town itself, it would be surprising if there were not support for the free-trade in the hinterland of Penzance. And indeed, a Madron man described how, when his father was apprenticed to a shoe-maker:

to vary the monotony of the work, however, they often turned out ... to Gorran or Portloe, ten miles away, to fetch home smuggled goods—chiefly brandy... On arriving home, the liquor was coloured the right shade with burnt sugar, after which it was returned to the kegs and sold to trusty customers.[44]

At Ludgvan, 2 miles north-east of Penzance, the customs officers could not sell seized liquor in 1748, because of the vast quantity smuggled in. Smugglers were asking 3s 3d a gallon for the illegally imported liquor: the reserve price on the seized goods was 5s 6d.

PRUSSIA COVE ■24

203-SW5527, 7m W. of Helston. The cove is approached along a minor road which leaves the A394 at Rosudgeon, some 7m W of Helston. There is a car-park a short walk from the bays.

The most famous smugglers of the Mount's Bay area, and perhaps of all Cornwall, hailed from Prussia Cove, which is just east of Cudden Point. The place actually takes its name from the soubriquet of one of the family who lived and worked here. John Carter was the self-styled 'King of Prussia', and together with two brothers, Harry and Charles, he ran an efficient and profitable smuggling operation that continued for many years.

John Carter is said to have got his nickname from boyhood games in which he regularly claimed to be the King of Prussia. The cove was formerly called Portleah, but gradually became known as 'the King of Prussia's Cove', and later just Prussia Cove or King's Cove on account of the Carter family's association with the area. The family used three small inlets for their business: Piskie's Cove on the west side, Bessy's Cove (named after the brewess who kept a beer shop on the cliff above), and King's Cove.

The spot has considerable natural advantages. It is:

... so sheltered and secluded that it is impossible to see what boats are in the little harbour until one literally leans over the edge of the cliff above; a harbour cut out of the solid rock and a roadway with wheel-tracks, partly cut and partly worn, climbing up the face of the cliff and either side of the cove, caves and the remains of caves everywhere, some of them with their mouths built up which are reputed to be connected with the house above by secret passages—these are still existing trademarks left by one

of the most enterprising smuggling gangs that Cornwall has ever known.

Certainly some of the fame of the family can be attributed to the autobiography written by Harry Carter. This was penned after he had seen the light, given up smuggling and retired as a preacher. The book is short, but still makes for heavy reading, rambling on for many pages. Nevertheless, Carter describes in the course of the narrative some hair-raising scenes.

One ill-fated smuggling trip took him to Cawsand—and almost to his death. As he guided the boat into the harbour, he assumed that the two small boats that came alongside were preparing to unload the contraband. Too late he realized they were from a man-of-war, and a fierce battle ensued. He was struck down, severely wounded, and left for dead, but after several hours his body was still warm although 'his head is all to atoms' as one of the guards observed. However, despite his injuries, he was able to crawl across the deck and drop into the water. Once in, he found—not surprisingly—that his stout swimming skill had deserted him, and he was forced to pull himself along ropes at the ship's side, until he could touch the bottom and crawl out of the water. On land, he was picked up, half dead, by local men:

My strength was allmoste exhausted; my breath, nay, my life, was allmoste gone... The bone of my nose cut right in two, and two very large cuts in my head, that two or three pieces of my skull worked out afterwards.

There was a bounty on Carter's head by now, and he fled from one safe house to the next, eventually taking refuge at Marazion and the farmhouse at Acton Castle. He lit fires only by night, so frightened was he of discovery, but recovered from his wounds in three months. That he even lived—let alone recovered—seems extraordinary when you remember that the incident took place in 1788.

Even before he took up the cause of Methodism, Harry Carter was an upright, honest and godly man, and the rest of the family appear to have been from a similar mould. Swearing and unseemly conversation was banned on their ships, and when living in exile in Roscoff, Harry Carter held church services every Sunday for the group of English smugglers in town.

John Carter had a reputation for honest dealing. A favourite story tells how he broke into the Penzance custom-house to rescue some confiscated tea stored there. His comrades were reluctant to help in such a risky venture, but John explained that he really had no choice. He had promised to deliver the tea by a certain date, and if he failed to fulfil his side of the contract, his reputation for honest dealing would be called into question. The excisemen, returning next morning to find the place ransacked, are said to have commented 'John Carter has been here, and we know it because he is an upright man, and has taken away nothing which was not his own'.

Clashes with the excisemen occur in abundance, naturally enough, but the most spectacular was probably an incident in which the smugglers fired a fusillade of shots at a revenue cutter from a battery of guns impudently stationed between Bessy's Cove and King's Cove. No damage was done, though the cutter returned fire.

Smuggling continued for some years after the King of Prussia had quit the throne. One later story tells of two men from the cove who were rowing their small boat home, the wind having dropped. They put in at Mullion, only to encounter a couple of excisemen on the beach. Offers of bribes were fruitless, so the rowing continued to Prussia Cove itself. Here, hidden from the preventives by a headland, they traded cargo with a fisherman hauling in his pots, and when met by the excisemen, were able to show a clean hand.[45]

Opposite: So many cartloads of contraband crossed Prussia Cove that the iron-bound wheels cut deep tracks into the rock.

MULLION COVE ■25

203-SW6617, 6m S of Helston on the B3296. The Chair is at
203-SW661169, overlooked by the cliff path a mile or so S of the village.

Mullion Cove at the east of Mount's Bay was a favourite landing-place for contraband, and the locals burned with loyalty for the free-traders. On one occasion here, Billy of Praow was bringing ashore contraband brandy, when the cargo was captured by a government brig. News of this disaster spread, and the local people raided an armoury at Trenance, and opened fire on the brig until the cargo was returned.

Another story centres around the Spotsman (the nickname of a prominent local smuggler). Returning from France with a cargo of brandy, the Spotsman succeeded in landing the goods between Predannack Head and Mullion Cove, at a spot known locally as 'the Chair'. However, the custom-house had organized a reception committee, which the Spotsman's friends told him about when he met them at Predannack, just as they were firing a furze beacon. A mad scramble back to the cliffs saved the day and the tubs were quietly moved off the rocks to a nearby mineshaft. When the customs men arrived on the scene, the coast was deserted; and despite the fact that they came within 100 yards of the hidden brandy, the excisemen were deceived and returned with only the smugglers' boat to show for the night's work. When the preventives departed the smugglers clambered down the cliffs and recovered their property undetected. Two tubs that had floated free were later picked up by a friendly fishing boat.[46]

The Spotsman was fortunate to escape capture or injury on that particular run, but he wasn't always so lucky—on another occasion he was slow to reply to a challenge by another smuggler, and was therefore mistaken for a revenue man and shot. Fortunately he lost only his thumb in the encounter.

It was Lieut. Drew, the chief coastguard for the Mullion area, who was credited with smashing the smuggling ring in the district. Drew and a fellow coastguard interrupted a run, but the smugglers melted away into the night. The two men clambered to the beach to find a rope leading out to sea. Pulling on the rope, they hauled in 100 tubs! Aided by reinforcements summoned with flares, the men marked the tubs and put them under guard. In the morning, a crowd gathered to watch the coastguards manhandle the contraband up the cliffs and take it to Gweek custom-house.

Drew interrupted other attempts to run goods in the area, notably at Angrouse Cliffs, where the firing of a furze beacon warned off the smuggling vessel hovering off-shore. Despite the warning, the preventives from Mullion and Penzance recovered nearly 100 tubs that had been sunk by the ship. By 1840 the game was effectively up.[47]

At Gunwalloe a little way to the north, caves on the beach were said to be linked by a tunnel to the belfry of a nearby church; and another passage joined the Halzephron Inn to Fishing Cove, the home of a local smuggler called Henry Cuttance.

PORTHLEVEN ▪26

*203-SW6225, 2m SW of Helston. Methleigh Manor is at
203-SW624264.*

Local legend tells that tunnels connect caves in the cliffs to Methleigh
Manor a mile or so away, and describe a chamber under the kitchen
floor 'big enough to accommodate twelve jolly smugglers'. The floor of
the Manor House was recently re-laid, and when workmen raised the
flagstone said to cover the chamber, they found to their disappointment
only a solid floor beneath. However, tales of tunnels hold more water,
perhaps literally. Tunnels cut in the bedrock do indeed exist at the
Manor; they channelled water from the hills down to the mill that still
stands in the courtyard. When dry, these tunnels could perhaps have
been used to store contraband.

There are rumours of further smugglers' tunnels leading from caves
in the harbour area and other places on the coast nearby. The cliffs
where some of them terminated are the site of many graves of drowned
sailors, including, no doubt, some unidentified smugglers. The
philosophy was that, since there was no way of determining whether
these victims of the sea were Christian or not, they weren't entitled to
burial in a churchyard. Stories of the drowned mariners make grim
reading, as this letter from a local vicar to the Lord of Methleigh Manor
illustrated:

> Dear Sirs,
> By the enclosed paper you will find that the number of dead
> bodies and of such parts of bodies as with respect to interment
> should we think be considered and paid for as such whole bodies,
> taken up within the precincts of your manor and buried there,
> after the last wreck amounts to 62. The extraordinary charge of
> two men attending constantly, one for 12 days, the other for 13
> days at 1/6, was thought to be necessary, in order to secure the
> bodies as soon as they should be cast ashore, from being torn by
> dogs etc, and to prepare graves for their immediate reception
> being at that time very offensive.
> The circumstance accounts for the great consumption of liquor
> without which the people would hardly have been prevailed with

to touch the broken bodies, and also for the pack and rope by
which they were drawn up over the cliff.[48]

The Ship Inn at Porthleven was rumoured to have numerous escape
routes; these must be very cunningly concealed, because a search by the
present landlord revealed no trace. However, an old local man recalls
how, while standing in the cellar, a draft of air drew the smoke from his
pipe into a fissure in the rock wall!

HELSTON ▪27

*203-SW6627, 10m S of Redruth. The Angel Inn is in the main street.
There is a well, and other original features inside the pub, and the yard
mentioned in the story still exists at the back of the pub.*

Buildings at Helston were frequently pressed into service to house
smuggled goods in transit from the coast, and an amusing story is told of
the Angel Inn. George Michell drove a cart-load of silk up to the pub,
but was met by the landlady, who warned him of a party of searchers
awaiting his arrival. Michell sent his son round to the yard with the cart,
walked brazenly into the bar and bought the crowd of searchers a drink.
Relieved that they had their quarry in sight, they accepted, and Michell
managed to spin out the conversation for a good while, lacing the talk
with flattery about the preventives' skill and insight. Eventually, they
heard a rumble of cart-wheels, and, rushing to the window, the searchers saw an old horse-drawn hearse driving off—which they dismissed as
a pauper's funeral. Needless to say, when the officers eventually got
round to searching Michell's cart, they found only innocent
provisions.[49]

MOUSEHOLE ▪28

*Mousehole (203-SW4626) lies just S of Newlyn. The pretty harbour is
approached down steep hills—park outside the village and walk in,
especially during the summer season.*

Mousehole is the most westerly of the Mount's Bay smuggling villages,

*St Ives is one of the few substantial
harbours on the north coast of
Cornwall. It is also the farthest west,
and thus the closest to sources of
contraband on the continent. Little
wonder, then, that the town had strong
connections with the free trade.*

and here too the excise authorities do not appear to have been particularly diligent. Contraband was carried around openly during the day—when asked why he had not apprehended the villains, one preventive assigned to the town said he had been pelted with stones and lay in his bed recovering.

This attitude did not go down well. Around 1780 charges were brought against the Mousehole officials for accepting bribes and cooperating with the smugglers. This is hardly surprising: Richard 'Doga' Pentreath of Mousehole was described by the Penzance collector of customs as 'an honest man in all his dealings though a notorious smuggler'. Another smuggler, Thomas Mann, was also described as honest.

THE ISLES OF SCILLY ■29

Prior to the development of tourism, the population of the Scillies was hard put to find any legal gainful employment besides fishing, which was in any case seasonal. Smuggling was therefore the mainstay of the islands' economy, and the Scillies were for a long time a valuable staging post for smuggling in the West Country.

This idyllic state of affairs came to an end with the establishment of a preventive boat on the islands in the early part of the nineteenth century. The boat was effective, and the almost immediate result was ruination for the inhabitants. In 1818 they petitioned the Prince Regent, and their plight caught the attention of the Magistrates of the Western Division of the Hundred of Penwith. This grand-sounding body sent what would now be called a fact-finding mission to the islands to find out whether the pleas of the islanders had any foundation. The conclusion drawn was that the islands' economy had indeed been destroyed, and that:

> some substitute should be provided ... When this powerful measure was adopted by the present administration, it never could be in their contemplation to crush forever a multitude of families on those islands; who had for generations been brought up in this mode of support, and whose proceedings must at least have been very mildly treated for many years ... the new System in the islands has destroyed almost every comfort of the unhappy sufferers.

The problem was at least partly solved by a cash injection to stimulate the fishing industry.[50]

THE NORTH COAST

Smuggling boats landed goods from the Continent on the south coast of the peninsula in all seasons, but the north coast was used for continental traffic principally during the summer, when the Atlantic storms had abated.

The coastline on the north is less favourable for landing smuggled goods: there are fewer gently-sloping sandy beaches, and many of the suitable coves are too exposed to the wind, making approach more hazardous. The heavy surf for which the area is now famous was another problem, breaking up the floating 'rafts' of roped-together tubs. The main advantage of a north-coast landing was its inconspicuousness: revenue vessels kept an eagle eye on the south coast, but were less vigilant on the north.

Smuggling activity on the north coast focused on traffic with the West Indies, and with various off-shore depots, such as Ireland, the Isles of Scilly and Lundy Island. Ocean-going vessels heading for Bristol found it a simple matter to keep a clandestine rendezvous with small boats off the Devon coast.

SENNEN AND ST JUST ■30

Sennen is at 203-SW3525, 8m W of Penzance. St Just is some 4m N.

At the extreme tip of Cornwall, Sennen was a centre of the free-trade. The inn was owned by the farmer who helped to finance local smuggling operations, with the help of the landlady of the inn, Ann George, and her husband. Dissatisfied with their lot, this unpleasant pair blackmailed the farmer, refusing to pay the rent on the premises. When they were evicted, they shopped their former employer, and he was sent to gaol for his involvement. Needless to say, this treason made the two informers highly unpopular, and had some considerable bearing on a later trial in the town.

This sequel came in 1805 when the excisemen impounded a large cargo—1000 gallons each of brandy, rum and gin, and a quarter of a ton of tobacco. As they struggled to remove the cargo, a large and hostile crowd built up, and a running battle ensued. The owner of the cargo eventually appeared in court charged with inciting the mob to riot. The main witness for the prosecution was Ann George, but she was regarded as such a malicious gossip that the case was dismissed.

A court case at St Just, a short way north of Sennen, amply illustrates a number of other interesting facets of the free-trade, in particular the financial arrangements made by smugglers in order to conceal the trail they left behind. Two smugglers from the town—Oats and Permewan—were very active around 1818. However, they took the precaution of employing a middle-man, who paid the merchants in France for the goods that they brought to Britain.

It appears that the middle-man, Pridham, got greedy, and kept the payments, instead of just his percentage. Furthermore, he threatened to report the smugglers to the authorities if they ended the arrangement. A meeting was organized, at which Permewan proposed to terminate the contract. To prevent prosecution based on the evidence of the greedy middle-man, Oats and Permewan hatched a cunning plan. The middle-man had met Permewan in person just a couple of times, so Permewan sent his brother to impersonate him. While the meeting took place, Permewan himself made a point of establishing the perfect alibi, by meeting as many people in the town as possible. So when the blackmailer made his accusations, his evidence was ruled out of court.[51]

ST IVES ■31

203-SW5140, 12m W of Redruth. Trencrom Hill is at 203-SW5136 on a minor road 2m SW of Lelant ■32. The cottages are at the end of a track leading away from the NT car-park. At St Erth ■33 , you can still see the bridge under which the Redruth man hid; it is by the churchyard at 203-SW549351.

St Ives Bay is the first inlet sheltered from the Atlantic storms, and it should come as no surprise to learn that north-coast smuggling started this close to Land's End. John Wesley noted of the town that 'well-nigh one and all bought and sold uncustomed goods'.

The collector of customs here was at one stage John Knill, who, it appears, dabbled in smuggling a little himself. While he was mayor (in 1767) he paid for the fitting-out of a privateer which was used as a smuggler. He also built a steeple nearby to serve as a landmark for his vessels, and left some curious provisions in his will to ensure that his memory lived on in the town.

One story links Knill to a boat loaded with china that ran aground at the Hayle side of Carrack Gladden. The crew escaped, and someone removed the ship's papers since they implicated Knill and a squire of Trevetho. Roger Wearne, the customs man of the time, helped himself to some of the cargo, but got no further with it than the ship's side. As he was climbing down, one of the locals noticed his bulging garments, and a few well-aimed blows ensured that the china was worthless.[52]

In St Andrews Street at St Ives once stood the Blue Bell Inn, which was frequented by a Dutch smuggler called Hans Breton. It was said that he was in league with the devil, and that he paid duty on just one keg of brandy. This, however, never seemed to empty, and lasted 22 years.

Like most of their fellow countrymen, the people of St Ives enjoyed a story that showed the smuggler as hero and the preventives as, at best, fools. One episode which reinforces this impression took place in 1851. Despite the considerable—and largely successful—efforts that had been taken to stamp out the free-trade locally, a notorious local smuggler called James 'Old Worm' Williams landed smuggled Irish whiskey close to the St Ives breakwater, and hid the barrels in fishing boats and pigsties near the water. Later that night, three carts collected the haul, and carried it openly through the streets, heading east. However, the carts attracted the attention of a coastguard drinking in the George and Dragon in the market place, and when he investigated, he was knocked to the ground, bound and gagged. After some time, though, he managed to get free, and went for help. The officer he called on galloped off to the toll-house on Hayle causeway, but the toll-collector denied ever seeing any wagons. (In fact, the smugglers had got new horses at Skidden Hill, and had made for Hayle and Redruth). The coastguard drew the conclusion that the smugglers had headed for Penzance, and he made a fruitless trip there.

All that remained in evidence was Williams' smack, the *St George*, which was still in the bay. The only crew-man left on board was a

John Knill, the eccentric collector of customs at St Ives, built a tall obelisk on a hill overlooking the town as a sea-marker for his ships. In his will he paid for a ceremonial procession from the town to the steeple every five years.

Prussian cabin-boy who apparently knew just three words of English, 'I don't know'. According to tradition, though, he had been threatened with murder if he told more. Eventually the customs authorities detained the boat on the rather feeble charge that the ship's name was partially hidden where it was painted on the stern.

A passage relating the incident appeared in the *West Briton*, headed 'Smuggling', and Williams took the unprecedented step of replying. He claimed that he was in St Ives harbour to take on board baskets of fish, and suggested that the coastguard in the George and Dragon had been drunk and simply imagined the carts. The letter appeared on 13 June 1851, and the vessel was released on the 16th.

The customs men were, however, nothing if not persistent. They discovered some tubs nearby, and found with them rope and chain that matched samples from the *St George*. Nevertheless, the case was dismissed for lack of evidence.

The cabin-boy, nicknamed 'Prussian Bob', settled in St Ives and became known as 'Old Worm's Fool' on account of his fine performance.

A St Ives historian argues that the town was the last outpost of the trade. In the 1870s a local boat called *Old Duchy* smuggled rum from Holland. The trips ended when the excisemen put spies among the fishermen involved in the trade, resulting in heavy fines all round.

The area around St Ives and to the east has its fair share of smuggling tales. At Trencrom Hill, Lelant, one of two granite cottages once known as Newcastle was used as a nineteenth-century kiddlewink—a beer-shop. Smugglers excavated a cave alongside for the concealment of contraband. The cottages still stand on the hill, but are private houses, and there is no public access to them. The church at Lelant was also used for the storage of contraband spirits.[53]

According to a St Erth legend, a Redruth man was being pursued by the excisemen, when he decided at St Erth Bridge that his exhausted nag could no longer carry both himself and the tubs. He dismounted and hid under the bridge, whipping the horse off at a gallop. When he heard the officer's horse pass overhead, the man emerged and walked home—the horse had arrived a good deal earlier.[54]

HAYLE ■34

3m SE of St Ives. The house with the tunnel lies close to Phillack at the end of a cul-de-sac on the N side of the inlet, at 203-SW562382. On the coast N of Hayle, the B3301 coast road to Portreath passes several landing-points: Hell's Mouth some 5m from Hayle, at 203-SW605430 was a landing spot; and Ralph's Cupboard (which took its name from a smuggler), 1m outside Portreath at 203-SW644452 was used for storage.[55]

Hayle was a popular landing-place for smugglers, and in the garden of the former local youth hostel there is a remarkable tunnel that was allegedly used for smuggling. A sloping trench leads down from ground level to the arched tunnel entrance, where the hinges for a gate or door can still be seen. The tunnel is still open, and runs due north for hundreds of yards. It is possible to walk along it only in a stooping posture, though in the last two centuries the average stature has risen considerably, so possibly seventeenth-century smugglers could have walked upright.

Many smugglers' tunnels prove disappointing, or just non-existent, but this one seems as authentic as any. It is the right shape; it runs towards the coast; it even has a drainage gulley along its length to keep the flat floor dry.

Among the local smuggling legends is a story of a smuggler who came to live in Hayle despite the fact that he was a stranger to the area. He was comparatively wealthy, but seemed always to suffer from the cold—he had a very pale complexion, and shivered even in summer. When he stood in the sun, it is said, he cast no shadow. When the man died, it emerged that he had made his money by giving false evidence against a fellow and claiming the reward. From that day on, the sun never shone on the perjurer.[56]

PORTHCOTHAN ▪35

200-SW8572. To reach the tunnel described below leave Porthcothan by the road on the N side, turning up the valley along footpaths, and keeping to the S side of the brook. Walk up the valley until a tributary joins the main brook at 200-SW865715, then follow the tributary for some 300 yards. The low entrance to the cave is halfway up the valley side on the right. Look carefully: it's well hidden in bracken and gorse in the summer.

To the east of the St Ives area, smuggling traditions are fragmented and occasional. This is perhaps to be expected, since most of the inland areas could be supplied with continental luxuries far more easily from the south coast than the north. Nevertheless, persistent stories link some of the north-coast towns and villages with the free-trade.

In *The Book of the West* the vicar of Morwenstow describes a cave used for concealing contraband a little way up the valley from Porthcothan Bay, just west of Padstow.

At Porth Cothan the cliffs fall away and form a lap of shore, into which flows a little stream. . . About a mile up the glen, is a tiny lateral combe. Rather more than halfway down the steep slope is a hole just large enough to admit a man entering in a stooping posture . . .

This smuggling tunnel at Hayle runs inland for hundreds of yards and it is still possible to walk along it, stooping slightly. A sloping trench conceals the entrance from view.

The cave is still in existence, but there is no trace of the extensive tunnel that the writer goes on to describe. Some of the details he wrote about over a century ago can still be seen though: there are notches near the mouth of the cave, into which smugglers lodged a beam of timber; they then heaped earth against the beam and covered the pile with furze to hide the entrance. The tunnel supposedly led to a farm on the hill half a mile away.

PEPPER COVE ▪36

200-SW855737. Take the B3276 Newquay to Padstow road, and turn off towards the coast about 4m outside Padstow, following signs to Treyarnon Bay caravan site, where there is ample parking. Walk across the beach, and S along the cliff path for about 600 yards. Pepper Cove is the third inlet.

Smugglers were essentially opportunists, and were prepared to run practically anything that would turn a profit. When pepper from the East Indies was taxed heavily, it became a popular item for the Cornwall smugglers, and the tiny inlet of Pepper Cove a little way north of Porthcothan takes its name from the barrels of spice that were landed there from smuggling ships.

It is an archetypal smugglers' cove. The entrance from the sea is narrow, and fringed with jagged rocks; once inside, a smuggler's vessel would be totally hidden by the high cliffs and therefore unloaded at a safe and leisurely pace. The beach is sandy and free of rocks, so it would have been a safe landing place once a vessel had negotiated the dangerous entrance. The gradient is sufficiently gentle that even a large boat could have been beached quite easily.

Nearby is Will's Rock, where smugglers left a revenue man to drown in the rising tide; amazingly, the officer lived to tell the tale.

PADSTOW ▪37

200-SW9275, 10m NW of Bodmin.

Here an Irish smuggling vessel chased an excise ship into the harbour, then hung out flags and fired guns as a victory signal. The smugglers sailed on to unload at Newquay, where the customs authorities were known to be very obliging about watching the wall.

In 1765 a beach 2 miles west of Padstow was in use as a landing-point, and William Rawlings wrote in that year to the Earl of Dartmouth that his servants encountered 60 horses carrying a cargo from the beach some 3 miles from St Columb, 'having each three bags of tea on them of 56 or 58lb weight'.

Another local story—perhaps apocryphal—tells how a farmer, spotted carrying a barrel of spirits by a distant exciseman, lifted a gatepost from its socket, dropped the tub into the hole, replaced the gatepost and greeted the man with a cheery wave.

BODMIN MOOR ▪38

Jamaica Inn is at 201-SX184768 on the A30 at Bolventor, Bodmin Moor, 10m outside Bodmin. Despite the many changes the inn has undergone, there is still a hint of the malice and ill-fortune so vividly portrayed in the book.

On the windswept wastes of Bodmin Moor Jamaica Inn is perhaps the best known of all smuggling haunts, thanks to Daphne Du Maurier's novel of the same name. It is surrounded by barren country and often hemmed in by chill winds and thick mists, and the approach is perhaps more spectacular than the building itself, which has been extended and modified over the years. The fame of the inn is not entirely fictional; it was probably supplied with contraband booze landed by Polperro and Boscastle boats.

Jamaica Inn, made famous by Daphne du Maurier's novel, stands high up on Bodmin Moor. It was probably supplied with contraband drink from Polperro and Boscastle boats.

CRUEL COPINGER

Port Isaac ■ 39 is at 200-SW 9980, 9m N of Wadebridge. Parking available on the beach at low tide (fee); at other times, park above the village and walk down the steep streets to the harbour area. Village centre closed to traffic during the high season.

Will you hear of Cruel Copinger?
He came from a foreign kind:
He was brought to us by the salt water,
He was carried away by the wind.

'Cruel' Copinger was the most notorious of Cornwall's many smugglers, and the Rev R.S. Hawker paints a vivid picture of Copinger's arrival in a furious storm. The population turned out in the hope of a wreck, and spied:

a strange vessel of foreign rig . . . in fierce struggle with the waves of Harty Race. She was deeply lade or waterlogged, and rolled heavily in the trough of the sea, nearing the shore as she felt the tide. Gradually the pale and dismayed faces of the crew became visible, and among them one man of Herculean height and mould, who stood near the wheel with a speaking-trumpet in his hands. The sails were blown to rags, and the rudder was appar-

ently lashed for running ashore . . . the tall seaman, who was manifestly the skipper of the boat, had cast off his garments, and stood prepared upon the deck to encounter a battle with the surges for life and rescue. He plunged over the bulwarks, and arose to sight buffeting the seas. With stalwart arm and powerful chest he made his way through the surf, rode manfully from billow to billow until, with a bound, he stood at last upright upon the sand, a fine stately semblance of one of the old Vikings of the northern seas.

The story continues in this vein, with baroque flourishes by the Reverend. Copinger grabbed the cloak from one of the old women on the beach (note the cruel streak), leapt onto a horse behind Miss Dinah Hamlyn, and rode off to her home, where he introduced himself to the girl's father as Copinger the Dane. The ship, meanwhile, sank from sight.

Copinger threw himself on the family's charity, wooed the girl, and appeared grateful for all they did for him. The father, though, sickened and died, and Copinger took over as head of the household. He married Dinah, and immediately 'his evil nature, so long smouldering, break (*sic*) out like a wild beast uncaged . . .'.

Copinger, it emerged, was head of a large and terrifying gang, half smuggler, half pirate. After the wedding 'all kinds of wild uproar and reckless revelry appalled the neighbourhood day and night'.

Copinger indulged in many daring exploits, but the Reverend Hawker mentions only a few specifically. One was to lure a revenue cutter into a channel near Gull Rock. Copinger piloted his ship, the *Black Prince*, safely ashore, but the revenue cutter went aground and all perished. To deter the excisemen on another occasion, the crew cut the head off a gauger and carried the body to sea.

Copinger terrorized the locality, capturing men who had offended him, and forcing them to work on his ship. This story finds confirmation in other sources: a 97-year-old man told a Penzance woman[57] that he was witness to a murder perpetrated by an associate of Copinger's, and that to prevent him from telling anyone he was abducted. He was released only when some friends ransomed him two years later.

Copinger amassed such a fortune that he bought a farm for cash in gold coin: 'Dollars and ducats, doubloons and pistoles, guineas—the coinage of every foreign country with a seabord'. The astonished lawyer reluctantly agreed to the payment by weight.

Copinger even controlled land transport, forbidding anyone to move on 'Copinger's tracks' at night. The paths converged at a headland called Steeple Brink, hundreds of feet below which was Copinger's Cave, where secret revelry was indulged in 'that would be utterly inconceivable to the educated mind of the nineteenth century.'

Copinger extorted money from his mother-in-law by tying his beautiful wife to the bedstead and threatening to whip her with a sea-cat unless the old woman paid up. He also whipped the vicar, and tormented a half-witted tailor, threatening to sell him to the devil. His union with Dinah produced a son who, though deaf and dumb, was as mischievous and cruel as his father, and who joyfully murdered a playmate when aged six.

Copinger's luck ran out, and he disappeared as he had arrived, in a violent storm. Standing atop Gull Rock, he waved his sword to an approaching craft and was eventually met by a boat in Harty Race 'with two hands at every oar; for the tide runs with double violence through Harty Race'. The boat picked him up at Gull Creek, and the crew struggled through the waves to the pirate vessel. A crew-man who flagged was cut down with a cutlass. The tale ends:

Thunder, lightning and hail ensued. Trees were rent up by the roots around the pirate's abode. Poor Dinah watched, and held in her shuddering arms her idiot boy, and, strange to say, a meteoric stone, called in that country a storm-bolt, fell through the roof into the room, at the very feet of Cruel Copinger's vacant chair.

Port Isaac features prominently in the legend of Cruel Copinger. The advantages of the spot to the free-trading community are still obvious today: the long sandy beach is protected by high, rocky promontories on either side, and the valley stretching away inland must have provided easy access for the large numbers of men and horses needed to transport contraband into the hinterland.

Especially unusual is the lifeboat-house and fishermen's shelter, a triangular building that protects a cobbled courtyard from the lashing Atlantic rain.

At the shelter you can buy excellent lobsters, a reminder that Port Isaac was for a long time one of only two substantial fishing villages along this stretch of the north coast—Bude was the other. The Bloody Bones Bar at a local pub is a shrine to smugglers.

MORWENSTOW ■40

190-SS2015, 5m N of Bude.

Cruel Copinger's biographer was the Reverend Hawker, vicar of this tiny hamlet. He wrote many tales of smuggling folk in the area, and one characteristic tale concerns 'The Gauger's Pocket' or the Witan-Stone (rock of wisdom) at Tidnacombe Cross. It is on the edge of the moor, near the sea '. . . grown over with moss and lichen, with a moveable slice of rock to conceal its mouth . . . a dry and secret crevice, about an arm's length deep. Smuggler Tristram Pentire, who tells the tale to the vicar adds:

> There, sir have I dropped a little bag of gold, many and many a time, when our people wanted to have the shore quiet and to keep the exciseman out of the way of trouble; and there he would go if so be he was a reasonable officer, and the byeword used to be, when t'was all right, one of us would go and meet him, and then say, 'Sir, your pocket is unbuttoned;' and he would smile and answer, 'Ay! ay! but never mind, my man, my money's safe enough;' and thereby we knew that he was a just man, and satisfied, and that the boats could take the roller in peace.

Tristram Pentire seems to have kept the location of the Witan-Stone a secret, because today, even knowledgeable locals at Morwenstow know nothing of the concealed hiding-hole.

CLOVELLY ■41

190-SS3124, 13m NE of Bude. Visit very early in the morning, or in the evening when the coach parties have left.

East of Hartland point, Bideford Bay provided a safe haven from the pounding westerlies. On the west of the bay the village of Clovelly, clinging to the cliff-face, had a notorious reputation as a smuggling haunt, and certainly many smuggler's luggers set out from the well-protected harbour there. A local legend about cannibals keeping tubs of salted human flesh in caves along the coast may well have been spread by smugglers to keep inquisitive visitors away from their hiding-places. Today, locals will point out the smugglers' cave to the curious; it is a good walk east along the shore from the harbour.

LUNDY ISLAND ■42

180/190-SS1345, 19m out of Bideford Bay

Lundy Island was at the centre of a massive tobacco-smuggling scheme that defrauded fortunes from the exchequer in the mid-eighteenth century. The mastermind of the fraud was a Bideford man called Thomas Benson. He had inherited considerable wealth from his father, including a fleet of ships plying regularly to the American colonies, and returning with tobacco. Benson's fortune flourished from the trade, and in due course he became Sheriff of Devon, and later MP for Barnstaple. His business activities, though, were not up to the standard expected of present-day public figures (though Benson was probably far from a black sheep by eighteenth-century standards). Benson conceived an elegant scheme to defraud the customs, involving both Lundy Island, which he rented from Lord Gower, and the steady flow of convicts who streamed through Bideford *en route* for the New World.

Benson's ships transported the miscreants across the Atlantic, but some got no further than Lundy. There Benson established a—perfectly legitimate—tobacco processing plant and storage facility. His smuggling activities revolved around the drawback system, whereby merchants who re-exported goods that they had imported could reclaim the import duty paid. Thus Benson would land tobacco on the mainland, pay duty, re-export it to Lundy and legitimately reclaim the duty he had paid. His trick, though, was to import the

To discourage the inquisitive, Clovelly smugglers spread stories of cannibals who lived on barrels of pickled human flesh. In reality, of course, the barrels contained fine French brandy.

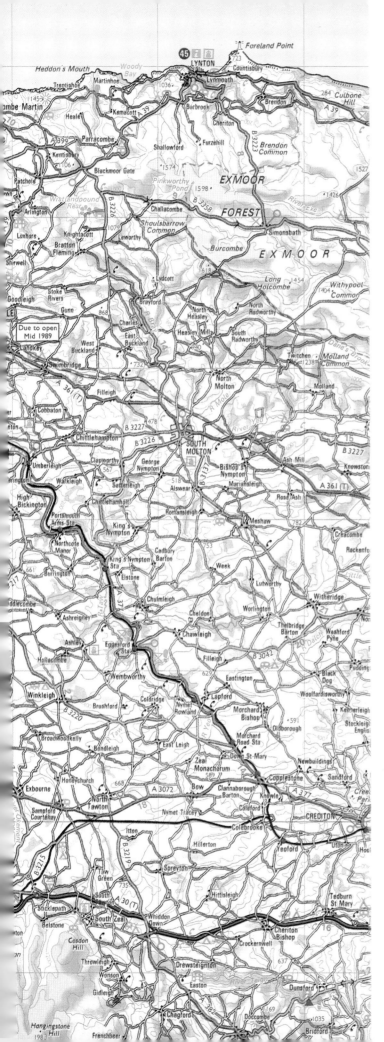

processed tobacco once more—this time illegally.

The defrauded customs men of Appledore, Bideford and Barnstaple were perplexed. 'We are at a very great loss how to act in this case . . .' they wrote in September 1751 '. . . as we cannot find that this island is within the limits of any port'. The problem persisted. The following year the board of customs feared that '. . . the island will become a magazine for smuglers (sic)'.

However, Benson's days were numbered. He had scuttled one of his ships to claim the insurance, and the government net was closing tighter on his customs frauds. In 1754 he fled to Portugal.

Two smugglers are known to have made Lundy their business centre. Thomas Benson of Bideford used the island to evade customs duty until 1754, and Thomas Knight moved here when he was ejected from Barry in 1785. This engraving of Lundy Castle was made in the period between the two Toms' residencies.

BARNSTAPLE ■43

180-SS5533, 34m NW of Exeter.

The Barnstaple custom-house staff must have considered their lot unlucky in the extreme. They were on the losing side whatever happened: when smugglers were popular, the customs men were villains. But when the local populace were at odds with the smugglers, the customs men were accused of being too slack in the execution of their duties. In 1746 the Barnstaple people believed that corn was being illegally exported (the corn laws made this illegal when the price of grain rose above a certain level). Of course, they looked to the customs men to prevent export and in April a mob took to the streets of the town.

The exporter, Major-General Campbell, had a licence to ship the corn, but the 'mobb' suspected this to be a forgery. The customs men themselves were in mortal danger, since they had to ensure that the grain was loaded legitimately. The mob burst into a granary in the town, and carried away 600 bushels of wheat. They 'patrol'd the streets beating old frying pans, canisters & blowing horns, threatening all who should offer to oppose them.' They even broke the window of the previous owner of the granary.

The mob however, may have been justified in their suspicions. Forged documents were commonplace as there was a centuries-old tradition of fraud at the port. In one particularly memorable medieval example, smugglers were loading contraband leather from the Barnstaple quay, in full view of a corrupt official. A visiting merchant drew the man's attention to the illicit activity with the words 'here it is, blind knave', but the official simply laughed.

The customs men also had to deal with wrecks, and this was another source of friction. When a ship called *Beulah* was wrecked near Barnstaple in 1764 the locals swarmed around, and one of them, the wife of

Richard Budd, assaulted the tide-surveyor with a ladle. The poor man was apparently unaware that she was the wife of the tenant of the local manor, and therefore entitled to salvage—she had lace and a candlestick in her apron. Also washed up was a small cask of rum which was doled out to the men who had helped with the salvage, 'they being exceedingly wet and cold'. Mrs Budd evidently also partook and got so drunk that she fell from her horse.

ILFRACOMBE ■44

9m N of Barnstaple (map 180). Access to Brandy Cove 180-SS505475 is through the National Trust estate of Langleigh Valley. Drive to Langleigh Lane on the W side of Ilfracombe and park before the 'Unsuitable for Motors' sign.

To reach Samson's Bay at 180-SS545485 park on the cliff top adjacent to the Ilfracombe coastguard station on the A399 coast road; take the coast path to the right of a prominent post with steps, then turn off the main path to the left after 300 yards or so. An overgrown track zigzags down the cliff to the cave.

Place names in the Ilfracombe area bear witness to the town's connections with the smuggling trade. On the east side of the town there is an inlet called Brandy Cove, and to the west, Samson's Bay is named after a famous local smuggler. The bay could be the model on which second-rate adventure-story writers base their 'Smugglers Cove'. A gentle sandy beach makes landing easy, and there are several deep caves which really were used for the storage of contraband. The beaches are visible only from the sea, and the entrances are covered at high tide. The cliffs above the beach are now overgrown with brambles, but a gully which cuts through the hill-side is deep enough to conceal even a thousand ponies carrying contraband inland. Was it coincidence that the coastguard station was sited nearby?

LYNMOUTH AND LYNTON ■45

180-SS7249, 15m NE of Barnstaple; Smuggler's Leap is above Lee Bay at 180-SS695490.

East of Ilfracombe the north coast of Exmoor is wind-swept and desolate, and there are few proper landing-places. Those that there are invariably played host to the free-traders. The fourteenth-century Rising Sun Inn at Lynmouth has a long-established reputation as a smuggler's pub, and on the way to Martinhoe the Lynmouth road passes close to a spot known as 'Smuggler's Leap'. Here, it is said, a revenue man and the smuggler he was chasing tumbled over the cliff together, locked in a desperate struggle. The smuggler had a small lead over his pursuer, but the King's horse was evidently of better stock than the smuggler's old nag, and capture seemed inevitable. In a last ditch attempt to escape, the smuggler reined the horse round, but the beast lost its footing. As the smuggler plunged over the cliff, he grabbed his adversary and they plummeted together to the rocks below.

THE BRISTOL CHANNEL

After the desolation of the Exmoor coast, the sheltered waters of the Bristol Channel are a haven of tranquillity. Bristol was for centuries England's second largest port, and in the eighteenth century handled the bulk of the transatlantic trade. So the majority of the contraband landed in the Bristol Channel came from the West Indies and the American colonies.

The simplest way to land goods illegally was of course to bribe the Bristol officials, and this practice certainly went on to a considerable extent. However, when corruption was impossible or too costly, the small ports to the west of Bristol were happy to harbour the smugglers, and buy their goods.

Not all the tobacco that came ashore in the Bristol Channel appeared by the usual (if illegal) route: some bobbed up on the beaches without the benefit of a boat. In 1736 the tide washed up hundreds of bales that had been tossed off the decks of in-bound ships. News of recent legislation to prevent smuggling reached the incoming vessels as they approached the coast, and the seamen, fearful of stiff penalties when they arrived, threw the goods overboard. Though the bales penetrated by seawater were of course worthless, dry bales were eagerly picked up by the local population and sold off.

At a time when contraband was pouring into Britain along the Bristol Channel, the port of Ilfracombe relied on just four unarmed customs officials to stop the illicit trade. Just below the spot where the artist stood to make this engraving lies Samson's Bay, the haunt of an Ilfracombe smuggler. The cave he used for storage still exists.

WATCHET ■46

181-ST0743, 15m NW of Taunton. St Audries Bay at 181-ST1143 is now approached across private land. Small entrance/parking fee for day visitors.

This quote from a history of Somerset provides an eloquent picture of smuggling in the Watchet area, and the involvement of the rich and famous, without need for amplification:

> Sir William Wyndham patronised the smugglers, the port of Watchet, his town, being used to escape the customs house at Minehead, and growing exceedingly rich from that cause. Col. Luttrell, who owned Minehead, was similarly indisposed to help the preventive officers... A century later the trade had reached formidable proportions when there was much smuggling from Ireland, Lisbon and the West Indies, and one hundred horses were sometimes waiting for the arrival of the cargoes, temporary hiding places for the goods being found under the floors of barns, in the thickness of farm-house walls, and in caves and holes along the coast.[58]

Contraband was landed not only at Watchet itself, but also at other accessible places nearby on the coast, including St Audries Bay a little way to the north.

WESTON-SUPER-MARE ■47

To reach Sand Point at 182-ST316659, leave the M5 and approach Weston on the A370, then turn off to the right and follow signs to Sand Bay. At the coast turn right (signposted Sand Point). Limited parking, then a walk. St Martin's Church, Worle, is on Church Road. Turn off the high street up the hill, and follow signs to the village surgery. The church is then approached across the graveyard. The tower is on the N side.

Close to Bristol, the channel coast has some features that enabled the Weston smugglers to run rings around the preventives. The peninsula of Sand Point juts out into the Bristol Channel, giving the land party a clear view of vessels approaching from all directions. The point was clearly visible from inland, too, and was therefore used as a signal station. The beaches at Middle Hope to the east of Sand Point were frequently used for landing contraband, and a scout group camping here in the 1930s discovered a secret tunnel. Unfortunately, they were made to fill it in before it could be investigated thoroughly.

Another signal point was at Uphill. Smugglers there lit beacons at the church, or on Worlebury Hill, to guide ships to an unguarded section of coast.[59] And at Worle the twelfth-century church of St Martin's contains a staircase that rises to an octagonal turret—according to local tradition smugglers stored contraband in a hiding-place (now disappeared) in the church roof.

Ships from the Caribbean had little difficulty in unloading a portion of their cargoes into small boats offshore, before heading for Bristol to declare the remainder. The smugglers' boats landed the goods here at St Audries Bay and at other secluded beaches up and down the coast.

BRISTOL ■48

Bristol was for centuries a centre for illegal import in the west. It was a port of considerable importance, although today silting of the docks has made normal trade virtually impossible.

Early Bristol smugglers were nothing if not brazen. In the sixteenth century, when Britain was at war with Spain, Bristol merchants were shipping out canon to the enemy. 'Culverin' guns were exported from the port by the shipload, along with ammunition. These guns were made in the Forest of Dean iron-foundries, and fetched a high premium abroad. The Spanish Armada was armed by its adversary.

In the Elizabethan era, Bristol was famous for wine smuggling from France and the Mediterranean. According to some reports only half the wine landed there paid duty, and the customs officers pocketed a £30 bribe for each ship that landed. It appears, though, that the income from this illegal source was not fairly divided—when a clerk threatened to inform on his superiors, he spent eighteen months in prison on a trumped-up charge of debt, and even when he reported the illicit dealings, no action was taken.

Attention in the seventeenth century, though, focused on the tobacco trade with Bermuda and Virginia, and the Bristol customs authorites were quick to profit from it. William Culliford investigated the port in the 1680s, and found a rat's nest of fraudulent officials. The only tide-waiter considered to be honest was blind!

The standard way to smuggle goods in was for the ship's master to keep two sets of accounts. One showed the true cargo: this was for the benefit of its owners. A second set of books was presented to the customs authorities with a nod and a wink. One example was a ship called the *Bristol Merchant*, which docked with 9½ tons of tobacco on board. It cost the crew £80 to get the customs officials to turn a blind eye, but this was less than half what they saved in duty. Pay-offs took place at Mother Grindham's Coffee House on Bristol quayside.

In the golden age of smuggling, Bristol was Britain's second port. Corrupt officials on the quayside were easily persuaded to turn a blind eye to illegal imports.

WALES AND WEST ENGLAND

BRISTOL TO CARLISLE

Information about smuggling in Wales and north-western England is not easy to find. Many of the official records compiled by the individual custom-houses were lost in the fire that destroyed the Thames-side custom-house in 1815. What records remain provide a rather scant picture of the activities of the free-traders.

The fact that there is so little information to be found, though, certainly doesn't imply that the citizens living on the coast between Bristol to Carlisle were any more willing to pay customs and excise duty than the inhabitants of other parts of Britain. This poem by the eighteenth-century poet and singer, Richard Lloyd of Plas Meini, sums up the simmering resentment in Wales:

> They've fixed the tax for the year today
> God would never have done it this way
> A tax when you die
> A tax when you're born
> A tax on the water
> A tax on the dawn
> A tax upon the gallows tree
> Even a tax on being free[1]

Certainly, the surviving correspondence between the customs board and the collectors of customs suggests that the level of evasion in this part of the country was fairly typical. However, by comparison with the south and east coasts of England, smuggling here was a comparatively minor problem, and the customs authorities were often more preoccupied with wrecking than with the deliberate running of goods.

A determined and ingenious smuggler can usually succeed in bringing goods ashore practically anywhere, but the geography of Wales, and the character of the Welsh provided the free-trader with some useful benefits. Much of Wales was (and is) remote and sparsely populated; the few preventive centres were widely scattered, and under-funded; there are plenty of gently-sloping beaches and sheltered coves, which made landing easy in some areas; and the traditional independence of the Welsh people, and their resentment of interference from England must have also been a considerable aid in concealment of smugglers' activities.

In what is now Cumbria, the majority of written information about smuggling comes from the legal side of the fence—court records provide particulars of sentences, and custom-house books note seizures in every detail. So the picture we get of the Cumbrian smugglers is a dry and rather dull official one, rather than the more human folk image that prevails in many other areas.

The official records paint a picture of considerable smuggling traffic off-shore, but rather less contraband actually crossing the coast. This is perhaps surprising, since Cumbria would seem to be ideally situated for smuggling: it is just a short distance from the Isle of Man, a major source of contraband, and borders Scotland. One possible explanation is that smugglers found it easier to land goods in Scotland than on the English side of the Solway, and had a ready market north of the border.

Certainly this explanation is confirmed by some of the comments in the local custom-house letter books. In 1733 the authorities at Whitehaven reported that they regularly saw small ships from the Isle of Man 'Steering up for the Scottish Border where they generally land without much opposition, then bring the goods on horseback in the night into England'. And nearly two decades later the collector of customs at the same port noted that, although large quantities of goods came in via Scotland, landings on the Cumbrian side of the Solway had declined.

Records of sales of seized goods provide a guide to the level of smuggling activity around the Cumbrian coast, and in some years the quantities are considerable. However, the source of much of this contraband was vessels seized at sea, so it's hard to distinguish between goods that would have been run into England, and those that were headed to Scotland.

As in Scotland, Cumbrian use of the word 'smuggling' covers not only illegal import and export, but also illicit stilling of spirits, which lies beyond the scope of this book. Certainly this fraud on the revenue was widespread in the eighteenth century and the smuggling yarns that are to be found in books—notably centred on one Lancelot Slee of Langdale—generally fall into this category. Nevertheless, relatively few stories of land smuggling have found their way into print, either officially, or through oral history. Perhaps the Cumbrian smugglers kept their lips tightly closed?

CONTRABAND AND ITS SOURCE

As happened elsewhere, the character of smuggling in Wales and the north-west varied in line with the prevailing taxation policies, but trading patterns had an effect, too. The south coast of Wales had two great advantages—proximity to Bristol, which was the main British port for trade with the New World; and a relatively high population eager to buy uncustomed goods.

It was a simple matter to transfer to small boats at least part of the cargo from inward-bound ships as they sailed serenely along the Bristol Channel, and then attribute the shortfall on arrival to 'spoilage' or 'lost in storms'. More often, bribery secured the silence of officials not only at Bristol but at official landing-places in Wales. When tobacco smoking came into vogue, many Welsh clay pipes were filled with Virginia leaf imported in this manner.

The Channel Islands was a major source of contraband entering Wales, and at least one Guernsey smuggler, Richard Robinson, had vessels off the coast of Glamorgan. He himself commanded the largest of these, and a smaller vessel was in the charge of his son Pasco. The pair were operating in the 1730s, principally landing goods on Flat Holm, for later onward shipment to Wales.

Smuggling in Wales received a boost with the Irish 'troubles' at the end of the seventeenth century. These led to a ban on civil shipping in the West, so honest residents were deprived of much of the cargo that would previously have been legitimately landed. Smugglers were happy to step into the breach and import the creature comforts that people had become used to.

North Wales and north-west England look out across the Irish Sea, and there is evidence to suggest that much of the contraband landed here came from Ireland. Heavy taxation on salt made this a favourite cargo for smuggling ships, and Ireland was a major source of rock-salt. As the incident at Conwy (see page 145) demonstrates, salt smuggling drew support from every part of the community. Recognizing that there was a problem, the authorities carried out a survey of the Welsh coast in 1740; a member of the salt board trudged warily from port to port, largely (and often prematurely) reporting 'no smuggling takes place here'.

Irish vessels didn't necessarily take the shortest route and may have avoided mid-Wales because of the risk of running aground on the sandy shallows which abound in the local bays.[2] Instead, many Irish ships made a longer trip through St George's Channel, to land goods on the south coast of Wales.

Besides being a major original source of some forms of contraband, Ireland was probably also used as a depot for goods brought in from the Continent. The trip from the Irish coast took only a matter of hours with favourable wind and tide, and an overnight stop in an Irish creek must have seemed an attractive option to exhausted crews who might otherwise face an opposed landing at the end of the long trip from France.

Ireland wasn't the only off-shore depot. Lundy Island to the south was heavily used by smugglers for storage and freight forwarding, and other islands—especially Ramsey, Skomer and Skokholm off the Pembroke coast—were probably used in the same way.

North Wales and northern England are conveniently close to the Isle of Man, and certainly much of the untaxed brandy quaffed on Anglesey and in Cumberland came into Britain via the three-legged isle.

Brandy may have been the first cargo smuggled into Wales, but one Victorian writer suggested that wool and corn export was rife in Wales long before import smuggling began. She wrote that: 'The almost impassable hills and cwms (dingles) were looked upon as protection against discovery'. She added that the people involved in wool export smuggling were chiefly landowners, whereas the illegal importers . . . 'of brandy, Hamburg spirit, tea and silk . . . were of a lower order, who frequently showed so much brutality that eventually they became a terror to the people'.[3]

It wasn't just luxury goods that smugglers brought to the eager Welsh and Cumberland markets. In some parts, grinding poverty and near starvation created a demand even for ordinary foodstuffs. Poverty cut both ways, though, and was exploited not only by the smugglers, but also by the preventive forces, who relied on information from paid informers.

Customs officers at Whitehaven were frequently less concerned with stamping out smuggling than with eliminating other ways of defrauding the Exchequer. Wrecks were frequent, and the Crown was entitled to claim duty from those who salvaged goods washed up on shore.

THE BRISTOL CHANNEL AND SOUTH WALES

This area had a changing role in the free-trade, but even before the smuggling explosion of the eighteenth century, the Bristol Channel was notorious for smugglers and pirates. The shape of the channel partly accounts for the ease with which vessels could avoid duty: when the King's men were being unusually diligent at Bristol, the ships' masters simply headed for the south Wales coast, and added only a few hours to their journey time.

CHEPSTOW ■1

162-ST5393, 12m N of Bristol.

This border town was the closest port to Bristol, and has a long history of illicit trade. The most colourful (and perhaps unlikely) era of smuggling at Chepstow was during the fifteenth century, when Chepstow ships carried on an illicit trade in Icelandic dried fish. In 1419, a storm wrecked more than two dozen English ships on the Icelandic coast, so the trade with the island must have been considerable.[4]

Though such evasion was really an incidental aspect of general trade,

'professional' smugglers were operating in the area as early as 1577. One, a Simon Fferdinando, smuggled some 100 'chestes of sugar', and unloaded them in the Roads of Penarth.

When Bristol customs officials became particularly diligent, sixteenth-century merchants directed their ships to Chepstow, where there were no customs staff.

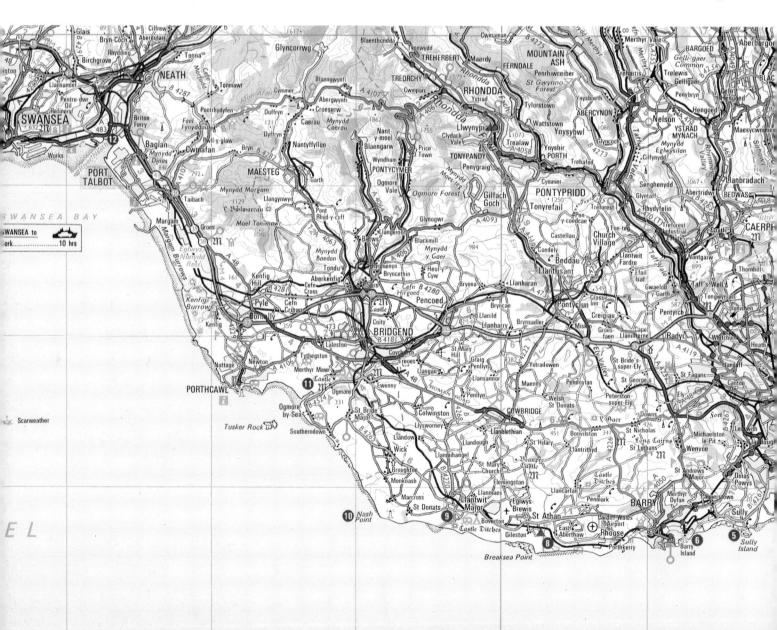

NEWPORT ■2

171-ST3088. St Woolos Cathedral is on the Stow Hill, some 1/2m S of the railway station. Skinner Street is a continuation of Bridge Street, near the Newport Bridge.

The big boost to the Newport smuggling trade was the craze for tobacco smoking. As early as 1649 the collector of customs at Caerleon seized '34 great rowles and 14 hand rowles of Barbathoes tobacco which was privately landed at Redwick, to the south east of Newport. The tobacco was about 2000 lb weight . . . and it was landed to defraude the State of Custome and Excise'.

The bustling Newport docks concealed a great deal of illegal trading. The Salt Survey commented that 'The Usk and the Ebbw received and sheltered many a smuggling craft . . . for Running'.[5] The opening of the Monmouthshire canal increased the amount of trade through Newport, and smuggling expanded, too. In 1804 the collector of customs admitted that 'the running of goods up the Usk has frequently been attempted and sometimes with success as we are assured'.

The success of the smugglers is hardly surprising in view of the resistance they put up when trade was threatened. The Newport authorities faced a daunting task as an incident in October of 1791 illustrates. A custom-house officer tried to board a small vessel (15–20 tons), anchored at the mouth of the Usk:

the persons on board her, with horrid imprecations, recited him, swearing that if he presumed to come on board, they would blow his brains out, and at the same time brandishing a cutlass and pointing a pistol, with horrid threats of his life, etc . . . There is 6 or 7 desperate ruffians on board . . . but we are assured she belongs to Barry Island, and built on purpose for smuggling.

This glimpse of a genuine smuggler is a rare one, and the records of the Newport custom-house provide much greater detail about the minutiae of life in the service of the King, and about every hair-pin seized by the preventives. The level of seizures listed, though, is no real guide to the amount of smuggling that went on, and this is amply illustrated by the fact that there was a rise in goods seized locally after 1830, a time when smuggling nationwide was on the decrease owing to changes in the levels of duty. Many of the merchant seamen found guilty of smuggling in this period were pressed into the navy, this in itelf being considered sufficient punishment.

Small seizures were common, but there were also a number of bigger hauls at Newport that provide an interesting if oblique insight into the way that the Newport smuggling trade was organized. A case in point was the 72-ton schooner ironically named *Good Intent*. This ship was owned by a consortium of five Newport businessmen, one of whom had strong links with the revenue services. The ship apparently plied a perfectly innocent trade with France, but when passing through Mount's

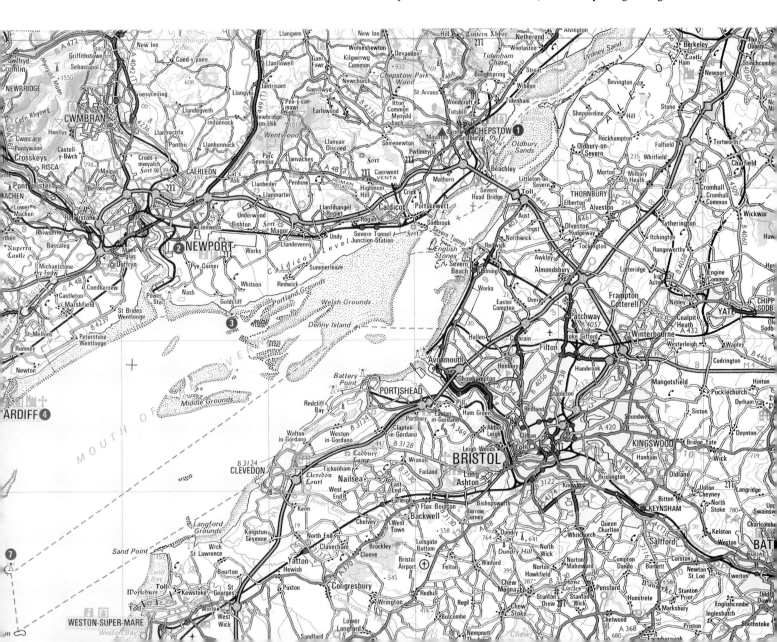

Bay in 1837 a close inspection by a revenue cruiser revealed that the intents of the captain and merchant owners were far from good. The schooner had false bulkheads concealing 1100 gallons of Brandy in 259 small kegs. The ship was cut up, and the master was sentenced to a long spell in Monmouth gaol. Significantly, the owners simply lost their ship.

Today there is little remaining to connect Newport with the smuggling of the eighteenth and nineteenth centuries, but Skinner Street was the site of an incident as late as 1867. A hawker stole a firkin of butter from a Mr Mathews' warehouse, and a search of his lodgings uncovered 70 lb of uncustomed tobacco. There is also a persistent rumour of a tunnel leading from the Ebbw River to St Woolos Cathedral.[6]

GOLDCLIFF ■3

171-ST372819, 5m SE of Newport.

This area was a popular landing-site in the late eighteenth century, and within a stone's throw of major markets at Cardiff and Newport. In 1784 customs officers seized nearly 10,000 lb of tobacco, and 40 gallons of brandy, and a couple of months later a further 130 gallons of brandy. Even today, the Goldcliff salt-marshes are criss-crossed by dykes and drainage ditches and are quite isolated. Houses are few and far between, and anyone landing goods over the sea wall could do so with little fear of interruption.

One report suggests that after running continental spirits via the Channel Islands, the smugglers collected the empty tubs, stuffed them with wool, and smuggled the wool out to France. This seems a little far-fetched, even taking into account that 'In order that the cargo should appear innocent, casks actually empty were placed on top in case the vessel should be intercepted by revenue cruisers'.[7]

CARDIFF ■4

171-ST1876.

The principal illegal imports at Cardiff were wine, spirits and tobacco,[8] but cargoes also included salt and some other extraordinary items: 14 lb of human hair were seized in 1733 by vigilant customs officers! It appears that the Cardiff customs authorities—or at least some of them—were in league with the smugglers, because a directive from London in February of 1690 admonished the Cardiff men and called for greater diligence in the execution of their duties.

Though some of the contraband may have been imported via the town quays with the connivance of the authorities, much of the tobacco was landed in the surrounding creeks, such as the Rumney River, and quickly distributed to the 80–100 illegal tobacconists in the town.

The local smugglers used the usual range of ruses to conceal their goods, and at one stage, importers of hillingstones (roofing tiles) were known to be hiding contraband under their bulky cargoes.

To the south of the city 'Penarth Bay is a member of the port of Cardiff' commented the Salt Survey, 'likewise a very convenient Place [for smuggling]'.

SULLY ■5

Sully Sound is at 171-ST1667, 3m or so E of Barry. Leave the B4267 on the outskirts of Sully, and turn down Beach Road. The Pot Inn has faded from memory, and the Manor House has been turned into flats, but the well remains, in the courtyard of the pub The Captain's Wife. Sully beach is a series of rocky shelves, and you can walk to Sully Island at low tide. Take care, though, as the currents can be lethal when the tide rises.

Sully was a port in the 1740s, but the law restricted foreign trade to Cardiff, so theoretically, Sully could only trade coastwise (with another British port). Nevertheless, quantities of goods, notably livestock, were landed on the beach at Sully, and stored in the yard of the Pot Inn.[9]

This hostelry was 'a regular smugglers' resort' and the ancient manor house had a well with a false bottom:

> the flow of water could be stopped, and what remained pumped out. Underneath the false bottom was a vault in which a horse and cart could easily have been turned. It was evident that smuggling had been carried on here extensively, but so secretly that it was not even suspected.

The salt surveyor commented about Sully Haven that 'This is also a very convenient Place for Running, and I am informed very much used to that purpose for Tea and other Custome Goods'.

BARRY ■6

171-ST1166, 8m SW of Cardiff.

Barry Island has a benign appearance today, but this hides a chilling history. It was once a true island, and the private domain of smuggler Thomas Knight. He put sturdy fortifications around the shoreline, and ran a fleet of heavily-armed smuggling ships from there, importing spirits and tobacco from the Channel Islands, and soap from Ireland. Knight probably arrived in Barry in 1783, in a 24-gun brig called the *John O Combe.*

Opposition from the customs authorities was at first nominal, and with support from local people, Knight quickly made the island his stronghold. The customs men may well have exaggerated the problem, but Knight was reputed to have a force of 60 to 70 men defending the island from uninvited interest.

Knight's influence grew rapidly, and within a year or so, the customs authorities had difficulty recruiting members, since the local population evidently had more respect for Barry's smuggling king than for the legitimate crown.

Knight's crews did not hesitate to fire on preventive vessels, and the crews of the revenue cutters evidently went in fear of their lives. On occasions the custom-house boats refused to give chase, the crew claiming justifiably that there was no pension scheme for customs men injured in the line of duty.

To counter this, a £10 payment was introduced for mariners who lost a hand or foot, and free medical treatment for any injury. Knight was implicated in the heavy seizure of tobacco at Goldcliff in 1784, and some indication of the importance attached to his influence in the area can be gained from the fact that the seized goods were taken to Cardiff under armed guard at considerable expense. The local people refused to help with the transport, because they were terrified of how Knight would exact his revenge.

Knight's reign was brief. In 1785 a concerted effort by the authorities dislodged him and he retreated to Lundy. His place was taken by another smuggler, named William Arthur (see page 134). Arthur proved as tough a nut to crack as his predecessor, and the local collector of customs estimated that it would require the efforts of 60 dragoons to make the island safe once more.

Other smuggling gangs subsequently made Barry Island their home and place of business, and outwitted the custom-house officers with the aid of the tide:

> At Barry . . . if they find the officer on the Iseland (*sic*) they land the other Side of the harbour. If [they find the officer on] the other Side of the harbour, they'll land on the Iseland, and the officer can't get over till the tide is out, wch may be five or six hours; and there is so much Cover on the Iseland, and such conveniencys for hiding of goods on the other side, that an officer has but poor chance to meet with em after they have landed.[10]

However, for reasons that are not entirely clear, the contraband trade from Barry had more or less petered out by the closing years of the eighteenth century.

FLAT HOLM ■7

171-ST2265, 6m E of Barry. The island is a nature reserve, with no regular public boat service. However, landing is permitted (on payment of a fee).

The strategic position of this small island in the middle of the Bristol Channel made it the ideal base for smuggling activity, with easy access to both English and Welsh sides of the channel. The island is clearly visible from the mainland in good weather, and the loading and unloading of cargoes was carried out in full view. However, the customs authorities were for many years powerless to stop the illegal trade, since they lacked a boat to take them out across the 6-mile stretch of water separating Flat Holm from Wales.

According to tradition, a small cave in the east cliff at Flat Holm was used for the storage of contraband, but the writer who commented in 1902[11] that 'men are still living who claimed to have seen (the cave) filled with kegs of brandy that had never paid the Queen's dues' had clearly not visited the island himself. The entrance to the cave is hardly large enough to squeeze into, and just a couple of barrels would have filled the chamber. Nevertheless, elsewhere on the island circumstantial evidence points to smuggling activity. An old mine shaft on the north side connects with a series of natural tunnels, and a sea-facing exit from the system has been cleverly filled with masonry and disguised as solid rock. These concealed chambers are well-hidden, and even on close inspection would pass for a derelict tin mine.[12]

ABERTHAW ■8

170-ST0366, 5m W of Barry.

Smugglers based on Flat Holm and Barry favoured Aberthaw as a landing-place. From here, they could easily ship goods onwards by land, for sale in Cardiff.[13]. The locals had a simple but effective method for avoiding capture:

> At Aberthaw and Barry when any boat goes out to em from thence, the Owners of em have always a spy on the Officer; and when they find him on one side of the river at Aberthaw, they'll land what they have of the other; and by reason there's no Boat in the service . . . and the officer obliged to go to a bridge about two miles round, they have time enough to secure the goods before he can get there. Nay, there is instances that they have Run'd goods in the daytime before the officer's face in this manner . . . At Ogmore River it is the same case, and so at Aberavon.[14]

LLANTWIT MAJOR ■9

170-SS9668, 11m W of Barry. The pub is in the middle of the village.

The Old Swan here was a smugglers' meeting place, and at the back of the pub a concealed staircase still leads up to what was once an attic storage space. The upstairs room adjacent to the staircase is much smaller than common sense would suggest, and the stairs are hidden in the wall. The entrance to the stairs can be seen through a small window overlooking the pub car-park, but there's no public access. There are also rumours of a tunnel leading from the cellars to the sea.

NASH POINT ■10

170-SS9168. Nash Point is on a toll road leading from Marcross. St Donats is at 170-SS9368.

Nash point was the site of a major seizure in 1833: 1,100 gallons of spirits were found in a house at Nash, believed to have come from the *Kate* of Bristol. This vessel had been anchored off Nash Point with a cargo of coal and suspicions had been aroused when it was observed that

the coal did not fill her hold to capacity. Local merchants were appalled that the sale of the seizure might cause prices of drink in the area to plummet, so the brandy was sold in London. A visit to the point confirms its suitability as a landing-place: the valley behind is wooded, providing perfect concealment for chains of ponies shipping the contraband inland.

Smugglers landing at Nash used the high tower at St Donat's Castle as a sea marker, and Henry Stradling, once the owner of the castle, employed the vantage point to keep an eye on shipping. According to one local yarn, Stradling was attacked on one of his regular trips to France by a privateer, and was held ransom. Though he was released, Sir Henry continued to hold a grudge against the pirates, and eventually captured the man who had made him suffer. The man's punishment was to be buried up to his neck in the sand of St Donat's Bay, and Sir Henry watched from his tower as the tide rose. Though colourful, this tale is probably a concoction of several local stories, since a similar fate reputedly awaited another local villain called Peter the Pirate!

THE OGMORE RIVER ■11

170-SS8676, SW of and passing through Bridgend.

Smugglers used the Ogmore River as an artery for shipping contraband up to Bridgend, as the salt surveyor wryly observed: 'here is a very convenient Bay for small vessels, and I find very great Quantitys of tea is Run here . . .'.

In 1737 smuggling here was so widespread that a local landowner wrote to the collector of customs in London, complaining of the activities of the smugglers. He commented that the Bridgend smugglers (most of whom were shoemakers) . . . 'have a bell for a signal, which they have agreed to ring if any of them should be apprehended, that the whole town may rise to rescue the prisoners'. The letter was provoked by a violent incident at Nash Point, where over 300 people, many of them armed, turned out to pillage a vessel that had run aground, laden with tobacco.[15]

The local smugglers' haunt was the New Inn, which stood close to a bridge crossing the Ogmore. It is said that when the inn was demolished, a concealed cave was discovered at one side of the kitchen, big enough to hold the whole of a ship's cargo; and that the garden was like a graveyard, because the barbarous smugglers had buried so many of their adversaries there.[16]

THE NEATH RIVER ■12

170-SS7393, 5m E of Swansea.

In the eighteenth century, coal ships from Neath were the principal smuggling vessels, trading with Ireland and returning with concealed contraband. What makes the Neath area exceptional though, and possibly unique, was the involvement of women in the trade. The local smugglers were led by Catherine Lloyd, who was the landlady of the Ferry Inn of Briton Ferry.

The women were evidently made of stern stuff, and when in 1726 a 'sitter in ye boat at Briton Ferry' seized some brandy and wine, four of the smugglers rescued their contraband, and 'abused' the revenue man. Eight years later Catherine Lloyd was still running the pub (now called the Bretton Ferry) and still smuggling. She made the mistake of offering contraband India cotton to an off-duty customs collector from Llanelly:

> Edward Dalton . . . Stop'd at the publick house to drink a Pint of ale, the woman of ye house, one CATHERINE LLOYD a widow not suspecting him to be an officer bro't out the s'd goods & offer'd the same to sale as India Goods, moreover told they were RUN GOODS she had secured the night before . . . Said Widdow is very well to pass in ye world & Suppos'd to have All Her Riches by Running of Goods for SHE is an old offender and NOTED SMUGGLER.

The trade continued through the century, still under the control of women. An anonymous informer wrote from Gower to the tidesman at Briton Ferry in 1758, giving the names of four women who had gone from Neath to Bridgewater to buy uncustomed tea. What is not clear from any of these accounts is the exact role of the women involved. Most probably, Catherine Lloyd would have been financing the operation and storing the contraband in the pub, rather than being a sea smuggler.

Later in the century it seems that the Briton Ferry smugglers had progressed from tea and cotton to brandy. In 1771, customs inspectors found 18 kegs of it on the sands at Briton Ferry, with ropes attached ready for carrying. They commented that the brandy came from Guernsey, and probably came ashore as a raft, 'as is the practice made use of by smugglers'. If this is true, it is a rare Welsh example of goods being rafted in.[17]

Guernsey smugglers continued to land goods in the area, and in November 1787 customs men seized the *Polly* of Guernsey at Neath Abbey. Their searches were interrupted by a mob of colliers and copper men who tried to storm the vessel, stoning the customs men. A second attack, at midnight, was repelled only by firing on the crowd.[18]

GOWER PENINSULA

The Gower Peninsula is conveniently close to the huge market-place of Swansea, yet is amply supplied with secluded bays and sandy inlets where it was a simple matter to bring contraband ashore unobserved. Swansea coal ships found it convenient in the late eighteenth century to be 'blown off course' to Ireland, where they could load up with salt and soap. On the return trip, Gower made a handy stopping-off point. Those that exported coal to the Continent did not return empty, either.

The chief preventive station was at Swansea, but the authorities were hampered by lack of facilities and money (as elsewhere in the country) and there is the usual run of letters to the board of customs in the vein of: If only we had a boat/a new boat/another boat/a bigger boat/we could do more. In this instance, the grievance is probably legitimate, and the ill-equipped preventives were no match for the local free-traders, as this complaint in 1730 illustrates:

> The smugglers are grown very insolent and obstruct our officers in the execution of their duty . . . the master and mariners of the ship Galloway . . . came up on deck with pistols and drawn cutlasses and refused them to rummage.

The smugglers presented Gower farmers with an interesting quandary. The landowners had no choice but to cooperate by lending their horses and barns, yet the demand for carriers and bat-men drove up wages locally.[19]

BRANDY COVE ■13

159-SS586874, 2m W of the Mumbles. Take the B4593 to Caswell. Leaving Caswell, the road bends sharply to the right at the top of a steep hill, then left about a mile farther on, then right again. At this third bend, turn left down a cul-de-sac and park at the end. Follow the farm track to reach Brandy Cove.

The name of this delightful and concealed cove requires no amplification, and acts as fairly damning evidence of the role the beach played in the free-trade. The cove is almost concealed by rocks, and is often deserted, even when tourists throng more accessible Caswell Bay just half a mile away.

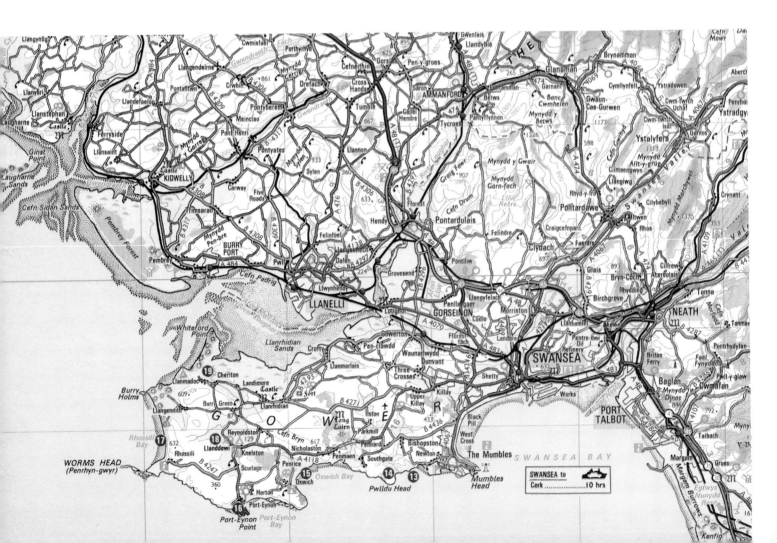

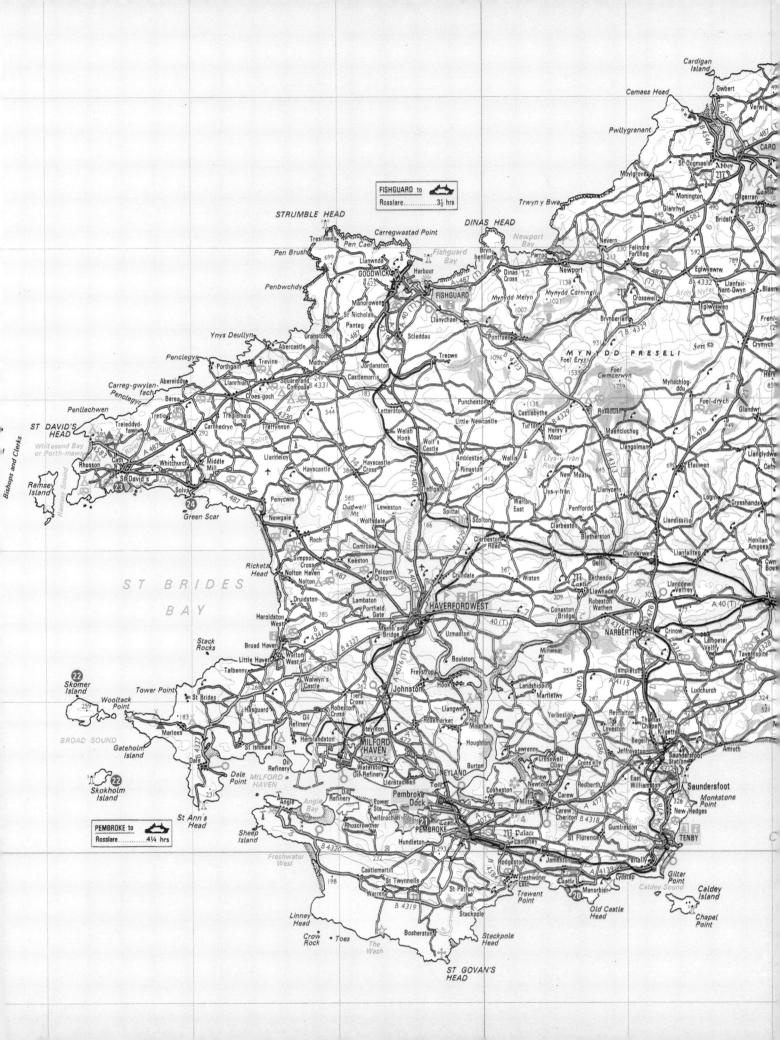

Even today Pwlldu Bay is extremely isolated, and its seclusion was even greater two centuries ago when Gower smuggling was at its height. A thriving company landed goods here before carrying them inland to the Highways farms for temporary storage.

PWLLDU AND THE HIGHWAY ■14

3m W of the Mumbles. The farms at Highway are either side of a minor road that leaves the B4436 at Pennard 159-SS5588. To reach Pwlldu Bay, continue along the road and park at the Southgate NT car-park at 159-SS555875, then follow the track for about 3m down to the isolated beach.

Central on the south coast of Gower, Pwlldu headland guided smuggling boats to the bay at its foot. The 300-foot high headland also provided a very convenient vantage point for keeping an eye on the opposition.

The name of the place is Welsh for black pool: a shingle bar blocks the river flowing into Pwlldu Bay, forming a pool. The house behind the pebble bank was once the Beaufort Inn. The landlord here was said to have made a convenient arrangement with the local smugglers; they used his cellars for free storage, but they never took out of the cellars

quite as many barrels as they rolled in. A cottage on the cliff path west of the beach was also used by smugglers, though it is now in ruins.

The bay was a hotbed of smugglers. One local writer claims that more contraband was landed here than anywhere else in the Bristol Channel. To the visitor the advantages are obvious. From the sheltered bay, transport inland was virtually invisible, the wooded Bishopston valley providing plenty of cover. From the valley, farms at Highway were used as staging posts, and as headquarters for the smuggling company. In the second half of the eighteenth century the gang was run by William Arthur of Great Highway Farm, and John Griffiths of Little Highway. William Arthur had been described as 'the most daring smuggler in Glamorgan during the eighteenth century', and at one stage he ruled Barry Island almost as a kingdom.

In 1786 there was a raid on Highway Farm by 12 revenue men but Arthur had been kept well informed, and the customs and excise officers were met with a stout defence: a 'Body of desperate fellows . . .

amounted to One hundred'. The King's men retreated with bruised pride. Two subsequent expeditions to capture Arthur failed in 1788.

A local tale relates how a customs officer arrived at one of the farms with a search warrant, and discovered a half-anker of brandy concealed in the attic. The officer sent for reinforcements and settled down to keep a close watch on the barrel. Meanwhile, the smugglers created a terrific row in the room below to conceal the noise as one of them bored a hole through the floor of the attic and the base of the tub, draining the contents into a barrel waiting below.

The farms at Highway still exist, some 400 yards west of the crossroads at Pennard. The present occupiers—one of whom is descended from smuggler Griffiths—knew nothing of the cellars,[20] and the buildings have been considerably changed over the last two centuries. The former occupant didn't entirely escape the attentions of the law: he paid a fine of £5 5s for concealing prohibited goods in 1789. However, in 1802, the Swansea Guide referred to him as 'a proprietor of considerable stone-coal and culm collieries on the Swansea canal', so he had clearly retired from the free-trade by the turn of the century.[21]

OXWICH SANDS ■15

159-SS5187, 8m from Swansea on the A4118.

Smugglers landed many of their cargoes at Oxwich Sands and an incident that took place there in 1804 is fascinating not only because it led to the break-up of the gang based at Highway, but also because it displays the näiveté of some of the smugglers. A smuggling cutter dropped anchor in the bay, and two of the crew rowed to the beach to ask directions to Highway. The two men walking on the beach gave the mariners detailed directions, and as the helpful locals ambled away the run began. By midnight most of the contraband had been carried to Highway, and hidden in cellars. A skin of earth concealed the entrance to the cellars.

Unfortunately the apparently casual passers-by were actually members of the preventive authorities, and in the early hours of the morning a raid started. Early searches were fruitless, but eventually the customs men discovered the hidden chambers, and seized 420 casks of spirits. Most of these were transported back to Swansea under guard, but 17 kegs never arrived—a crowd of 200 local people waylaid the convoy, and had to be pacified with a drink from the barrels. Even when the guard on the barrels was increased to 50 men, the spirits weren't safe; the commanding officer knew that his men would help themselves to the booze, so the soldiers were given permission to drink what they liked while on guard.

PORT EYNON ■16

At the end of the A4118, 13m from Swansea. The Salt House is at 159-SS469845, close to the beach car-park, and the spectacular Culver Hole is on the far side of the headland at 159-SS465845.

On the southernmost tip of Gower, the ruined Salt House is today the only reminder of a powerful dynasty that dominated smuggling there for a century or more. The Lucas family have a long and distinguished history—Sir Charles Lucas fought for the King in the Civil War, and was executed under Cromwell's instructions. The family had some black sheep, though, notably John 'of fine and bold front and very comely in the eye but lawless and of fierce and ungovernable violence'. John spent nine years roaming abroad, 'engaging his handes in much violations of all laws.' When he returned to Gower, he set to fortifying Ye Salte House:

> ... with the battlement and walls thereof all around reached even unto the clift and the rocks on the edge of ye wilde parte of ye foreshore near unto Porth Eynon and storing said stronghold with arms and also rebuilded and repaired another stronghold

In the 1720s Swansea smugglers had so much influence that they were able to have the senior customs officers of the port summoned for jury service on the day when they landed a large cargo in the harbour!

135

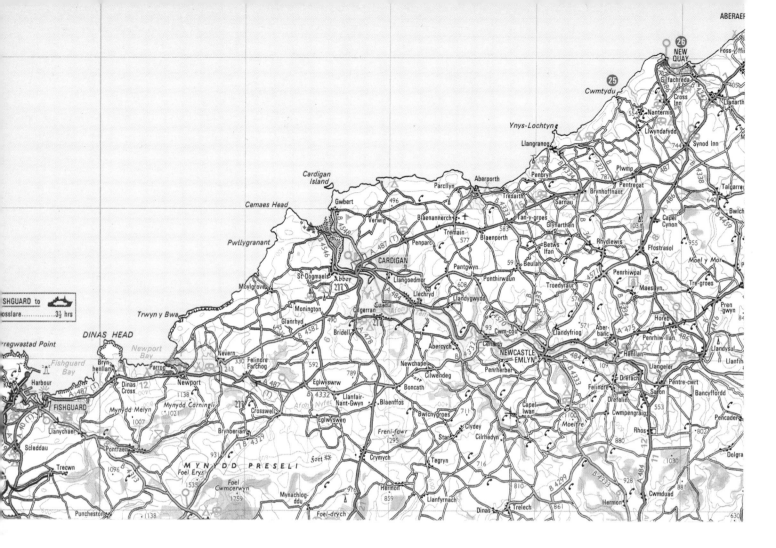

called Kulverd Hall [Culver Hole] ... [he] connected the two strongholds by a passage under the grounds where of no man was told ye mouthe. He became outlaw, engaged in smuggling matters secoured ye pirates and ye French smugglers and rifled ye wrecked ships and forced mariners to serve him ... He was assisted by George ap Eynon of Brinefield and by Robert de Skurlege, and a band of ruthless young men gathered round them.[22]

John Lucas wasn't all bad, though. It is said that all his law-breaking abroad was done 'in the King's name' and that he used the spoils of his smuggling trips to support the Gower poor.

There are local stories of a hidden cache of contraband in the vast cellars below the ruins, and secret passages in the area 'some of them big enough for a man to ride through on horseback'. Another local legend has smugglers using pigeon post to give advance warning of their arrival,[23] but this story probably started because Culver Hole was at one time used as a pigeon loft, quite separately from its role as a contraband store. Kulverd, the root of the place name, is old English for pigeon.

The church at Port Eynon was used as a hiding-place for contraband around the time of the battle of Trafalgar—kegs were hidden in the altar—and at other times the goods were buried in the sand-dunes.

The spectacular Culver Hole at Port Eynon on the Gower Peninsula is the epitome of the smuggler's cave. A masonry curtain wall guards the entrance to this cave which runs deep into the cliff.

RHOSSILI ■17

159-SS4190, at the extreme W of Gower.

This gently curving beach was a natural Gower landing-spot, and smuggling continued here long after it had been stamped out at Port Eynon by the stationing of a preventive boat and a force of eight stout 'Sea fencibles'. Eventually, though, the preventives realized what was going on at Rhossili, and by 1805 had become a little more watchful. There were various clashes on the sands, and it seems the two sides were fairly evenly matched, with about equal numbers of home and away wins. In June, the customs officers seized 115 kegs, but three months earlier they didn't fare so well—two preventives were man-handled by a smuggling gang and severely beaten. One was locked up in William Stote's cottage in Middleton.[24] The Stote family were the most prominent Rhossili smugglers: a popular (though possibly apocryphal) story concerns two customs officers who asked Mrs Stote for stabling for their horses. She realized that they had probably come to search for a cargo of run spirits that were concealed nearby, so she delayed them with a drink. When they commented that the spirits were too strong, she topped up their glasses from the kettle on the stove. This, however, also contained spirits, and the customs men soon fell asleep. At this point Mrs Stote was able to raise the alarm, and the hidden contraband was dispersed.

OLD HENLLYS ■18

Park near Llanddewi church at 159-SS460891, then follow the track that passes the church for about 1 mile.

Local tales tell of a 2-mile long tunnel leading here from Rhossili Bay, and while the tunnel story may seem unlikely, the isolated farmhouse was the home of the Mansell family, who were well known locally for their smuggling interests.

NORTH GOWER ■19

Brandy Cottage is close to Cheriton. Park near the Britannia pub at 159-SS446933 and walk up the hill towards Llanmadoc. Take the footpath on the right signposted Whiteford Burrows. Brandy Cottage is the last white-painted house on the left.

Most of the smuggling on Gower took place along the south coast, but there is an occasional reminder in the north. Brandy Cottage overlooking the west end of Landimore Marsh was built at the end of the eighteenth century specifically for smuggling purposes. However, the entrance to the huge cellars rumoured to be underneath the cottage must have been well-hidden, for their location is now lost.

Tucked away on the edge of a marsh, Brandy Cottage is easy to overlook. When its smuggling owners had filled the ample cellars with contraband, there was plenty of scope for concealment in the vast dunes of Whiteford Burrows nearby.

WEST AND MID-WALES

Pembroke smuggling has a long history. French traders were bringing uncustomed wine into Pembrokeshire ports as early as 1611, according to a contemporary document.[25] In the seventeenth and eighteenth centuries, smuggling vessels traded openly with Caldey Island, south of Tenby and:

> Cargoes (generally French Brandy) were run into every southern bay from Tenby to Dale . . . The town of Tenby too was deeply implicated in this illicit business. Probably a vast number of persons in all stations of life were implicated. The story goes that when a cargo was in, and the revenue men alert, or the weather squally, teams were requisitioned right and left, not infrequently the squire's carriage-horses were found in the morning sweating and exhausted; but a mysterious keg of excellent eau de vie stood in the hall, so no questions were asked.[26]

SWANLAKE AND MANORBIER ■20

The Castle at Manorbier is at 158-SS064977, 6m W of Tenby. Swanlake Bay is just to the W. Sunny Hill, where the Swanlake tubs were hidden, is on the Ridgeway, about 1/2m NW of Manorbier station. Another favourite landing-place nearby was Bullslaughter Bay, at 158-SR940943.[27]

At Swanlake a smuggling story of treachery and loyalty dates from 1825. A Swanlake man confided in his wife that a local smuggler, Mr J, had temporarily stowed barrels in their cellar, and the following day the wife went downstairs, counted the barrels, and set off to inform the local customs officials, calculating that she would receive a reward of some £200. En route through Manorbier, she told a friend of her plan, who in turn told Mr J himself. The smuggler rallied his troops, the Swanlake house was cleared within an hour or so, and the contraband being transported to Sunny Hill and elsewhere. The reactions of the customs officers at their discovery—or lack of it—were not recorded.[28]

A well at nearby Manorbier castle was used as a storage place by smugglers, and the place 'was honeycombed with smugglers' cellars'.[29] You can still peer down the well and see the entrance to a smuggling tunnel leading to the sea.

Local stories revolve around the castle as the centre for smuggling activity in the area. A persistent tale features Captain Jack Furze, who arrived in Manorbier around 1800. He was . . .

> 'a jolly-looking seaman patrolling in the grounds of the castle . . . those who were favoured with his calls of an evening, liked his society immensely. He told them that 'he had saved a few pounds, and thought of taking the farm that was to be let in connection with the old castle'.

The sailor had a small brig, which he intended to keep running while farming and digging for coal. It emerged, though, that his mining and farming activities were merely a front for smuggling, and the castle cellars were being used for storing contraband.[30]

Jolly Jack Furze continued trading at Manorbier for some time, but eventually things began to get uncomfortable. As Jack's ship *The Jane* was heading for the coast one day, one of the King's ships appeared on the horizon. *The Jane* tacked away, but:

> at a critical moment the King's ship caught the wind, and came onward so fast and so ably that the Saucy Jane was brought within range of her stern chaser. Then a storm of shots flew into the Jane and about her deck, making the little craft to reel again and the crew to look despondingly at the captain . . . but with the dexterity of a hare the Jane doubled then shot on its way. For an hour the unequal contest continued. The dusk was now creeping steadily on, necessitating to the cruiser a determined effort, or, in the darkness, their prey would escape. So putting on all sail, the pursuer dashed onwards, then, pausing, raked her fore and aft; but still Captain Jack was inexorable. 'Run below, you lubbers!' he said to his men 'or lie down on the deck, I'll manage the brig myself,' and alone at the helm, seeming to have a charmed life, unhurt, while the iron hail cut up his rigging, or made matchwood of his deck, he continued to double and tack until the welcome darkness settled down, and the cruiser, fearful of the coast drew off from pursuit.
>
> Tradition says that Captain Jack . . . exclaimed 'I told you so, you beggars, the timber is not spliced that'll run down Jack Furze!'

However, this was too close a shave for the smuggler, and he soon settled to a quieter life.

The castle at Manorbier still has tunnels and cellars that are well suited to the storage of contraband. However, it is unclear whether Captain Jack Furze, the occupant around 1800, adapted the premises for the purpose or simply took advantage of existing facilities.

PEMBROKE DOCK ■21

Bentlass is at 158-SM961017. Turn off the B4320 at Hundleton. You can see where Truscott tried to cross; the channel is a mere trickle at low tide, and a ferry once operated here. See map on page 133.

In the 1830s, smuggling in Pembroke was organized by one William Truscott, known romantically as 'The King of the Smugglers', but his reign came to a violent end at Pembroke Dock in 1834. He had been captured at a cave used for storage at New Quay, 'a sequestered little inlet near St Govan's'. He managed to escape, and fled as far as the Pembroke River, which he tried to cross to Pembroke Dock from Bentlass. Here the customs men shot and wounded him and he drowned.

The case aroused more than the usual amount of interest, because it appeared that the revenue officer who fired at Truscott did so the instant he ran into the water, and that the officers ignored the injured man's cries for help. The jury at the inquest judged that the conduct of the King's men 'was highly reprehensible, cowardly and cruel'acte'.[31]

ST BRIDE'S BAY

Solva is at 157-SM8024, 4m E of St David's.

That the villages around St Bride's Bay were involved in the free-trade is beyond doubt; Skomer and Skokholm islands to the south ■22 were used as smuggling depots, and smugglers at St David's ■23 (for both sites see map on page 133) to the north scuttled a government ship in 1770:

The Pelham cutter, in the service of the customs . . . was attacked by two large smuggling cutters and a wherry, and, the officers being obliged to quit it, was boarded by the crew of the wherry. It has since been found at St Davids, with several holes in the bottom, and almost rifled of everything. The Commissioners have offered a reward of £200 for the conviction of any of the offenders.[32]

However, the most persistent stories from this area centre on Solva ■24 (see map on page 133), where houses are reputed to have concealed cupboards and shafts that were used to hide contraband.[33]

Two stories in particular are concerned with the smuggling of salt and tallow, and both implicate people respected in local society. The Baptist chapel was lit by candles made from tallow smuggled into Solva harbour, and . . .

One evening, the chapel being lighted with those candles, by some means or other, the excise officer became aware of it, and he suddenly appeared and comandeered all the candles, leaving the congregation in the dark.

The tax on salt was a particular burden to the local fishing industry, which relied on salt for preservation.

It was sold about 1s [5p] a pound about the first half of the eighteenth century. There was also much smuggling carried on in the salt line, and the smugglers supplied the country with salt at 4d [1.5p] per lb. Their usual time for doing business was at night,

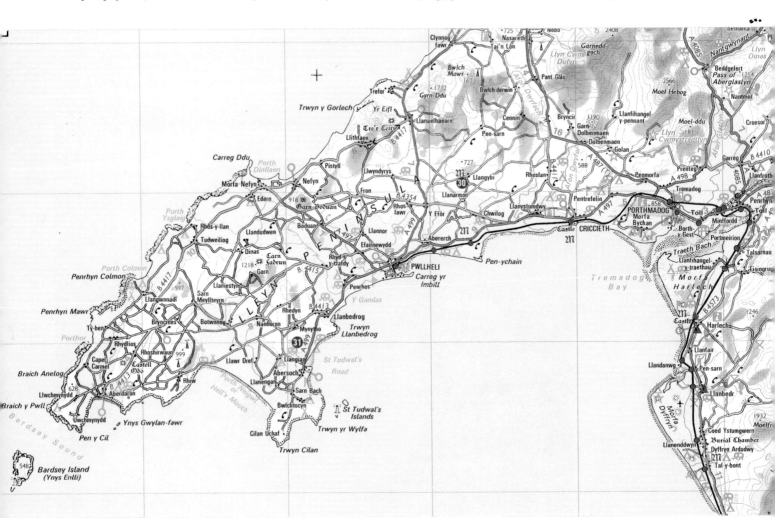

and much liquor was supplied by the same traders at a low price.[34]

One day a spy informed Mr Raymond, the justice, who lived in Bank House [Solva] that a vessel had just come in and that they had salt smuggled aboard. Mr Raymond, who privately sympathised with the poor smugglers and was anxious not to convict the smugglers in this case, came slowly over the hill, roaring like a lion. 'I'll punish the rascals! They shan't thieve from his most gracious majesty, my beloved king. I'll salt the d-ls'. Those in the vessel below heard every word—as he intended. Hailing the men and demanding a boat, he hunted the vessel through. Needless to say, no salt was found. But tradition says that the specific gravity of the salt water in Solva harbour that evening was much heavier than usual.[35]

FISHGUARD TO NEW QUAY

Cwmtydu ■25 is at 145-SN3557, 2m SW of New Quay (map on page 136).

Salt smuggling was rife on this part of the coast, in particular at New Quay, the little bay of Cwmtydu, and at Fishguard. The Salt Survey commented that there were many small creeks around Fishguard, where vessels were able to land contraband unobserved: 'The Country People in General Favoureing the smuglers . . . I think a Boat here absolutely necessary both on Salt and Customs Acco' as much Soap as well as Salt is Run here.'

Smugglers importing salt at New Quay ■26 (see map on page 136) clashed with customs officers from Aberdovey in 1704. The eight officers met with stout opposition from 150–200 locals who were unloading salt from three barques on the beach. In self defence, they fired over the heads of the crowd, who then redoubled their attacks. The customs officers then fired into the crowd, severely injuring one of them. At daybreak, the 'Rabble' returned with the police, and had two of the customs men arrested and charged with injuring the smugglers. It's not recorded whether they secured a conviction.

CARDIGAN BAY

Pen-y-bont Bridge is at 135-SN686715, where the B4340 crosses the Afon Ystwyth at Llanafan.

Smuggling in Cardigan Bay took place primarily between Aberdyfi and Borth-y-Gest, a small village close to Portmadoc.[36] However, farther south the Trefechan district of Aberystwyth ■27 was reputed to have been a haunt of smugglers and other low criminals, and the best known of the local smugglers was a man called Jolly. He landed contraband on Tanybwlch beach, running it up the Ystwyth valley to Llanafan. The

When west Wales revenue men were particularly alert, smugglers used Skomer Island as a convenient offshore warehouse for their stock-in-trade.

The estuary of the Mawddach gave the Barmouth smugglers quick and easy access to the Welsh hinterland: the town of Dolgellau was some 8 miles away by water.

journey onward to England was said to be completed by drovers. According to legend, the gang led by Jolly clashed with the revenue men at Pen-y-bont Bridge, Llanafan ■28 and 'a bloody battle ensued. The tale says that the smugglers attempted to escape through Pont-rhyd-y-groes, leaving dead and dying comrades.'[37]

The Mawddach estuary to the north has a well-established reputation for smuggling as ships could move contraband directly inland as far as Dolgellau. Court records for the Barmouth ■29 area substantiate the stories. A pub adjoining Llanaber church a mile or so from Barmouth was used to store contraband, and in the churchyard itself, graves known locally as Cistfaen, (table tombs) were reputedly used for temporary storage. For sites 27, 28 and 29, see map on page 137.

Ships from Barmouth traded particularly with Spain, importing spirits, wines and silks for the fine houses in the area. At Barmouth, the smugglers would transfer goods to smaller boats for onward movement up the river. This trade was sufficient to merit building a custom-house in the town.

A favourite hiding-place for contraband was a headland called Trwyn Glanmor. A creek there reputedly leads to a cave.[38]

THE LLEYN PENINSULA

St Cybi's well ■30 is at 123-SH427413, 5m NE of Pwllheli. Park by Llangybi church and follow signs along a footpath to reach the well. Castell March House ■31 stands at 123-SH315295 between Abersoch and Llanbedrog on the A499, almost opposite The Warren. Both sites are on the map on page 140.

At the north of Cardigan Bay, this area had a rare advantage for smugglers in the days of the square-rigged ships: its two coasts made running feasible whatever the direction of the wind. Porth Dinllaen on the north was a destination for many of the eighteenth-century smuggling ships, and one popular local story tells how a group of villagers from the surrounding countryside met a revenue officer while they were returning home loaded with spirits. They were, however, able to persuade the innocent man that the tubs actually contained holy water from Saint Cybi's well.

On the south side of the peninsula, an amusing yarn links Castell March House and its master with the local smuggling fraternity. In the seventeenth century the owner, a knight called Sir William Jones, was plagued by a forceful butler who proved impossible to dismiss. Attempts to sack him were treated as jokes, so Sir William hatched a plot to be rid of the man. He hired local smugglers to kidnap the butler and dump him in some distant part. However, the plot misfired, because once on board the smugglers' ship the butler made himself indispensable, and eventually took over as the ship's master. To exact his revenge, he turned the tables on his employer, returning to Castell March, seizing Sir William with the aid of the crew, and forcing him to suffer the same fate as he had once wished on his irritating servant.

The holy water of St Cybi's well on the Lleyn Peninsula provided at least one smuggler with a convenient excuse for his illegal activities.

WALES AND WEST ENGLAND

ANGLESEY AND NORTH WALES

Moelfre ■32 is at 114-SH5186 and Amlwch ■33 at 114-SH4492 on the NE coast of Anglesey.

Smuggling to Anglesey probably reached its zenith in the middle of the eighteenth century,[39] and was largely unhampered by the efforts of the excise authorities. One contemporary writer described the coast-waiters of Anglesey as 'Two fools, one Rogue, one Bully and one Numbskull'.[40]

In 1763 the master of a revenue cutter outlined how the Anglesey smugglers worked. They travelled as passengers on the first available boat to the Isle of Man, often independently, then, after a rendezvous on the island, hired an Irish wherry to take the cargo back to Anglesey. The wherries had crews of nine or ten, and the smugglers added a further six to eleven. They scheduled a landfall in the early hours of the morning, and simply enlisted local help with unloading, which took an hour or less. Farmers were in league with the smugglers, and had carts and other transport waiting; they also served as lookouts, with tinder-dry warning beacons at the ready.

When the Isle of Man returned to the Crown, the smugglers who had been trading with the island instead chose north-east Ireland as their base, in particular Port Rush. The sources of contraband were Belle Ile, Lorient and Roscoff.

Left: *Sir William Jones of Castell March House near Abersoch suffered an unfortunate fate at the hands of his butler and a crew of smugglers.*

Below: *A custom-house at Beaumaris guarded the Menai Straits and though in the 1770s staff were conscientious and diligent, they were no match for the smugglers. The collector of customs wrote that 'No officer dared approach them, for they always send armed men to deliver goods in safety'.*

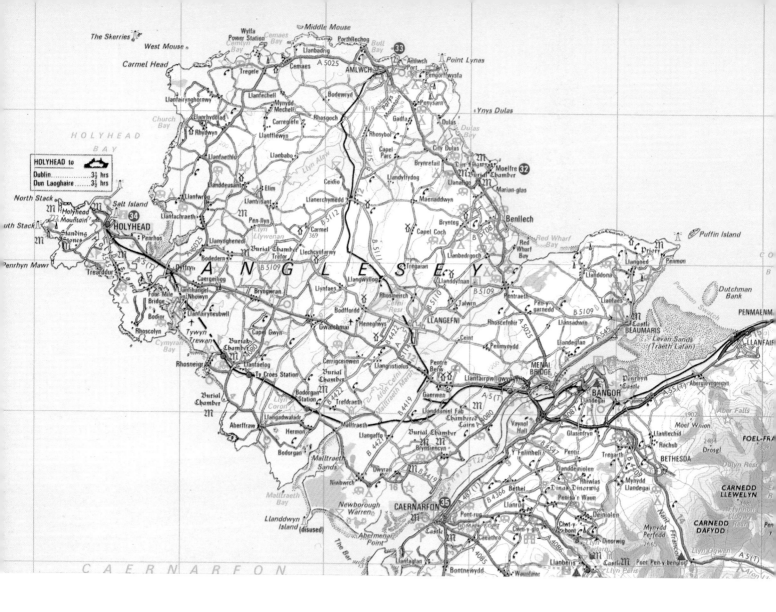

They abandoned the small ships they had used to ply to and fro between Wales and the Isle of Man, and instead took to bigger craft with better arms. These larger vessels forced the smugglers to use different tactics—they could not be beached as the smaller ships could, and their greater draft made certain passages impossible. Lavan Sands and Caernarvon Bar, for example, were risky, and the smugglers looked to the deeper waters at Moelfre and Amlwch. The larger ships were formidable opponents for the preventives, though, and in 1770 the revenue cutter Pelham was captured at Port-Ysky Bay by a smuggler colourfully named Jack the Bachelor. It was plundered and wrecked on the rocks at St David's (q.v.).[41]

Some smuggling still went on in small ships, as the following account, written in 1798, makes clear. Significantly, it additionally implicates a customs official from Amlwch in the trade. Fourteen people from that village had shares in a 25-ton sloop, including the doctor, and the custom-house officer. They made a trip to the Isle of Man—supposedly a holiday—and on their return, a search of the ship revealed seven dozen bottles of wine and 4 gallons of rum. The crew excused themselves by saying that they'd bought the contraband for personal consumption on the trip, but that the weather had been too bad to open the hold.[42]

Though goods smuggled into Anglesey moved onwards to the mainland, much was consumed on the island itself. One writer commented in 1760 that the drink of the island was 'todi'—a sweetened mixture of brandy and water.

The diarist William Bulkeley, who lived in North Anglesey in the mid-eighteenth century, was perhaps an unlikely imbiber of todi. Unlike that other famous diarist of the period, Parson Woodforde (see page 170) Bulkeley saw smuggling from both sides of the fence, since he sat on the bench at Beaumaris. In his capacity as JP he was lenient towards smugglers, and tried to discharge them without punishment at every opportunity. However, there is no evidence in his diaries that pressure was brought to bear to secure lighter sentences.

Bulkeley regularly bought smuggled goods. From a Flintshire man plying between the Isle of Man and Wales, the squire bought French brandy at 5s a gallon, white wine and good claret. In 1750 he wrote that:

> On account of a very penal law being passed last Session of Parliament against the running of soap and candles, there will soon be no soap to be had, but what comes from Chester at 7d a pound. I bought today of a woman in that business 20 lb almost (which I am afraid is the last I shall have of her).[43]

Bulkeley probably bought smuggled salt, too. The sea salt factory on Salt Island in the centre of Holyhead ■34 mixed in smuggled rock salt to improve the quality of the product, and then passed the salt off as wholly of local origin.[44]

144

CAERNARFON ■35

114/115-SH4862 at the SW end of the Menai Straits.

Smugglers in this area continued to enjoy popular support throughout the eighteenth century. In July 1783 several were captured and imprisoned at Caernarfon after a sea chase in which one of their number died, but after just one night behind bars the smugglers were released by the local JPs. With incredible cheek, the freed men then immediately attempted to prosecute the customs man who had shot their crew member.[45]

CONWY ■36

115-SH7777, 2m S of Llandudno.

An incident on the sands here in 1712 gives considerable insight into the relationship between smugglers, the revenue forces, and the local establishment. A smuggled shipment of salt arrived and the local population turned out *en masse* to collect it. They arrived with carts to carry off the contraband, and at the head of the procession was a baronet and JP, Sir Griffith Williams. A lone customs officer had the misfortune to observe the spectacle, and immediately lay down in the sand in case he should be seen himself. He was spotted

and the smugglers beat him, blindfolded him and tied him up. He was imprisoned in a hen-house for a day and a night, and fed a diet of buttermilk—hardly a terrible punishment. When he reported the incident, the official could get nothing done about his ill-treatment, let alone about the smuggling, because he was accusing people who, if not well placed themselves, at least enjoyed the protection of the wealthy and famous. His enthusiasm, and that of his predecessors, may in any case have been open to question: one customs officer at the Great Orme went for 30 years without a seizure and was 'effectively redundant'.

THE DEE RIVER

The Llety Gonest Inn is on the A548 between Talacre and Mostyn (map 116) ■37. The Quay House at Connah's Quay ■38 is at the end of Dock Road, a turning off the A548 on the western outskirts of Connah's Quay. Connah's Pool can be reached by walking up a path at the side of the pub. Take a right turn up an alley, then first right towards the Dee, and down a flight of steps. Pen-y-Llan Rock and the pool are on the left (map 117).

Running goods in Dee estuary had been made virtually impossible by the mid-eighteenth century owing to silting, which had been accelerated by dredging to make the Dee navigable as far as Chester: the 1740 Salt

Survey reported that 'The sea has of late years filled the Channel so much that vessels of Burthen cannot come up as formerly, and by all I can learn there is no Running of any Kind in these parts'.[46]

There were, however, some inland centres: Rhuddlan became a minor depot, and at Talacre a cargo of fine French wine was seized at the Great Barn, and taken to the Lletty Gonest Inn. During the night, a party of 'Mostyn colliers' kidnapped the revenue men guarding the goods, and rescued the wine, which had been intended for the local gentry. The son of the landlord observed wryly that the 'colliers' wore valuable diamond rings, and fine clothes underneath their dirty rags.[47]

Connah's Quay, close to Chester, was named after a famous Welsh smuggler, as were Connah's Cave in Pen-y-llan Rock, and Connah's Pool below it. Connah himself was reputed to have been the landlord of the Quay House.[48]

OWEN WILLIAMS

One Welsh smuggler carved his niche in history not by the extremity of his exploits, but by the fact that he wrote them down. He thus joins Jack Rattenbury and 'The King of Prussia' in that select band of smuggler/autobiographers. The National Library of Wales purchased the manuscript of Williams' story in 1982, and a brief summary of it appeared in the Library's Journal in 1985.[49]

Owen was born in Nevern, Pembrokeshire, in 1717, the son of a wealthy farmer. His wayward nature was evident from an early age; his father wanted him to go into the church, or into law, but he rejected both these plans, and made his distaste for farming abundantly clear, too. When he was fourteen or fifteen he ran away to Haverfordwest to join the crew of a ship trading with Bristol. The novelty of the sailor's life soon wore off; tired of being a skivvy and whipped when he stepped out of line, Williams returned to the farm, but found this suited him even less. On his father's land he was just a labourer, and clearly aimed for something better.

After a second false start on a Bideford ship, his father bought Owen a ship of his own. The sixteen-year-old sea captain soon began to exhibit another side to his character—as a philanderer. He began a debauched affair with a maid, which prompted his father to take back the vessel. Williams retaliated by marrying the girl, and at this his long-suffering father returned the ship, together with cash to set Owen up in business.

Williams traded legally for a while, but was clearly seduced by the rags-to-riches stories of the smugglers he mixed with on the dock-side. He tried his hand at smuggling goods in from the Isle of Man—and got caught on the first trip. He lost his ship and everything he owned, and fled to the West Indies, where he joined a smuggling ship called the *Terrible*.

From this point on, the narrative adopts a tone that shows Williams in a heroic light that is perhaps not entirely true to the facts. The *Terrible* engaged a Spanish ship in battle, and Owen dispatched 25 of the crew by rolling a powder keg, fuse fizzing, onto the deck of the Spanish coaster. Despite a wound to his head, Williams was soon back in Barbados, indulging in various licentiousness with the local ladies, and then later we find him on various smuggling trips in the area. On one of these he was captured by a British man-of-war, but was judged to be such a brave fellow that he was appointed midshipman, and stayed with the vessel for 20 months. Homesickness eventually set in, though, and Williams returned home to set up a legitimate business with his own boat. He dallied with various local women, and fell out with his wife, who turned to drink.

As the years went by, Williams' catalogue of adventures grew: he returned to smuggling, with considerable success; aiding an Aberystwyth friend, he led a large party which laid siege to a local mansion. Owen secured the surrender in heroic manner by loading a wagon with gunpowder, setting light to the wagon, then rolling it under the balcony of the building. Later he masqueraded as a baronet off the Isle of Man, and played double-agent as a customs officer with a lucrative side-line in smuggled goods. He fell in love with a young Manx girl, but was prevented from marrying her by his own reluctance to get a divorce, and by the fact that she was a minor.

Williams, like so many smugglers, had a remarkable ability to smile through adversity. Losing his boat and virtually everything he owned through the treachery of a crew member, he raffled a cow and was thus able to raise £30.

The Llety Gonest Inn, between Talacre and Mostyn.

Smuggled goods came up the River Clwyd to Rhuddlan, and for a while the town was an entrepôt depot for the smuggling community. In the late 1760s the Rhuddlan boat-yards began to construct fast and sophisticated cutters which the smugglers used to outsail the customs vessels.

His fortunes soon changed, and with help from the Manx girl (whom he was then passing off as his wife) Williams bought a new yacht, and resumed smuggling. In 1744, though, the authorities were on his tail, and Owen's ship was attacked in Cardigan. Despite overwhelming odds, the ship's crew escaped, but killed four men, including a customs officer, in the showdown.

By this time, Owen Williams must have been notorious. Even the Isle of Man authorities, who were noted for their leniency, joined in the search, and Williams and his young sweetheart had to escape from the island on an Irish oyster boat. On the run in Ireland, they posed as peddlers until the heat died down, and then travelled back to Wales, to Ireland again, and eventually to the Isle of Man. Here, his luck ran out, and he was captured and brought to trial in Hereford.

Owen Williams must have been a remarkable character, because he defended himself in the trial against 'a very severe prosecution' and was acquitted, largely because of his eloquent defence.

A free man again, Williams resumed a career which interleaved legitimate trading with smuggling and privateering. He became a castaway, wracked by fever on the Barbary coast, and lost his wife in a shipwreck. He went back to Cardigan to recuperate from the recurring effects of the tropical disease, and eventually fell in with James Lilly, a Cardigan fencing master.

Owen Williams lived such a full and colourful life that the end of the story seems like a sordid anticlimax. Though the details are unclear, it seems that Lilly and Williams had burgled a house in Nevern, and had been spotted in Cardiff. Running from the hue and cry, Williams shot the leading pursuer—the Cardigan post boy—then turned his gun on his companion, Lilly. He was hanged in 1747, aged just 30.

ISLE OF MAN

The Isle of Man had a thoroughly deserved reputation for smuggling. For three centuries it was a private domain, outside of the control of the Crown, and even today the island maintains a degree of autonomy that is unparalleled on the British mainland.

Henry IV granted trade freedom for the island to Sir John Stanley in 1405, and the status of the Isle of Man was theoretically that of a kingdom quite separate from the rest of England (or Britain, after the act of union incorporated Scotland in 1707). The monarch of the island was for centuries known as King of Man.

The Isle of Man operated a free-trade policy, and regarded the English customs duties as protectionist. Smuggling on the island in the early eighteenth century took the form of merchants exporting goods to the Isle of Man from mainland Britain, and claiming the 'drawback'—a refund of import duty paid. The now uncustomed goods were then shipped back to England. This system grew rapidly, and eventually ocean-going ships began to sell direct to the Manx—a simple drawback fraud had become wholesale smuggling.

A major industry of the island was brewing. The brewers on the Isle of Man bought malt in England, and brewed strong beer for sale to ships setting off for the New World. Much of their production, of course, found its way back to the English and Scottish mainlands. Scots customs officials complained about the loss of revenue this caused. Since the Manx brewers bought raw barley, they didn't pay malting duty—neither did they pay duty on the beer they brewed. At one stage it was estimated that 40 per cent of all British beer was brewed in the Isle of Man, though this estimate should probably be taken with a pinch of salt.[50]

A letter in the *Gentleman's Magazine* in 1751 rained abuse on the island, calling it 'the greatest STOREHOUSE or MAGAZINE for the French'. In the same letter the correspondent lists as the principal contraband wine, brandy, coffee, tea and 'other India goods' and the sources as Denmark, Holland and France.

Manx apologists for the trade point to the fact that the local parliament, the Tynwald, took steps to stop illegal trading, and that it was not Manx themselves who were guilty of the accusations—it was bad folks from the mainland, especially Liverpool merchants, and 'Irish bankrupts and fugitives' who were the bad apples.

In all fairness, the English customs vessels did not endear themselves

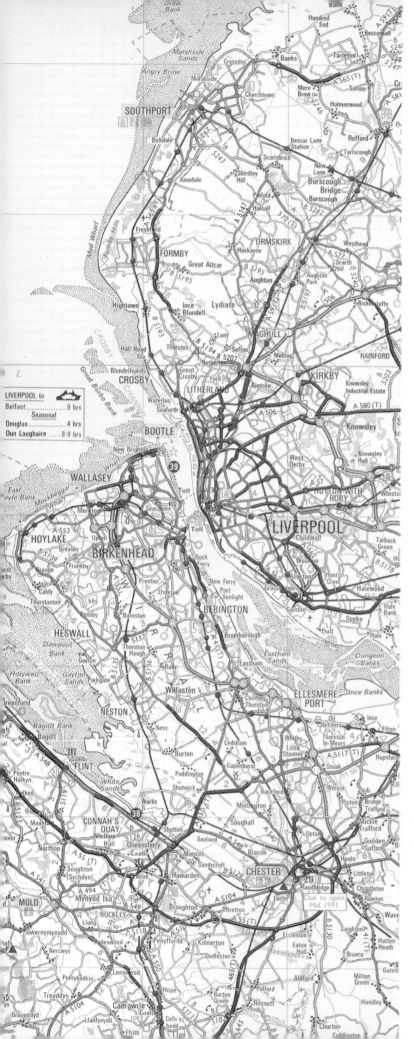

to the Manx, and there are various accounts of how customs cruisers harassed legitimate merchants going about their honest business. In one instance the customs men swarmed aboard a wherry that had brushed against her side, and, finding no cargo, stripped the crew of their clothes, and robbed a passenger of 25 guineas. This incident caused a near riot, and could not have engendered much sympathy for the crown.

If the smugglers who used the island as a depot did not enjoy local support (and it's hard to avoid the suspicion that in actual fact they were made quite welcome by the locals), then they certainly got a warm reception on the mainland. The Scottish customs authorities complained that . . .

> their correspondence with the common people of these coasts . . . on the South and North sides of the Solway Firth is so well established, that the least appearance of danger from thence is conveyed to them by signals which, at the same time, inform them to what parts they may with safety steer.

The Manxmen continued to take advantage of unrestricted (and uncustomed) trade through until 1765. In that year the crown finally regained control.

The sale of the island back to the English crown was not a popular move, and was carried out in some secrecy. In the short term it led to a rise in the cost, and a fall in the standard of living for the islanders, considerable emigration, and a fall in land values.

Not all Manx smugglers made a fortune. Myles Crowe was once a schoolteacher, but was persuaded to invest what little capital he had accrued in a smuggling enterprise. He was successful for a while in his trade with the Solway, but an informer revealed his 'cog-hole' to the customs authorities, and Myles was a ruined man. He spent some time living in Kirkcudbright and working as an assistant to more fortunate free-traders. He returned annually to the Isle of Man, to collect the rent from some small property he owned there, investing the income in contraband. These enterprises were hardly more successful. On one occasion his breeches, stuffed with tea, burst as he was boarding a ship in Douglas Harbour; and on another trip, he was overcome by the narcotic effect of tobacco wrapped round his body next to the skin!

In old age the smuggler manqué became an assistant ferryman, plying from Kirkcudbright to Castelsod, and died a miserable end at the hands of a poisoner who sold his corpse for dissection.

NORTH-WEST ENGLAND

According to a revealing customs report dated 1750:

> Smuggling into the coasts around Liverpool . . . is generally from the Isleman (sic) . . . in small boats that never appear on the coast but fall in with the land just in the dusk of the evening, that by their observations they may run in the night time into the place intended for the discharge of their goods where persons are always ready to assist and convey them to a proper place of safety . . . [51]

One such place of safety was undoubtedly a Wallasey pub called Mother Redcap's ■39, which stood 'on the promenade between Egremont and New Brighton ferries'. At that time Wallasey was wild and desolate:

> Wirral up to the middle of the 18th century was a desperate region. The inhabitants were nearly all wreckers and smugglers—they ostensibly carried on the trade or calling of fishermen, farm labourers or small farmers . . . Then for smuggling: fine times the runners used to have in my young days. Scarcely a house in North Wirral that could not provide a guest with a good stiff glass of brandy or Hollands—Formby was a great place for smugglers. [52]

Until 1765 the British Crown had no jurisdiction over the Isle of Man, and Manx smugglers were free to do pretty much as they pleased. The island developed into an off-shore depot for goods smuggled in from the Continent and from Ireland.

That part of Wallasey was separated from the rest of Wirral by a tidal pool, so the pub was free of unwanted observers on the land side.

Mother Redcap's was riddled with storage places, and was stoutly defended against attack. The door was 5 inches thick, and heavily reinforced, and the windows had shutters in a similar style. A customs officer who succeeded in entering the door could be precipitated into the cellar via a trapdoor on the threshold: forcing the door released a catch that opened the trapdoor.

Opening the front door closed off the entrance to one of the rooms, so visitors unfamiliar with the layout of the pub would either walk upstairs, or into the north room, unaware of a second ground floor room to the south. Numerous other hiding-places were concealed in a well and in the chimney-breast.

The proprietor of the inn, Mother Redcap herself, was said to be 'a comely, fresh-coloured Cheshire-spoken woman . . . a great favourite with the sailor men'. The inn was popular not only with smugglers, but also with lonely revenue men, who, to avoid suspicion, were entertained with the same hospitality as any other customer. This sometimes caused difficulties for the smugglers:

They were thus installed on one occasion when the smugglers were desirous of getting a cask of rum or some other merchandise away from one of the hiding places, but were prevented by the unwelcome presence of the officer. So it was arranged that one of the smugglers was to creep down to the shore from the Moor, and lie down in his clothes in the water, at the edge of the receding tide. The attention of the solitary officer at Mother Redcap's was called to the supposed body which had been washed ashore, and he made his way to it as quickly as possible. He had removed the watch, and was going through the pockets when the corpse came to life, sprang up, and laid out the surprised officer. By the time he had come to, the rum had been removed from Redcap's, and started its journey to the moss. No blame could be attached to the 'drowned man' who said he was walking along the shore, when he must have had a fit, for the next thing that he became aware of was that he was lying in the sand with his pockets being rifled.[53]

Thomas Stowell's grieving wife was reputed to have herself carried his heavy tombstone from their home on the Isle of Man to erect it over his grave at Bowness on Solway.

CUMBRIA[54]

Fifteenth-century records of smuggling cover the export of wool from Cumberland across the border to Scotland, and by sea to Ireland. In 1423 abbot Robert of the Cistercian abbey at Furness was accused of smuggling wool out in a 200-ton vessel from Piel Fowdray to Zealand. Wool export smuggling in Cumbria continued as late as 1788, when nearly 3 tons were seized and sold at Carlisle.

In the early eighteenth century, most of the smuggling activity in Cumbria seems to have been of an amateur nature—the crews of fishing vessels and colliers bringing in the odd barrel as a treat for the family. Persecution (or just prosecution) of those guilty of these minor tax evasions was seen in an extremely bad light by the local populace, and the price of over-zealousness was a transfer for at least one customs officer from Ellenfoot (Maryport).

Customs records provide a fairly typical picture: a mixture of success against impossible odds, mundane trivia of custom-house life, and tragic battles involving brutality and loss of life. Some of the accounts make interesting reading, though. An excise cutter, *Badger*, challenged a ship close to the Isle of Man in 1791, but was no match for the crew. The commander of the preventive vessel was shot through the legs, and the smugglers swarmed aboard the *Badger*, throwing the small arms into the sea. As they departed, they robbed the captain and mate of everything except a shirt each, and stole the sails. When the *Badger* reached Douglas harbour she was described as 'a wreck'.

The enormous majority of contraband that crossed the sea borders into Cumbria arrived on the Solway Firth, yet there are very few mementoes of the free-trade in the area. At Bowness on Solway ■40, there is a smuggler's tombstone in the churchyard. Approach Bowness from Carlisle along the coast road (caution, liable to flooding), and on entering Bowness, turn left

Above: *Furness Abbey was derelict when this engraving was made in the nineteenth century, but four centuries earlier the monastery was thriving, and the abbot was a smuggling pioneer. He evaded an export tax on wool by selling it in Zeeland, rather than through the official channels in the staple town of Calais.*

Right: *Maryport was strategically situated close to the mouth of the Solway Firth, and much of the work of the customs authorities based in the port involved the interception of smuggling vessels bound for the Scottish shore. Little contraband was landed on the English side.*

at the pub to reach the church. Thomas Stowell's grave is on the right of the path, under a Yew tree.

At Burgh by Sands, ■41, Longburgh House looks out over the Solway, and is reputed to have been built from the proceeds of smuggling. Legend has it that the right-hand first-floor window above the front door was used as a signalling place. Today it's a blind window, backed by a hollow-sounding, unusually thick wall. To find the house at 85-NY308589 (it's not open to the public), turn left after passing through Burgh on the road from Carlisle. The junction is just before the cattle grid that separates the village from the tidal road. The house is on the right after about 300 yards.

Longburgh House near Burgh-by-Sands, which is supposed to have been built from the proceeds of smuggling.

THE EAST COAST

LONDON TO BERWICK

East-coast smugglers dealt mainly with Holland and northern France. Trade links with Holland in particular had historical connections dating from the time when English wool was systematically smuggled out to Holland to avoid the legal staple in France. In the golden age of import smuggling the most important commodity was over-proof gin: enormous quantities came over from Schiedam, where the stills produced several million gallons of spirits a year. However, the east coast trade in strong 'Geneva' was not to the exclusion of other products—most of the heavily-taxed products that made up the smugglers' stock-in-trade elsewhere in Britain were landed here too.

The Dutch applied their legendary business skills and trading acumen to smuggling with as much alacrity as they did to any legal venture: the bulky tobacco took up too much space in the ships' holds, so the companies supplying the contraband found it profitable to invest in tobacco presses for compacting imported leaves into smaller bales. When British vessels proved inadequate to the task of ferrying goods across, they bought their own ships to move the goods across the North Sea. Trade in contraband took place either afloat, or at the destination in England.[1]

The pattern of landing and distribution in England along the east coast changed with the evolving policies of prevention. For example,

the Suffolk coastline was well-supplied with good beaches which suited the open landing of contraband—a technique that worked well in the eighteenth century while the preventives dozed in the distance or were open to bribes. As the net tightened in the early nineteenth century, though, smuggling intensified among the creeks and estuaries of Essex, where activity was less easily observed, and where tubs could be secretly sunk in the murky waters for later collection.[2]

Although tactics changed with time, the general character of the free-trade in the east of England did not. In the east, the involvement of the local population was most often as haulage contractors, landing goods that were brought to the country by foreign entrepreneurs. This was in marked contrast to the south-east, where the whole operation, including financing, was the concern of big smuggling companies. Perhaps because of this, east-coast smuggling was not marked by the same violence as its counterpart south of the Thames.

However, the scale of the smuggling operations was similar. Some indication of the extent of smuggling in this part of Britain may be gleaned from a document which relates to the period 1 May 1745 to 1 January 1746. This details all the runs which came to the attention of the customs officers—the total must have been much more. The area

At Corringham the Bull Inn has a longstanding reputation as a bastion of the smuggling trade, with numerous places for storing contraband, all of them well hidden.

covered was the county of Suffolk. 4,550 horses are mentioned, and based on the assumption that a horse could carry 1.5 cwt, the loss of duty would have been over £58,000, and the amount of currency sent overseas to pay for the goods, £43,000.[3] In today's terms, this was the equivalent of some £26 million.

NORTH THAMES ESTUARY

Contraband entering the Thames estuary reached its eager buyers on the north shore along devious routes. Much London-bound cargo would be shipped directly to the city, to be unloaded surreptitiously at illegal quays; or openly, with a payment to ensure that the customs officials turned a blind eye. Other free-traders might 'break bulk' near the mouth of the estuary, and transfer their stocks to smaller boats such as coasters and colliers for transport up the river. One stratagem that was avoided where possible, though, was to unload far from the city, and send goods overland to their destination; transport on water was so much quicker and cheaper than haulage overland that this approach could make a serious dent in the profits of a smuggling adventure.

The contraband that did come ashore on the Essex side of the river was therefore usually destined for consumption locally. Though the banks of the Thames were nowhere near as densely populated in the eighteenth century as they are today, there were significant markets for the smugglers' fare, notably in the areas of Rayleigh, Leigh-on-Sea, Hadleigh and Southend. Points farther north would have been more easily supplied from the winding Crouch and Roach estuaries.

CANVEY ISLAND ▪1

Opposite South Benfleet 178-TQ7883.

Low-lying Canvey Island is within just a few miles of Rayleigh, Leigh and Hadleigh, and was therefore a convenient spot for landing goods. It was for centuries little more than a glorified mud-flat—unhealthy for living on and poor grazing land—so smugglers could go about their business watched only by sheep. However, the free-traders of Canvey must have sensed that their isolation was soon to end when the Dutch were invited to build a sea wall around the island.

Though the Dutch influence made Canvey more habitable, the connection with Holland probably increased smuggling activity rather than reducing it. The Dutch engineers who built the dykes were well connected with merchants and manufacturers in the Low Countries, one of the principal sources of goods smuggled into Britain, and they quickly established a thriving and untaxed business. An additional incentive for the Dutch smugglers was the position of the island, within easy reach of both the Kent and Essex coasts, and close to the mouth of the Thames.

All this activity didn't go unnoticed; a writer of the 1860s[4] observed that '. . . the island 70 years ago was a noted place for smuggling', and that contraband liquor was said to have been stored in Canvey Church.[5]

Dutch influence on Canvey persisted for a long time, and much of the architecture echoed the style of Dutch buildings. Only a couple of examples still stand, notably the Dutch Cottage on Canvey Road, which is now a museum.

THE LOBSTER SMACK[6]

On reaching Canvey Island follow the A130 (signposted Seafront); turn right at the King Canute down Haven Road.

This old weather-boarded pub by the sea wall is an enduring link with the golden age of smuggling. It was a notorious haunt of smugglers, who would simply nip over the sea wall to unload the ships as they arrived, then ship the goods inland to Rayleigh and Hadleigh. There has been a pub on site since 1600, and the present building, which was constructed in the early eighteenth century, is possibly the oldest structure on Canvey.

Dickens wrote innocently enough of The Lobster Smack in 1880 in *Dictionary of the Thames from Oxford to the Nore*, noting that it was 'comfortable and unobtrusive' and that 'boating men are frequently accommodated with bed and board'. But he adds that 'smuggling still continued and this part of the Essex coast has a history of runs carried out by "gentlemen"'.

The pub is also rumoured to be the model for Sluice House in *Great Expectations*.

CORRINGHAM AND FOBBING ▪2

Corringham is 4m S of Basildon at 178-TQ7183. Turn off the A13 down the B1420 and continue straight on, following signposts. The pub is by the church. At Fobbing, 1m or so to the east, the marshes are not hard to find. Park close to the church at 178-TQ710834, and walk down the road until you see footpath signs.

The winding creeks of Fobbing Marshes,[7] made navigation hazardous, but unobserved landings correspondingly easier, and much contraband came ashore here to satisfy those gasping for a taste of cheap high-quality spirits from Holland and France. The Bull at Corringham is said to have had sunken chambers under the yard, caverns under the hearth, and other hiding-places for illicit goods.

HADLEIGH AND LEIGH-ON-SEA ▪3

Hadleigh is on the A13 S of Rayleigh. To reach Hadleigh Castle at 178-TQ810861, turn down Castle Lane—near Hadleigh Church on the London-bound section of the one-way system that encircles the town centre. Leigh-on-Sea is a district of Southend at 178-TQ8486. Daws Heath 178-TQ8189 is on a minor road that leads north from the Southend-bound side of the Hadleigh one-way system. The heath is about two miles north of Hadleigh, at the point where the road swings round to the left.

Slipping into the nearby marshes around Canvey and Corringham, smuggling vessels kept a sharp eye out for signals from the shore, and the ruins of thirteenth-century Hadleigh Castle made an ideal vantage-point for a shore party equipped with a flash. From this commanding position overlooking the river, a lantern was capable of sending messages as far as Cliffe Marshes in Kent on a dark night. There were

A tunnel from Hadleigh Castle to the estuary half a mile away provided Thames smugglers with a handy way to transport contraband inland unobserved; a lantern high on the crumbling towers was visible on the Kent shore.

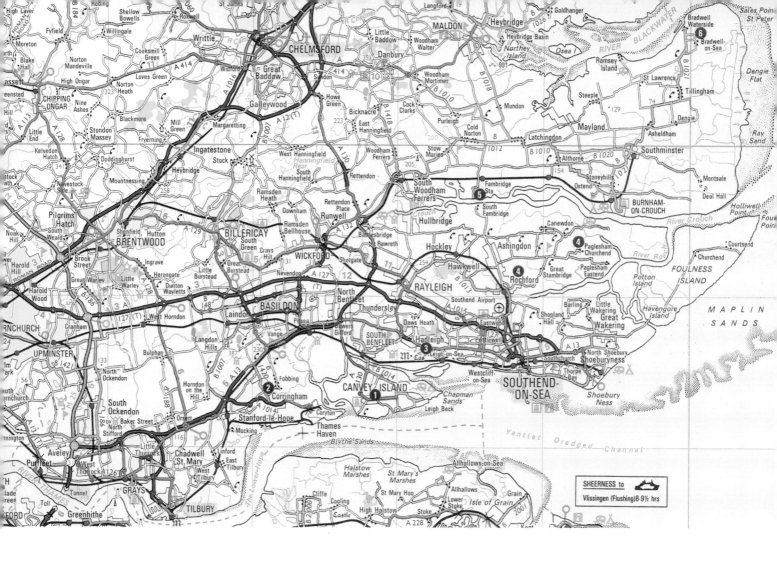

rumours too that the castle had at one time been adapted to better suit the intentions of the smugglers:

> It is said that there formerly existed a subterraneous passage from the castle to the bed of the river, but its mouths are now stopped up, and little or no traces of it are (sic) to be found.

> Leigh . . . is seen to great advantage, as well as the estuary of the Thames, and the distant hills of Kent.[8]

The view of Leigh would have been a valuable asset, since the smuggler standing on the crumbling parapets may well have been signalling not only to a ship in the Thames, but to accomplices in Leigh-on-Sea. The town was known to be a haunt of the smuggling fraternity, and when in 1892 the Peter Boat Inn in Leigh High Street burned down, few were surprised to discover a big cellar with direct access to the waterside adjoining the Alley Dock. A path from the dock ran up to Daws Heath—a notorious area for lawless highwaymen, transients and drifters.

THE CROUCH

Not all the south Essex smugglers favoured a landing in the Thames. Those who were intrepid enough to navigate the treacherous sandbanks to the north of the Thames estuary could soon lose themselves in the network of channels around Foulness Island. The low-lying coastal land is criss-crossed with dykes, and if local legend is to be believed, these waterways once linked up, providing a navigable link between the Crouch and the Thames estuaries.[9]

This area undoubtedly gained in popularity as the customs net tightened around the coast in the early years of the nineteenth century. Eighteenth-century smugglers found it easy to prevail over the preventives by sheer force of numbers, but as this became less and less practical, the secrecy provided by the Essex mists and dykes looked more attractive.

ROCHFORD AND PAGLESHAM ■4

Rochford is 3m N of Southend at 178-TQ8790. Paglesham is 4m E of Rochford, at 178-TQ9293. From Rochford, follow minor roads to Great Stambridge, then signposts to Paglesham.

Smuggling was so vigorously pursued in the Rochford area that the region's reputation persisted well into this century. One writer commented in 1909 that:

> The whole district is honeycombed with traditions concerning smuggling . . . The tower of Rochford Church was used to store gin, Hollands and tea—the cavity under the pulpit was known as The Magazine.[10]

But it was a tiny hamlet outside Rochford that was the smuggling capital of the district. At Paglesham, most of the population was alleged to have been involved with the free-trade in one way or another.[11] Several locals were ship-owners, and used oyster-fishing or legitimate cross-Channel transport as a cover for smuggling. In 1783 the Maldon custom-house reported that William Dowsett of the village owned two vessels which he used for illegal trade, and that his brother-in-law, Emberson, also operated a small ship. Another member of the Dowsett family traded from the *Big Jane*, a heavily-armed lugger that was frequently in skirmishes with the King's men. The most notorious figure, though, was William Blyth.

Blyth—alias King of the Smugglers, or Hard Apple—was village grocer and churchwarden. Evidently he found it difficult to separate the two roles, since he often wrapped groceries in pages torn from the parish record books.

Other stories about Blyth are more exotic. In one he drank two glasses of wine in the local pub, the Punch Bowl, then calmly ate the glasses. Another yarn has Blyth playing cricket on the local green with fellow smugglers Emberson and Dowsett. Though the men took off their coats for the matches, they took the sensible precaution of laying out their guns and swords ready for interruptions from the excisemen. In the course of one of these matches, there was an unscheduled break of another sort: a bull charged the team. Blyth grabbed it by the tail, and set about the animal with a cudgel. The terrified animal fled with Blyth clinging on, vaulted over a hedge and ditch, then collapsed and died.

On one occasion Blyth's boat was captured during a run, and the cargo transferred to a revenue cutter. On board the cutter, Blyth started drinking with the crew, taking full advantage of his legendary head for alcohol. Before very long, the officers and men were fuddled by drink, and Blyth restored his cargo to its rightful home.

Another story has the smuggler in irons, captive on board a revenue cutter. The ship grounded on the Dogger Bank, and the captain appealed to Blyth for help. He replied, 'might as well be drowned as hanged', but was eventually prevailed upon to get the boat off.

The Paglesham smugglers were so well known that they seem to have practically operated a ferry service across the Channel. John Harriott, a well-known writer and traveller from Great Stambridge, close to Paglesham, described[12] how he had acted as 'chaperon' to two ladies who needed to visit France in 1786, and wished to return home. He knew that the Paglesham men plied to Dunkirk, so he went there in search of them:

> purporting to get home to Essex by the nearest passage, I took my road to this port, being pretty certain of finding smuggling vessels from that part of England, with whom I made no doubt of obtaining a ready passage to within a few miles of my house.

Harriott did indeed hitch a lift across the Channel, and was dropped off less than 2 miles from his home. His account is made more colourful by his description of the time he spent drinking at the inn before the Paglesham smugglers arrived. While waiting he handed his pistols, 'my constant travelling companions', to the landlady, and thus gave a nearby group of free-traders the impression that he too was a smuggler. They told him that the Essex men, 'Emberson, Bligh (*sic*) or Brown', were expected imminently, and Harriott sat down to drink with them. When he refused to drink a toast to the destruction of the revenue services, Harriott was assaulted by his fellow drinkers. He wagered that he could prove that the oath was a false one, and proceeded to argue that without revenue men and laws to prevent or tax imports, there would be no smugglers and they would all be poorer men. Harriott's eloquence persuaded them and the smugglers incongruously drank a toast to 'revenue laws and officers for ever'! What makes this story still more extraordinary is that Harriott was himself a local magistrate.

Paglesham is still largely unspoiled, with a row of weather-boarded white houses. You can still see the pub were Blyth ate his wine glasses, and wander round the Norman church of St Peter where contraband was hidden in the vestry.[13] Three pollarded elms at Pound Pond near East Hall were also used as a hiding-place—£200 worth of silk was concealed in the trees at any one time. Many footpaths criss-cross the flat fertile fairyland around, and the place and pub names are reminders of the intimate associations with the sea that the area enjoys: The Anchor, The Ferry Inn, Seafarmer.

THE CROUCH TO THE BLACKWATER

The narrow isthmus of land between these two estuaries is isolated and unspoiled even today. There are many shallow inlets and vast tracts of low marshland and saltings which would have made evasion a simple matter. The coastline is desolate and isolated, and the ditches treacherous—especially at night—to all except those local folk who knew the routes inland from the shore. The east-facing shore between Bradwell and Holliwell Point remained a favourite landing-place right up until the middle of the nineteenth century.

Most land lies below the 20m contour, and on a clear night a lantern on a high point could be seen many miles off. A few local high points still carry names that point to their former function: Beacon Hill at Saint Lawrence was used by smugglers for signalling to Salcott-cum-Virley on the other side of the Blackwater estuary, and possibly also to Tiptree Heath.

NORTH FAMBRIDGE ■5

Turn S off B1012 at Cold Norton, some 4¹/₂m E of South Woodham Ferrers. After passing the North Fambridge station continue straight on where the road bears right to reach the Ferryboat Inn at 168-TQ857970.

This small village was once linked by ferry to its namesake on the opposite bank of the Crouch, and eighteenth- and nineteenth-century Essex smugglers would have regularly used the short-cut to avoid a long detour to the nearest bridging point much farther up the river. Today the only reminder of the link between the two villages is the name of the Ferryboat Inn. The white-painted fifteenth-century inn is haunted by the ferryman's ghost,[14] and smugglers' tunnels used to run to Blue Farm and Smugglers' Cottage nearby.

BRADWELL ■6

At the mouth of the Blackwater Estuary 168-TM0010. Take the B1021 from Burnham, and continue to its end to reach Bradwell Quay. To get to St Peter's Chapel (168-TM031084) turn off the B1021 to the right (signposted). At the next T-junction turn right into Bradwell-on-Sea, then left along a road by the church. Continue for about 1¹/₂m, and park at a farm (signposted). The chapel is about 600 yards away along a firm path.
Parking at Bradwell Quay is restricted during weekends and bank holidays in summer season only.

There are still a few reminders of the age of smuggling in this desolate and wind-swept peninsula: the simple chapel of St Peter at Bradwell was frequently used as a storage-place for smuggled goods, and the tower made a handy high point for a beacon. The chapel was originally founded on the remains of the Roman fort of Othona, and has existed in some form on the site since the seventh century; its use as a smugglers' hiding-place probably ensured its survival.

Bradwell Quay is a pleasure marina now, but two centuries ago the hustle and bustle of the working quayside drew smugglers to the spot. They met in the Green Man, and planned their illicit crossings to Holland there. Nearby Pewit Island was sometimes used for storing contraband.

Bradwell was notorious for smuggling even before illegal imports began. As early as 1361, local residents were accused of smuggling out wool (they were eventually acquitted); and nearly two centuries later a return of 'abettors and assisters of pirates' and 'receivers or conveyors of pirate goods' named five local men who were said to have landed goods illicitly at Bradwell, Stansgate and Ramsey Stone. As late as 1930 there were people living in Bradwell who could still remember Hezekiah Staines, a local constable, who was reputed to have been a kind of smuggling double-agent—he was a special constable by day, and a smuggler by night.[15]

THE BLACKWATER TO THE STOUR

The Reverend Baring-Gould chose this area as the setting for his epic novel of smuggling and intrigue. In *Mehalah* we read that:

> The mouth of the Blackwater was a great centre of the smuggling trade: the number and intricacies of the channels made it a safe harbour for those who lived on contraband traffic. It was easy for those who knew the creeks to elude the revenue boats and every farm and tavern was ready to give cellarage to run goods and harbour to smugglers.

> . . . Between Mersea and the Blackwater were several flat holms or islands . . . and between these, the winding waterways formed a labyrinth which made pursuit difficult.

MERSEA ISLAND AND AREA ■7

Mersea Island 168-TM01 is about 6m S of Colchester via the B1025. The Dog and Pheasant is on the outskirts of East Mersea. The Peldon Rose is on the Mersea–Great Wigborough Road at 168-TL989168. Fingringhoe is some 4m SE of Colchester at 168-TM0320.

Two pubs in this area were certainly more than happy to conceal the smugglers' stock in trade, though not necessarily in the manner that Baring-Gould described. On Mersea Island, the seventeenth-century Dog and Pheasant pub was much used by smugglers, and the nearby mainland pub, the Peldon Rose, which was built 200 or so years earlier, was also involved in the free-trade. Storage at the Rose was not in the cellar but in the pond alongside—there was a large well hidden in the middle of the pond, and weighted tubs of spirits could be lowered down this on ropes until the revenue men had completed their searches.

At Fingringhoe *en route* from Mersea to Colchester there is a grisly reminder that not all smuggling trips ended in success and wealth for the participants. A local smuggler was hanged just outside the churchyard there, and buried on the spot. An acorn placed in the mouth of the corpse grew into the spreading oak tree that now stands on the spot.[16]

Above: *The Bradwell area is among the most isolated places in southern England, so the smugglers who used St Peter's Chapel there as a storehouse and signal point could do so with little fear of discovery. A beacon hung in the tower was clearly visible for miles inland and out to sea.*

Left: *The Rose at Peldon, Essex was deeply involved in smuggling. There was a large well hidden in the middle of the pond into which goods could be lowered by rope.*

SALCOTT-CUM-VIRLEY ▪8

168-TL9513, 4m E of Tiptree on minor roads.

The twin villages of Salcott and Virley also feature in *Mehalah*: the marriage of the principal characters Mehalah and Elijah Rebow takes place in the now-ruined church at Virley. The churches are also steeped in legends associating them with non-fictional smugglers; from the church towers signals could be flashed to Tiptree Heath, and to Beacon Hill on the other side of the Blackwater estuary. There was always a good attendance for the service at Virley because the congregation was swelled by local smugglers who turned up to keep an eye on the contraband they had concealed in various parts of the church![17]

According to one local fable, villagers found a customs boat floating off nearby Sunken Island with a crew of corpses—all 22 men had their throats cut from ear to ear. The bodies were buried in the local graveyard, with the hull of their up-turned boat over the graves.

TIPTREE ▪9

168-TL8916, 9m SW of Colchester on the B1022. The heath is on the S side of the town. Paternoster Heath is 2m E of Tiptree at 168-TL9115, N of the B1023 Tiptree road.

Smugglers moving their goods inland used the heathlands around Tiptree to trade and store their goods, and possibly to rest their horses before moving on to the larger market in Colchester. Tiptree Heath was notorious, and gypsies and squatters held auctions of smuggled goods there.[18] For storage, they dug shallow holes in the sandy soil, and covered the packages with turf and brushwood.

There were many other safe houses and storage depots in the area; for example, on Paternoster Heath at Tolleshunt Knights a pond was used for sinking tubs as late as Victorian times.

GOLDHANGER ▪10

168-TL9009, 3$\frac{1}{2}$m E of Maldon on the B1026.

Goldhanger was sufficiently distant from Maldon to escape the attentions of all but the most diligent officers stationed there. A favourite trick of the Goldhanger smugglers was to float rafts of tubs down the Blackwater, and land them at Mill Beach opposite Northey Island. In 1960 one local man described the route that smugglers used to bring goods inland:

They used ter (*sic*) go up Blind Lane into Wash Lane then up to Witham. Or Green Lane, down on the beach, up there, through Long Wick Farm to Tolleshunt Major, either to the Church, the Bell Inn, or Rentner's Farm. Up Joyce's Creek they'd come, and land their Hollands, lace and tobacco, and shove the brandy down in the cellars at Joyce's Farm, or Cobbs.

At night, my mother used ter tell me, they'd ride up Fish Street carrying brandy on horses whose hooves had been muffled with cloth. But them days has gone. They went out about 40 years ago with the fishing. They're all buried now like my granfather's stuff under the gardens of Goldhanger Hall.[19]

Many of the place names mentioned in the account can still be picked out on the 1:25 000 map.

WITHAM ▪11

168-TL8215, 15m SW of Colchester.

Though much extended, the sixteenth-century Spread Eagle pub in Witham town centre still retains a reminder of the cunning of the smugglers, who would have been innocently refreshing themselves at the bar when the revenue man walked through the door. A concealed well that

The villages of Virley and Salcott were chief landing places for contraband and horses and donkeys were kept in larger numbers for the conveyance of the spirits, wine, tobacco and silk to Tiptree Heath. Virley church, now in ruins, was used for storage.

was once accessible only from the roof pierces the pub from attic to cellar. Climbing on the tiles, the smugglers would lower their goods down the shaft on ropes. To make the shaft visible to present-day drinkers, a small window has been installed in the bar.[20]

A pub at nearby Braxted was the headquarters of a gang of smugglers operating in the mid-nineteenth century. Led by the pub landlord, they used a Maldon smack called *The Providence*,[21] which berthed at Tollesbury.

TOLLESBURY ▪12

168-TL9510, 7m E of Maldon on the B1023. Old Hall Marshes are on the peninsula NE of the village. Turn N off the B1023 along North Road, then turn right off the road a mile or so along—signposted Old Hall Farm. This leads to Old Hall Creek.

Like so many of the ports and landing-points on the Blackwater, Tollesbury supports a wealth of legends about smuggling. For a long time, the nearest custom-house was Maldon, and the staff there were greatly overworked, so the Tollesbury smugglers would have been free to come and go pretty much as they pleased. When the authorities became more vigilant, contraband was simply thrown overboard at one of the many creeks and inlets punctuating the estuary, to be collected when the coast was clear.

There was always a chance, of course, that goods hidden in this way would fall into the hands of 'honest' men, and be turned in to the authorities. In 1819 one such man, Daniel London, was dredging (probably for shellfish) and hauled up a large number of tubs of spirits that had been sunken in Old Hall Creek. He spent most of the night loading the tubs into his boat, and in the morning he sailed up to the Maldon custom-house with 152 tubs. For somewhat suspect reasons, though, he overlooked 11 more, leaving them in Mill Creek, where they 'were liable to be found by any other dredger, of which there were many near'.

When he got home a reception committee of smugglers was waiting for him, and not unnaturally wanted their property. Being reasonable men, they offered to pay him half of what the goods were worth, but Daniel foolishly declined. At this point the angry mob threatened to lynch him and his son, so the pair of them retreated indoors. When the Maldon comptroller of customs arrived, Daniel—now in fear of his life, no doubt—owned up to the other 11 tubs, and was promptly accused of smuggling and thrown into Chelmsford Gaol. In gaol, things went from

The picturesque yacht stores at Tollesbury vividly evoke the maritime tradition of the village. The nearby creeks were much used for landing goods from the continent.

bad to worse: the other prisoners assaulted him, and he eventually lost his boat, the *George and Anne*.

The story is told[22] in letters and petitions to the customs authorities, and 170 years later it is difficult to unravel the truth. The authorities were evidently convinced that London was in league with the smugglers, and pointed out that he had a previous conviction for the offence. On the other hand, the unfortunate dredger was clearly not popular with the smugglers, either!

Old Hall Creek is now heavily silted, but at one time there were wharfs there, as rotting timbers and skeletal boats in the mud testify. When business was thriving, there was a waterside pub that had huge cellars for storage of contraband and the sea-wall hid the free-traders from view as they unloaded. The pub was long ago converted to houses as the torrent of thirsty smugglers turned—like the waters in the creek—to a trickle.

In 1779 the windows of the pub would have commanded a good view of a large cutter landing goods at one of the wharfs, and perhaps one of the drinkers was the customs officer from Tollesbury, Edward Abbot. He intercepted a labourer called William Tabor, who was carrying tea and gin which had been unloaded from the boat. Tabor tried to negotiate freedom from prosecution, but this was refused and the labourer was convicted and fined. To get his own back, Tabor accused Abbot of embezzling some of the seized goods (which the revenue man quite likely did). His attempt to discredit the officer failed, however, and when asked to appear before the local collector of customs, the smuggler lost his nerve.

Modern Tollesbury is a working waterfront. Pleasure boats are today much in evidence, but there are some working vessels too, and there are four beautifully restored traditional yacht stores which form the centrepiece of the waterfront, reminding the visitor of the long-standing links with the sea.

COLCHESTER ▪13

168-TL9925 N Essex. Old Heath is at 168-TM0123 on the SE outskirts of Colchester.

The customs authorities in Colchester had a doubly onerous job. In addition to the town's local small-time smuggling villains, they also had to put up with the attentions of free-traders whose goods had been confiscated some considerable distance away. The 'desperate villains' who used a combination of low cunning and brute force to gain access to the customs-house in 1748 were probably members of the Hadleigh gang (see page 163), but since they were never caught, there is no way of

knowing for sure. However, what is clear is that they were determined to reclaim 60 oilskin bags containing 1,512 lb of tea, which had been seized earlier at Woodbridge Haven. They did so by the elementary device of impersonation. In the early hours of the morning, two men claiming to be customs officers arrived at the Hythe quay in Colchester[23] and asked to be taken to the custom-house. There they were joined by 30 armed smugglers, who broke open the custom-house and took away the tea.

The most notorious of the home-grown Colchester smugglers (if only because a tract[24] was published describing his life and crimes) was probably John Skinner, alias Saucy Jack or Colchester Jack. As the tract explains:

> Skinner was accounted as great a smuggler as any in the county of Essex; tho' the better to difguife his Way of Life he rented two Farms, known by the Names of the Tan Office and Cox's Farm ... at Old Heath.

Skinner's nickname 'Saucy' was well earned. He was by all accounts quite a rake, and on one occasion '... had been at a Bawdy House for ten Days fucceffively, and had fpent 60 or 70l, when he fhould have been at home minding his Bufinefs.'

Skinner spent money wildly, working his way through his wife's substantial fortune, then casting her on the parish, where she went to work in the poor-house. When he'd squandered his wife's money, he bought the King's Head Inn at Romford, 'and had a very pretty trade, particularly among smugglers. Understanding what large Profits were gain'd in the Smuggling Way he left his Inn and commenc'd smuggler'.

This trade apparently went well for Saucy Jack, but in the end, his violent temper was his undoing. He had smuggled some goods in May 1744 in partnership with his servant, one Daniell Brett, and it appears that Brett had cheated Skinner by betraying where the contraband was hidden. When Skinner discovered this, he flew into a rage, and swore he would kill Brett. One witness testified that 'he anfwered this Examinant in a great paffion, and fwore bitterly that let him find (Brett) where he would he would fhoot him dead that night'.

Saucy Jack returned home to Old Heath just before midnight in a confused state, then rode off to Colchester to fetch a surgeon. While he was gone, Brett appeared with a stomach wound; from the description, he appeared to have been shot at point-blank range. However, the loyal servant would not reveal who had shot him. Despite medical attention, the man died the following day, and Saucy Jack was tried for murder and found guilty. In gaol, Skinner made a vain attempt to cheat the gallows by stabbing himself in a rather inexpert way with a small knife. He was nevertheless hanged, but was too weak to utter any last words, which must have come as a blow to the printer of the tract, since the cover page (perhaps printed in advance of the contents) clearly promises the reader a gallows confession.

CLACTON ▪14

168/169-TM1715, 15m SE of Colchester.

The heyday of smuggling in the Clacton area was in the eighteenth century, before prevention had really gathered momentum, but goods continued to be landed openly and in daylight until well into the nineteenth century. There was good access to the shore, especially via Holland Gap, making it easy to assemble a large and mobile force of men on the beach to unload the goods. Though the runs themselves were largely unopposed, the local preventive officers nevertheless succeeded in recovering some of the contraband—particularly if it had been hidden nearby or buried. Some of the discoveries were involuntary; in 1721, the ground gave way under the feet of customs officer D'Oyley, revealing a cache of 19 half ankers of Brandy!

The smugglers seem to have enjoyed genuine partnership and cooperation with the farmers and labourers along the coast here, in stark contrast to the intimidation and coercion that was needed to extract

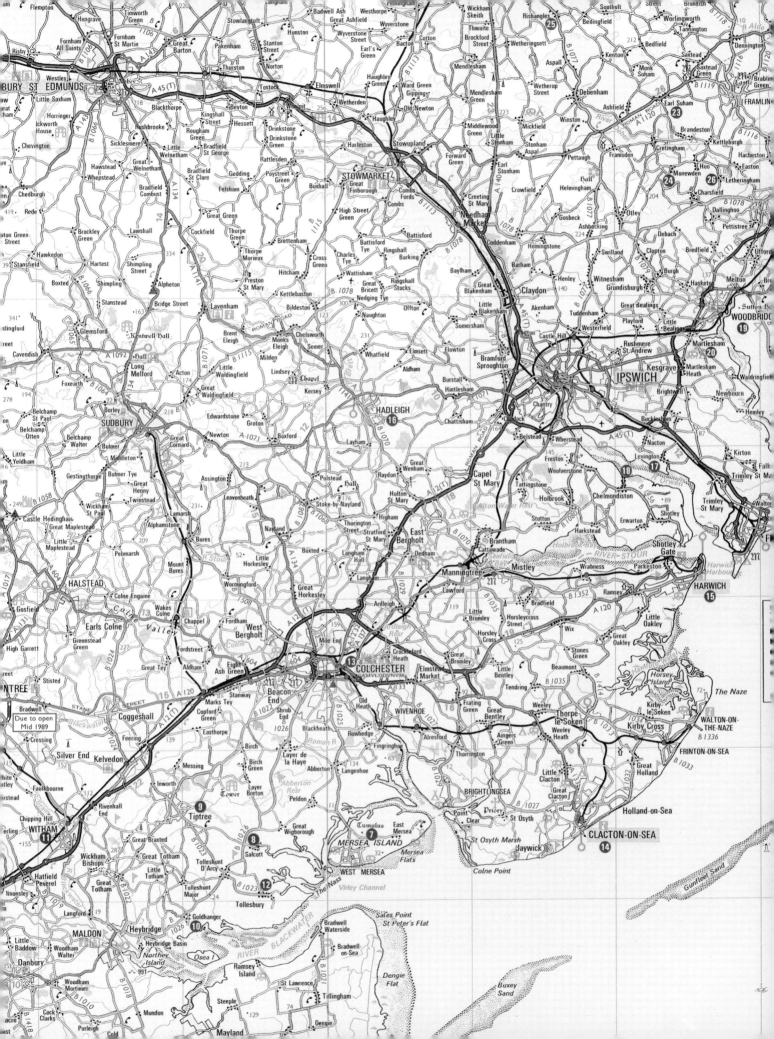

'cooperation' on some other coasts. A story from Great Holland illustrates the way the relationship worked. A farmer was fond of a drop of gin, and a party of London smugglers who worked the area were happy to supply his tipple. He simply asked them to 'leave the lane gate locked' as a signal that his barrel was running low. In return for this kindness, the farmer provided stabling and feed for the smugglers' 15 horses.[25]

Payment in goods was the rule—on another occasion labourers working on the sea-wall at Christmas time received gin as a reward for helping smugglers land a cargo. The payment was clearly more than sufficient, because one of their number fell off a plank bridge into Holland Brook, and his colleagues were so drunk that they had difficulty fishing him out. Unable to carry the poor man home, they simply propped him up against a hay-stack and covered him up. He froze to death in the cold December night.[26]

One Clacton smuggler prospered more than most. George Wegg the Elder was outwardly a very respectable figure, but was reputed to have made much of his substantial fortune as a smuggler.[27] He owned a house next to the Ship Inn in Clacton; in 1870, renovation to this building revealed enormous cellars, with a concealed entrance reached from a brick kitchen. These cellars would have been used for storing the contraband brought from George Wegg's ships, which were met at The Black Grounds, Sea Lane, or The Haven.[28] There were other depots pending onward movement to Colchester, at Rill Cottage and at Dawson's. In the Colchester area, Wegg owned: Jaywick, a farm; Cross House; Millers, and East Hill House.

HARWICH AREA ■15

169-TM2531, 16m E of Colchester. The White Hart is on Manningtree High Street at 169-TM105319.

Much of the smuggling on the Stour involved the postal packets based at the river's mouth. Though these ships were supposed to carry only the mail, passengers and their luggage, few would complete a journey without taking on a small private adventure. The passengers were as

guilty as the crews of the packets. The collector of customs at Harwich complained bitterly in the mid-eighteenth century about the quantity of lace and needlework brought in by ladies of the court, 'enough to supply all the milliners shops in and around London'.

Smuggling also went on in Harwich in the traditional manner. In 1811 a ship ran aground in the shallows off the Landguard fort, and the crew threw overboard 600 tubs of spirits in order that the ship would draw less water. The soldiers from the fort took full advantage of the situation, and four of them died of the drink.

Not all the smuggling vessels unloaded their cargoes in the mouth of the estuary, though. Some travelled up-stream as far as Manningtree, where the White Hart, a sixteenth-century inn, had a tunnel that led underground from the cellar to the Stour estuary.

SUFFOLK

The major centre for smuggling in Suffolk was perhaps surprisingly not on the coast, but some 40 miles inland: the charming market town of Hadleigh gave its name to one of Suffolk's most successful smuggling gangs. At full strength, the gang numbered 100 men, each turning out with two horses. Such a force would have been almost unstoppable, even when the customs authorities had military support. Certainly, the precise descriptions of the gang's activities recorded in the custom-house letters suggests that the authorities could do little more than watch and count the horses:

20 May	70 horses with dry goods landed at Sizewell
27 May	27 horses with wet goods and 36 loaded with tea landed at Sizewell
11 June	60 horses most with brandy, 53 with tea
2 July	83 horses with tea, 9 waggon loads wet goods
12 July	50 horses tea
17 Sept	120 horses—100 smugglers
10 Nov	50 horses dry goods, 1 cart w/wet goods
23 Nov	at least 40 horses, mostly dry goods.

In 1811 Harwich soldiers posted at the Landguard Fort shown here could barely believe their luck: a smuggling ship went aground, and the crew threw overboard hundreds of tubs of spirits.

Bear in mind that this list is far from comprehensive—it is likely that an equal amount of contraband was landed unobserved.

The gang frequently clashed with the preventive forces, but the biggest battle took place in 1735. The gang's store-house at Seymor (Semer) had been discovered, and the customs authorities, backed up by the military, took the cache to the George Inn in Hadleigh, for overnight storage. This was an outrage that the gang could not take lying down, and 20 or so smugglers soon presented themselves at the inn to demand the return of their goods. In the battle that followed a dragoon was shot dead, and others injured; the gang rode off into the night with their prize.

The authorities recognized 17 of the smugglers, and two were hanged for firing pistols in the battle. This did not deter the rest, though, and 12 years on the leader of the gang, John Harvey, was committed to Newgate prison, and eventually transported for seven years. Even this setback was temporary—the following year the gang broke open the King's Warehouse in Ipswich to rescue their goods.

HADLEIGH ▪16

8m W of Ipswich at 155-TM0242.

Some of the places associated with the Hadleigh Gang are still in existence. You can visit the George Inn, on the main road through Hadleigh; and Pond Hall (155-TM0541) on the Hadleigh to Duke Street Road, was home of gang leader John Harvey.

THE IPSWICH AREA

Levington ▪17 is 6m SE of Ipswich at 169-TM2339. To reach Pin Mill, ▪18 (169-TM206379) leave Ipswich on the B1456 Shotley Road; in Chelmondiston turn left after the Forester's Arms. Pin Mill is reached by a single track road. Parking may be difficult on summer weekends.

The principal urban market for contraband in Suffolk was Ipswich, which could be conveniently reached by the Orwell, or—when that was being watched—by a short overland hop from the river Deben. The banks of the Orwell are linked with numerous smuggling legends and associations that act as reminders of the illegal traffic between Ipswich and the coast. At Levington the Ship Inn had a cupboard under the eaves that was used as a place of concealment; and 'at Pin Mill, the riverside portion of the parish of Chelmondiston, the Butt and Oyster Inn is said to have been a favourite resort of smugglers'.[29]

WOODBRIDGE AREA

Woodbridge ▪19 is at 169-TM2749 8m E of Ipswich. The tide mill is open to the public most days between June and October and at Spring and Easter bank holidays. The wheel can be seen in operation on these days at times dictated by the tide. Phone Woodbridge (0473) 626618. To reach Martlesham Creek ▪20 take the A1214 from Ipswich towards Lowestoft. In the Martlesham area, watch for a turning on the right signposted 'Sandy Lane'. Continue along this minor road for a few hundred yards, then park by the signpost indicating a footpath to the creek.

The Deben River that laps at the doorstep of Woodbridge was well used by the smuggling fraternity, though not always with complete success. At Woodbridge Haven in 1739 a smuggler's cutter was stranded by the tide and the preventive services were able to seize brandy and tea. With extraordinary cheek, the smugglers not only raised affidavits for the recovery of their goods, but also contrived to have the master of the grounded cutter press-ganged into serving on *HMS Boyne*. This of course prevented him testifying against the smugglers.

Today Woodbridge's most notable feature is its tide mill—one of two British examples in working order. It dates from the twelfth century, ceased commercial working in 1957, and was fully restored in 1982.

Martlesham Creek, just a couple of miles away from Woodbridge, was used as a waterway for transporting small boat-loads of contraband. Phillip Meadows, rector of Great Bealings, was reputed to have cooperated with the smugglers[30] by leaving his stables unlocked, with the chaise and harness ready. Since the owner of the chaise was so well respected locally—and effectively above suspicion—the smugglers were thus able to travel around the district quite freely, and used the chaise to collect cargoes ferried up Martlesham Creek.

LEISTON AREA ▪21

156-TM4462, 4m E of Saxmundham. Many of the places described can still be located, in particular the White Horse Inn, Leiston Common Farm just E of Leiston, at 156-TM456632, and the Parrot and Punchbowl pub at Aldringham, 156-TM445609. See map on page 165.

From the account of the activities of the Hadleigh Gang, it is clear that the coast near Leiston was the focal point for smuggling in Suffolk. Many of the traditional anecdotes and yarns feature the village, and even in verifiable accounts of smuggling incidents some of the action takes place in the area. Leiston's principal advantage was the proximity of Sizewell. Today, Sizewell's only claim to fame is the nuclear power station sited on the low coastline, but two centuries ago the landscape looked quite different. The sea was flanked by spectacular cliffs, and the most convenient route through them was via Sizewell Gap, just a couple of miles from Leiston. From the cliffs, goods would be carried inland along an ancient trackway crossing Westleton heathlands, or hidden in Minsmere levels.[31]

The document that details the runs by the Hadleigh Gang makes frequent references to Sizewell. This entry is typical:[32]

> June 15th—80 horses mostly with tea landed out of Cobby's cutter at Old Chapel about 2 miles from Sizewell: at the same time 34 horses all loaded with Tea landed out of the May Flower cutter and 20 next morning out of the same at Sizewell.

(There is a suggestion that Cobby, who owned one of the boats involved, was one of the smugglers who broke into the Poole customhouse, and was ultimately hanged and his body displayed on a gibbet at Selsey Bill.)

Of the countless local tales about the free-trade, one yarn in particular is extremely vivid, and gives an unusually detailed glimpse of how the local smugglers operated. Furthermore, the particulars of the story have been verified by several writers.

Small boats filled with contraband rum at Sizewell Gap had little difficulty losing themselves in the brackish lakes and marshes of the Minsmere levels.

The story is set in the summer of 1778, when a group of smugglers brought in a cargo of gin. They landed the 300 tubs undetected, shipped it a couple of miles inland in six carts, and stored the contraband in a barn at Leiston Common Farm, under the watchful eye of Crocky Fellowes, a trustworthy accomplice.

All would have been well had the cache not been found by another local of Leiston, the club-footed 'Clumpy' Bowles. Either Bowles did not have the same sympathy for the local smugglers, or he smelt a reward, because he reported the find to the local revenue man, Read. Realizing that he'd need some support if he was going to separate the spirits from their owners, Read tried to summon a pair of dragoons who were billeted at the White Horse[33] in the village. The dragoons were drunk, so Read looked elsewhere for reinforcements. He sent for two dragoons from the inn at Eastbridge, but the landlady there plied the two men with spirits before they left, so their assistance was equally useless.

Read eventually got together some help, and the party was met at the locked door of the barn by Crocky Fellowes and two chums—Sam Newson and Quids Thornton. The three men kept Read and his party occupied while twenty of the smugglers moved the tubs through an adjoining hay-loft and onto waiting carts. When the work was complete, the three men guarding the barn unlocked the door, admitted the revenue officers . . . then locked them inside. The carts trundled off to Coldfair Green, a mile south-west of Leiston.

Here the smugglers had another hiding-place waiting. A dung-heap concealed a trap-door which led to a sizeable underground vault. The tubs were bundled in and the dung moved back into position; the finishing touch was to eliminate all the cart tracks and footprints by driving a herd of sheep over them. This subterfuge seems to have been sufficient to outwit the revenue men, but the tale is not yet over.

Some time later, the gang returned to recover their cache. They shovelled the manure away from the door and opened the vault. Despite warnings from Crocky Fellowes, they didn't wait for the foul air from the dung to disperse before descending, and three of the gang were overcome by the fumes; two of them died as a result.

News of the deaths travelled fast, and eventually reached the ears of a revenue officer at Saxmundham. He guessed that the smugglers would move the tubs to Aldringham, probably to the Parrot and Punchbowl. He was right. He rode to the pub with two (sober) dragoons, and caught the smugglers red-handed.

However, while their gin was hidden, the gang had not been idle. They soon found out who had informed on them, and at nine o'clock one night two of them arrived at the crippled breech-maker's house on the Yoxford Road close to Leiston High Street. They dragged Clumpy from the house and took him on horseback to somewhere a little less public. There they gagged him with the bung from a beer barrel and savagely whipped him. They threw the apparently lifeless body over a hedge, but Clumpy was clearly a man of some stamina. A farm labourer found him, and took him to the Green Man at Tunstall, where a servant recognized the bung with which Clumpy's assailants had gagged him; she had lent it to a man called Tom Tippenham. Clumpy's testimony, and this corroborative evidence earned Tippenham and his accomplice a two-year stretch in Ipswich prison.[34]

EASTBRIDGE ■22

156-TM4566, 2m N of Leiston. See map on page 165.

The pub at Eastbridge, the Eel's Foot Inn, had a long-standing association with the free-trade, but also served as a billet for dragoons. This irony would certainly account for the behaviour of the landlady in the account of the Crocky Fellows incident above. Generally the pub seems to have managed to maintain an uneasy truce between the two opposing sides, though sometimes there were lapses. Thirty years before the Leiston deaths, preventive men supported by a detachment of fusiliers had clashed with smugglers at Eastbridge in mid-December. The smugglers proved superior, and the authorities retreated to the nearby Eel's Foot. Evidently exhausted by the struggle, the smugglers arrived at the same pub half an hour later to refresh themselves. Lieutenant Dunn, commanding, ordered his men out, and they fired on the smugglers who were stabling their horses in the yard, thus driving them off. Two of the smugglers were captured and sent to London for trial.

In a barn here at Leiston Common Farm smugglers concealed a thousand gallons of contraband gin in 1778. When an informer revealed the site of the cache to the revenue men, the smugglers locked them up in the barn, and made off for a safer hideout.

Theberton, just a mile or so west of Eastbridge, was also used as a point of storage and concealment; kegs were stored under the altar-cloth of the church there, according to contemporary correspondence![35]

EARL SOHAM AND AREA

Earl Soham ■23 is at 156-TM2363, 3m W of Framlingham. Street Farm is just off the green at Earl Soham, on the road leading south. Monewden ■24 is 4m NW of Wickham Market 156-TM2358. Rishangles ■25 is 4m N of Debenham at 156-TM1668 and Letheringham ■26 lies 2m NW of Wickham Market at 156-TM2757.

The Roman road leading towards Stowmarket from the Suffolk coast was a convenient and well-used route for contraband heading inland. Its progress was only sporadically interrupted by the customs authorities, but nevertheless the passing carts did not go unnoticed. Earl Soham on this route was the home of William Goodwin, a surgeon. Goodwin lived at Street Farm for the second half of the eighteenth century and the early years of the nineteenth, and he meticulously recorded contraband passing through from Sizewell Bay to points farther west. In the summer of 1785, he noted that, in less than a week, twenty carts had passed by carrying 2,500 gallons of spirits. In February of the same year, five carts carrying 600 gallons passed in the course of just one morning. On 23 February, though, the smugglers were not so lucky, and they lost six carts loaded with spirits to the preventive services.

The enormous quantities of contraband being moved along the Roman road can be partly accounted for by the state of Britain's other roads. Their condition was generally appalling, and at their worst during the winter. Until major road-building programmes began in the 1790s, the Roman roads that criss-crossed the country would have been the only reliable way of transporting heavy wagons. On other roads carts often foundered in the mud.[36]

There are stories associated with other villages close to Earl Soham. At Monewden, the sexton of the local church was in league with the smugglers, and in February 1790 the revenue services seized 9 tubs of spirits that he had hidden behind the ten commandments in the church.[37] The parson, sexton and clerk at Rishangles to the north were also reputed to be involved in the trade, and repairs to St Margaret's church in 1858 lend some credence to this story: under the pulpit workmen found the remains of kegs and bottles. The interior of the pulpit was accessible only from outside the church, and the clerical gang had evidently used it as a secure storage place for their contraband. The church is now a private house.

At Letheringham Mr Hart was robbed and 'cruelly beaten' on 1 December 1791 by one James Marr, a smuggler of Charfield. Marr was apprehended, but hanged himself in Ipswich New Gaol while awaiting trial.[38]

ALDEBURGH AND THE ALDE ■27

156/169-TM4656, 6m SE of Saxmundham. The Alde estuary stretches away to the S.

The villages and towns along the meandering Alde all saw their fair share of the free-trade. Sudbourne was the home of a particularly brazen smuggler, Richard Chaplin. On his retirement, he placed an advertisement in a local newspaper that must surely have been calculated to cock a snook at his traditional rivals, the revenue men. It is worth reproducing in full:

Richard Chaplin, Sudbourne, Suffolk, near Orford, begs to acquaint his friends and the public in general That he has some time back declined the branch of smuggling and returns thanks for all their past favours. To be SOLD on Monday August 6th at the dwelling house of Samuel Bathers, Sudbourn, the property of Richard Chaplin aforesaid. A very useful Cart fit for a maltster,

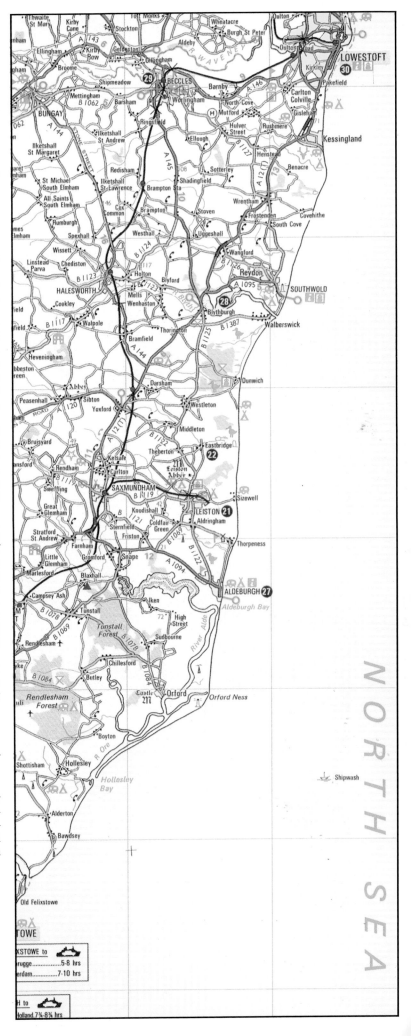

ashman or smuggler—it will carry 80 half ankers or tubs—one small ditto that will carry 40 tubs; also very good loaden Saddles, three Pads, Straps, Bridles, Girths, Horse-cloth, Corn-bin, very good Vault and many articles that are useful to a smuggler.[39]

Aldeburgh itself was deeply implicated in the free-trade. Lord Orford once commented that the only man in Orford who was not a smuggler was the parson. And though there is little to connect Snape with smuggling directly, it was nevertheless the scene of at least one unfortunate clash between the smugglers and the preventives. When Jeremiah Gardener came across a gang of desperate smugglers near to Snape in 1727 he made the mistake of challenging them, despite the overwhelming odds. The smugglers fired on him, so he drew his sword, but this proved no deterrent. His assailants cut off his nose, and if he hadn't crawled off and hidden behind a hedge, poor Jeremiah would not have escaped alive.

The remoteness of Orford made it a valuable spot for landing goods unobserved. The port was controlled by a customer and a searcher from Aldeburgh, and these officials visited Orford just a couple of times a week. As late as 1856 one local ship's master observed that by timing the visit carefully, any would-be smuggler could spend two days in Orford harbour unloading an incoming cargo—perhaps wine—and loading a new one for export to the Continent. The King's Head at Orford was used as a storehouse for goods run at Hollesley Bay.

Coastal erosion and a nuclear power station have changed the face of the coast at Sizewell, but in the 18th century high cliffs overlooked the sea.

THE BLYTH RIVER ▪28

The Blyth enters the sea at Southwold, 8m E of Halesworth at 156-TM5076. Blythburgh is on the A12 where it crosses the Blyth, at 156-TM453753. Blyford is 2m from Blythburgh on the Halesworth road at 156-TM424765.

Waterways of all descriptions provided routes for smuggled cargoes to move inland, and the Blyth served the purpose well. Dunwich, close to the river's mouth, was a popular landing-spot, and at Blythburgh in the roof of the White Hart there is a small window looking across the marsh[40]—a convenient place to put a light to signal to the string of small boats ferrying goods onward to their customers. A couple of miles upstream Blyford made a convenient stopping-off point for the kegs of brandy as they moved onwards. The Queen's Head was noted for many smuggling associations, and contraband was stored in a recess above the fireplace.[41] Another hiding-place was the church, where the pews and altar were used for concealment; but St Andrew's Church at Westhall some three miles to the north provided an even better-kept secret —kegs were hidden in the valley roof between the two ridges.

This tiny window in the roof of the White Hart at Blythburgh provided a convenient place to put a lantern as a signal for boats ferrying contraband inland up the Blyth River.

BECCLES ■29

156/134-TM4290, 8m W of Lowestoft.

The landlord of the Queen's Head at Blyford (see above) in the mid-eighteenth century was John Key, and as he became more and more deeply involved in the smuggling trade so his business as a publican must have looked increasingly like small beer. Eventually he gave up the licensed trade altogether, moving to Beccles where he took a house at Swines Green on Smugglers' Lane near St Anne's Road, 'Where five crossways meet'. The house was adjacent to a large barn, and both buildings had numerous places for hiding contraband. The buildings were standing in 1931 but described as being in dilapidated condition. Smugglers' Lane was an artery along which contraband moved into the town from the coast and from landing-points at Barnby and Worlingham on the Waveney River,[42] and perhaps Key took a fancy to the house when helping to move cargoes landed at Dunwich. Contraband also came in along the road from Covehithe, and possibly Benacre, which was a favourite landing-spot for the Hadleigh Gang.

Key played a prominent part in Beccles smuggling, and left behind a number of anecdotes. In one of them,[43] revenue officers met up with Key at Brampton Church six miles from his home, as he was returning from a run. Key spurred his horse onward, but near the Duke of Marlborough Inn, Weston, one of the officers shot John's horse (which he had borrowed for the occasion) from under him. Key completed the journey on foot, arriving just before the King's men. To his delight he found a horse very similar to the one he'd been riding, grazing contentedly near his home, so he hurriedly locked it into the stable and donned his nightclothes on top of his working garments. When he heard the inevitable knock on the door, he was able to lean out the window and shout innocently enough, 'Wha' d' ye want?'. When the revenue men replied 'where's your horse ... didn't we shoot him less than half an hour ago?', John directed them to the stable, thus providing himself with an apparently waterproof alibi.

Despite his ingenuity (or perhaps because of it) Key's stay in Beccles ended badly, for in 1745, smugglers dragged him from his bed, believing that he had informed on them. They stripped and beat him, then tied him naked to a horse and rode off. A reward of £50 for information elicited no response, and the man was never seen again.[44]

Smugglers' Lane is now called Wash Lane, and leads from 'Swine's Green to the Ellough Estate, and ... on past Castle Farm'.[45] Codlins or Codling Wood in Beccles, between Ellough Road and Worlingham boundary, was once a dump for contraband.

LOWESTOFT ■30

156/134-TM5493, 38m NE of Ipswich.

Despite the relative importance of Lowestoft as a port, there are relatively few references to smuggling activity locally—and those that do exist have a familiar ring to them. One author[46] gives an account of how contraband was smuggled ashore using the subterfuge of a coffin. In 1910 a French boat encountered a watchful body of preventives, so they pretended that a British passenger on the ship had died, and wished to be buried locally. The coffin, of course, contained contraband, and when permission had been granted and the 'body' interred, it could be secretly dug up again.[47] This story may well be apocryphal, since other writers tell very similar stories about different ports around the country.[48]

A more credible story recalls a visit to a vessel involved in the contraband trade, and describes how those involved kept to the letter of the law, if not the spirit:

We went together aboard one of the small trading ships belonging to that town, and as we were on shipboard we took notice of two of the seamen that were jointly lifting up a vessel out of the hold: when another seaman that stood by, clapped one of them

on the shoulder, and asked him why he did not turn his face away? (for he was looking down as he would see what he and his fellow were lifting out of the hold). Upon which he turned his face away. The meaning of which we soon understood to be this: that he would be obliged to swear he *saw nothing* taken out of the hold; not that he *took nothing* out of it.[49]

NORFOLK

Northern East Anglia would seem to be ideally placed for trade with the Low Countries, but apart from the usual official records of the customs and excise authorities, smuggling stories are few and far between. Perhaps the sparseness of the population accounts for this. The tight-knit communities would be reluctant to spill the local secrets to a stranger even a century or more later; perhaps the thinly-scattered villages made too lean a market for the smugglers; or maybe the Norfolk free-traders were simply better at concealing their activities than their colleagues elsewhere in Britain.

There are a couple of exceptions to the conspicuous Norfolk silence about the free-trade—and significantly, both of them were men of the cloth.

YARMOUTH AND GORLESTON-ON-SEA ■31

134-TG5207, 18m E of Norwich. Corton Cliffs are adjacent to the golf course at Gorleston.

Now a southern suburb of Yarmouth, Gorleston-on-Sea was the home of the Reverend Forbes Phillips, who wrote widely about the free-trade. His most notable work was *The Romance of Smuggling*, which he penned under the pseudonym of Atholl Forbes in the early years of the twentieth century.

In the book he refers to the High Street vicarage where he lived:

I live in a house that was constructed with a view not only of the Yarmouth Roads and the North Sea, but a further one of plundering the Revenue ... Beneath my feet as I write are large and roomy cellars, once used for the storage of imported goods, and until a few years ago a subterranean passage connected these with a landing stage by the waterside; and let the full truth be told, the designer of all was the vicar of the parish.

Under the guidance of the town's smuggling vicar, the manse at Gorleston was constructed with huge cellars and a tunnel to the waterside, with a view to 'plundering the revenue'.

Forbes Phillips relates various anecdotes about local smugglers, and his predecessor at the vicarage features prominently. One tale tells how, in the course of a landing, a newcomer to the parish arrived, and was horrified to find that goods were being illegally landed. 'Smuggling! Oh, the shame of it! Is there no magistrate to hand, No justice of the peace? . . . Is there no clergyman, no minister?' The innocent man's enquiries are silenced when one of the locals pointed out the vicar holding a lantern.

The author asserts that all the stories in the book are true, and there are a few other local yarns that support the smuggling reputation of the stretch of coast between Yarmouth and Lowestoft. Just a little to the south of Gorleston, the south end of Corton Cliffs was a popular landing spot, and during a run there, the landing party detained a preventive officer whom they caught snooping by pushing his head down a rabbit hole, then hammering a stake into the ground between his legs to prevent his escape.[50]

Yarmouth proper was a local centre for the revenue services, and the scene of much activity and battling between the preventives and the free-traders. A lot of the contraband came ashore in the treacherous Yarmouth roads, where smuggling vessels would sink the tubs for local fishermen to collect.[51] An alternative strategy that was employed farther up the coast was simply to wait for low tide, when the sea ebbed away a mile or more. A beached smuggling vessel would then appear in toy-like scale on the horizon and kegs of brandy or parcels of tea could be tossed overboard with impunity, to be carried back to the shore hidden under cart-loads of kelp. An approaching customs man could be spotted long before he reached the rendezvous.

At Yarmouth ended a bloody skirmish between the revenue cutter *Ranger* and a heavily armed smuggling vessel, which had begun at Robin Hood's Bay. The two ships were fairly evenly matched, in terms of arms and crew. The *Ranger* fired over the lugger's bows (a signal that they should stop and prepare for customs inspection) but the lugger instead returned fire. The fight continued for 90 minutes, and when the *Ranger* got the upper hand the smugglers abandoned ship. They left behind a substantial cargo valued, with the vessel, at £10,000: 507 ankers and 945 half-ankers of geneva; 206 bags of tea; 9 boxes of playing-cards; 27 bales of tobacco; and 47 bales of silk bandana handkerchiefs.

In the course of the battle, two smugglers and three revenue men were killed, and seven preventives were wounded, three so seriously that they had to be pensioned off. The bodies of the three officers were taken to The Wrestler's Inn, which can still be seen in Yarmouth market place, and were buried the following Sunday in St Nicholas's churchyard. Despite a £500 reward the smugglers were never captured.

WESTON LONGVILLE ■32

133-TG1115, 9m NW of Norwich.

James Woodforde was the parson at Weston Longville at the very height of the smuggling era, and he kept a careful diary in which he noted every detail of life in a rural community in the mid-eighteenth century. Today it makes fascinating reading, if only for the matter-of-fact way in which he deals with aspects of life that are now remote and almost forgotten. This approach extends even to smuggling and smuggled goods. Like the clergy elsewhere in Britain, Parson Woodforde was not averse to a little smuggled tea, though as far as we know he was simply a customer of the smugglers, and did not provide any sort of help and assistance to them. We read that in March 1777:

> Andrews the smuggler brought me this night about 11 o'clock a bag of Hyson Tea 6 Pd weight. He frightened us a little by whistling under the parlour window just as we were going to bed. I gave him some Geneva and paid for the tea at 10/6 a Pd.

The parson regularly bought smuggled gin, brandy and tea, not only from Richard Andrews, but also from Clerk Hewitt of Mattishall Burgh, and from the blacksmith at Honingham, Robert 'Moonshine' Buck. Not all of Woodforde's suppliers of brandy and gin were as happy to show their faces as those that he names in his diaries. On at least one occasion the parson describes how a knock took him to the door, and he discovered a couple of kegs waiting for bottling; by the time he peered out of his window, whoever delivered them had disappeared into the shadows.

In 1730 smuggling gangs were landing goods unhindered on the East Anglian coast. So great were their numbers and support from local people that effective opposition was impossible, as two Yarmouth revenue men learned to their cost. When they boarded a Dutch brigantine in their search for contraband, the ship's master cut the anchor cable and sailed away with the two men on board. They were never seen again.

THE NORFOLK BROADS ■33

Horsey Mill is 9m NE of Acle at 134-TG457222 on the B1159. Sutton Broad is at 134-TG3723 some 6m W.

Once contraband had been landed on the Norfolk shore, the Broads provided an elaborate and intricate system of distribution. Barges plying a perfectly legitimate trade were happy to take on board a little extra cargo that provided a higher return than a hold full of coals. The wherrymen who plied the Broads evolved an ingenious semaphore system to warn of the approach of the customs authorities:

> If a search was suspected by those on the watch . . . warning was sent by a runner to the nearest marshman. If his mill was turning he would stop it at the St Andrew's (diagonal) cross, then wait until those at the next mill had seen him and done the same. Then he would let the mill turn again. If there was no wind the boy would be sent up to climb on the sail, and his weight used to turn the mill to the required position . . . The clear signal would be telegraphed using the St George (square) cross on the mill sail.[52]

Horsey Mill was reputedly used in this way: a message could travel from Yarmouth to Horsey in a quarter of an hour—much faster than a customs man could ride.

When a wherryman saw the sails stop turning, he would sink his tubs in the broad, marking the spot with a float made of reeds. The marshman at the mill would pick up the contraband later, and share in the proceeds. There was a risk attached to this procedure—sometimes the kegs would drift free and be lost. This possibility was avoided by lobbing the tubs into a drainage ditch; the mill gradually pumped the water along the ditch, so that the tubs were delivered directly to the marshman.

Mills were useful for other purposes beside signalling. In communities where no one ever locked their doors (if the doors had locks at all) mills were among the few places that could be secured without arousing suspicion. Close to Stalham Dyke a mill was used as a storage-place in this way; the contraband hidden there came into the country between Horsey and Happisburgh. When space ran out at the mill, kegs were sunk in nearby Sutton Broad.[53]

THE SMUGGLERS' ROADS OF NORTH NORFOLK

The last part of the route described below is still marked on large-scale OS maps as 'Smugglers' Lane'. To reach it, leave the A1075 at Shipdham on the Bradenham Road, and just before the Lord Nelson pub, fork right along Mill Street. Cross the first ford, then fork right and continue up the hill past the grand entrance to Bradenham Hall. Opposite the farm offices take the minor road on the left, and follow it straight down, past some derelict farm buildings. At the T-junction turn right, then left, skirting the wood. At the end of the wood, Smugglers' Lane crosses north to south at 132-TF915105 ■34.

Overland transport of contraband was used when waterways were unavailable, but was generally regarded as unreliable. When they did travel overland, smugglers favoured green lanes and ancient trackways, out of sight of the main thoroughfares. Peddar's Way,[54] which runs south-east from Hunstanton, was widely used, and the section north of Massingham used to be known as Smugglers' Way for the same reason. The same label was attached to other routes:

> Across the barren wastes of Bodney there is a sandy trackway known as the 'Smugglers' Road' which appears originally to have been . . . connected with the road from Swaffham to Hillborough, with a junction about a mile north of the above-named place . . . A Smuggler's Way . . . left Peddar's Way at Pettigards, but is lost before crossing the Necton-Hale Road . . . it reappears as a grass lane to the Hale Fox Cover . . . is again lost, but conti-

nues as a lane which runs into West End, West Bradenham, where it turns sharply north east, follows the highway to the cross-roads, and runs for some distance as a sunken lane . . . it starts again inside the edge of Bradenham [Great] Wood, whence it runs to Fransham and Litsham.[55]

If convoys of wagons and horses rolling along these roads attracted too much attention, old superstitions provided plenty of ways of discouraging further interest. Old Shuck the ghost dog is a persistent Norfolk legend that, like the cannibals of Clovelly, the smugglers used to advantage. Shuck is an enormous black dog with one glowing eye, and fiery breath. Anyone who sees Old Shuck is sure to die within a twelve month. Norfolk smugglers took advantage of the gullibility of the villagers and tied a lantern round the neck of a black ram, sending it running off through the fields to frighten nosey locals when a smuggling run was due on the coast nearby.[56]

HAPPISBURGH ■35

133-TG3731, 6m E of North Walsham

The manor house here was the headquarters of a smuggling gang, and an early nineteenth-century apparition that troubled Happisburgh might well have been dismissed as the gang's attempts to frighten off unwelcome attentions—had it not been for the grisly sequel. The ghostly figure had no legs, and his head was almost severed, hanging by a thin strip of flesh. Dressed as a sailor, the ghost approached from Cart Gap on the coast, and 'walked' along the main street carrying what appeared to be a bundle of clothes.

Two of the braver farmers followed the ghost, and saw it disappear down a well. The following day a volunteer was recruited, and was duly lowered down the well on a rope; he returned to the surface clutching a sack, tied at the neck. The sack was opened, revealing a pair of human legs, hacked off at the thighs. Further descents (involving a different volunteer!) revealed the remainder of the corpse, dressed exactly as the ghost had been, with his neck almost cut away, so that the head dangled on a thread.

By piecing together other evidence the local people deduced that Dutch smugglers had landed at Cart Gap, and in a drunken quarrel one of their number had had his throat cut with unnecessary vigour. His murderers had cut off his legs to make transport of the body from the place of death simpler.[57]

OVERSTRAND ■36

133-TG2440, 2m E of Cromer. Mill House is at 133-TG254404 on the B1159 coast road, close to a communications beacon, and on the coast side of the road. Mill Lane is now a footpath leading up the hill opposite.

The Old Mill House, Overstrand, had a squint (spyhole) placed to provide a view of the sea in the direction of Holland. Outside the house it was at head height, but indoors it would have been inconspicuously at floor-level, perhaps concealed by a flap in the skirting board or a conveniently-placed piece of furniture.

The fruits of the landings close to the Mill House were often buried in a ploughed field on the right-hand side of Mill Lane at the brow of a hill. The field was known locally as Hickerman's Folly after a riding officer from Cromer who was rash enough to try and interrupt smuggled goods that were being 'harvested' from the fresh-turned earth. For his troubles he was pulled from his horse, gagged and blindfolded, and tied to a gate as the contraband was ferried down Hunger Lane, and possibly on to a Rookery Farm at Gimmingham, where there were secret hiding-places under the lawn.[58]

At Gimmingham there is today no trace of Rookery Farm, though the lawn at Rookery Farm in Trunch nearby bears traces of uneven grass growth that suggests tunnels and hidden caverns.

WEYBOURNE ▪37

133-TG1143, 3m W of Sheringham.

The coast between Sheringham and Weybourne was popular for landing goods because ships could anchor closer to the shore than anywhere else in the area. There was also a convenient gap in the cliffs through which goods could be easily transported.[59] On Weybourne beach there was so little cover for the waiting land party that the men were reputed to bury themselves neck-deep in the shingle until the smuggling vessel appeared on the horizon.[60] This story perhaps stretches the credulity to the limits, but the fact that it is also told of Suffolk locations adds at least a little weight:

> A boy going down to a lonely part of the beach one evening was asked by a man if he would like to earn a sovereign . . . the latter forthwith dug a hole in the beach and making the boy lie down in it, covered him up to the chin with beach. 'There' said he 'You lie there and don't move till you hear a whistle blow and then do you get up and do the same as others do'. By and bye the whistle blew, and jumping up the boy saw . . . hundreds of men unseen before coming up out of the beach all round. Then a boat ran ashore and her cargo was unloaded and carried away inland.[61]

The owner of much of the inland areas at Weybourne (William J. Bolding) reputedly turned a blind eye to goods landed on the beaches bordering his property, and was rewarded with a couple of tubs left discreetly on his doorstep.[62]

STIFFKEY AREA ▪38

132-TF9743, 4m E of Wells.

Smugglers around Blakeney and Wells during the early nineteenth century were nothing if not brazen. In the Stiffkey district, they were led by a man called John Dunn. Dunn arranged a landing on one occasion in 1817 on the sands at Wells during a race meeting—at that time the horses ran on a track along the sand. The preventive men saw the landing, but when they tried to seize the tubs, they were attacked by the gang. Heavily outnumbered, the customs men appealed for help from a yeomanry major in the crowd. With mounted friends he formed an improvised cavalry charge, and succeeded in clouting with his riding whip—among others—the local baker. The smugglers escaped with all but six tubs despite this spirited opposition.[63]

The same Major Charles Loftus related that he chanced upon 15 carts standing by near Morston. The smugglers informed him that they'd been expecting a signal all afternoon from a smuggler off-shore, and had sent accomplices to the Swan at Cley-next-the-Sea to get the dragoons there drunk. The men commented 'We can tie up the preventives but we don't like them dragoons' pistols and swords'.[64]

There is ample evidence to suggest that the revenue services were as unpopular in North Norfolk as they were elsewhere in the country; the usual stock of local stories portray the customs and excise service as fools or worse. One enduring story concerns a farmer from Blakeney who was caught carting smuggled goods up from the coast and had had several good horses confiscated. The beasts were due to be auctioned,

Horseracing on the fine, flat sands of Wells was interrupted in 1817 by a smuggling run. The outnumbered revenue men enlisted help from the local gentry, but the smugglers nevertheless escaped with most of their haul.

and the astute farmer went along, knowing that at that time his animals would be starting to moult. Counting on the ignorance of the sea-faring customs men (obviously not riding officers) he pulled at the hair of one of the horses. Naturally it came away in his hand and he told the supervising officer, 'Whoi, the poor brute have gotten t' mange and all tudde-runs'll ketch it ef you int keefful'. Naturally, an examination of the other horses proved that his worst fears had been realized, and he was able to take the horses off the man's hands for £5 before the mange spread to the mounts of the riding officers themselves![65] Another version of this yarn has it that the horses belonged not to one farmer, but to the whole village—everyone had lost horses when the run was raided.

OLD HUNSTANTON ■39

132-TF6842, 14m NE of King's Lynn. Snettisham is some 4m S. Both graves are clearly marked with white-painted boards.

The antagonism between the Norfolk smugglers and their opponents in the revenue services ran much deeper than punch-ups on the beach and harmless tricks involving horses. A visit to the church of St Mary the Virgin at Old Hunstanton illustrates this. In the graveyard are buried two soldiers who were killed in battles with smugglers. The epitaphs read:

> In memory of William Webb, late of the 15th D'ns, who was shot from his Horse by a party of Smugglers on the 26 of Sepr. 1784
> I am not dead but sleepeth here,
> And when the Trumpet Sound I will appear
> Four bulls thro' me Pearced there way:
> Hard it was. I'd no time to pray
> This stone that here you Do see
> My Comerades Erected for the sake of me.

> Here lie the mangled remains of poor William Green, an Honest Officer of the Government, who in the faithful discharge of his duty was inhumanely murdered by a gang of Smugglers in this Parish, September 27th, 1784.

Two smugglers were caught in the battle that killed Webb, and when brought to trial there was, according to contemporary accounts, 'no doubt' of their guilt. Nevertheless, against all the evidence, a jury found them not guilty. The prosecuting counsel demanded and got a new trial, but again the new jury displayed its sympathy with the smugglers and returned a second not guilty verdict.[66]

Another tale from Snettisham, set in 1822, illustrates how much support the free-traders enjoyed. A smuggling boat landed 80 tubs, and when the preventives impounded them, the local population turned out in a band of over 100 people to rescue the goods . . . 'armed with bludgeons and fowling pieces'. The smugglers escaped along the Peddar's Way, at a time when virtually nobody else used the track.

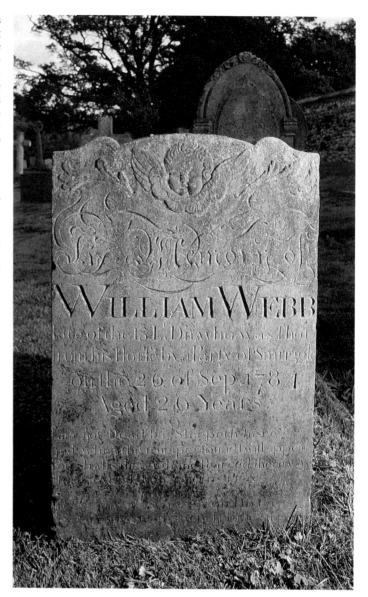

William Webb's gravestone at the church of St Mary the Virgin in Old Hunstanton.

LINCOLNSHIRE

Like Kent, Lincolnshire was a major sheep farming area, and early smuggling in the two counties ran on similar lines, even down to the 'owlers' nickname. The principal haunts of these seventeenth-century smugglers were coastal hamlets such as Grainthorpe and Saltfleet, and villages in the marshes not far from the sea—Irby in the Marsh was one such depot.

In common with other areas, import smuggling in Lincolnshire gradually superseded wool exports. Dutch gin was a favourite commodity, and Dent's Creek on the Humber saw so many Dutchmen passing through that locals called the area Little Holland.

Nineteenth-century smugglers, though, favoured tobacco. This was imported in convenient-sized bundles weighing 50–100 lb, making the bales instantly identifiable from the legal stuff, which was packed in vast hogsheads weighing 1300 lb.

The illegal tobacco was frequently disguised as perfectly legitimate cargo, and manhandled from the coast to Lincoln for manufacture into cigars or snuff—the villagers of Louth and Horncastle were especially adept at this journey. Transport by cart was less energetic, but required more care; the convoy had to travel by night, with the contraband stored in safe houses during the day. Places of concealment included: a hen house at Stewton close to Louth, on Vicarage Farm; at a house between Ashby and Horncastle; at Claxby under a potting shed in the Hall gardens; and the Midge Inn between Horncastle and Wragby. Routes inland led from Mumby Chapel to Claxby, following Burlands Beck; and from Theddlethorpe to South Thoresby, then over the Wolds.

Smuggling in south Lincolnshire seems to have continued very much longer than in southern England, perhaps because of the isolation of the most popular landing beaches, and the difficulty of patrolling the long coastline from preventive stations that were frequently undermanned.

SKEGNESS ■40

19m NE of Boston. The Vine Inn (now Hotel) is at 122-TF564619. Leave the town centre travelling S on Drummond Road. After ³/₄m, you'll see the hotel signposted to the right. See map on page 172.

Here the task of prevention fell on the shoulders of a riding officer from Boston; his other responsibilities meant that he was unable to visit the town daily. If his inspections coincided with a run, he might find himself entertained at a local hostelry, while the locals unloaded the small boats that were beached between Seacroft and Gibraltar Point. These vessels plied between the beach and the smuggling cutters, unloading various contraband cargoes, typically gin, tobacco, snuff, tea and sugar.

The haunt of the Skegness smugglers was The Vine Inn, and here in 1902, building work revealed a skeleton dressed in uniform with brass buttons carrying the royal crest. This was probably the body of a revenue man who disappeared in the early years of the nineteenth century. It was in the Vine that the unfortunate man was last seen alive. The room where the skeleton was found is now the Grill Room.

The most famous (or notorious) of the Skegness smugglers were Thomas Hewson and James Waite. Hewson was a tailor by profession, but left his family in his native Anderby to take up the free-trade. Among other dark deeds, he was suspected of the murder of a young man of Sloothby. Hewson was known to have lured the lad away from his employer, and was caught with a watch belonging to the youth. However, the body was never found. James Waite was caught for smug-

gling numerous times, and had three boats confiscated and sawn in half. When he was not awaiting His Majesty's pleasure he lived at Ingoldmells, in a house picturesquely named Leila's Cottage (now a prominent pub called The Ace). Waite's renown can be judged from the fact that Skegness coastguards at one time carried in their watchboxes a portrait of the man, captioned 'James Waite, the notorious smuggler'.

The coast north of Skegness to Saltfleet was another popular stretch for landing goods. Boats were unloaded on the beach, and the contents transferred to carts. These were then hauled through gaps in the sand dunes, known as 'pullovers'. Ingoldmells was for a long time a favoured landfall, and as late as 1846 Dutch vessels were still landing tobacco on the beach there.

MABLETHORPE ■41

122-TF5085, 11m E of Louth. Bleak House is at 122-TF493870 in North End. See map on page 172.

Contraband landed on the beaches here could not always be spirited away immediately, and tubs were frequently buried in the dunes to await later collection. Early this century a partly decayed barrel of tobacco was unearthed in the sands; the owner had clearly been unable to return to claim his cargo, or perhaps had failed to take accurate bearings to locate the hiding-place among the drifting sand-dunes.

Oliver's Gap was a regular highway for smuggled goods, and two local smugglers had houses near here. Ned Bell lived at Bleak House,

Caves at Flamborough Head were widely used to conceal smuggled imports from the Continent. Flamborough fishing boats bought the contraband at sea from French vessels, then hid the bales and barrels in the caves until the coast was clear.

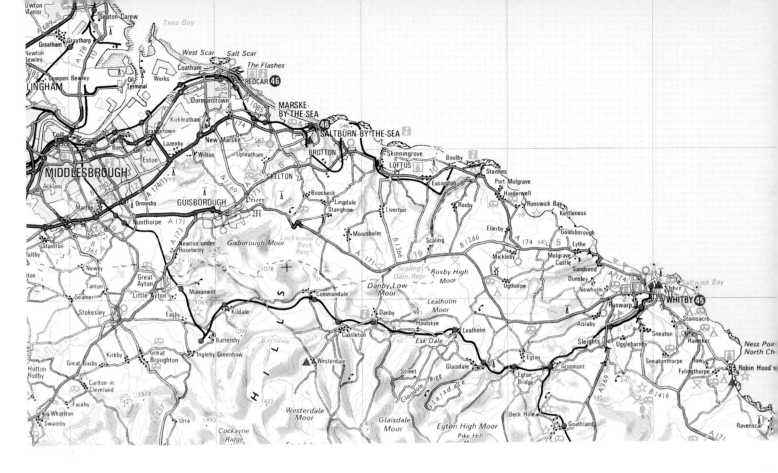

and is reputed to be buried in the family plot at Theddlethorpe St Helens some three miles north;[67] a direct descendant still lives in Bleak House. William Twigg lived at North End Farm, which also still stands. To the north a mile or so, a brick cottage called the Curlew, half hidden by the dunes, was home to another smuggling family, though it was demolished earlier this century.

YORKSHIRE AND THE NORTH-EAST

The Yorkshire coast is some 200 miles from Holland across the wind-swept north sea, so it is not entirely surprising to find that Yorkshire smugglers crossed to the Continent less often than those who simply had the narrow Channel to negotiate. However, in the late seventeenth century and the early years of the eighteenth, there was a brisk export trade in wool and sheep snatched from contented grazing on the lush Yorkshire Ridings. And certainly as the century wore on, the ships crossing to Holland returned loaded with tea, gin and brandy.

Yorkshire lacked the vast and concentrated market of south-east England, and much of the early eighteenth-century smuggling activity was piecemeal, with big, heavily-armed luggers hovering off-shore as floating supermarkets, to service demand from the coastal fishing villages and farming hamlets. Hull, though, was the exception. It had the considerable advantage of a large population eager for contraband goods, and the city was at the root of a vast distribution system formed by the Ouse and Trent Rivers. In terms of its importance as a port, Hull ranked behind only London and Bristol. Much of the town's trade was in coal, exported to Holland, and moved coastwise to London, and cargoes of smuggled goods slipped into the town quay in the black holds of ships returning in ballast.

Hull's involvement was nothing new: as far back as 1394 a merchant there was caught smuggling a barrel of honey and 200 oranges! Such evasion was petty, though, in contrast to later, more substantial frauds: the poundage due was just tuppence ha'penny, which suggests that early smuggling was habit—merchants just didn't want the aggravation of paying duty.

HORNSEA ■42

107-TA2047, 14m NE of Hull.

Many of the coastal towns and villages to the north of Hull have stories to tell: at Hornsea the crypt of St Nicholas' Church was said to have been inhabited by a witch called 'Nanny Cankerneedle', who was made homeless by the parish clerk who wanted to use the crypt to store barrels of brandy. He was caught out two days before Christmas in 1732, when a hurricane blew sheets of lead off the church roof, wrapping them around high trees in Hall Garth. The clerk was struck dumb by the shock of being discovered just as he was stashing away his casks, and he died just months later.

FLAMBOROUGH ■43

101-TA2270, 4m NE of Bridlington. The pub is on the High Street.

A Flamborough anecdote relates how, in 1844, a lad took a horse from Sewerby to The Rose and Crown (then calling the Bending Mule) at Flamborough. The boy, Robin Jewison, met a customs officer near the mill at Croft's Hill, and the officer quizzed him about what he'd seen. 'Nothing untoward' was the boy's reply.

When he reached the pub, there was the sound of men moving kegs in the cellar, but the landlord was nowhere to be seen, and his wife explained that he was sick in bed. However, on his return, the lad met a cart with rags tied over the wheels, pulled by a horse with hooves similarly muffled, and in the dark he heard the 'sick' landlord address him: 'Now then Robert, we've seen a lot o' thoo leately, an' we're alus pleased to see thi, but thoo tak oor advice, see nowt, an' hear nowt, an' some fine day thi old granfayther may find summat tiv his likin' iv his corn bin'. This prediction soon came true, and just the next day the boy's gradfather discovered in his granary at Sewerby Fields a tub of brandy.

Flamborough Head is dotted with caves that were associated with smuggling, and one of them—Rudston Church Garth—is reputedly connected by a tunnel to the church mentioned in its name. Another cave is simply called The Smugglers' Cave, though an elderly local comments that 'We called it that when I was a lad to amuse the visitors. The cave that was really used was Dovecote (now called Pigeon-Hole)'.

SCARBOROUGH ■44

101-TA0488 The Three Mariners is on the quayside, tucked away behind Horace Cherry's amusement arcade. Open 10–6 daily from Spring Bank Holiday to end of September. Admission 30p.

George 'Snooker' Fagg dominated Scarborough smuggling in the 1770s. His schooner, the *Kent* was armed to the teeth, with sixteen four-pounder guns, and a dozen swivels. The local revenue cruisers were no match for this sailing fortress and hesitated to engage the ship, even when it was clear that smuggled goods were being openly sold.

Fagg was so cock-sure that he invited the revenue men aboard the *Kent* one summer's day in 1777 when trading with the massed ships in Bridlington Bay. Fagg had sent a message across to the revenue cruiser to enquire how they were fixed for provisions. Hearing that stocks were low, the cheeky smuggler entertained several of the revenue men on board the *Kent*, sending them back with a free half-anker sample of gin.

Less than a month later, relations between the preventives and their adversary were less cordial. For once the revenue men were able to muster a force sizeable enough to tackle the *Kent*. Acting on a tip-off, two revenue ships closed on the *Kent* off the coast near Filey. The captain of one of the cruisers ordered Fagg to 'heave to, or we will fire', and was greeted with a cheery reply of 'fire away, you bouggers, and be damned to you!'.

The ensuing battle was agonizingly prolonged because the wind had dropped to the gentlest of breezes. Out-gunned for once, the *Kent* attempted to flee and nearly succeeded. But just as the smugglers were drifting out of range, a naval frigate appeared, and then another. In the dying wind, Fagg resorted to desperate tactics. He put his men in small rowing-boats, and ordered then to tow the badly damaged schooner. When defeat was clearly inevitable, the surviving smugglers surrendered, and were taken on board the revenue ship. The *Kent* was sailed

into Hull by her captors, and the substantial cargo of tea and spirits unloaded into the customs warehouse.

The Yorkshire smugglers were by all account a popular lot—or to put it another way, the revenue men were as unpopular locally as they were elsewhere in the country. One of the few ways that the customs men could secure the cooperation of local people was with the aid of prize money from seizures—greasing a few palms locally quickly loosened tongues.

The widespread use of informants led indirectly to an orgy of brutality in Scarborough, and to a trial that attracted as much attention in Yorkshire as the trial of the Hawkhurst Gang did in Kent.

The story started with a fairly routine seizure. Acting on information from an informer, revenue officers seized a boat-load of tubs just north of Scarborough in August 1822, but the smugglers who were rowing them in from the lugger anchored off-shore escaped capture.

In the normal course of events, the story would have ended here; the loss of just one boat-load of gin was regarded as an acceptable risk. However, the local customs authorities weren't satisfied, and cast around for people who knew a little more about the run. Billy Mead from Burniston came forward, and implicated a wool merchant called James Law. Law was certainly a smuggler, but claimed that on this occasion he was innocent, and that Billy Mead was lying. The case eventually went to the King's Bench in London, and Law won his case against the informer—Mead was found guilty of perjury.

This caused merriment in Scarborough, but also much bitterness. The Scarborough smugglers were looking for revenge, and the target for their violence was a woodman named James Dobson, who had given evidence against Law the smuggler. Dobson visited Scarborough on market day, 13 February 1823, and was met by a mob baying for blood. He was severely beaten, breaking his ribs, rolled around in a dog kennel, then paraded through the streets tied to a ladder. He would probably have died had he not been rescued by a couple of farmers.

Law was apparently involved in the violence, and a witness at the subsequent trial gave evidence that Law kicked Dobson to the ground at the Old Globe, shouting 'damn him, kill him, he is an informing devil'. Whether this is true or not, Law had certainly been drinking in

The Three Mariners Inn at Scarborough was constructed so that smugglers drinking there had a perfect view of the harbour entrance, and could therefore spot their ships arriving, or revenue vessels putting to sea.

The smugglers in the picture-postcard town of Robin Hood's Bay were protected by a tight-lipped local community, and supported in clashes with the authorities by local quarry workers.

the town that day, because he and some friends rode drunkenly home on the night of the 13th, making a point of stopping outside the Burniston house of Billy Mead, the convicted informer. The drunken group hurled abuse at the dark windows, but it appears that Mead was prepared for trouble. He smashed a window of the house and fired a pistol out into the dark. The shot hit Law, who was taken severely wounded to the Dodsworth Farm in Harewood Dale.

This fanned the flames of public anger. The following day, a mob several hundred strong attacked one of Billy Mead's friends who had given evidence at Law's trial for smuggling, and practically killed him. In a separate incident, a group laid siege to the house of a local customs man.

When Law died, Billy Mead was put on trial for murder. For obvious reasons the trial polarized local opinion, and created a great deal of interest. The jury heard that a Burniston girl had warned Mead that Law was after his blood, and, perhaps swayed by this evidence, they took less than half an hour to find the man guilty of manslaughter. Mead served just two years for the crime, and was wise enough to leave the area when released. He subsequently pursued a profitable career as a confidence trickster in Leeds.

Today, The Three Mariners Inn is a smugglers' inn *par excellence*, though it has been converted to a shrine to the free-trade. It once had four entrances, including a tunnel that led away from the cellars. There is an abundance of low-ceilinged corridors and concealed cupboards, and the front windows provide a perfect view of the harbour entrance, despite the fact that buildings crowd in around the tiny house.

NORTH YORKSHIRE

The principal north Yorkshire smuggling ports towards the end of the eighteenth century were Staithes, Whitby and Robin Hood's Bay. All three were close-knit communities where the inside information essential for successful action against the smugglers was hard to come by. At Robin Hood's Bay the local free-traders enjoyed the support of the alum-workers from the nearby quarries, and even itinerant labourers were happy to throw in their lot with the local people and form a temporary, but effective alliance. In 1779 the building of a sea-wall brought

hundreds of workers into the area, and these men lived in Redcar, Coatham and Eston, where they joined local smugglers and formed large gangs to ship goods inland virtually unopposed despite the efforts of the local customs officers.

WHITBY ▪45

94-NZ8911, 17m NW of Scarborough. Church Street, Whitby, is at the heart of the old smuggling district.

At Whitby, subterfuge was the rule in distribution of the contraband. The housewives of the town would go to market wearing loose-fitting garments, and return with buttons bursting, having stuffed their clothes with contraband goods. Mrs Gaskell, who lived in Whitby for some time, commented on 'The clever way in which certain [Whitby] women managed to bring in prohibited goods; how in fact when a woman did give her mind to smuggling, she was more full of resources, and tricks, and impudence, and energy than any man'. She also observes that even a couple of quaker brothers in the town bought smuggled goods, and that 'Everybody in Monkshaven smuggled who could, and everyone wore smuggled goods who could.'[68]

The *modus operandi* of the local smugglers in the late eighteenth century was to 'hover' off the coast in large ships (itself an illegal activity) and send signals to the land. Fishermen would then sail out in their small boats, a design known locally as cobles, to pick up the contraband goods. In this respect the methods and organization of the Yorkshire smuggling groups paralleled that of the gangs in the south of the same period.

One collector of customs at the town summed up the situation succinctly in 1783:

Very great quantities of prohibited goods have been Run, spirits, tea, etc., are loaded into boats and cobles which are guarded by a great number of armed men who are totally defiant of the [customs] Officers, and the Country People, many of whom follow no employment but this illicit practice, are constantly in waiting, and being armed with Bludgeons, etc., and provided with Horses, immediately convey the Run goods to some distant place. Vessels are generally of the Cutter or Lugger kind, which we have reason to believe are often built in Kent, and are generally between seventy and one hundred and fifty tons, with crews of 15 to 25 men.

The revenue men stood little chance of success when faced with such opposition: 18 six-pounder carriage guns was not an unusual compliment of arms. The master of one of these ships was asked whether he didn't fear the customs cutters, and simply tapped his pistols in reply.

SALTBURN AND REDCAR ▪46

Redcar lies 6m NE of Middlesbrough at 94-NZ6124. Saltburn is 4m to the SE

The section of coast between Saltburn and Redcar was almost as notorious as the Whitby area, and some of the coastal towns were turned over almost entirely to the free-trade, smuggling principally brandy. The preventive forces naturally did all they could to stamp out the traffic, but the honest officers must often have felt they were fighting a losing battle.

Two Redcar officers had particular reason to feel bitter. They heard gunfire one spring night in 1779, and headed for the beach to see a smuggling vessel lashed to the revenue cutter that had captured it. As they watched, though, a small boat, heavily laden, set off from the ships and headed for the beach. There, the crew unloaded some 200 gallons of spirits, but fled when the riding officer and his boatman appeared.

Delighted, and eagerly anticipating a supplement to their meagre pay, the pair counted the barrels, then one set off to fetch a cart. His colleague, left to guard the haul, was somewhat dismayed when he saw to his astonishment that the revenue men were rowing a party of smugglers to the shore. The group landed and soon collected their tubs,

threw them back into the boat, and headed off along the coast. Clearly this was not what the revenue had in mind, for a revenue boat set off in hot pursuit. However, when they caught up with the small boat, the customs men set the smugglers free with half their haul of tubs—satisfied with the reward for the remainder of the cargo on board the confiscated lugger (336 half-ankers of spirits). It emerged that the smugglers had come to an agreement with their captors, and the riding officer and boatman left without reward or arrest.

The Ship Inn at Saltburn was the centre for the free-trade on this stretch of coast, and the landlord, one John Andrew, was 'the King of the Smugglers'. He also owned the nearby White House, and in the stables there hid contraband in a chamber under one of the stalls. When the place was to be searched, the stable lad had strict instructions to put in that stall a mare that could be counted upon to kick viciously at any stranger. Adjoining houses were reputedly linked to the pub by a tunnel.

The smuggling landlord owned a cutter called the *Morgan Rattler*, (though this may have been a mis-reading of the *Morgan Butler* that operated from Stockton around the end of the eighteenth century). In the course of a long career landing illegal cargoes, he had many brushes with the law and spent a spell behind bars when caught on a run at Hornsea. He died in 1835.

BORDER AREAS

North of Newcastle, the character of the free-trade begins to change, and the influence of Scotland becomes apparent. Much of the contraband activity in the border areas consisted of through transport of scotch, but there was also a thriving trade in gin from Holland, and in salt.

Whitby women, according to Mrs Gaskell, applied themselves to smuggling with more tricks, impudence and energy than any man. The whole town supported the free-trade, including two Quaker brothers.

BOULMER ■47

81-NU2614, 3m NE of Alnmouth.

This tiny village probably owes most of its notoriety not to actual smuggling exploits, but to a local rhyme that commemorates the trade. It begins, 'Jimmy Turner, of Ford didn't think it a sin, to saddle his horse on a Sunday and ride to Boulmer for gin'.

Succeeding verses feature other Boulmer smugglers. One of the best-known was the gypsy 'Wull Faa', who was famous not only for the cargoes of gin he brought in, but also for his skills in the boxing ring and on the violin. His promising musical career came to an untimely end, though, on a smuggling trip that went badly wrong. Pursued by the customs men, Will urged his horse over a wall near Littlemill, only to find its hooves effectively anchored in a bog. Will turned to fight, holding off the customs man's cutlass with his cudgel. Only when this had been whittled to a match-stick and his right hand cut to the bone did he surrender, with the plaintive cry 'Ye've spoilt the best bow hand in Scotland'.

This led to the verse:

> There is a canny Will Faa o' Kirk Yetholm,
> He lives at the sign o' the Queen;
> He got a great slash i' the hand
> When comin' frae Boulmer wi' gin.

One of the local tracks that the Boulmer men used is still in existence—it leads from Kirk Yetholm up the valley of Bowmont Water to Elsdonburn, to College Valley, Kirknewton, and then to Boulmer.[69] Carrying the goods across the Cheviots, the team were frequently guarded by a pair of bulldogs, one at the front and one bringing up the rear.[70]

The Fishing Boat Inn at Boulmer was the HQ for the local smugglers, and the landlord owned an armed smuggling lugger called the *Ides*, which he operated with a crew of two dozen. To unload the ship demanded considerable manpower, and since a large band of smugglers would have been conspicuous in such a small village, the carriers hid in the dunes while waiting for the ships to arrive from the Continent. The signal to get to work was a fiddler parading round the streets playing:

> O but ye've been lang awa'
> Ye're welcome back again.

Beadnell, Bamburgh and Spittal were favourite landing-places. Lamberton, Mordington and Paxton Tolls were 'notorious depots'.[71]

Jimmy Trotter was another legendary smuggler in the area, and was condemned to death for the theft of a horse. His strength was legendary, and it is said that when chained to a huge block of stone in gaol, he jerked the chain free of the block and carried it across the cell to block the door. He escaped from the gaol, but was recaptured when he dallied to thank the jailer's wife for her kindness.[72]

Though Boulmer is best remembered for its gin trade on account of the rhyme, salt for curing pork or fish was also regularly smuggled both across the border, and from the coast inland, and there are many local stories that centre around salt smuggling. One author wrote in 1909 that a friend recalled childhood memories of a woman of the village appearing at the door, to announce simply, 'He has come', before hurrying on to tell others that the salt man had arrived in town.

Salt was retailed by the local women who would carry it around in sacks on their backs. If the excise man caught them, a deft slash with a knife would spill the cargo. The contraband goods travelled as discreetly as possible, and a path among the hills near Newton Tors was known locally as Salters' Path.[73]

SCOTLAND

In Scotland whisky dominates the story of smuggling, for the word has a dual meaning. To a Scot, 'smuggling' meant not just illegal import and export, but also illegal distilling. We are primarily concerned with coastal aspects of the free-trade, and the subject of illegal stilling has been dealt with thoroughly in other books. However, the excise officers charged with the responsibility of stamping out stilling were also concerned with illegal imports, so it would be remiss to ignore the subject completely.

Most of the stilling went on in the glens, where there was a plentiful supply of the clean fresh water needed for soaking the grain prior to malting. After several days soaking in a burn, the grain was spread out on a warm floor and allowed to sprout. The sprouted grain was roasted and ground to make the malt, which was mixed with hot water to create the wort. After fermentation, the wort was boiled in a copper container, and vapour condensed in a spiralling tube, called the worm, to make the spirit.

All this was legal (though taxable) until 1814, when small stills of less than 500 gallons were prohibited. The response from the highlanders was, needless to say, not very sympathetic, and much of the public fury was vented against the officially approved distillers, who were hugely outnumbered by illicit manufacturers. In 1778 there were eight legal stills in Edinburgh—and an estimated 400 working without payment of duty.[1]

As much of the stilling process as possible was carried out in the heather rather than on the hearth, and the stills were hidden in caves and hollows on the hillsides. Smoke curling up from the peat fires gave away the location of the stills, and it would be these plumes that the exciseman was seeking.

He had an unpopular task, because the trade had wholehearted support from every section of the community, including in some areas even the clergy. The Rev. Andrew Burns, the minister of Glen Isla, for example, was clearly in sympathy with the illegal distillers of whisky.

His house overlooked the hotel where the excisemen would stop for refreshment before continuing with their searches further up the glen. The minister would keep his eye on the arriving party, and when the last of the group disappeared inside, the Rev. Burns would amble from his garden leading his pony, as if to set it grazing further up the glen.

Once out of sight, though, he'd leap on the bare back of the nag, and gallop with all possible haste to the nearest house where he'd borrow a saddle and reins. Then the pair would charge on up the valley, the reverend waving his hat at every bothy that housed an illicit still, shouting, 'The Philistines be upon thee, Samson!'[2]

Not all the illegal hooch was consumed locally; much was moved south of the border, often in very odd containers. 'Belly canteens' for the transport of spirits held 2 gallons and were made of sheet iron. They gave the female wearer a convincing if somewhat rigid appearance of advanced pregnancy.[3] Another container was made to look like a passenger riding pillion behind the horse-borne smuggler—a leather head completing the illusion.

IMPORT AND EXPORT

Smuggling in the sense of cross-coast trade certainly went on, but the business was on nothing like the same scale as in southern England. Poverty and the sparseness of the population accounts for this in part—with the exception of the principal towns, the market for costly foreign luxuries in Scotland was very restricted.

Perhaps in response to these circumstances, the smugglers concentrated on the import of staple goods that were heavily taxed. Salt in particular was an essential for preserving meat and fish over the harsh dark winter months, and great quantities of salt entered the country, principally from Ireland, via the west coast.

Along with the salt, of course, came other forms of contraband, because import smugglers used Ireland as a warehouse and staging-post on their way from the Continent, especially after control over the Isle of Man returned to the Crown. Tea and tobacco came in this way, and were then transported to the Scottish cities on horseback: to move a box of tea or a bale of tobacco from Galloway to Edinburgh in the early eighteenth century cost 15s.[4]

The character of Scottish smuggling was to a certain extent moulded by the Act of Union in 1707. Prior to this date, there was a wide discrepancy between duties north and south of the border, and the Scots had taken advantage of this situation to smuggle highly taxed goods into England. When the two countries were united, duties on some products north of the border increased sevenfold. The taxes were seen by the Scots as oppressive, and resistance to them positively patriotic. Walter Scott commented:

> Smuggling was almost universal in Scotland, for people unaccustomed to imposts and regarding them as an unjust aggression upon their ancient liberties, made no scruple to elude them whenever it was possible to do so. ·

The clan system, the powerful Scots church and Jacobite sympathies further united the population behind the smugglers, and made it unlikely that a free-trader would be found guilty in a jury trial. Even when the customs men managed to secure a conviction, the fines were paltry.

Antagonism between the revenue men and the Scottish population often turned to violence, the most famous example probably being the Porteous riots in Edinburgh, which were triggered off by the execution of a smuggler in 1736. Wilson, the condemned man, had gained popularity when he helped a colleague escape from the Tolbooth gaol, and a mob gathered to jeer at the gallows. They insulted Captain John Porteous, the officer in charge of the guard, and pelted him with mud. The terrified Porteous fired into the crowd, resulting in several fatal injuries. Although he was sentenced to death for the shooting, there was a rumour that he would be pardoned, and a party, wearing disguise, broke into Edinburgh prison and lynched Porteous from a signpost. Prominent Edinburgh figures were implicated in this barbaric but

highly popular murder, and as a result Westminster imposed a £2000 fine on the city.[5]

After the Union, the Scots customs and excise system was modelled on the prevailing English system, and abuses were imported along with the bureaucracy. At Edinburgh, for example, customs officers at the city gates checked permits of goods arriving from the ports and did not hesitate to seize even the most mundane objects if they could expect to make a few pennies from the sale. One zealous officer even seized a worn pair of gloves![6]

Left: *When an Edinburgh smuggler called Wilson helped a colleague escape from the Old Tolbooth shown here, he set off a train of events that was to lead to the famous Porteous riots. It was at Wilson's hanging that Captain John Porteous gave the order to fire into the angry crowd.*

Below: *From the Solway Firth smugglers supplied much of south-west Scotland with continental luxuries, and even shipped goods onward to Edinburgh.*

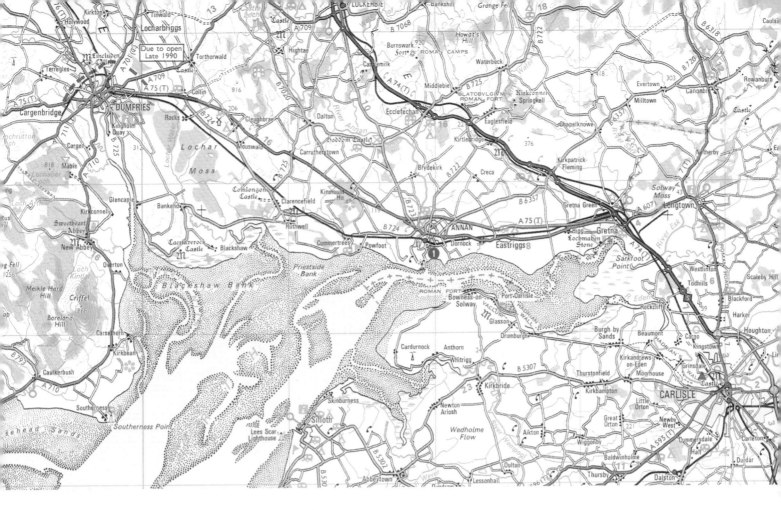

The methods used by Scottish smugglers were broadly similar to those in use elsewhere in the British Isles, with a few small variations. For example, to signal to ships at sea during the day, smugglers sometimes stretched a bed sheet on the roof of a croft or a peat-stack, a practice that doesn't seem to occur elsewhere. The danger of chance discovery by routine patrols, while low in England, was virtually negligible in Scotland, so open, unopposed landings were the rule, and the tub-men or lingtow men on the beach would be interrupted only if an informer had named the time and place of the landing.

Robert Louis Stevenson described the scene at a typical landing: 'There, against the sun which was then dipping, we saw the free-traders with a great force of men and horses, scouring the beach.'[7]

Tubs were rarely sunk, possibly because it was unnecessary, or perhaps because surf crashing on the rocky Scottish coastline would soon destroy a raft of tubs.

SOLWAY

Annan ■1 is off the A75 8m W of Gretna; Waterfoot and Kenziels are just S of the town at 85-NY1965. Ruthwell is 8m farther W.

There is a wealth of stories and legends about smuggling on the north coast of the Solway, and it seems clear that the enormous majority of goods smuggled into Scotland were landed here. The proximity of the Isle of Man gave the local smugglers a considerable advantage over their competitors elsewhere on the coast. The island was effectively a free-trade area for many years (see page 147), and the shortest crossing to the Solway was less than 30 miles. The sailors of south-west Scotland needed no encouragement to exploit this valuable trade link, and often sailed from the island in fleets of ten or more small ships and boats, in order to saturate the coast with landings, and outwit the overstretched customs and excise services.

Walter Scott wrote of the area that 'Few people take more enthusiastically to the "free-trade" than the men of the Solway Coast'. Another writer observed that 'Every little village along the Wigtownshire coast has its local tradition of some episode connected with the daring deeds of the smuggling fraternity'.[8]

A number of these little villages developed a special reputation for smuggling: Annan Waterfoot, Kenziels, Ruthwell, and Borgue (near Kirkcudbright) were particularly noted, and the minister at Anwoth, Gatehouse, was sacked for being involved in the smuggling trade.[9]

Some of these villages would also have been familiar to Scotland's most famous revenue man, Robbie Burns. Burns was appointed to a post at Dumfries in 1791, on a salary of £50 a year, and one of his superior officers there commented that, although he was not 'a bustling, active gauger . . . he does pretty well'.

The best documented incident in which the poet took part happened at Annan. A smuggling lugger was stranded on the sands nearby, and Robbie Burns was posted to keep watch while his superior officer went for help. During his long wait Burns composed a rhyme which suggests that his loyalties were more than a little divided:

> We'll mak' our maut an' bre our drink,
> We'll dance, and sing, and rejoice, man
> An' monie thanks to the muckle black De'il
> That danced awa' wi' the Exciseman!

Burns took the surrender of the ship when the dragoons arrived, and his biographer describes the incident in euphoric terms. Custom-house records, though, portray his actions in a slightly more mundane way, pointing out that the ship was listing badly, and could not therefore use its cannons on Burns or the advancing infantrymen. Nor were Burns' later actions seen in such a heroic light by his superiors. When the smugglers' ship was broken up, he bought four brass cannons, and sent them to France as a token of sympathy with the French

Revolutionaries. This act earned him some disfavour when the cannon was impounded at Dover.

At nearby Ruthwell in 1777, a tide-waiter learned that a notorious smuggler called 'Morrow of Hidwood' had returned from the Isle of Man. Tracks in the sand confirmed that a landing had taken place, and the waiter and a police constable went to the man's house, finding there a substantial amount of tobacco. They were preparing to carry it away when a multitude of women pounced, making off with the contraband. To make matters worse, the revenue man was imprisoned in Hidwood House. When he escaped and returned to his headquarters, he received little reward for his bruised body and ego, and was sent back to the scene with ten men. This time they had more success, and located one pack of tobacco in a ditch. Nevertheless, they still had to run the gauntlet of 'A monstrous regiment' of women armed with clubs and pitchforks. Some of the women were tried at the circuit court, but revealingly were discharged because witnesses for the prosecution pretended to 'entertain malice against the prisoners'.[10]

This tale seems to show women in a role that is fairly typical of Scotland at this time—supporting their men folk, or attacking the revenue men, but not actually carrying out the illegal acts themselves. The same sort of attack also took place at Glenhowan, near Glencaple, the following month.

CAPTAIN YAWKINS
(aka Dirk Hatteraick)

The Abbey Burn ■2 mentioned in this account is at Port Mary 84-NX7545 near Dundrennan Abbey.

Dirk Hatteraick's cave ■3, reputedly used by Yawkins, overlooks Wigtown Bay [Map 83]: follow the A75 from Gatehouse of Fleet towards Newton Stewart, and ¹/₂ mile past the turning on the right marked 'Holy Cairn', take a track off the road to the left. Follow this down, and take the left fork into a meadow; when the track runs out at the wood's edge, go down onto the shore. Continue along the beach in the same direction across a burn. About 300 yards farther on, an outcrop of rock juts out to sea, and just after this there's a wooded valley and a track ascending to the cave. Descent into the cave is not for the old or stout; take a change of clothes if you plan to enter. There is no trace remaining of the sleeping platform smugglers built at one end, or of the special pigeon-holes that once existed for the storage of the oddly-shaped Dutch flagons. Dirk Hatteraick's Cove ■4 is another name for Torrs Cove at 83- and 84-NX6744 (danger area) overlooking Kirkcudbright Bay on its east side. A cave here used to have a door fitted, with a stone lintel above.

Various colourful figures crop up in the many smuggling legends of the Solway area, but with hindsight, Captain Yawkins stands head and shoulders above the rest. His exploits read like fiction, and Walter Scott indeed used him as the model for his character Dirk Hatteraick in the book *Guy Mannering*. Some of the stories about Yawkins are verifiable, but others—such as the allegation that he had traded his own soul and a tenth of his crew with the devil—seem decidedly dubious.

All are entertaining, though. A typical tale has Yawkins and his crew buying a bullock at Drummore Bay on the Mull of Galloway watched by a revenue cutter. The officer on the cutter declines a roast-beef supper on board Yawkins' *Black Prince*, but they arrange a picnic ashore. When the customs officer admires the smuggler's gun, he is presented with it as a gift, followed rapidly by a decanter and glasses. Yawkins wryly comments that, since the officer had the only thing he values, he may as well take everything else.

There are many other stories. The tale that Yawkins kidnapped a revenue man and sailed him over to Amsterdam echoes other verified accounts from elsewhere on the coast. In another he was landing a cargo at Drummore (some accounts place the incident at Manxman's Lake near Kirkcudbright) when two revenue cruisers appeared, one from the north and one from the south. Yawkins cast off, replaced his pennant with a mast-head cask to identify his chosen trade, and sailed directly between the two ships, close enough to toss his hat onto one and his wig onto the other. While this may be an exaggeration, it is worth remembering that carriage-guns were useless unless the target was broadside on to the ship, so there may well be a germ of truth in the yarn.

Yawkins was such a larger-than-life figure that when he had brushes with the law, the official accounts of them rather pale in comparison with the images perpetuated in myth and legend. Often Yawkins appears off-stage. In 1787 a run by Yawkins was interrupted by an 'Admiralty cruizer'. The local customs authorities heard gunfire off the Abbey Burn at around 10pm, and discovered that the Admiralty ship had indeed intercepted a smuggling lugger—but not before 17 boxes of tea had been unloaded and spirited away on the backs of waiting horses. The captured lugger had on board 80–90 boxes of tea, 400 ankers of spirits, and 'a quantity of silks and tobacco'. A postscript adds that the lugger 'was commanded by the noted Yawkins and that she was loaded at Ostend'. Yawkins' lugger, the *Hawke*, was delivered to the Liverpool authorities, but was found to be so leaky as to be of no use, and the ship was broken up.

Dirk Hatteraik's cave is now hemmed in by young trees, but when it was in regular use, the cave would have given its namesake a splendid view over Wigtown Bay.

SCOTLAND

DUMFRIES ■5

84-NX9776, Carsethorn ■6 is at 84-NX9959 10m S of the city, and Southerness Point ■7 is at 84-NX9754 off the A710.

The centre for prevention in the Solway area was Dumfries, where there was a substantial legal import trade mainly in tobacco from Virginia, wine from Oporto, and some timber from the Baltic. Food imports, though, were banned by law, and in times of famine grain and oatmeal from Ireland won the local people over to the cause of the smugglers.

Tobacco smuggling at the port eventually became so extensive that by 1760 the legal traders in the town had been driven out of business. Duties on spirits in Scotland were lower than in England until the mid-nineteenth century, so even legitimate imports to Dumfries (conveniently close to the border) were then clandestinely moved into England.

The silting-up of harbours around the Solway served the interests of the smugglers because trade could take place legally only through the Royal Burghs, but the routes to them had become too clogged with mud to accommodate ocean-going ships. Cargo was thus transferred to barges for the last stages of the journey, but somehow, not all of the goods unloaded found their way into the official custom-house quay. For example, goods travelling to Dumfries on the Nith River were

unloaded at the port of Carsethorn, and frequently completed their journey overland—to arrive untaxed via illicit salesmen, instead of properly inspected and duly levied at the custom-house quay. On one occasion excisemen at Carsethorn found tubs of spirits at North Carse Farm and followed footprints in the snow to the local manse, where they located the minister's son with snow on his boots.

The authorities took great trouble to prevent such activities; Southerness Point at the mouth of the Nith estuary holds a dominant position overlooking the Solway, and was therefore a natural choice as the site of both a lighthouse and preventive station. Both can still be seen.

The custom-house at Dumfries was of course the principal headquarters for activity against the smugglers, but at times the collector there despaired of any effective action being carried out against the free-traders. In the summer of 1761 he wrote:

> If smuggling is not more frequent . . . the insolence and audacity of the smugglers is certainly much increased. Since the departure of two companies of Highlanders . . . [the smugglers] ride openly thro the country with their goods in troops of 20, 30, 40 and sometimes upwards 50 horses suffering no officer to come near to try to discover who they are, far less to seize their goods.

Thirty years later:

> . . . the business is of such a nature that it is not possible to

Abbey Burn on the Solway Firth, the scene of an interrupted smuggling run by Captain Yawkins in 1787.

187

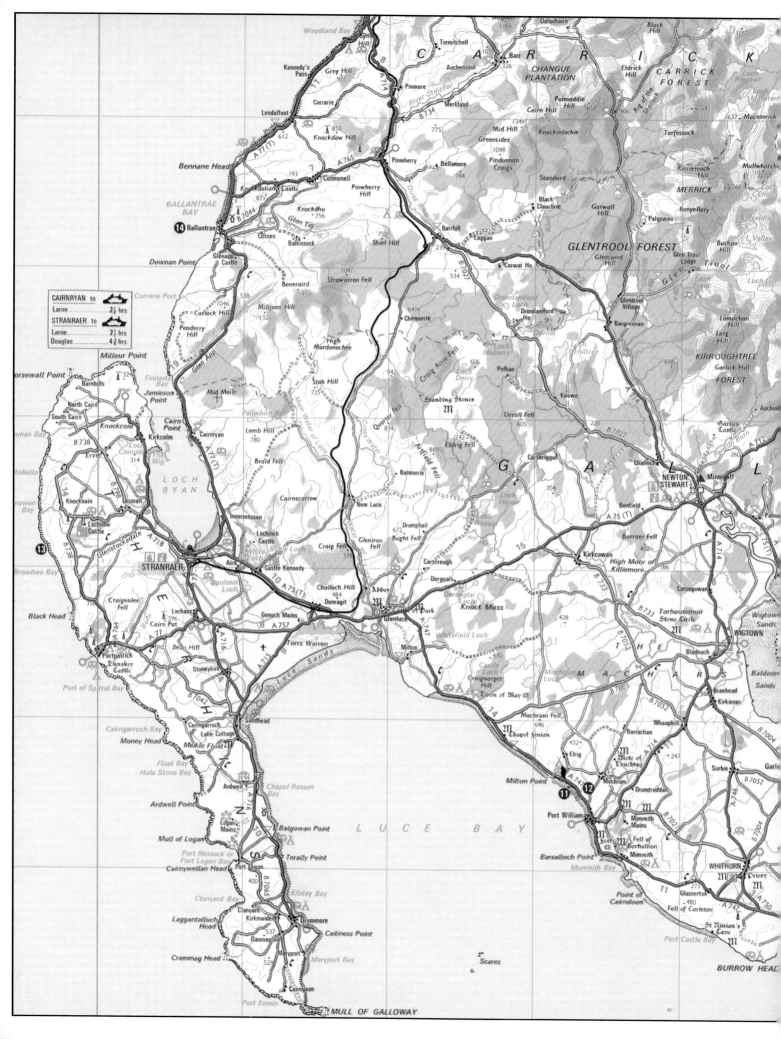

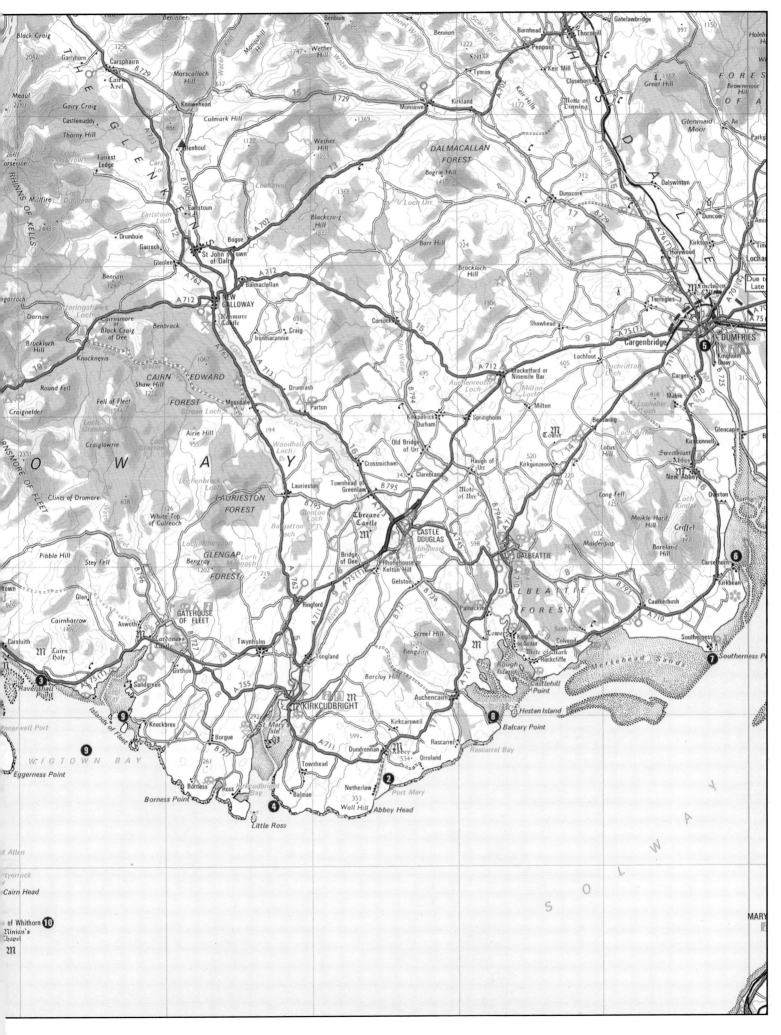

These Solway smugglers are unloading their cargo close to the mouth of the Nith; the string of pack animals was probably destined for Dumfries.

ascertain very certain information [but] in the course of the last year, five cargoes were imported as under:

1st—A sloop from Guernsey, name the 'John and Mary', carrying about 350 packages of tobacco and spirits, the different quantities of each not know but may be valued at £1200–1300

2nd—The same sloop another trip taken by Captain Cook off Annan loaded with 1071 gallons brandy, 177 gallons rum, 549 gallons geneva, 8837 lbs Tobacco and 679 lbs tea appraised at £1310/12/9

3rd—A brig from Guernsey supposed to carry 7 or 800 packages but the different species not known but believed to consist of a sorted cargo of tobacco, rum, brandy and Geneva and may be valued at £1900–2000

4th—A sloop from Ostend name unknown, carrying 350 or 400 packages of a sorted cargo, the contents unknown but valued at £12 or 1300

5th—A cutter from Ostend name the 'John and Jenny' carrying also a cargo of Tobacco and spirits, the different species unknown values also at £1300

Total £7210/12/9
Besides the above we have no doubt that very considerable quantities of tobacco and spirits have been carried up the Firth into this district from the different repositories and hiding places on the coast of Galloway where importations are made but it is impossible for us to ascertain either the extent or value.

These dry statistics, though, hide some ingenious activity by the local smugglers, including horse training worthy of a circus:

Individuals . . . had frequently seen one famous troop of these quadrupeds, heavily laden, at day-dawn, with contraband goods, unattended by any human being, and preceded by a white horse of surpassing sagacity, scouring along the Old Bridge, down the White Sands, and through the streets of Dumfries, without any one daring to interrupt their progress . . . on one or two occasions, when some individual more officious than the rest

rashly attempted to intercept the leader of the troop, the wily animal either suddenly reared and struck its opposer to the ground, or by a peculiar motion swung the kegs with which it was loaded with so much violence that no one durst approach within its reach.'[11]

KIRKCUDBRIGHT AREA

84-NX6850 The Barlocco Caves at 84-NX7846 are hard to reach without a boat. Balcary House overlooks Balcary Bay ■8 at 84-NX8249 near Auchencairn.

The whole area around Kirkcudbright has a reputation for the free-trade, but Rascarrel Bay and Abbey Head were particularly notable. At Balcary Bay, Balcary House was built with vast cellars that could accommodate the burden of 200 horses used on a run. The house was built by a smuggling company that called itself Messrs Clark, Crain and Quirk.

To the west, the Barlocco caves include the vast but well-hidden Black Cave and White Cave; the Black Cave was used by an intrepid smuggler called 'Wild' Watt Neilson. The mouth of the cave is vast—100 feet wide and 50 high—and though constantly filled by the sea even at low tide, sailing into it is a simple matter only on a calm day.

Watt was renowned for his ability to enter the cave in any weather, but one night even he found his seamanship tested to the limits. Worse than the weather, a revenue cutter was bearing down on Watt's boat, the *Merry Lass*. As it drew closer, the smuggling crew saw that the revenue ship was in the charge of Captain Skinner; though Watt had never met Skinner, the captain was the 'maist feared man' in the service of the King.

Wild Watt hatched a plan. He stayed in a small boat, posing as an informer, and sent the *Merry Lass* around the coast to the Waterfit (*sic*) at Annan, where the confederates of the smugglers would be waiting to unload the cargo at double-quick pace.

Watt's plan worked. He claimed to be the brother of the gauger at Boggle's Creek (the gauger himself was being 'entertained' for the duration of the run by the landlord of Fell Croft) and offered to pilot the ship up the Solway in hot pursuit of the *Merry Lass*. A deal was struck, and Watt took the helm. With the sails full, the lugger sped along into an area of the Solway that was unfamiliar to the King's men; nevertheless, they had the *Merry Lass* in good sight until a cloud crossed the moon. At that very instant, the smuggling boat rounded the headland, and . . . 'wi' a' sails brailled she was cuddling intae the shadows amang a cluster o' ither boats in the Annan'.

When the *Merry Lass* disappeared, Captain Skinner began to get impatient with his informer. But known only to Wild Watt, things were happening in the shadows of the Annan. Two small boats appeared in the river mouth, and when Skinner hailed them, threatening to pepper them with grapeshot, they quickly surrendered. In the commotion, none of the revenue men noticed the *Merry Lass* (now unloaded) slipping out to sea, 'ready tae tack and rin wi' the turn o' the tide'. The revenue men had their eyes fixed on the two small boats, apparently laden with rolls of tobacco, sacks of salt, and barrels of brandy.

The situation began to change, though, as the outraged boatmen were hauled aboard, hurling abuse at Skinner for interrupting an honest night's work. Far from ferrying contraband, they were simply rowing provisions to the farms at the head of the Solway: 'As ye kenna reach them when the tide is oot, can ye think o' onything mair sensible than tae gaun when the tide is in, and the folk stervin' for their meal?' Sure enough, the tubs contained only herrings, the sacks innocent oatmeal, and the 'tobacco' turned out to be dried fish. Watt chuckled at the captain's discomfort and surreptitiously swung himself over the side and into one of the small boats. The 'wronged' boatmen returned to the oars, and they made haste back to the *Merry Lass*. The duped revenue men watched helplessly as the smuggling ship hauled an empty half-anker to the mast-head, and swept out of the channel on the tide.[12]

Kirkcudbright itself has a history of smuggling—or, more precisely, of resistance to it. The Tolbooth there held many desperate and violent smugglers who were unlucky enough to get caught. Those who were found guilty were hanged in the town.

One who got away was Billy Marshall who, besides smuggling, followed the callings of gypsy and robber. Among his aliases he counted the King of the Gypsies, and Caird (gypsy) of Burullion (after the area he controlled). He died aged 120, and was buried in St Cuthbert's churchyard. However, his gravestone has now been removed.

WIGTOWN BAY ■9

Ardwall Island at 83-NX5749 can be reached on foot at low tide. It is close to Knockbrex, 6m W of Kirkcudbright.

Wigtown Bay is really the estuary of the Cree River, and concealing inlets made detection here unlikely. Ardwall Island, just a few hundred yards from the east coast, was a useful headquarters—one of the bays on its perimeter was known locally as Smugglers' Bay. Dirk Hatteraick's Cave also overlooks Wigtown Bay (see page 186 for location).

Wigtown and Creetown at the north Wigtown Bay were both hotbeds of smuggling. One vivid account tells how in 1777 a defiant procession of 100 or more smugglers led twice this number of horses within a mile of the town, despite the attentions of 30 soldiers who had been sent to stop the run. An eye witness described how four horses were overcome by the smell of tobacco and the heat of the day, and dropped down dead.

Clark, Crane and Quirk was a smuggling company based here in Balcary Bay. From their substantial cellars beneath Balcary House they would have been well-placed to supply the wealthy households of nearby Kirkcudbright.

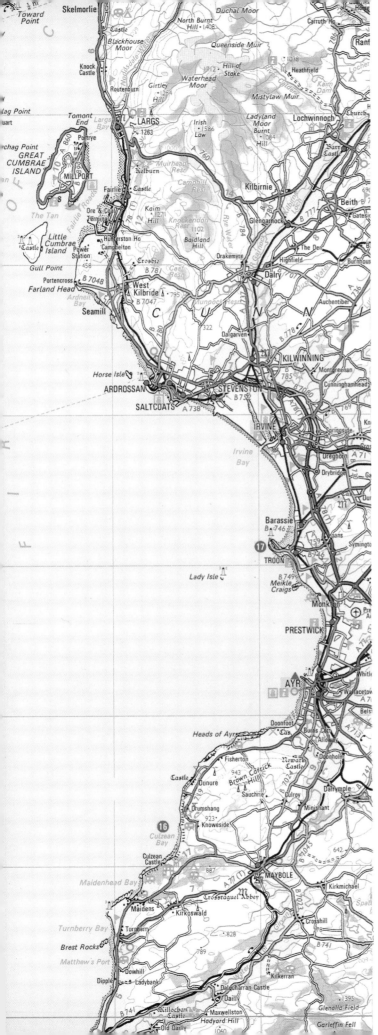

ISLE OF WHITHORN ■10

83-NX4736, 3m SE of Whithorn. Now an island in name only. The channel has been filled with silt, though you can still identify the places described in the story, and the yarn makes more sense on the spot than it does in print.

On the west side of Wigtown Bay the Isle of Whithorn overlooks a narrow inlet, which was at least once used by smugglers to effect a cunning escape. Their ship was sighted off the Mull of Galloway, and a revenue cutter gave chase.

The two ships sped round nearby Burrow Head and the smugglers made for the harbour under the Isle of Whithorn—effectively a cul-de-sac. Seeing this, the revenue men shortened sail and made a leisurely entrance to the harbour. When they had tied up, they were astonished to find no trace of the ship which they had minutes before been hotly pursuing. The smugglers had skilfully piloted their vessel out of the harbour through a channel so narrow that it was normally passable only to small boats. They had the full tide on their side, it is true, but low water revealed what a tight squeeze it had been; the ship's keel had cut a deep furrow in the shingle lining the channel.

LUCE BAY

Philip and Mary Point ■11 is at 82-NX325455. High and Low Clone Farms ■12 are at 82-NX3345 off a minor road, signposted Mochrum and Barrachan, that joins the A747 about ½ mile N of Port William. There is no public access to either farm.

This bay close to the mouth of the Solway has some gently sloping beaches, and a great deal of contraband came ashore here. Not all of it was unopposed: one clash that was particularly humiliating for the preventive forces took place just off Philip and Mary Point on the east side of the bay.

Local troops heard about a landing, and lined up on the beach, while the two smugglers' luggers, armed with a total of 36 guns, and with a complement of 100 men, hovered off-shore. The smugglers shouted to the troops that they should retire a little, as a run was about to take place, and they did not care to be observed too closely. The alternative—a fight against far superior forces—was declined, and the dragoons retreated. When the excisemen returned sometime later, a row of barrels was waiting for them on the shoreline as a reward for their cooperation with the smugglers.

Most of the buildings in the area had hiding-places for a tub or two, and some still bear mute witness to the illegal activities that took place here.

At Clone Farm, on the outskirts of Port William, the 'brandy-hole' was covered by a fireproof trapdoor—the farmer lit a fire in the kiln above it when he expected a visit from the revenue men.[13] The 'farmer' was actually a smuggler in disguise, for the farm was the headquarters of a smuggling company, and an underground passage from the cellar of the farmhouse led to the nearby beach. The passage was revealed to the authorities by an informer, whose life was spared only by luck. A sniper from the betrayed smuggling gang would have shot him as he walked on the beach if the traitor's female companion had not kept stepping into the line of fire.

At the farm in 1777 there was a haul of 80 chests of tea, 140 ankers of brandy, and 200 bales of tobacco.

The farmer there can still point out evidence of the brandy holes: a combine harvester parked over an underground chamber began to sink into the ground, and a depression in the farmyard bubbles as water seeps into the tunnel below. The entrances to the tunnel and brandy hole have long been lost, though.

Stair Haven close to Glenluce was also much used by smugglers, and other favourite landing spots in the bay were Crow's Nest and the Bay of Auchenmalg below Sinniness Head.

MULL OF GALLOWAY

Salt Pans Bay ∎13 is at 82-NW965615. From the junction of the B738 and the B7043 near Lochnaw Castle, take the B738 N, then take the first minor road on the left, just beyond a radio beacon. Follow the road past a castle, then take the footpath to the bay.

Parts of the Mull of Galloway are south of the Scotland/England border, and the whole region was an isolated (and therefore discreet) place to ship in contraband. On the west side, the area round Laggantalluch Head, especially Breddock Bay, was a popular spot. Low Clanyard farmhouse supposedly had a cellar with an entrance in a nearby bank.

A major contraband item along this coast was salt, which at one stage carried a tax burden of 15s a bushel. The principal source of rock-salt was Carrickfergus in Ireland, just 35 miles away, and ships landed the salt at Float Bay, Ardwell Bay and Clanyard Bay. Farther north, Salt Pan Bay was an occasional landing-place.

At Dally Bay a smugglers' haul was rescued by an attractive local Amazon, Maggie McConnell. She charmed the one exciseman left on guard into shaking her hand, then wrestled him into an arm lock and blindfolded him with an apron until the goods had been restored to the smugglers and carted away!

BALLANTRAE AND AILSA CRAIG

Some 15 miles north of Stranraer, Ballantrae ∎14 was at one time the centre for a vast smuggling ring, and the local fishermen helped land and conceal the cargoes of brandy, tea and tobacco:

> ... vessels, then called Buckers, lugger rigged, carrying twenty and some thirty guns, were in the habit of landing their cargoes in the Bay of Ballantrae, while a hundred Lintowers, some of them armed with cutlass and pistol, might have been seen waiting with their horses and ready to receive them, to convey the goods by

unfrequented paths through the country and even to Glasgow and Edinburgh.[14]

Off-shore to the north, Ailsa Craig ∎15 (see map on page 192) was reputedly a smuggling base, and McNall's Cave was used by a smuggler for storage—he is even said to have lived there. The cave is 100 feet deep, 12 wide and 20 high. A later inhabitant was one David Bodan, who, it is said, took on and defeated six revenue men when they backed him unarmed against a rock.[15]

THE FIRTH OF CLYDE

Goods discharged on the sheltered beaches here soon found their way inland to Kilmarnock and Glasgow. Ayr itself was the destination for contraband coming in from Ireland at Dunure and Culzean Bay ∎16 near Maybole (see map on page 193) were landing-places largely for Irish whiskey, which was known locally as 'Arran Water'.

Prestwick and Monkton were also well-known landing-places, and the minister of the parish was once accused of keeping the tide-waiter out of the way during a run by drinking with him. On the Irvine road outside Monkton smugglers called at a house (probably now in ruins) called Rum How.

TROON ∎17

70-NS3230, 6m N of Ayr. See map on page 193.

This town enjoyed the strongest reputation as the smuggling centre for the surrounding area. Troon Bar provided shelter from the wind, and the smuggling ships would be run up the sands at Barassie Burn, on the Barassie shore. At low tide the luggers were left high and dry, and could be unloaded easily using horse-drawn carts which moved inland

The Galloway coast admirably suited the needs of Manx smugglers seeking a convenient landing-spot on the mainland. It was remote enough to escape the attentions of all but the most diligent customs man; and at the southern end, Galloway is actually south of some parts of England, so a border crossing by sea was quick and safe.

along Dundonald Glen and along the road crossing Clevance Hill.

Contraband came from the Isle of Man until the island was returned to the Crown, and also from other parts of Scotland. Whisky was the cargo for this domestic trade, and was landed at Port Ronnald, which was reached by a road that had been paved specifically for the convenience of the smugglers' carts.

If the goods could not be run inland immediately, they were stored locally. Many of the houses of Troon are reputed to have brandy holes, or concealed rooms for the storage of contraband, and others have double gables for the same reason.

Opposition to smuggling came not only from the customs and excise authorities, but also from the redcoats stationed at Ayr and Irvine. Clashes were frequent, and despite the strength of the opposition, the King's men often came off worse than the smugglers, who armed themselves with loaded whips and 'kents' (fearsome oak cudgels, 5 feet long and weighted with lead).

There are many local yarns about clashes, and as usual these show up the smugglers in an undeservedly good light. One tells how a group of smugglers had run some goods from the coast of Troon inland through a valley in the Dundonald Hills, by the Awt or Aut—a hanging wood. They encountered a detachment of dragoons, and seeing their adversaries, Tam Fullarton, a man renowned for his 'strength, courage and dexterity', volunteered to hold off the soldiers while his comrades escaped. He stood behind a dry-stone wall, and hurled it rock by rock down onto 'the red anes'. Only when the smugglers were well away did Tam melt away into the woodlands, earning himself the accolade 'the man who threw a stane dyke at the sodgers',[16] and this rhyme remains as testimony to his actions:

Tam Fullarton, who hailed from Loans
A Hector when he took to stones,
Declared that 'wi' a dry stane dyke
At hand, he wad ha'e skailed the bike'.
That night Tam was not slack nor slow,
But dealt and warded many a blow.

Despite the conflict between the collectors and evaders of duty at Troon, there are some touching stories that show the two groups in a human light.

In one incident, smugglers led by one James McAdam had successfully crossed the swollen Irvine River, when an exciseman on the far bank ignored the smugglers' warnings that the river was dangerous, and dived in to try and cross. He was swept away by the current, and his life was saved only because McAdam himself plunged into the water and hauled the man out.

In contrast to the numerous local anecdotes about smuggling,[17] accounts from the custom-house make possibly more objective reading. This one is dated 1764:

Between 7 and 8 in the morning, they discovered a boat coming for the Troon, which proved to be a small Isle of Man one, and which they believed contained foreign spirits. She was no sooner arrived than about 100 men, mounted on horses, having large sticks in their hands, accompanied by some women, instantaneously came down from the country, and took possession of the Troon and although the officers immediately made an attempt to seize said boat and spirits, they could by no means get access to her for the mob, who threatened to put them to death if they offered to touch her or what was in her. [The officers] at length, however, laid hold of their carts, with six casks of spirits in each, but had no sooner made a seizure than they were attacked by one ————, servant to ————, in Loans of Dundonald, and by three other men unknown to them, disguised in sailors' habits: all were provided with great sticks, who deforced them of the seizure, while others drove off the carts and spirits, swearing every moment to knock them down, and sometimes lifting up their sticks ready to lay on blows.[18]

GREENOCK ■18

63-NS2776, 20m W of Glasgow. See map on page 196.

Battles between the excisemen and smugglers or their customers were at their fiercest when the cargo consisted of food, and the mob were hungry. At Greenock there were riots when ships brought in food from Ireland in 1770:

A most violent and outrageous mob has risen at Greenock and by force broken open the hatches and carried away the sails of the vessels laying in that harbour laden with oatmeal . . . and taken and carried away all the said meal despite of whatever could be done to prevent it.

The complement of twenty dragoons could hardly control the mob of 5000. A magistrate who tried to intervene would have been thrown over the quay had he not been caught and dragged into the custom-house.

THE KINTYRE PENINSULA ■19

Campbeltown is at 68-NR7220. See map on page 192.

The centre of prevention in this remote part of Scotland was Campbeltown, and most of the anecdotes that survive centre on it. The Campbeltown smugglers used Sanda Island as a stronghold and off-shore base, and imported such quantities of foreign spirits that Scots distillers complained that their trade was being damaged. The central figures in the business were thought to be the Breckenridges of Ireland's Red Bay:

When the vessels employed in this traffic appear in the channel there are boats of theirs in waiting towards the said Mull as if fishing, but with a view of receiving their illegal importations.

The Campbeltown custom-house records are a catalogue of defeat, but the low-point for the preventives must surely have been in autumn 1792 when the authorities seized the smuggling sloop *Nancy and Peggy* in the Sound of Kilbrannan. The events that followed read like a tragicomedy. The crew succeeded in recapturing their ship, and forced the mate of the custom-house cutter and two others into a yawl (small rowing-boat) which overturned, drowning the mate. The remainder of the cutter's crew fired on the *Nancy and Peggy*, and she was eventually taken once more, and brought into Campbeltown.

The three senior smugglers were thrown into gaol (which already held a group of debtors) but the leader, John King, escaped almost immediately through the negligence of the soldiers guarding him. His description sounds comic enough: '35, 5'8", brown short hair, florid complexion having a sulky countenance and did not look any one straight in the face but with the tail of his eye'.

The guard was redoubled, the gaoler dismissed, and the keys were thrust upon the reluctant collector of customs.

Two weeks later one of the debtors escaped, followed after a further twelve days by another of the smugglers. The last remaining smuggler from the *Nancy and Peggy* took four more days to get away; he cut a hole in the floor and lowered himself into the courtroom below, escaping through a window!

As at Greenock, periods of hunger led to riots when a ship carrying dutiable food arrived at Campbeltown Quay. When a boat from Ireland docked at the port with a cargo of oatmeal, which the customs authorities refused to allow to be landed:

. . . a parcell of women headed by one Brown, an old soldier assembled with a piper playing, went to the quay and boarded the vessell, deforced the tydesman, unriged her and proceeded to take the meall . . . the comptroller who lives a little distance from the office and is obliged to go through a great part of the town was attacked by some women who give him very abusive and threatening language.

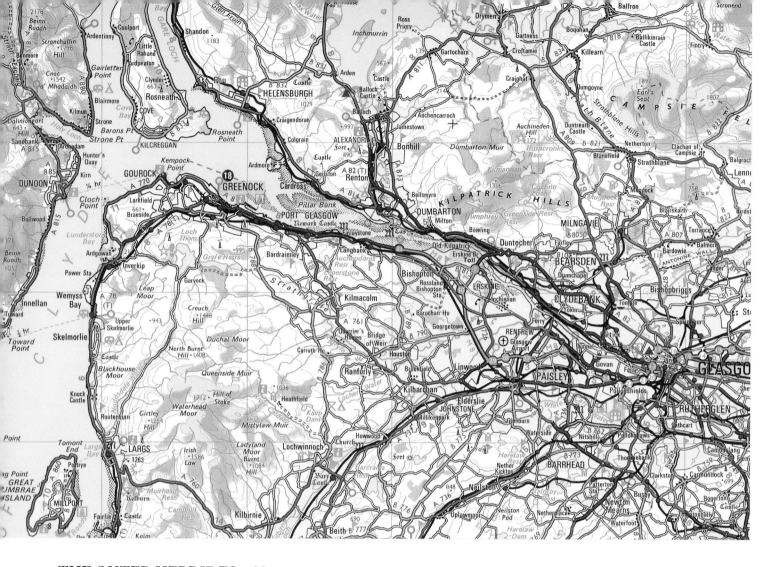

THE OUTER HEBRIDES ■20

The Monach or Heisker Islands off the coast of North Uist were used as a smuggling depot, though a far from satisfactory one. According to some reports, the swell in 1791 was so heavy that two ships took a fortnight to land 1500 ankers of brandy and gin. The smugglers stored the goods in houses on the island, but because of bad weather were only able to take goods off piecemeal, as local demand warranted.

South Uist was immortalized in Compton MacKenzie's book *Whisky Galore*. In real life, the ship loaded with booze was *The Politician*, and ran aground between Eriskay and South Uist in the early hours of 4 February 1941. For the true story, read Arthur Swinson's book, *Scotch on the Rocks* (1963).

THE EAST COAST AND BORDERS

To visit Salter's Road ■21 at 66-NT423627, leave Edinburgh on the A68, and after going through Pathhead turn left at the sign 'Fala Dam 1'; then take the first left, signposted Costerton. Salter's Road leads down the hill across Salter's Burn. Salter's Wood is on the left of the road.

Sauter's Ford, 6m E of Selkirk ■22, is more accurately located in Border country, at 73-NT558264. Leave Lilliesleaf travelling E on the B6400, and follow the road right at the T-junction, then left. Where the main road bears right again, instead turn left to reach the ford.

Illegally stilled whiskey and contraband salt brought in from Ireland created a flourishing transport trade across the Cheviot Hills, so in the border areas smuggling tales are to be found surprisingly far from the

Salt seems an unlikely contraband cargo, but before refrigeration it was needed in large quantities for preserving food and it was highly taxed. The salt smugglers are remembered in place names such as Sauter's Ford shown here.

196

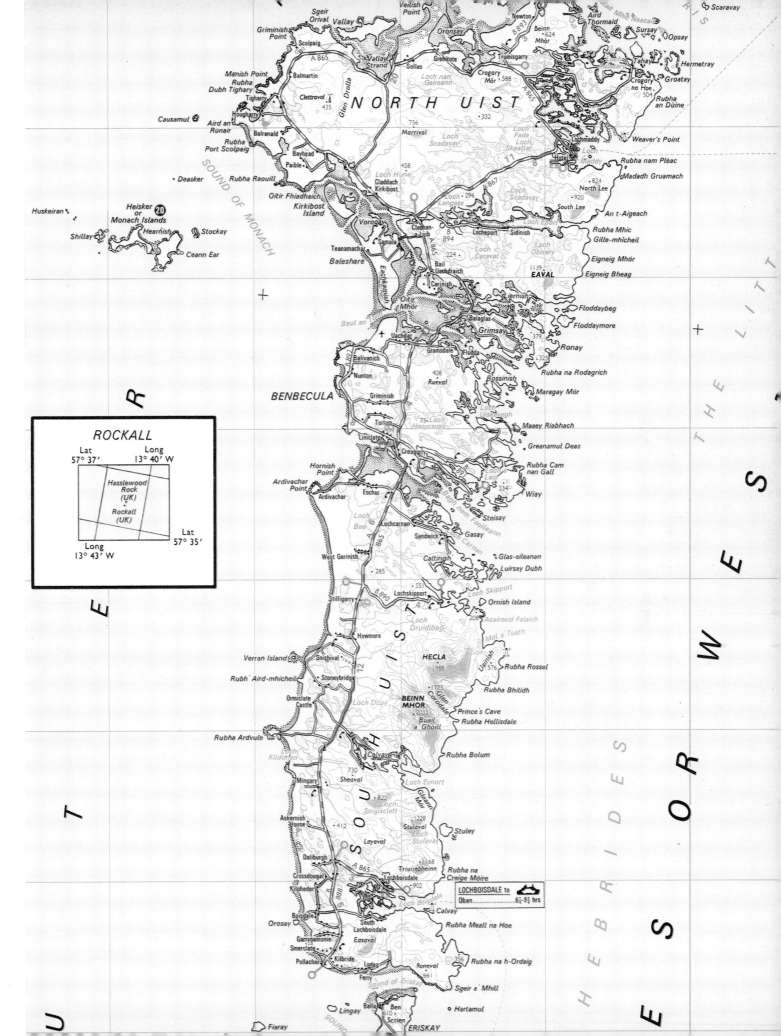

coasts. Kirk Yetholm, close to Coldstream, and Newcastleton were storage places for the salt in transit,[19] and at Town Yetholm between one in five and one in six people were at one time involved in smuggling.

The yarns that are passed down about the border smugglers are populated by colourful figures—Turkey Wull, John of Skye, Jock o' the Deck. All of them carried their contraband cargoes on horseback along the green lanes that criss-cross the Cheviots. In some places there are still reminders of the trade: there's a path called 'Sauter's Road' near Pathhead, and in Roxburghshire 'Sauter's Ford' crosses the Ale Water. Sites 21 and 22 are on the map on page 200.

HAWICK ▪23

79-NT5015. The Auld Brig Pool can still be seen, though the eponymous inn has now gone. See map on page 200.

This border town supplied carriers. One tale tells how a smuggler from Hawick, Alexander Mitchell, was resting with his father at Carter Toll Bar, on the way back from Boulmer, when he spied approaching customs men. The gin was hidden in a hay-loft, and the two ran up to ensure that none would fall into the hands of 'the Philistines'. In the dark of the loft the battle was confused, but the two men—both of whom were stocky and tall—fought off the threat. The fight didn't end without injury: the son was bitten in the leg, but bravely bore the attack without a murmur. After the battle his father commented: 'A've left the marks o' ma teeth on yin o' their legs at ony rate!' and his son sighed, 'It was me ye bate, father! Was aw no guid game no te squeel?'

Another Hawick smuggler, Wat the Candlemaker, lived at 2, Tower Knowe. He was a prominent local merchant, and had a reputation as a practical joker. He had acquired a barrel of gin, but word reached him that the customs men were on his trail. He took the gin to the house of a friend whom he trusted, and sank a tub filled with water in the Auld Brig Pool behind his house, then spread rumours around the town to the effect that the much-hunted gin could be found in the pool. Triumphantly the government men swooped, carried the barrel back to the weigh house, and broached it to sample the quality. The first jug was symbolically offered to Wull the Cutler, who had recently been a victim

of one of the candlemaker's tricks. Needless to say, as soon as Wull sipped, he knew he'd been tricked again.

The story ends with a twist. Wat the Candlemaker's friend who had been trusted with the contraband refused to give it up, and Wat had no redress, since he could hardly complain to the authorities.[20]

EYEMOUTH ▪24

67-NT9464, 8m N of Berwick. See map on page 202.

On the east coast close to the border, the rambling style of the architecture of Eyemouth has been attributed to the need for concealment: in the eighteenth and nineteenth centuries smuggling was rife in the town.

> An immense contraband trade was carried on along the coast of Berwickshire . . . the precipitous cliffs, creeks and caves providing the essentials for successful free-trade.

The numerous alleyways of Eyemouth served as escape routes for smugglers landing goods from boats in the bay, and a number of houses had secret cellars and passages. According to some reports, the place was riddled with passages like a Swiss cheese, and there was more of the town below ground than above. The centre of the trade in the eighteenth century was a house that is now the library. Passages ran underground to the adjacent premises, and stairs near the top of the house concealed a compartment big enough to store a tub or a few bottles. Just around the corner in Chapel Street there were underground windings leading from the shop on the corner opposite the butchers.

Gunsgreen Mansion (now the golf club across the harbour) was reputed to have an opening in its walls which formed a slipway giving direct access to the sea, and from the opening a passage led into the house. Beneath the lawn there was a vast cellar and according to tradition, tunnels led to a cottage on Gunsgreenhill above the mansion, and on to Burnmouth. Indoors, there were tales of concealed passageways, and 'a massive grate or fireplace, which, by moving some knob or lever, could swing out of its place like a gate being opened. This strange contrivance was the door-way into a secret passage'.

Among the most popular landing spots near to Eyemouth were

To accommodate the huge volumes of contraband landed at Eyemouth harbour and beach, the local people constructed vast basements and cellars, so that there was more of the town below ground than above it.

Scootie Cove near Hurker's Haven, between Eyemouth and Burnmouth; Coollercove, near Killiedraughts; and St Abb's Head, where recesses in the headland served to conceal cargoes.

DUNDEE ■25

See map on page 205. The smuggling trade in the Tay area was principally with Holland and Scandinavia. A typical incident in December 1724 involved the *Margaret of Dundee* which arrived in the port from Rotterdam with just a half-load of cargo. This aroused suspicions that the remainder might have been run nearby, and a search 5 miles west of Dundee revealed 8 casks of wine hidden in a barn. The party of customs officials quizzed a labourer threshing in the barn but learned nothing, so they left a guard of four men there to protect the seizure. This proved a wise precaution, because at about 9pm a group of 40 people attacked the guard with staves and pitchforks, injuring the sergeant, but failing to take the wine. Some Dundee vessels travelled from farther south. In 1766 the Dundee customs officers seized the French smuggling sloop

Friendship, and took the precaution of removing all sails, tackle and provisions. Nevertheless, the wily crew got a new set of sails and yards made on-shore, and sneaked out of the harbour at midnight.

Other incidents point less directly to trade with France. In 1738 Dundee smugglers bringing casks of French brandy from Arbroath met a land-surveyor and three other customs officers at the Muire of Craigie (now an industrial estate). The land-surveyor was separated from the party, armed with only a sword, and he was beaten so badly that the smugglers left him for dead, taking their cognac with them.

Whisky, though, was more often the cargo, especially in the late eighteenth and early nineteenth centuries. In the summer of 1816, for example, seven North Highlanders smuggled whisky across the Tay in the early hours of the morning, and hid in woodland near Birkhill House waiting for a chance to load the 19 kegs onto a cart for transport south. Customs men landed at Balmerino, captured the cargo, and took the barrels back to their boat. While they were doing this, the smugglers mustered eleven extra men and attacked the seven officers with sticks and stones. However, they were beaten back by the King's men, who were armed with cutlasses and guns.

The bustling port of Dundee was the centre of Tayside smuggling. The illegal cargoes came in not only from the ports of Dundee's traditional trading partners—Scandinavia and Holland—but also from as far afield as France.

PERTH ■26

See map on page 205. The harbour here was very unfavourable, and subject to silting, but smuggling nevertheless went on in the town, and was boosted by considerable anti-English feeling and a strong Jacobite element.[21] The customs authorities were never popular, and they frequently had to be supported by the military.

Help from the dragoons proved an effective deterrent, as an incident that took place in 1725 illustrates. Perth customs officials met a group carrying uncustomed goods, but orders to the smugglers to stop were ignored. The comptroller of customs sent for reinforcements, and meanwhile succeeded in keeping an eye on one of the hogsheads. It was taken into a pub called the *Thistle*, so the customs authorities put a guard on the door, and searched the place. However, the search was interrupted and on returning to the yard, the group found that one of the sentries had been separated from his comrades and was lying on the ground apparently dead. He had been cut and half strangled. This prompted a general alert among the soldiers, which so frightened the runners that they abandoned their hogshead near the cross.

Gunsgreen Mansion at Eyemouth reputedly once had a story-book hiding place for contraband: it was concealed by a fireplace, which on operation of a secret lever, swung open like a gate.

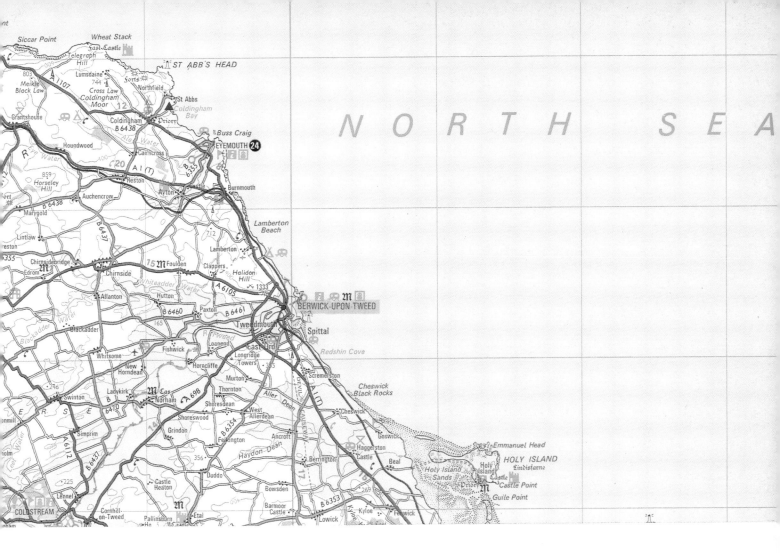

MONTROSE ■27

See map on page 205. As at Perth, Jacobite sympathies caused problems for the customs authorities here— and made friends for the smugglers. The port was famous for its legitimate commerce in tobacco, flax and corn, but the town also did a roaring trade in contraband goods. Much of this took place quite openly on the town quay, but when officials could not be bribed there were plenty of suitable landing-places up and down the coast, with secluded coves and wide sandy bays to suit a vessel of practically any shape or size.

Much of the smuggling was of salt for curing fish caught locally. The regulations governing salt imports were enormously complicated, and even a twentieth-century historian of the customs and excise commented that he could not see how the local fishermen managed to cope with the complexity of the laws governing the use of salt.

Brandy came in through the port, too. In 1709:

there is a clandestine trade of running brandy &c . . . carry'd on by Dutch and Danish ships to the prejudice of the Revenue and due not in the least doubt that the same is countenanced and encouraged by the merchants, skippers and others . . . for their own private advantage . . . Brandy is imported in anchors and half anchors to the number of 1000 or 1200 at a time.

Though many of these barrels were seized, they didn't all stay long in the Montrose custom-house:

This morning between the hours of 12 and 2 the door of His Majesty's Warehouse was broke open and 107 ankers of brandy . . . carried away. At 2 O'clock in the morning when the guard came to relieve the two centrys that were placed at the warehouse door they found the door open, the centrys gone, their muskets lying near the warehouse and one of the bayonets lying broke before the door . . . we went round the town and finding everything quiet . . . sent some souldiers to the [golf] Links to patroall where they found the two centrys lying tied neck and heel. The officer asked them why they had left their posts, they told him that 14 or 15 men had come upon them with clubs and other weapons and had knocked them down and tyed them . . . and afterwards dragged them to the links.[22]

Not all robberies of the custom-house were so blatant. In May 1734 smugglers retrieved 60 ankers of brandy by tunnelling through the wall from the cellars of the shipbuilders, Dunbar's, next door. The sentries outside heard nothing, and despite the fact that the barrels were rolled through Dunbar's house, and out the window, 'Mr Dunbar pretends he knew nothing of it which is very odd'.

ABERDEEN ■28

See map on page 205. Aberdeen was the major east-coast port, even in the eighteenth century. The whale fishery there was the principal industry, but smuggling ran a close second at some stages. In 1788 it was estimated that there were three luggers and two small sloops smuggling goods into Aberdeen—totalling 350 tons. Each made six trips a year, employing 100 men, smuggling spirits and tobacco—200 hogsheads a year. The annual overheads were judged to be £10,000 or more.

The customs authorities were hard pushed to contain such a trade. They had a coastline of 72 miles from Cullen to Catterline to manage, and constantly complained about lack of resources. The collector commented in 1721 that:

> the dangerous smuggling trade carried on at the creeks of this port which is now come to a very great height, we having account that two other ships . . . are arrived upon the N creeks of this precinct in ballast both of which we have good ground to believe are come from Bordeaux load with wine and brandy which they have run upon this coast.

Besides wine and brandy, the principal cargoes smuggled into the town were the old favourites tea and tobacco, but wool was also moved from Aberdeen around the Scots coast to other towns, and on overseas from there. The port record books point to a fascinating diversity of other goods seized:

80 ankers containing 672 gallons of brandy
5½ hogsheads and 11 ankers containing 446 gallons of brandy
35 matts containing 3059 lb leaf tobacco
10 small casks containing prunes
4 small casks containing raisins
2 small casks containing figs
1 small cask of currants
2 small casks of sweet liquorice
3 small casks of white soap
2 hampers of earthenware
2 casks containing molasses
1 anker of coarse oil
1 cask black pepper
1 small matt of twine
32 firkins and 10 half-firkins of soap
6 casks of anniseed
22 reams of writing paper
7 casks of white starch
111 bars of Swedish iron.

This was for November 1721 (though the period over which all this was seized is not stated).

Smuggling ships would by preference favour a landing-place where they could unload their cargo unobserved, away from Aberdeen itself. Favourite spots were Catterline, or Collieston and Newburgh to the north. At Collieston two smuggling syndicates operated, supplying spirits that 'were sold in every tavern between Peterhead and Aberdeen'. If the smuggling ships could not simply land goods at the creeks around Aberdeen, they would hover off-shore, and ferry the contraband to the beaches in smaller boats, stopping at several points on the coast to make deliveries.

The trade enjoyed the support of some highly-placed figures in the town, and interference from the customs authorities was frowned upon, as the King's men learned to their cost in the summer of 1744. On the basis of information received, they had sent out a party to the Denburn to ambush smuggled goods coming into town. There, though, the customs men were set upon by armed men dressed as women, and in the affray the son of a prominent Aberdeen merchant was killed. As a result of the clash, the smugglers escaped punishment, but two tide-waiters were arrested and thrown in the Tolbooth, and several days later the collector of customs (the most senior custom house official) was sent to join them.

A favourite trick of the Aberdeen-bound smugglers was to obtain a bill of lading for Bergen. Since this was the legal point of import for dutiable goods bound for Scandinavia, the smugglers caught running contraband on Scotland's east coast simply claimed to have been blown

Jacobite sympathizers in Montrose were such a threat that the controller of customs there considered he could carry out his job effectively only if several score of soldiers were constantly within hailing distance.

Aberdeen smugglers brought in a huge assortment of goods: not only the traditional spirits and tobacco, but also liquorice, starch, writing paper, figs, soap, earthenware, twine and pepper.

off-course. Another equally popular trick was a false declaration of cargo value, though this required the collaboration of the tidesmen. The ruse was eventually stamped out by sending the land-surveyor along to supervise the unloading (1721).

Smuggling in the Aberdeen area was all but eliminated after 1825, but a few French boats, ostensibly fishing for herring, succeeded in bringing in goods much later in the century.[23]

SLAINS ■29

Slains churchyard is just outside Collieston at 38-NK0429. The grave is by the bell-rope which hangs on the outside of the church (See map on page 208).

Caves in the coast between Aberdeen and Peterhead were widely used for storing smuggled spirits, and near Collieston and Slains, 1000 ankers of foreign spirits were landed monthly at the start of the eighteenth century. The caves at Slains were particularly extensive, and at a dance on a farm close to Slains Castle, the earth gave way, dropping the dancers into the cavern beneath.[24]

The smugglers also hid contraband on the beaches, digging elaborate pits deep in the sand big enough to hold up to 300 tubs of gin. The precautions taken by the smugglers seem extraordinary. An account written in 1858[25] describes how the barrels were taken from the lugger to a temporary resting-place while the pit was dug. Sand from the pit would be turned on to two pieces of sail-cloth—dry sand from the surface on one, and the damper sand from below onto the other, so that the com-

pleted hiding-place would not be betrayed by a change in the colour of the dunes. The pit was lined with bricks or timber, and the roof was always at least 6 feet underground, because the probes used to locate hidden caches on the beach were 6 feet long. Once the labourers had been paid off, the 'partners' in the run themselves transferred the barrels to the pit, sealed the entrance, and took bearings to landmarks so that they could locate the hoard. Within hours, wind-blown sand would cover all traces of activity.

Even this elaborate procedure was not a sure guarantee of security, and if an informer revealed information about the cargo the consequences were often catastrophic, and sometimes fatal. A simple gravestone in the Slains kirkyard is now the only visible reminder of a 1798 run that went disastrously wrong:

information of this [landing], together with that of the intended transfer of the cargo to the interior during the succeeding night was conveyed to the exciseman. Anderson, the officer in question, having secured the assistance of two others, proceeded in the evening to a spot about a quarter of a mile north of the Kirk of Slains, where the cart with the booty was expected to pass. Soon after the officers had taken up their position the carts were heard approaching, but, as usual, preceded by several avant couriers to 'clear the way'. One of these, Philip Kennedy, a man of undaunted courage and resolution, was the first to encounter [the excisemen]. Seeing the danger, he seized hold, successively, of two of the officers, calling to his companions to seize the other.

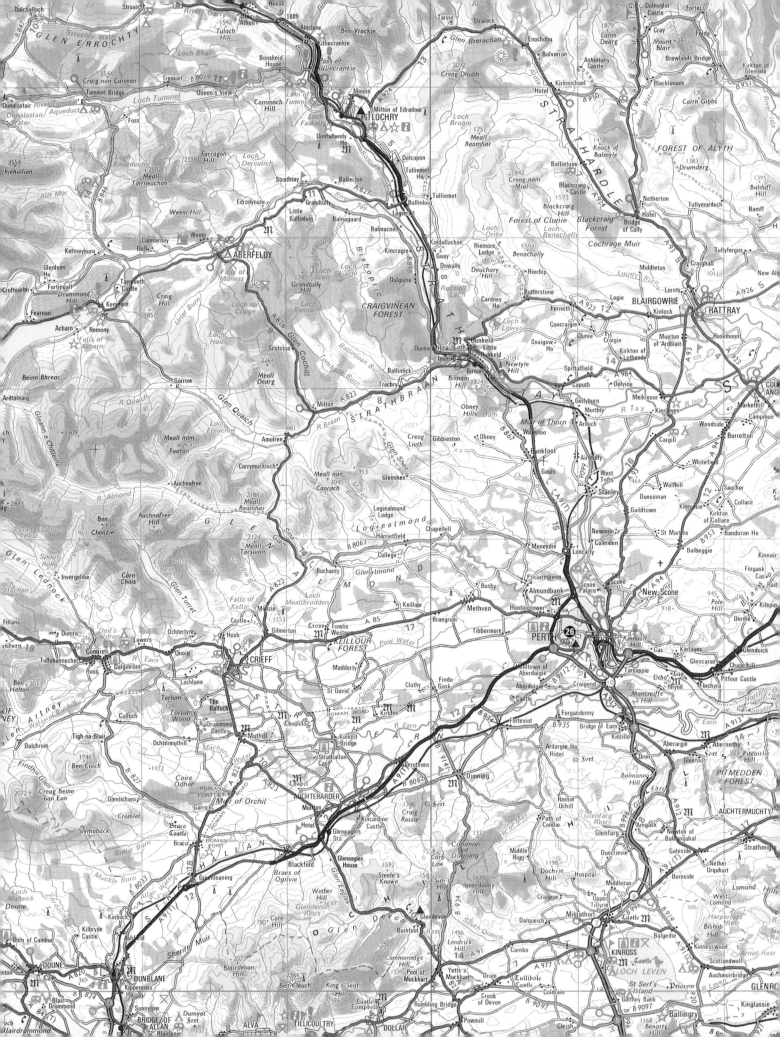

But these, possessing neither the courage nor the devotedness of poor Kennedy, decamped, and hid themselves among the tall broom which at that time clothed the neighbouring braes. Anderson, the officer who was still at liberty, attacked Kennedy, who was still holding on to his prisoners, and, with his sword, inflicted repeated wounds on his head; but Kennedy still kept his grasp on the prostrate officers, and Anderson was observed to hold up his sword to the moon, as if to ascertain whether he was using the [sharp] edge, and then, with one desperate stroke, cleft open the poor fellow's skull. Strange to say, Kennedy, streaming with blood, made out to reach Kirkton of Slains, a distance of nearly a quarter of a mile, where, in the course of a few minutes, he expired. His last words were 'If all had been as true as I, the goods would have got through, and I should not now be bleeding to death'.[26]

Anderson was tried for murder in Edinburgh, and acquitted.

A dance on a farm near Slains Castle ended abruptly: the roof of a smuggler's cavern below the farm gave way and the earth swallowed up the dance floor.

THE MORAY FIRTH ▪30

Castle Stuart is 4m NE of Inverness at 27-NH7449 on a turn in the B9039 road to Dalcross Airport.

A considerable amount of smuggling took place in the creeks around the twin ports of Banff and MacDuff: at Redhythe, 2 miles from Portsoy, coals were landed, and at Cullen coals were imported, and tiles and bricks exported; and at Macduff grain and fish were exported, and again, coals came in illegally.

Merchants from Elgin financed much of this trade, and one of them sent these highly specific instructions regarding smuggling procedures in 1710:

> I have ventured to order Skipper Watt . . . to call at Caussie, and cruise betwixt that and Burgh Head, until you order boats to waite [for] him. He is to give the half of what I have of the same sort with his last cargo, to any having your order . . . The signal he makes will be all sails furled, except his main topsaile; and the boats you order to him are to lower their saile when within muskett shott, and then hoist it again; this, lease he should be surprised with catch-poles.[27]

West from Elgin, Petty Beach ▪31, 5 miles east of Inverness was a popular landing-site. According to local legend, an elaborate code system alerted the smugglers to danger: when goods had been landed, one of

Wealthy merchants financed smuggling trips by vessels berthed in Banff. Returning laden from the Continent, the ships unloaded in quiet creeks a discreet distance from the town.

their number would take a snuff-box into an Inverness tobacconist. If the coast was clear, the shopkeeper filled the box. If he half-filled it, there were excisemen about. Nearby, Castle Stuart was the home of Bailie Stuart, the most intrepid and wealthy of the local smugglers.

ORKNEY AND SHETLAND

According to the collector of some Orkney fireside yarns:[28]

> It is not more than 50 years (ie 1820) since smuggled gin is said to have been disposed of quite publicly in a bank in town: and forty years ago some heavy cargoes were landed in Kirkwall, which were disposed of to hotel-keepers and others.

Most of the smuggling on Orkney, though, consisted of illegal malting of Barley and stilling of whisky, and many of the tales speak of how wiley Orcadians concealed their stills and steeping malt from the prying eye of the gauger. There are exceptions to this rule, such as the most renowned of Orkney's smugglers, George Eunson. He started his adult life as a cooper's apprentice, but soon became restless, and took command of a smuggling ship. He was too greedy, however, and soon the ship's owners were looking for a new master. For Eunson, there followed a succession of adventures, featuring besides smuggling, the press gang and privateering. Eunson eventually found himself back on Orkney, and embroiled in a political dispute which had divided the island. One faction contrived to have Eunson made officer of excise, and in this post he pursued the smugglers with all the vigour of poacher-turned-gamekeeper.

His principal targets were the local magistrates, who were widely suspected of smuggling, and he made many enemies among the upper classes of the island. When he took one step beyond the law, the magistrates were quick to pounce, and Eunson was locked up for ten weeks without trial. He later sued them for £2,000 apiece, and wrote a diatribe against the 'Petty Tyrants, or Grinders of the Poor' which was published in 1788. Eunson did not stay revenue man for long: he returned to smuggling, with a lucrative side-line as a pilot.

Gin landed here at Lerwick and elsewhere in the Shetlands consumed so much of the islanders' cash that there was actually a shortage of money during the 1790s.

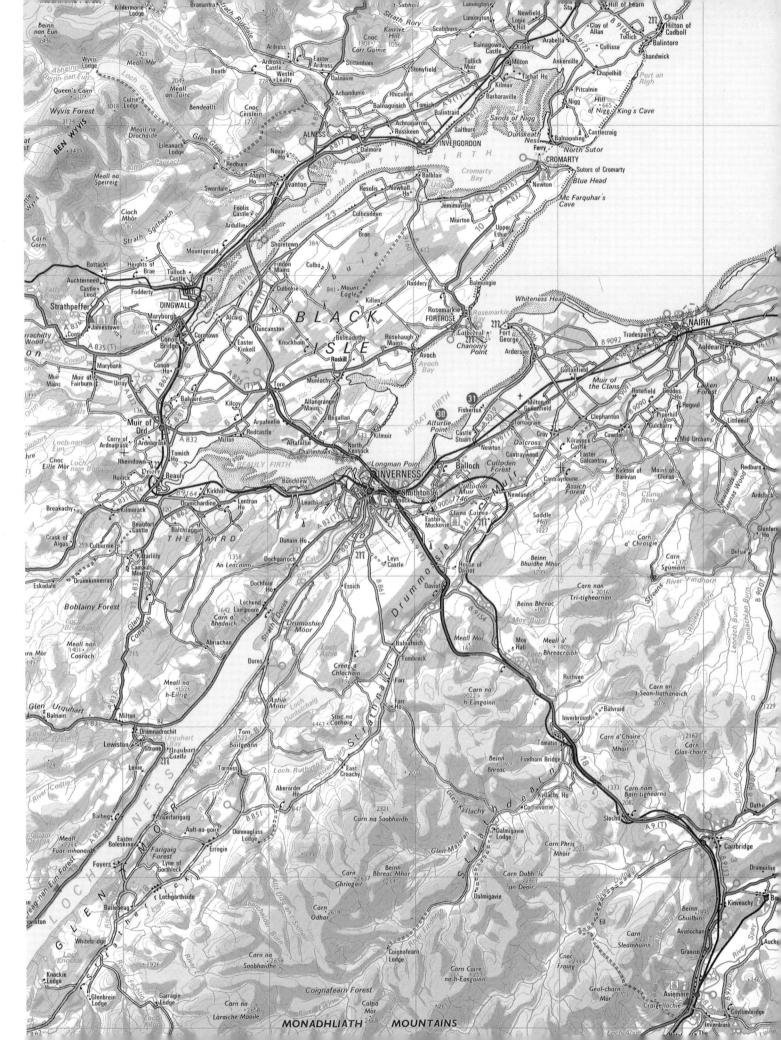

Lerwick, capital of the Shetland Isles. The distance from sources of contraband did not deter the people of the Shetland Isles from smuggling.

It was in this role that he died on a man-of-war.

A smuggler from Kirkwall shared George Eunson's surname, though the two were not related. Mansie Eunson was especially noted for his sense of humour, and his ability to squeeze his way out of the most desperate situations. One story which illustrates his wily nature tells of how Mansie wanted to bring in some kegs from Deerness, and hatched a plan to be rid of the opposition. He knew that a local villager was in the pocket of 'the gaugers' so he confided in this untrustworthy individual that he would cross the Bridge of Wideford between midnight and 1 am with the kegs on the back of three horses. The excisemen hid under the bridge and, shivering with cold, were glad to hear the sound of horses' hooves at around one. Sure enough, it was Mansie, but he was on his way out of town, carrying empty kegs. He explained to the waiting excisemen that he'd taken the spirits into town earlier that night, but that it seemed a pity to leave them out in the cold until dawn.

SHETLAND

The numerous inlets and hills of the Shetland islands favoured the smugglers' purposes, and the considerable distance from the principal sources of contraband does not seem to have acted as a deterrent. Much contraband came in from France, Holland and even from Spanish ships, but it is hardly surprising that this was supplemented by a thriving trade in contraband timber that was carried on with Norway, principally through Bergen.

The pattern of smuggling in the Shetland Islands had its ups and downs, as elsewhere, with foreign wars and high taxes providing tem-

porary boosts. A time-honoured technique frequently used by largely legitimate traders was simply to avoid declaring dutiable goods at customs, and this practice was so widespread as to be almost an expected part of everyday trade in the islands. A cargo from Hamburg in the mid-eighteenth century was declared as consisting of 'salt, lines, iron and tar', all commodities that attracted little or no duty at that time. The cargo invoices tell a different story; half the cargo was made up of corn brandy, cognac, claret and other wines.

This sort of smuggling trade was principally amateur, and was supplemented by small-time illegal trade among foreigners visiting the islands. Shetland coastal towns were ports-of-call for many sea-going vessels that stopped to take on food and water. For example, at Lerwick's summer fair there was a thriving business in barter, with fresh victuals and clothing exchanged for brandy and tobacco.

In the 1760s, large-scale gin smuggling began. In 1764–5 the customs authorities made a vain attempt to get all ships to unload at Lerwick in order to make detection easier, and by 1770 the trade had become sufficiently lucrative for businessmen from outside the island to take an interest. The gin ships were often bound for the Faroes, and used the weather as an excuse to shelter in the Shetlands, where they took the opportunity to unload some of their cargo.

The gin trade was largely run by merchants known as the 'Rotterdam gentry' (Rotterdam was the centre of the gin trade), whereas the 'Hamburg gentry' of local landowners organized the small-time smuggling of necessary everyday items such as tea, carrying out a little gin smuggling as a sideline. The landowners withdrew from this part of the trade in 1791, leaving the field open for entrepreneurs and merchants.

In the late eighteenth and early nineteenth centuries most of the smuggling ships came from Hamburg, Bergen, Christiansand and Rotterdam, and the main commodities imported were timber, tea, tobacco and spirits. A Royal Navy blockade of foreign ports between 1807 and 1814 more or less brought smuggling to a standstill but there was an explosion of activity between 1814 and 1823. Shetland merchants over this period took less active parts in the trade, and instead relied on international smuggling rings based in London (Ewarth and sons), Holland and west Norway. The thriving business was stamped out only by a concerted government effort, a drop in the duty on spirits, and by the rise of home stilling. In the years that followed, the principal sources of smuggled goods were the many fishing vessels that constantly plied the waters around the islands. Indeed, there is some evidence to suggest that the cod fisheries around the Shetlands were established as a cover for illegal import.

It's possible to get a taste of how Shetlanders mixed smuggling with legal trade by following the course of a typical trip, the *Catharine*, in 1814. The ship first sailed to Orkney, and loaded up with an illegal cargo of meal, which was landed at Bergen, where a load of hides and tallow (legal) was waiting. This travelled to London, and from there it was just a short cross-Channel journey, loaded with coils of rope (legitimate) to pick up a cargo of 600 ankers of gin from Rotterdam. This was then run in Shetland, and the coils of rope were bound for Orkney. The process would have continued had the smugglers not been caught and the vessel seized at Kirkwall.

The impact of smuggling on the economy of the Shetlands was considerable, though possibly at times exaggerated. Between 1796 and 1798 there was actually a shortage of money on the islands because so much had been paid out by merchants buying gin; and the minister of Unst at one stage reported that gin imports were worth half the rent of the island. One writer complained that illegally imported gin had 'drained the poor of this country . . . of every shilling they could spare or raise'. Ultimately, the poverty of the islanders contributed to the decline of the smuggling trade.

For an excellent and detailed account of the smuggling trade in the Shetlands, read *Shetland Life and Trade, 1550–1914* by Hance D. Smith (1984).

Exaggeration is not unknown in smuggling yarns, but one tale from the Orkneys has to take the prize for the most unbelievable. A Harryman had hidden a barrel of contraband liquor in the stables, forgetting to tell his wife, who tied up the horse as usual that night. It so happened that the barrel was open, or easily opened, and the following morning they found the horse stretched out stiff and apparently lifeless. Lamenting, they resolved to make the best of a bad job, and dragged the animal out and skinned it. Soon afterwards, the horse—which had been merely drunk—got up and started eating. The farmer had recently slaughtered and skinned some sheep, so he quickly covered the horse with the hides, 'it being cold'. The hides stuck and grew, and the horse gave the farmer several stones of wool each year.[29]

A Hoyman renowned for his muscle was smuggling in 4 ankers of spirits to Stromness, when he was caught red-handed. As he arrived at the harbour, he saw several gaugers peering down at him. He decided to brazen it out, and lodged a barrel under each arm, grabbing the remaining two by the rims. He did this so effortlessly that the gaugers assumed the barrels to be empty.[30]

In a rare appearance in print, Shetland smugglers feature in this humorous engraving as the captors of Dr Prosody.

NOTES

A SMUGGLING RUN

1 Gregory King, 1688, quoted in Trevelyan, 1944.
2 Duncan, 1841.
3 *Maritime Wales*, 10.
4 Ibid.
5 Smith, G., 1983.
6 Banks, J., 1873.
7 Trevelyan, G.M., 1942.

THE SOUTH-EAST

1 Though in linguistic terms the corruption is unlikely, regional usage tends to confirm this idea: most postal addresses containing the word 'owler' are in the traditional wool-producing and manufacturing areas of Britain (Source: PO postcode database computer).
   Of Britain's six breeding species of owl, only one, the short-eared owl, shows even a slight preference for these areas, and the three commonest species—the Barn, Little and Tawny owls—are more or less evenly distributed throughout England and Wales.
   (Sharrock, J.T.R. *Atlas of Breeding Birds in Britain and Ireland*, British Trust for Ornithology/Irish Wildbird Conservancy, 1976).
2 Heron-Allen, E., 1911.
3 Philip, A.J. (n.d.).
4 Personal communication, Wally Roberts, Blue Circle Heritage Centre.
5 Bygone Kent, 1980.
6 Finch, W.C., 1929.
7 Morgan, Glyn H., *The Romance of Essex Inns*, 1963. Benton, Philip, *History of the Rochford Hundred*, 1867.
8 Finch, op.cit.
9 Finch, op.cit.
10 Harvey, W., 1983.
11 Harvey, W., 1971.
12 Williams, N.J., 1959.
13 Douch, J., 1985, quoting the Crown Solicitor.
14 Fanny Burney.
15 Author's additions and amplifications in square brackets.
16 *Morning Post*, 31 October 1781, quoted by Douch.
17 Williams, op.cit.
18 Waugh, M., 1985.
19 Church brochure.
20 A lantern-carrying bodyguard.
21 Author's additions and amplifications in square brackets.
22 Piper, A.C., 1970.
23 Pagden, F., 1948.
24 Parry, J.D., 1783.
25 Richards, B.F., 'Smuggling in Sussex 100 Years Ago', *Sussex County Magazine*, quoted by Hufton and Baird.
26 Banks, J. 1873.
27 Alfred Bryant of Enfield, quoted by Henry Cousins, 1911.
28 Fleet, C. 1878.
29 Musgrave, C., 1981.
30 Ibid.
31 Middleton, J.A., 1979.
32 Knox, J., *View of the British Empire*, quoted by Cheal, 1909.
33 Cheal, H., 1921.
34 *Memoirs of Edward Snewin*, annotated by Smail.
35 John Cox, letter in the parish magazine, January 1988.
36 Heron-Allen, op.cit.
37 *Topographical and Historical account of Hayling Island*, 1826.
38 Morley, G., *Smuggling in Hampshire and Dorset 1700-1850*, 1983.
39 Fleet, op.cit.

SOUTHERN ENGLAND

1 Dowling, R.F.W., 1978.
2 Ibid.
3 Mew, F., 1986.
4 Dowling, op. cit.
5 Mew, op. cit.
6 Morley, G., 1983.
7 *Hampshire Notes and Queries*, Vol. 9, pp. 104–5.
8 *Hampshire Notes and Queries*, Vol. 9.
9 *Milford-on-Sea Record Society*, 1912.
10 *Hampshire Notes and Queries*, Vol. 9.
11 *Tour of England*, 1724.
12 *Hampshire, the County Magazine*, Vol 26, No. 1.
13 *Hampshire Notes and Queries*, quoting Wise, *New Forest*.
14 *Hampshire, the County Magazine*, Vol. 8.
15 *Sic*.
16 *The Gentleman's Magazine*, 29 November 1902.
17 Arnold-Foster, D., 1938.
18 Oakley, E.R., 1942.
19 *Westminster Journal*, 23 January 1748, quoted by Dowling.
20 *Hampshire Notes and Queries*, Vol. 9.
21 *Hampshire, the County Magazine*, Vol. 8.
22 Treves, F., 1906.
23 *Somerset and Dorset Notes and Queries*, Vol. III.
24 *Hampshire, the County Magazine*.
25 Oakley, E.R., 1944.
26 *Miniature War Games*, June 1987.
27 White, A., 1973.
28 Arnold-Foster, op. cit.
29 Warner, R., *Literary Reflections*, quoted by Short, B.C., 1969.
30 Chackfield, K.M., 1978.
31 3rd Earl of Malmesbury, *Memoirs of an Ex-minister*, quoted by Short.
32 Chackfield, op. cit.
33 Rodney Legg advances this theory in an introduction to Short.
34 Malmesbury. The incident took place around 1780.
35 Young, D.S., 1957.
36 *Salisbury and Winchester Journal*, 1726, quoted by Short.
37 *Hampshire, the County Magazine*, Vol. 12, No. 1.
38 Roberts, G., 1823.
39 Society of Dorset Men in London, 1959–60.
40 Short, op. cit.
41 Hardy, W.M., 1978.
42 Ibid.
43 Treves, op. cit.
44 Legg, R., 1972.
45 Dorset Natural History and Antiquarian Field Club, Vol. XVI, pp. 55–8, quoted in *The Greenwood Tree*.
46 *Somerset and Dorset Family History Society*, Vol. 5, No. 2.
47 Hardy, E., 1955.
48 Guttridge and Morley differ.
49 Treves, op. cit.
50 Society of Dorset Men in London, 1955.
51 Warne, C., 1856.
52 Goddard, C.V., quoted in Omand.
53 Lloyd, R., 1976.
54 Treves, op. cit.

SOUTH-WEST ENGLAND

1 John Cornish, in his introduction to Carter, H., 1900.
2 Coxhead, J.R.W., 1956.
3 Cornish, op cit.
4 Jenkin, A.K.H., 1932.
5 George Borlase in 1753, reported in the Lanisley Letters, *Journal of the Royal Institute of Cornwall*, XXIII, pp. 374–9.
6 Cornish, op. cit.
7 Oppenheim, M.
8 Borlase, op. cit.
9 Rattenbury, J., 1837.
10 Morshead, J.Y. Anderson, *Transactions of the Devonshire Association*, 1903, quoted by Coxhead.
11 Coxhead, op. cit.
12 Ibid.
13 Baring-Gould, S., 1899.
14 Harper, C.G., 1907
15 Hippisley Coxe, A.D., *A Book About Smuggling in the West Country*, 1984.
16 Morshead, J.Y. Anderson, *History of Salcombe Regis*, quoted by Coxhead.
17 Delderfield, E.R., 1948.
18 Paccombe Hill is at SY1690, 1m or so NE, just N of the A3052.
19 2m SW of Sidmouth.
20 *Western Times and Gazette*, 11 May 1956.
21 Coxhead, op. cit.
22 Hippisley Coxe, op. cit.
23 Ibid.
24 Devonshire Association.
25 Ibid.
26 Page, J.L.W., 1895.
27 Hippisley Coxe, op. cit.
28 Baring-Gould (n.d.).
29 Couch, J. 1871.
30 Quoted by Noall, C., 1971.
31 Possibly Pencarrow Head, which overlooks Lantic Bay, 1m E of Fowey.
32 Vivian, J., 1969.
33 Hippisley Coxe, op. cit.
34 Vivian, op. cit.
35 Hippisley Coxe, op. cit.
36 Noall, op. cit.
37 Hippisley Coxe, op. cit.
38 *Cornwall Gazette*, 29 April 1801.
39 Gay, S.E., 1903.
40 Ibid.
41 Jenkin, A.K.H., 1932.
42 Ibid.
43 Penzance custom-house book.
44 Jenkin, op. cit.
45 Jenkin, op. cit.
46 Harvey, E.G., 1875.
47 Vivian, op. cit.
48 *The West Briton*, reprinted in a mimeographed information sheet supplied by the present owner of Methleigh.
49 Jenkin, op. cit.
50 Vivian, op. cit.
51 Jenkin, op. cit.
52 Matthews, J., 1892.
53 *Windsor Magazine*.
54 Jenkin, op. cit.
55 Hippisley Coxe, op. cit.
56 Graham, F.M., 1967, quoting Bottrell, W., *Traditions and Hearthside Stories of West Cornwall*.
57 Miss M.A. Courtney.
58 *The History of the County of Somerset*, University of London Institute of Historical Research.
59 Knight, F.A., 1902.

WALES AND WEST ENGLAND

1 Quoted by Thomas, David of Bangor, 1952, and kindly translated by Hugh Denman.
2 Watkins, K.C., 1975.
3 Trevelyan, M., 1893.
4 Waters, I., 1977.
5 Salt Survey.
6 Dawson, J.W., 1932.
7 Ibid.
8 Chappel, E.L., 1939.
9 Spencer, M.R., 1913.
10 Cardiff custom-house letters to the Board.
11 Knight, F.A., *The Sea-Bord of Mendip*, 1902.
12 My thanks to the Flat Holm project, and especially the Project Officer, Dr D.H. Worral, and the Island Warden, Andrew Gibson, for letting me visit the island and ferrying me out.
13 Awbery, S.S., 1954.
14 Cardiff custom-house letters to the Board.
15 Letter from Robert Jones of Fonmon Castle, Glamorganshire, to the Commissioners of His Majesty's Customs, 10 December 1737, quoted by Trevelyan.
16 Spencer, op. cit.
17 Phillips, D.R., 1925.
18 Ibid.
19 Mostly from Edmunds, G., 1986.
20 Personal communication.
21 Phillips, op. cit.
22 *Archaeologia Cambrensis*, 1920, p. 339.
23 *Country Quest*, 1976.
24 Tucker, H.M., 1951.
25 John, B., 1976.
26 Bell, G., 1888.
27 Mathias, A.G.O., 'Smuggling Days', *Telegraph Almanack*, 1930.
28 Local Pembroke newspaper (name not supplied in press-cutting book), 28 July 1939.
29 Bell, op. cit.
30 Wilkins, C., 1879.
31 Mathias, op. cit.
32 Letter from Edward Stanley to Richard Sutton, 12 May 1770, published in the *Pembrokeshire County Guardian*, 27 April 1901.
33 John, op. cit.
34 *Pembrokeshire County Guardian*, 28 June 1902.
35 Unattributed, Haverfordwest library clippings file, 7 March 1924.
36 Owen, H.J., 1950.
37 Llowarch, 'Weird Wonders of Wales', *Cambrian News*, 1986.
38 Owen, op. cit.
39 Eames, A., 1981.
40 *Maritime Wales*, 10, quoting from Lewis Morris.
41 Calendar of Home Office Papers, 1770–72, 129, quoted in the *Pembrokeshire County Guardian*, 27 April 1901.
42 Custom-house letters to the Board.
43 Roberts, B.D., 1936.
44 Glazebrook, 1967.
45 *Maritime Wales*, 10.
46 Customs and Excise.
47 *Maritime Wales*, 10.
48 Ibid.
49 *Cylchgrawn Llyfrgell Genedlaethol Cymru*, Vol. 24, No. 1, 1985.
50 Qualtrough, J.K., and Scatchard, 1965.
51 Jarvis, R.C., 1954.
52 Stonehouse, 1836.
53 Woods, E.C., 1927.
54 Gibbon, R.T., 1983.

THE EAST COAST

1 Benham, H., 1986.
2 Ibid, p. 18.
3 Brown, A. Stuart, 'Smuggling in Suffolk', *East Anglian Magazine*, Vol. XIX, 1969 (January and March).
4 Benton, P., 1867.
5 Burrows, J.W., *Southend on Sea and District: Historical Notes*, 1909.
6 Shore, H.N. and Harper, C.G., 1923.
7 Martin, F., *Rogues' River*, 1983.
8 *A Guide to Southend*, 1824 (by A Gentleman).
9 Morgan, G.H., 1963.
10 Burrows, J.W., 1909.
11 Benton, op. cit.
12 Harriot, J., *Struggles through Life*, 1815.
13 Church brochure.
14 Thornton, D., 1977.
15 Brown, H., 1929.
16 Frith, R., 'Smuggling on the Blackwater', *East Anglian Magazine*, Vol. XX, 1960–61, p. 534.
17 Millatt, T.B. (n.d.).
18 *East Anglian Magazine*, Vol. XX.
19 Ibid.
20 Roe, F., 1929.
21 Thornton, op. cit.
22 Ibid.
23 Smith, C.E., 'Tea and the Free-traders of East Anglia', *East Anglian Magazine*, Vol. XV, July 1956.
24 *The Life and Behaviour of John Skinner, Who Murdered Daniel Brett, His Servant*, Anon., 1744.
25 Brown, A.F.J., *Essex People, 1750–1900*, quoted by Benham.
26 Ibid.
27 *East Anglian Magazine*, Vols. V and VII.
28 Solly, A.R., 'From Smuggling to Respectability',

East Anglian Magazine, Vol. XV, July 1949.
29 Dutt, W.A., 1909.
30 Thompson, L.P., 1968.
31 Dutt, op. cit.
32 Brown, A. Stuart, op. cit.
33 The White Horse Inn was at one stage the home of a Mrs Gildersleeves, a notorious smuggler and wife of the landlord. She is reputed to have used a void under the platform of the local Friends Meeting House as a storage place for contraband.
34 Chandler, L., 1960.
35 Letter from Edward FitzGerald to Charles Keene, quoted by Thompson.
36 Fussel, G.E., 'A Suffolk Surgeon and the Sizewell Smugglers', *East Anglian Magazine*, Vol. XII, July 1953.
37 *East Anglian Magazine*, Vol. XII, July 1953.
38 Ibid.
39 Fussell, G.E., *F.R. Hist. S. Earl Soham*.
40 Thompson, op. cit.
41 Ibid.
42 Lawson, G.H., 'In Smuggling Days', *Norwich Mercury*, 19 September 1931.
43 'WF', 'East Anglian Notebook', *Eastern Daily Press*, 16 October 1946.
44 Smith, op. cit.; more detail in Lawson, op. cit.
45 Elliot, C.R., 'Smugglers' Walks around Beccles', *East Anglian Magazine*, Vol. 35.
46 Dutt, op. cit.
47 Brown, A. Stuart, op. cit.
48 Graham, F., *Famous Smuggling Inns*, 1966. However, Thompson evidently found it sufficiently credible to repeat (p. 40). The story is also told about Lymington.
49 Whiston, W, *Memoir of the Life of Dr Samuel Clarke*,

(author's italics).
50 'Suffolk Coast', 'Smuggling in Norfolk', *Eastern Daily Press*, 29 December 1926.
51 Ward, A.J., 'Against the Law', *Eastern Daily Press*, 18 October 1963.
52 *Eastern Daily Press*, 18 October 1963.
53 Suffling, *History and Legends of the Broads District*.
54 Peddar or pedder is synonymous with, and predates, the modern 'peddler' or 'peddlar'.
55 *Eastern Daily Press* or *Norwich Mercury* (unattributed on cutting supplied), 14 April 1970.
56 Dutt, op. cit.
57 Suffling, op. cit.
58 Dutt, op. cit.
59 'JH', 'Smuggling in Norfolk', *Norwich Mercury*, 21 July 1923.
60 Reported by David Clarke in 'Norfolk Contraband', *Eastern Evening News*, 1 October 1973.
61 'Suffolk Coast', op. cit.
62 *Eastern Evening News*.
63 Cooper, E.R., *East Anglian Magazine*, Vol. III, January 1938, p. 160.
64 *East Anglian Magazine*, Vol. III, January 1938.
65 *East Anglian Magazine*, Vol. XV, July 1956.
66 *East Anglian Magazine*, Vol. XIX, 1969.
67 Personal communication with Bell's great-great nephew.
68 Chadwick, E.H., 1913.
69 Fergus, D., *The Countryman*, Summer 1981.
70 Ibid.
71 Sheldon, F., *History of Berwick on Tweed*, 1849.
72 Lang, J., *A Land of Romance*.
73 Nevill, H.M. *A Corner in the North – Yesterday and Today with Border Folk*, 1909.

SCOTLAND

1 Thomson, W.S., 1910.
2 Grewar, D., 1926.
3 Simmons, J., 1975.
4 *Weekly Scotsman*, 13 June 1908.
5 Sillett, S.W., 1970.
6 B.R. Leftwich, librarian. 1921, output records—customs and excise library.
7 Masters of Ballantrae.
8 *Gallovidian Annual*, 1931.
9 Ibid.
10 McDowall, W., 1867.
11 Ibid.
12 Warrick, M., 'Salt Spray', *Galloridian Annual*, 1936–7.
13 Another writer, Irving, places this trick at Drumtrodden.
14 Simmons, op. cit., and Hewat, K., 1898.

15 Hewat, op. cit.
16 Ibid.
17 Cuthbertson, D., 1927.
18 Mac Kintosh, I.M., 1969.
19 Fergus, D., *The Countryman*, Summer 1981.
20 Ibid.
21 Perth outport records.
22 Custom-house records for October 1789.
23 Clark, V.E., 1921.
24 Allardyce, J., 1913.
25 Pratt, J.B., 1981.
26 Ibid.
27 Dunbar, E.D., 1865.
28 Around the Orkney Peat Fires.
29 Smith-Leask, J.T., 1931.
30 Ibid.

BIBLIOGRAPHY

This bibliography is reasonably comprehensive, though there are a few footnoted references that do not appear below. The bibliography starts with general works, then continues with regional titles. Books on smuggling that are in print, or fairly common on the secondhand market are marked with a ●.

GENERAL

Atton, H., and Holland, Henry Hurst, *The King's Customs*, 1908.
Chatterton, E. Keble, *King's Cutters and Smugglers 1700–1855*, 1912.
Cleugh, James, *Captain Tom Johnstone*, 1955.
Cross, Arthur Lyon, *18th Century Documents*, 1928.
Denning, Roy, *Crime and Punishment*, Vol. 2, 1960.
Duncan, *History of Guernsey*, 1841.
Economic History Review, 2nd series, Vol. X, 1958.
Economic History Review, 2nd series, 1958.
Farjeon, Jefferson J., *The Compleat Smuggler*, 1938.
Forbes, Athol, *The Romance of Smuggling*, 1909.
Fraser, Duncan, *The Smugglers*, 1971.
Graham, Frank Moore, *Famous Smuggling Inns*, 1966.
Graham, Frank Moore, *More Smugglers' Inns*, 1969.
Hay, Douglas, *Albion's Fatal Tree*, 1977.
James, G.P.R., *The Smuggler*, 1908.
Nicholls, H., *Honest Thieves*, 1973.
Phillipson, David, *Smuggling, a History 1700–1970*, 1973.
Pringle, P., *Honest Thieves*, 1938.
Ruskin, J., *The Harbours of England from Drawings by Turner*, 1856.
Scott, James Maurice, *The Tea Story*, 1964.
Shore, Henry N., *Smuggling Days and Smuggling Ways*, 1892.
Shore, Henry N. (Baron Teignmouth) and Harper, Charles, *The Smugglers; Picturesque Chapters in the History of Contraband*, 1923.
●Smith, Graham, *King's Cutters*, Conway Maritime Press, 1983.
Stanfield, *Coastal Scenery*, 1820.
Thompson, E.P., *The Making of the English Working Class*, 1970.
Trevelyan, G.M., *A Shortened History of England*, 1942.
Trevelyan, G.M., *English Social History*, 1944.
●Williams, Neville John, *Contraband Cargoes—Seven Centuries of Smuggling*, Longmans, Green & Co., 1959.
Wood, George Bernard, *Smuggler's Britain*, 1966.

THE SOUTH-EAST

Banks, John, *Reminiscences of Smuggling*, 1873.
Barham, Richard, *The Ingoldsby Legends*, 1901.
Brent, Colin E., *Smuggling Through Sussex*, 1977.
Bullen, Mark, *Ill-Gotten Gains: The Romance and Tragedy of Sussex Smuggling 1700–1850*, 1978.
Bullen, Mark, *Sussex Coast Blockade for the Prevention of Smuggling*, 1982.
Bygone Kent (Canterbury), February 1980.
Cantium, *Smuggling in the Cinque Ports in the 16th century*, 1970.
Cheal Jnr, Henry, *Ships and Mariners of Shoreham*, 1909.
Cheal Jnr, Henry, *Story of Shoreham*, 1921.
Clark, Kenneth Michael, *Smuggling in Rye and District*, 1977.
Cousins, Henry, *Hastings of Bygone Days*, 1911.
●Douch, John, *Smuggling, the Wicked Trade*, Crabwell Publications/ Buckwell Publications, 1980.
●Douch, John, *Smuggling: Rough Rude Men*, Crabwell Publications/ Buckwell Publications, 1985.
English, John, *English's Reminiscences of Old Folkestone Smugglers*, 1889.
Finn, R., *The Kent Coast Blockade*, 1971.
Finch, William Coles, *The Medway River and Valley*, 1929.
Fleet, Charles, *Glimpses of Our Ancestors in Sussex*, 1878.
Gaselee, John, *Napoleon Encouraged Thames-side Smuggling*.
Gentleman of Chichester, A., *A . . . History of the . . . Murders of Mr William Galley . . . and Mr Daniel Chater*, 1779.
Harvey, Wallace, *Whitstable . . . and the French POWs*, 1971.
Harvey, Wallace, *The Seasalter Company*, 1983.
Heron-Allen, Edward, *Selsey Bill*, 1911.
Home Counties Magazine (London), Vol. XIV.
●Hufton, Geoffrey, and Baird, Elaine, *Scarecrow's Legion*, Rochester Press, 1983.
Kent County Library, *Smuggling in Deal*, 1984.
Lapthorne, William H., *Smuggler's Broadstairs*, 1970.
●Martin, Frank, *Rogues River*, Ian Henry Publications, 1983.
Middleton, Judy A., *History of Hove*, 1979.
Musgrave, Clifford, *Life in Brighton*, 1981.
Pagden, Florence, *History of Alfriston*, 1948.
Parry, J.D., *Historical and Descriptive Account of the Coast of Sussex*, 1833.
Philip, Alex J, *History of Gravesend*, (n.d.).
Piper, A. Cecil, *Alfriston*, 1970.
Sayer, C.L., *'The Sayer Manuscripts: a Transcription of Extracts from The Collier Papers'* (1742), a notebook compiled by John Collier, Surveyor General of the Riding Officers for the County of Kent, 1733–56.
Smail, Henfrey, *Glimpses of Old Worthing*, 1945.
Sussex County Magazine, Vol. 4.
Warter, J.W., *Sea Board and the Down*, Vol. 1, 1860.
●Waugh, Mary, *Smuggling in Kent and Sussex 1700–1840*, Countryside Books, 1985.

SOUTHERN ENGLAND

Anon., *Topographic & Historical Account of Hayling Island*, 1826.
Arnold-Foster, D., *At War with the Smugglers*, 1938.
Bettey, J.H., *Dorset*, 1974.
Carson, Edward A., *Smugglers and Revenue Officers in the Portsmouth area in the C18*, 1974.
Chackfield, Kathleen Merle, *Smugging Days*, 1969.
Chackfield, Kathleen Merle, *Smugging Heritage around Bournemouth*, 1978.
Cornish, J.B., 'Annals of the Smugglers', *Cornish Magazine*, Vol. I.
Dowling, R.F.W., *Smuggling on Wight Island*, 1978.
Farquharson-Coe, A., *Hants and Dorset's Smugglers*, 1975.
Gentleman's Magazine, 1802.
●Guttridge, Roger, *Dorset Smugglers*, Dorset Publishing Company, 1984.
Hampshire Countryshire, Vols. 1 and 2.
Hampshire Notes & Queries (Winchester), Vol. 9.
Hampshire, the County Magazine (Ringwood), Vols. 8, 12 and 26.
Hardy, Evelyn, *Thomas Hardy's Notebooks*, 1955.
Hardy, William Masters, *Smuggling Days in Purbeck*, 1978.
Hutchings, Richard J., *Smugglers of the Isle of Wight*, 1985.
Legg, Rodney, *Purbeck Island*, 1972.
Lloyd, Rachel, *Dorset Elizabethans*, 1976.
MacGregor, R., *Life of R. MacGregor*, 1823.
Mew, Fred, *Back of the Wight*, 1986.
Milford-on-Sea Record Society, *An Occasional Magazine*, November 1912.
Miniature War Games, June 1987.
●Morley, Geoffrey, *Smuggling in Hampshire and Dorset 1700–1850*, Countryside Books, 1983.
Notes and Queries for Somerset & Dorset, Vols. II–IV, XVIII and XXIX.
Oakley, Eric Russell, *A Guide to Christchurch Priory*, 1920.
Oakley, Eric Russell, *The Smugglers of Christchurch, Bourne Heath and the New Forest*, 1944.
Omand, W.D., *Chideock, Its Church*, 1965.
Page, William, *Victoria County History of Dorset*, 1908.
Parry, J.D., *History and Descriptive Account of . . . Sussex*, 1833.
Roberts, George, *History of Lyme Regis and Charmouth*, 1823.
Short, Bernard Charles, *Smugglers of Poole and Bournemouth*, 1969.
Society of Dorset Men in London, *Dorset Year Book 1955–60*.
Somerset and Dorset Family History Society, *The Greenwood Tree*, Vols. 4 and 5.
Somerset and Dorset Notes and Queries, Vol. III.
Sussex Archaeological Collection, 1858 and 1902.
Sussex County Magazine, Vols. 4 and 8.
Sydenham, John, *History of Poole*, 1839.
Treves, Frederick, *Highways and Byways of Dorset*, 1906.
Warne, Charles, *Ancient Dorset*, 1856.
White, Allen, *Eighteenth Century Smuggling in Christchurch*, 1973.
Windsor Magazine, September 1919.
Young, David S., *Story of Bournemouth*, 1957.

SOUTH-WEST ENGLAND

Baring-Gould, Sabine, *A Book of the West*, 1899.
Baring-Gould, Sabine, *Devonshire Characters* (n.d.).
Bottrell, William, *Traditions and Hearthside Stories of West Cornwall*, 1870.
Carter, Harry, *Autobiography of a Cornish Smuggler*, 1900.
Couch, Jonathan, *History of Polperro*, 1871.
Coxhead, James Ralph Winter, *Smuggling Days in Devon*, 1956.
Delderfield, E.R., *Exmouth Milestones*, 1948.
Devonshire Association, *Transactions*, Vol. 67.
Farquharson-Coe, A. *Devon's Smugglers*, 1975.
Gay, S.E., *Old Falmouth*, 1903.
Graham, Frank Moore, *Smuggling in Cornwall*, 1964.
Graham, Frank Moore, *Smuggling in Devon*, 1965.
Graham, Frank Moore, *Cornish Smuggler's Tales*, 1967.
Harper, Charles George, *Haunted Houses*, 1907.
Harvey, E.G., *History of Mullyen*, 1875.
Hawker, R.S., *Footprints of Former Men in Far Cornwall*, 1870.
●Hippisley Coxe, Anthony D, *A Book About Smuggling in the West Country*, Tabb House, 1984.
Jenkin, A.K.H., *Cornish Seafarers*, 1932.
Jenkin, A.K.H., *Cornwall and Its People*, 1945.
Jones, Penny, *Smugglers' Tales*, 1983.
Knight, Francis A, *The Sea-bord of Mendip*, 1902.
Matthews, J., *History of St Ives*, 1892.
Newcombe, Lisa, *Smuggling in Cornwall & Devon*, 1975.
●Noall, Cyril, *Smuggling in Cornwall*, D. Bradford Barton Ltd., 1971.
Oppenheim, M., *Victoria County History of Cornwall*,
Page, J.L.W., *Coasts of Devon and Lundy*, 1895.
Rattenbury, John, *Memoirs of a Smuggler*, 1837.
Vivian, John, *Tales of Cornish Smugglers*, 1969.

WALES AND WEST ENGLAND

Aberystwyth and Cardiganshire Archaeological Society, *Ceredigion*, Vol. VII, 1972.
Archaeologia Cambrensis, 1872, 1920 and 1939.
Awberry, Stanley C., *Let Us Talk of Barry*, 1954.
Bailey, Francis A., *History of Southport*, 1955.
Bell, G, *History of Little England beyond Wales, 1888*.
Chappell, Edgar L., *History of . . . Cardiff*, 1939.
Country Quest (Wrexham), August 1976.
Customs and Excise, *Choice Chips of Revenue Lore, Quoting 'Extracts from a Report of a Survey on the Coast of Wales by a Member of the Salt Board', 1740*, 1877.
Cylchgrawn Llyfrgell Genedlaethol Cymru, Vol. 24, No. 1, 1985.
Dawson, James W., *Commerce and Customs of Newport & Carleon*, 1932.
Eames, Aled, *Ships and Seamen of Anglesey*, 1981.
Edmunds, George, *Gower Coast*, 1986.
Ellis, H. Rees (ed.), *Rhwng mor a mynydd*, 1961.
Gibbon, Ronald T., *To The King's Deceit*, 1983.
Glazebrook, *Anglesea and the N. Wales Coast Book*, 1967.
Gower Journal (Swansea), Vol. XXIV, 1973.
Historic Society of Lancashire & Cheshire, *Transactions*, 1927.
Irving, Gordon, *The Solway Smugglers*, 1977.
Jarvis, Rupert Charles, *Customs Letter Books of . . . Liverpool*, 1954.
John, Brian, *Pembrokeshire*, 1976.
Lancs and Cheshire Antiquarian Society (Manchester), *Transactions*, Vol. 58, 1945.
Manx Museum, *Journal of the Manx Museum* Vol. VII, No. 88, 1976.
Maritime Wales, 10.
Myles Crowe the Smuggler, reprinted from the *Journal of the Manx Museum*, Vol. VII, No. 88, 1976.
Owen, Hugh J., *Treasures of the Mawddach*, 1950.
Phillips, D. Rhys, *A Romantic Valley in Wales*, 1925.
Qualtrough, John Karran, and Scatchard, *That Island*, 1965.
Rees, David, *Gower Anthology*, 1977.
Roberts, B. Dew, *Mr Bulkeley and the Pirate*, 1936.
Spencer, M.R., *Annals of S. Glamorgan*, 1913.
Stonehouse, *Recollections of Old Liverpool*, 1836.
Thomas, David of Bangor (formerly of Tal-y-Sam), *Hen Longau Sir Gaernarfon*, 1952.
Trevelyan, Marie, *Glimpses of a Welsh Life and Character*, 1893.
Tucker, H.M., *Gower Gleanings*, 1951.
Vale, Edmund, *World of Wales*, 1926.
Waters, Ivor, *Port of Chepstow*, 1977.
Watkins, K.C., *Welsh Smugglers*, 1975.
Wilkins, Charles of Merthyr Tydfil, *Tales and Sketches of Wales*, 1879.
Williams, Stewart, *South Glamorgan—A County History*, 1975.
Wood, John Maxwell, *Smuggling in the Solway*, 1908.
Woods, E. Cuthbert, *Smuggling in Wirral*, 1927.

THE EAST COAST

Anon., *Life and Behaviour of John Skinner*, 1746.
Baring-Gould, Sabine, *Mehallah*, 1903.
●Benham, Hervey, *The Smugglers' Century*, Essex Record Office, 1986.
Benton, Philip, *History of the Rochford Hundred*, 1867.
Border Magazine, Vols. 15, 28 and 32.
Brown, Herbert, *History of Bradwell on Sea*, 1929.
Burrows, J.W., *Southend on Sea and District: Historical Notes*, 1909.
Chadwick, Ellis H., *Mrs Gaskell, Haunts, Homes and Stories*, 1913.
Chandler, Lewis, *Smuggling at Sizewell Gap*, 1960.
Countryman (Idbury), Vol. 86, No. 2.
Dalesman, The (Clapham, Yorks), Vol. 37, No. 5, 1975.
Dutt, William Alfred, *Norfolk and Suffolk Coast*, 1909.
Dykes, Jack, 'Smuggling on the Yorkshire Coast', *East Anglia Life*, 1978.
East Anglian Magazine, T/1938, IV/1949, IX/1953, I/1956, 1959–61, 1969, VIII/1974, 1976.
Eastern Daily Press.
Eastern Evening News.
●Jarvis, Stan, *Smuggling in East Englia, 1700–1840*, Countryside Books, 1987.
Kime, Winston, *Skeggy*, 1969.
Knights, E.S., *Essex Folk*, 1935.
Lincoln Local History Society, *Lincolnshire Magazine*, Vol. 4.
Lincolnshire Life, Vols. 8, 14.
Millatt, T.B., *A Short History of the Parish Church of St Mary the Virgin, Salcott-cum-Virley* (n.d.).
Monthly Chronicle of N. Country Lore, June 1891.
Morgan, Glyn H., *The Romance of Essex Inns*, 1963.
Newcastle upon Tyne Society of Antiquaries, *Archaeologia Aeliana*, Vol. 43.
Norfolk Fair, 6/1980, 1/1984, 1–2/1968.
Norwich Mercury.
Robinson, David N., *Book of the Lincolnshire Coast*, 1983.
Roe, F., *Essex Survivals*, 1929.
Roscoe, E.H., *Guide to Mablethorpe*, 1889.
Thompson, Leonard P., *Smugglers of the Suffolk Coast*, 1968.
Thornton, David, *Plough and Sail*, 1977.
Weaver, Leonard, *The Harwich Story*, 1975.

SCOTLAND

Allardyce, John, *Bygone Days in Aberdeenshire*, 1913.

Anderson, George, *Kingston on Spey*, 1957.

Clark, Victoria E., *Port of Aberdeen*, 1921.

Cullen, L.M., *Anglo-Irish Trade*, 1968.

Cuthbertson, David, *Smugglers of Troon*, 1927.

Dixon, David Dippie, *Upper Coquetdale*, 1903.

Douglas, George Bourne Scott, *History of the Border Counties*, 1899.

Dumfries & Galloway Natural History & Antiquarian Society, *Transactions*, 1926.

Dunbar, Edward, *Social Life in Former Days*, 1865.

Dundee, *Dundee and Dundonians 70 Years Ago*, 1892.

Eunston, George, *Ancient & Present State of Orkney*, 1788.

Fleet, Charles, *Glimpses of our Ancestors*, (Vol. I), 1878.

Gallovidian Annual (Dumfries), 1921, 1931, 1936–7.

Grant, James (compiler), *Records of . . . the County of Banff*, 1922.

Grewar, David, *Story of Glenisla*, 1926.

Hall, James, *Travels in Scotland*, 1806.

Harriott, John, *Struggles through Life*, 1815.

Hawick Archaeological Society, *Transactions*, 1968.

Hewat, Kirkwood, *In the Olden Times*, 1898.

Imlach, James, *History of Banff*, 1868.

Kirkwall Antiquarian Natural History Society of Orkney, *Orkney Miscellany*, Vol. III.

Lang, Jean, *Land of Romance*, 1910.

McDowall, William, *History of Dumfries*, 1867.

MacIver, Daniel, *An Old-Time Fishing Town*, 1906.

Mac Kintosh, Ian M., *Old Troon and District*, 1969.

McLean, Charles, *The Fringe of Gold*, 1985.

Neville, Hastings M., *A Corner in the North*, 1909.

Pratt, John B., *Buchan*, 1981.

Sillett, Stephen W., *Illicit Scotch*, 1970.

Simmons, Jean, *Scottish Smugglers*, 1975.

Smith, Hance D., *Shetland Life and Trade*, 1984.

Smith-Leask, J.T., *A Peculiar People and Other Orkney Tales*, 1931.

Spencer, Marianne Robertson, *Annals of S. Glamorgan*, 1913.

Thomson, William S. (of Govan), *The Smuggling Era in Scotland*, 1910.

PLACE NAME INDEX

Numbers in *italics* refer to illustrations